WELCOME TO TRANQUILITY

BOOK TWO

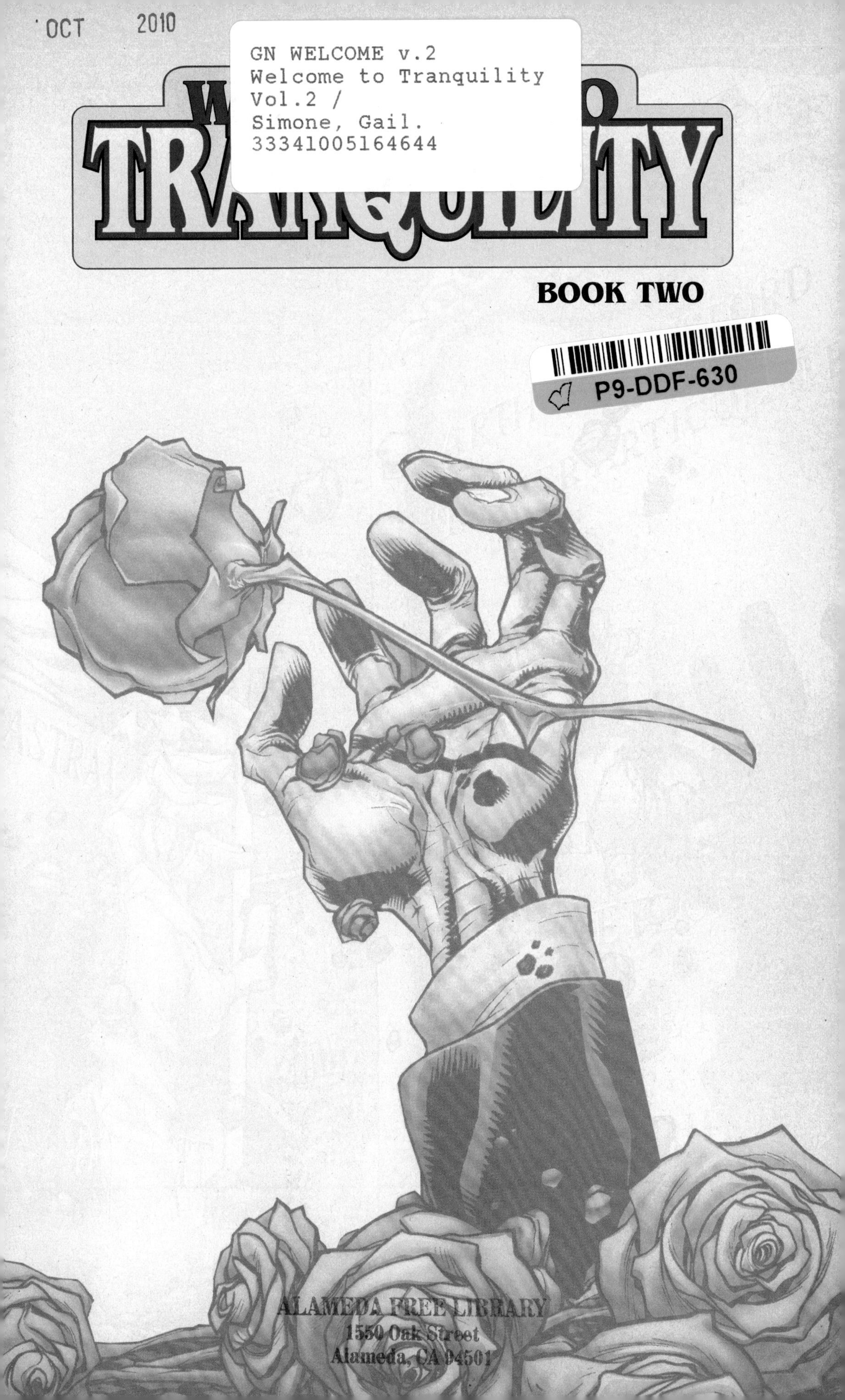

Gail Simone: Writer

Chapter One
Neil Googe: Main Story Artist
Steve Molnar: Backup Story Penciler
Dan Davis: Backup Story Inker
Carrie Strachan: Colors
Travis Lanham: Letters

Chapter Two
Neil Googe, Jason Pearson, ChrisCross, Georges Jeanty, and Peter Guzman: Artists
Carrie Strachan: Colors
Travis Lanham, Pat Brosseau: Letters

Chapter Three
Neil Googe: Main Story Artist
Leandro Fernández: Backup Story Penciler
Francisco Paronzini: Backup Story Inker
Carrie Strachan: Colors
Travis Lanham: Letters

Chapter Four
Neil Googe: Main Story Artist
Scott Shaw!: Backup Story Penciler
Mike Kazaleh: Backup Story Inker
Carrie Strachan: Colors
Travis Lanham: Letters

Chapter Five
Neil Googe: Main Story Artist
Irene Flores: Backup Story Artist
Carrie Strachan: Main Story Colors
Tony Aviña: Backup Story Colors
Travis Lanham: Letters

Chapter Six
Neil Googe: Artist
Carrie Strachan: Colors
Travis Lanham: Letters

**Collected Edition Cover and Original Series Covers by
Neil Googe and Carrie Strachan
Character designs by Neil Googe**

Jim Lee, Editorial Director • John Nee, Senior VP—Business Development • Ben Abernathy, Editor
Kristy Quinn, Assistant Editor • Ed Roeder, Art Director • Paul Levitz, President & Publisher
Georg Brewer, VP—Design & DC Direct Creative • Richard Bruning, Senior VP—Creative Director
Patrick Caldon, Executive VP—Finance & Operations • Chris Caramalis, VP—Finance • John Cunningham, VP—Marketing
Terri Cunningham, VP—Managing Editor • Alison Gill, VP—Manufacturing • David Hyde, VP—Publicity
Hank Kanalz, VP—General Manager, WildStorm • Paula Lowitt, Senior VP—Business & Legal Affairs
MaryEllen McLaughlin, VP—Advertising & Custom Publishing • Gregory Noveck, Senior VP—Creative Affairs
Sue Pohja, VP—Book Trade Sales • Steve Rotterdam, Senior VP—Sales & Marketing • Cheryl Rubin, Senior VP—Brand Management
Jeff Trojan, VP—Business Development, DC Direct • Bob Wayne, VP—Sales

WELCOME TO TRANQUILITY Book Two, published by WildStorm Productions. 888 Prospect St. #240, La Jolla,
CA 92037. Compilation and character design sketches Copyright © 2008 WildStorm Productions, an imprint
of DC Comics. All Rights Reserved. WildStorm and logo, all characters, the distinctive likenesses thereof and
all related elements are trademarks of DC Comics. Originally published in single magazine form as Welcome
to Tranquility #7-12 copyright © 2007, 2008. All Rights Reserved.

DC Comics, a Warner Bros. Entertainment Company.

ISBN: 978-1-4012-1773-0

CHAPTER ONE

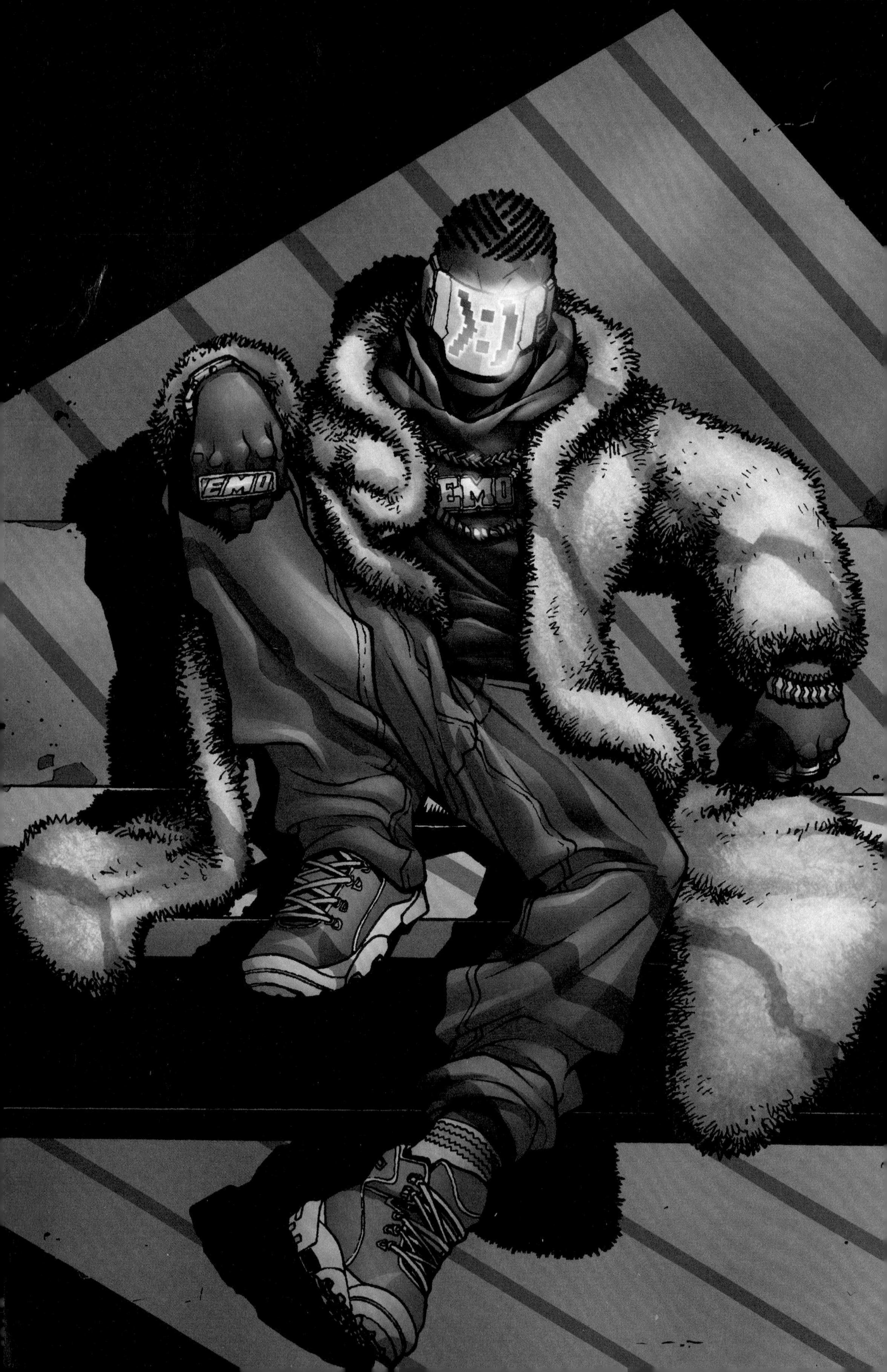
EMO
EMO

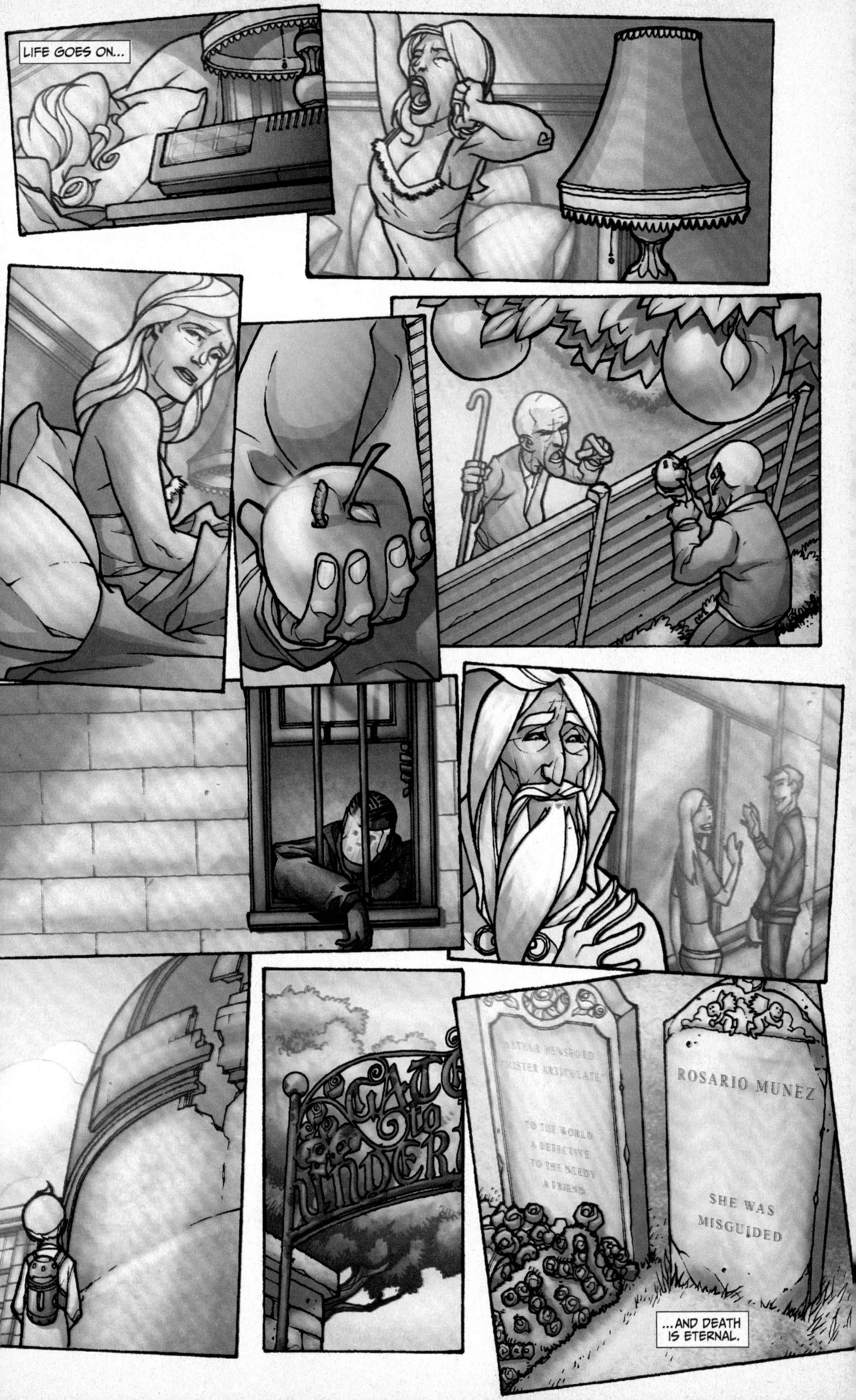
LIFE GOES ON...
ARTHUR HENSFORD
"MISTER ARTICULATE"
TO THE WORLD
A DETECTIVE
TO THE NEEDY
A FRIEND
ROSARIO MUNEZ
SHE WAS
MISGUIDED
...AND DEATH
IS ETERNAL.

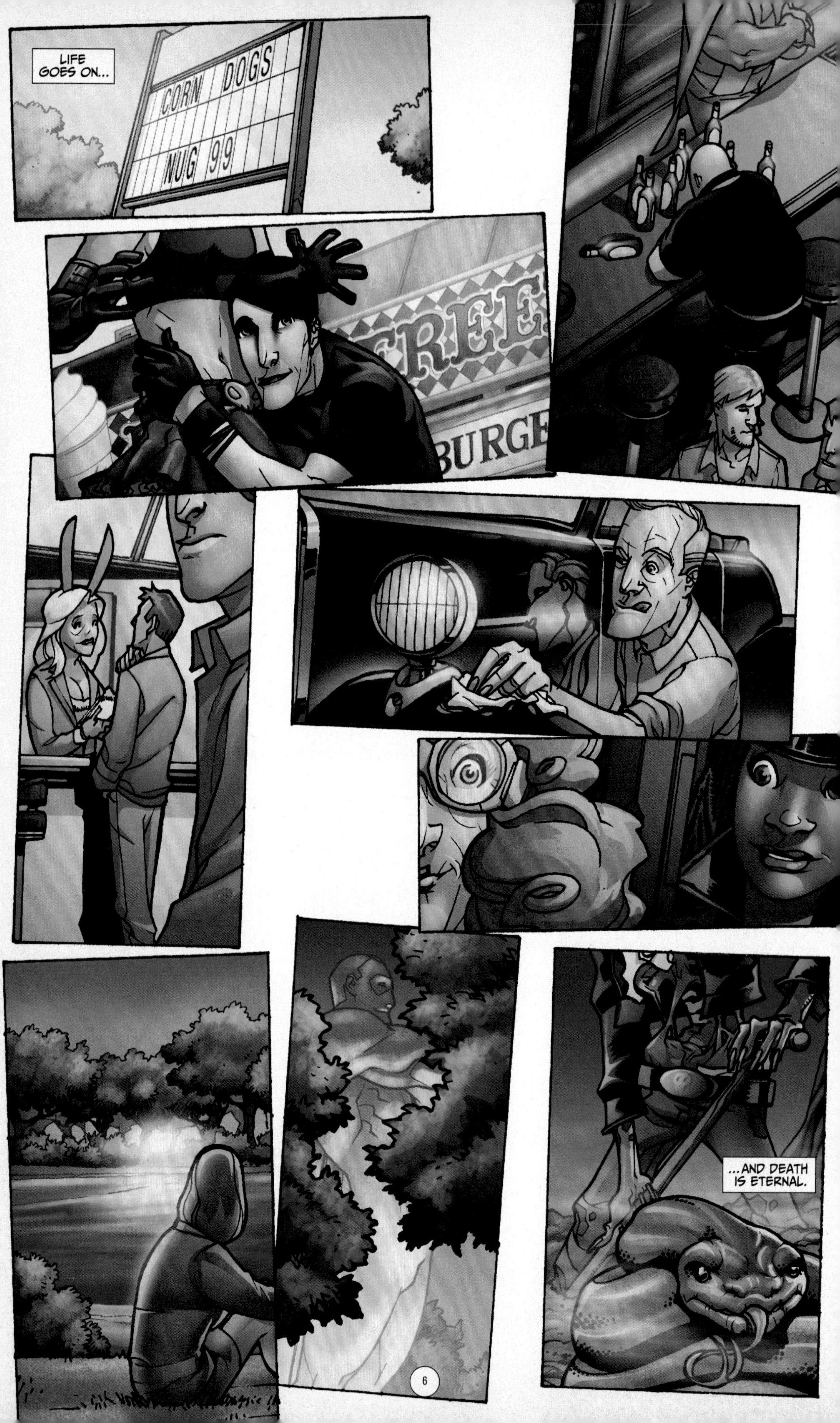
LIFE GOES ON...
CORN DOGS
NUG 99
...AND DEATH IS ETERNAL.

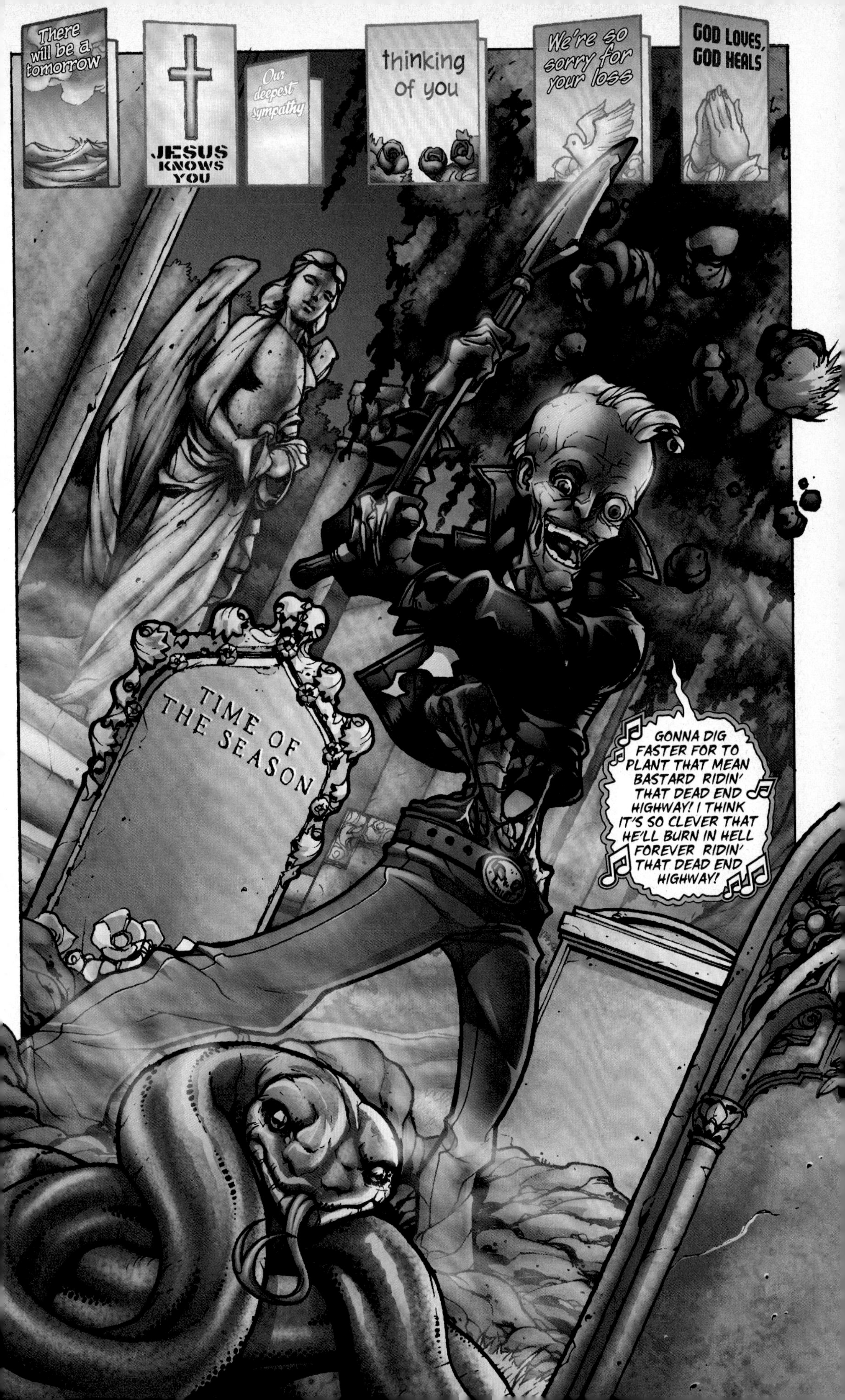
There will be a tomorrow
JESUS KNOWS YOU
Our deepest sympathy
thinking of you
We're so sorry for your loss
GOD LOVES, GOD HEALS
TIME OF THE SEASON
GONNA DIG FASTER FOR TO PLANT THAT MEAN BASTARD RIDIN' THAT DEAD END HIGHWAY! I THINK IT'S SO CLEVER THAT HE'LL BURN IN HELL FOREVER RIDIN' THAT DEAD END HIGHWAY!

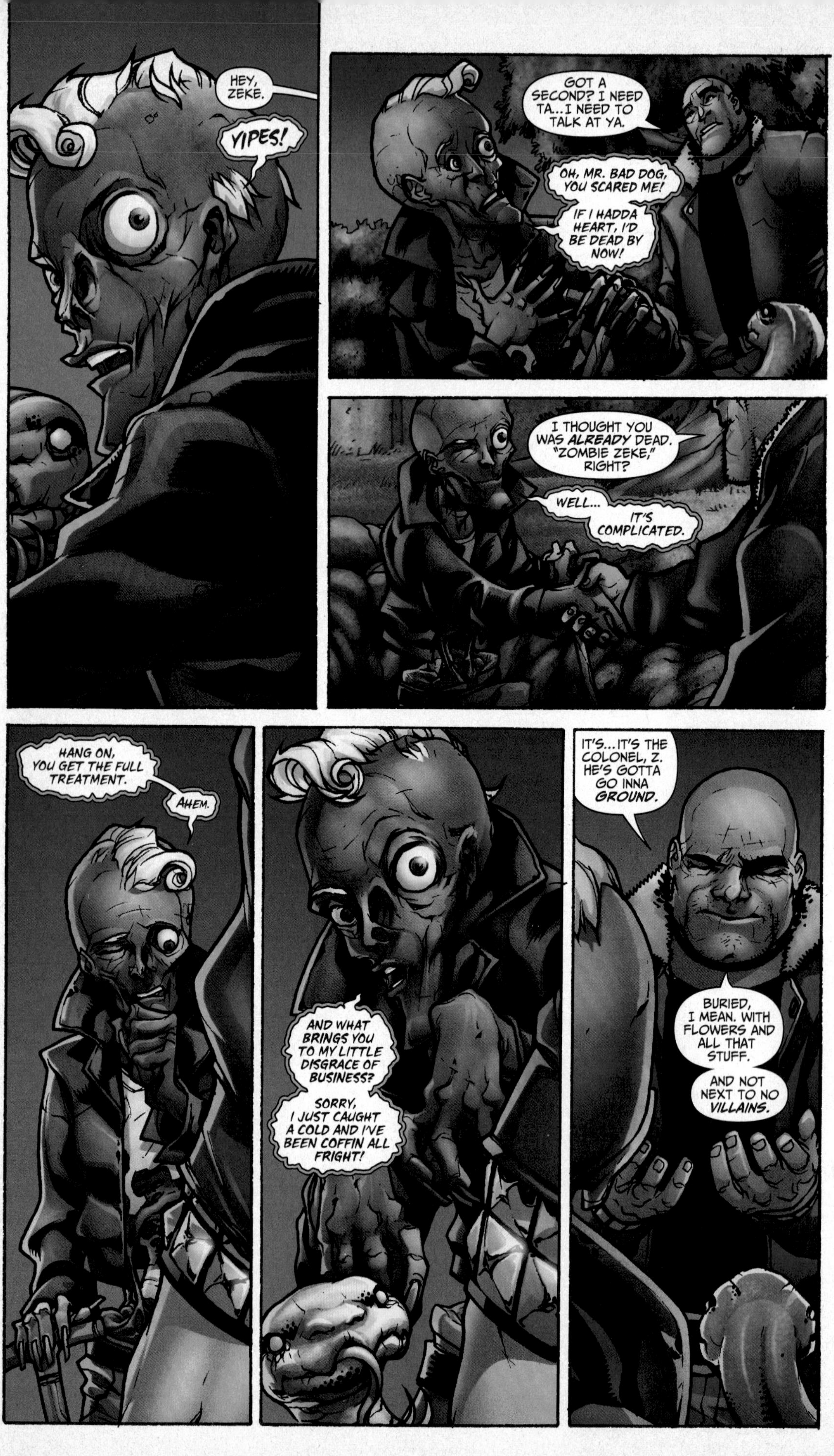
HEY, ZEKE.
YIPES!
GOT A SECOND? I NEED TA...I NEED TO TALK AT YA.
OH, MR. BAD DOG, YOU SCARED ME!
IF I HADDA HEART, I'D BE DEAD BY NOW!
I THOUGHT YOU WAS ALREADY DEAD. "ZOMBIE ZEKE," RIGHT?
WELL... IT'S COMPLICATED.
HANG ON, YOU GET THE FULL TREATMENT.
AHEM.
AND WHAT BRINGS YOU TO MY LITTLE DISGRACE OF BUSINESS?
SORRY, I JUST CAUGHT A COLD AND I'VE BEEN COFFIN ALL FRIGHT!
IT'S...IT'S THE COLONEL, Z. HE'S GOTTA GO INNA GROUND.
BURIED, I MEAN. WITH FLOWERS AND ALL THAT STUFF.
AND NOT NEXT TO NO VILLAINS.

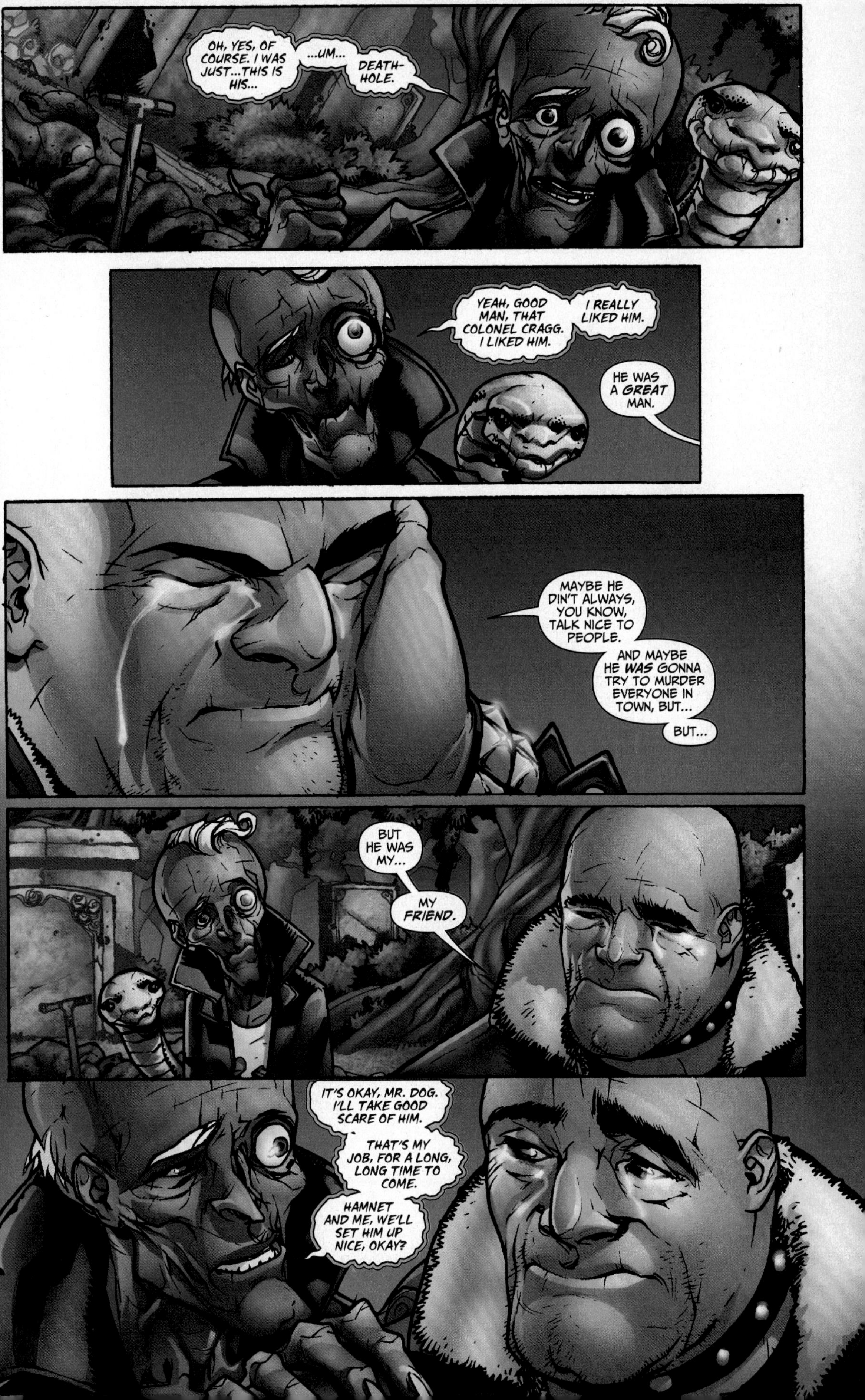
OH, YES, OF COURSE. I WAS JUST...THIS IS HIS...
...UM...
DEATH-HOLE.
YEAH, GOOD MAN, THAT COLONEL CRAGG. I LIKED HIM.
I REALLY LIKED HIM.
HE WAS A GREAT MAN.
MAYBE HE DIN'T ALWAYS, YOU KNOW, TALK NICE TO PEOPLE.
AND MAYBE HE WAS GONNA TRY TO MURDER EVERYONE IN TOWN, BUT...
BUT...
BUT HE WAS MY...
MY FRIEND.
IT'S OKAY, MR. DOG. I'LL TAKE GOOD SCARE OF HIM.
THAT'S MY JOB, FOR A LONG, LONG TIME TO COME.
HAMNET AND ME, WE'LL SET HIM UP NICE, OKAY?

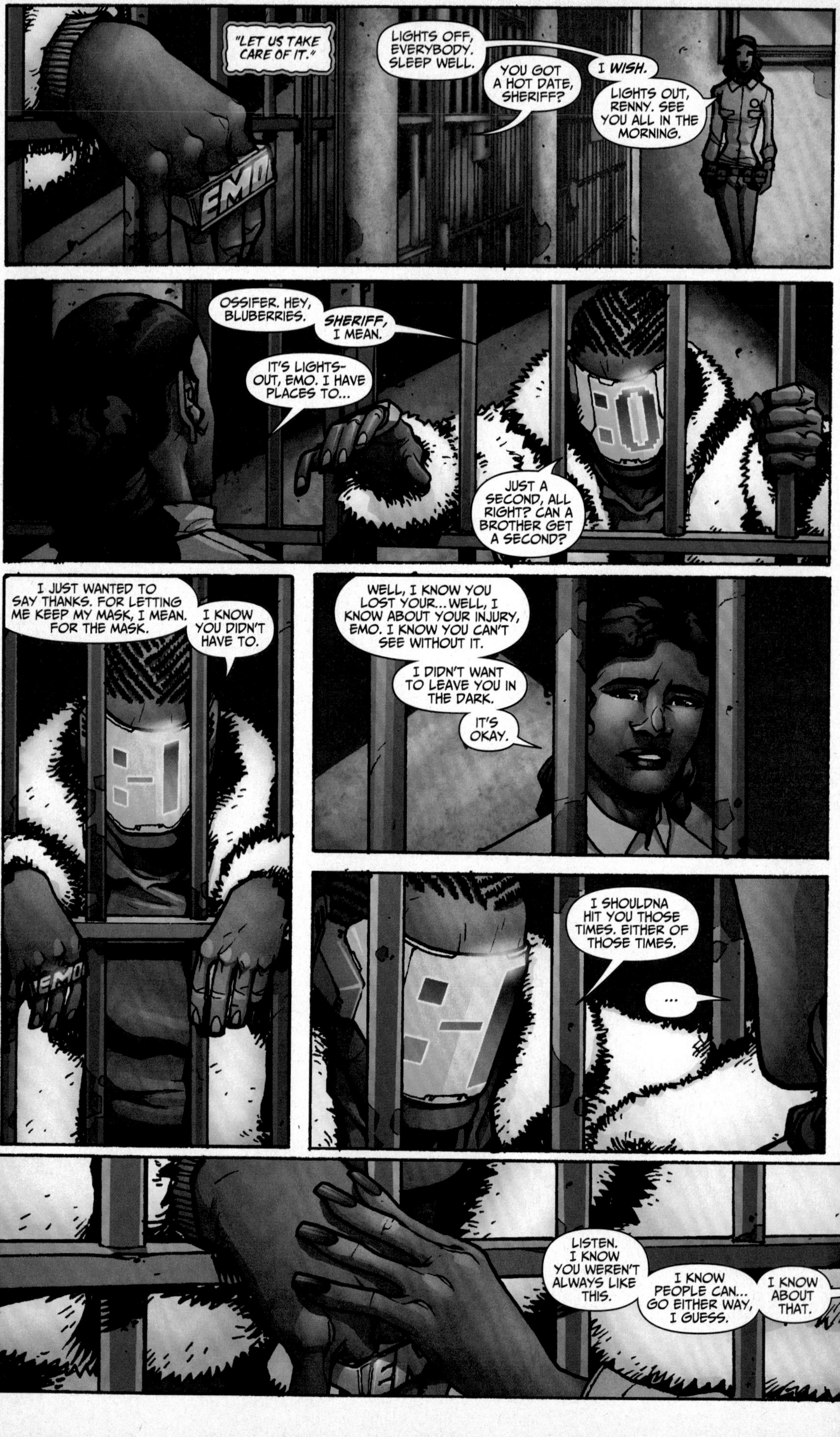
"LET US TAKE CARE OF IT."
LIGHTS OFF, EVERYBODY. SLEEP WELL.
YOU GOT A HOT DATE, SHERIFF?
I *WISH*.
LIGHTS OUT, RENNY. SEE YOU ALL IN THE MORNING.
OSSIFER. HEY, BLUBERRIES.
SHERIFF, I MEAN.
IT'S LIGHTS-OUT, EMO. I HAVE PLACES TO...
JUST A SECOND, ALL RIGHT? CAN A BROTHER GET A SECOND?
I JUST WANTED TO SAY THANKS. FOR LETTING ME KEEP MY MASK, I MEAN. FOR THE MASK.
I KNOW YOU DIDN'T HAVE TO.
WELL, I KNOW YOU LOST YOUR... WELL, I KNOW ABOUT YOUR INJURY, EMO. I KNOW YOU CAN'T SEE WITHOUT IT.
I DIDN'T WANT TO LEAVE YOU IN THE DARK.
IT'S OKAY.
I SHOULDNA HIT YOU THOSE TIMES. EITHER OF THOSE TIMES.
...
LISTEN. I KNOW YOU WEREN'T ALWAYS LIKE THIS.
I KNOW PEOPLE CAN... GO EITHER WAY, I GUESS.
I KNOW ABOUT THAT.

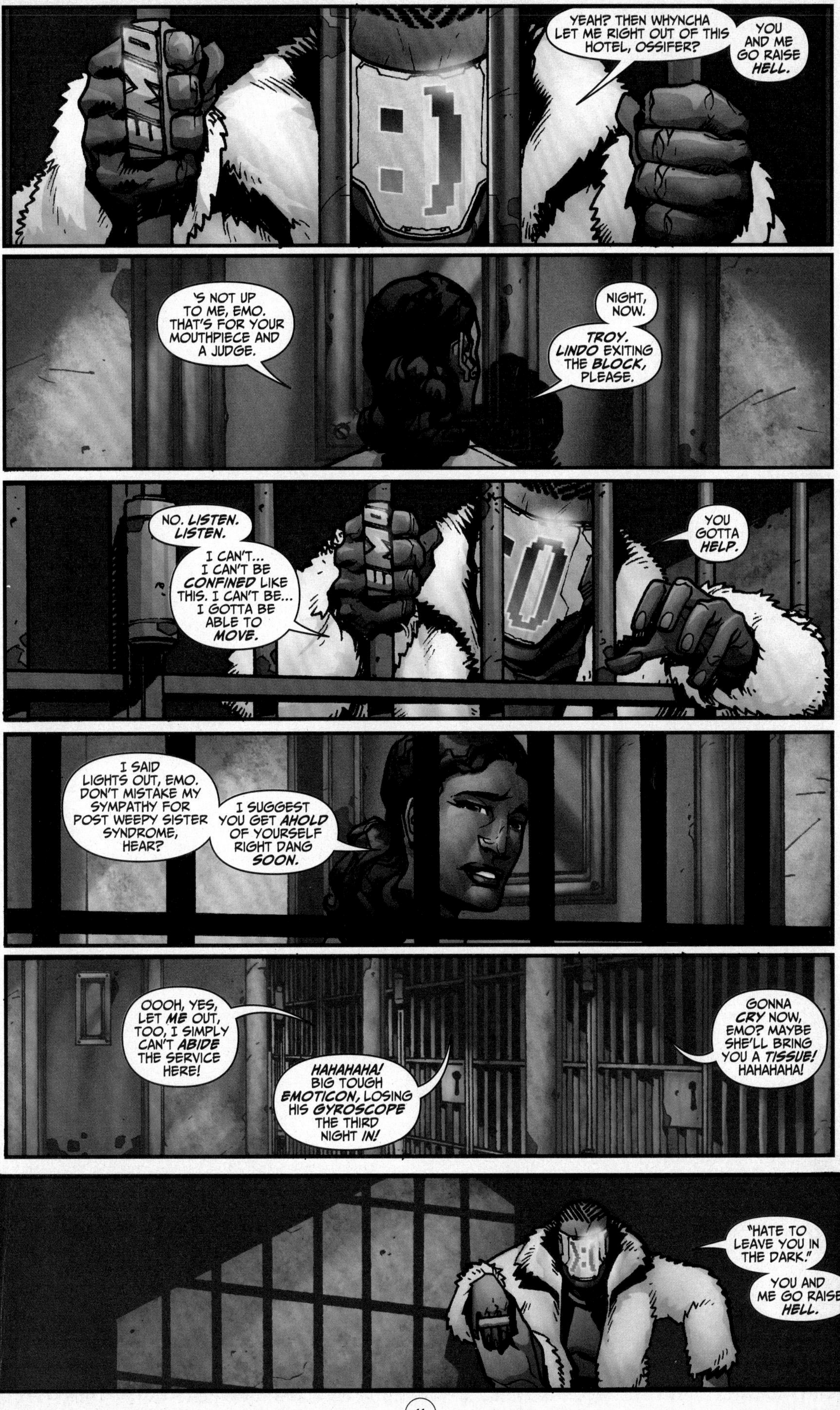
YEAH? THEN WHYNCHA LET ME RIGHT OUT OF THIS HOTEL, OSSIFER?
YOU AND ME GO RAISE **HELL.**
'S NOT UP TO ME, EMO. THAT'S FOR YOUR MOUTHPIECE AND A JUDGE.
NIGHT, NOW.
TROY. LINDO EXITING THE ***BLOCK,*** PLEASE.
NO. ***LISTEN. LISTEN.***
I CAN'T... I CAN'T BE ***CONFINED*** LIKE THIS. I CAN'T BE... I GOTTA BE ABLE TO ***MOVE.***
YOU GOTTA ***HELP.***
I SAID LIGHTS OUT, EMO. DON'T MISTAKE MY SYMPATHY FOR POST WEEPY SISTER SYNDROME, HEAR?
I SUGGEST YOU GET ***AHOLD*** OF YOURSELF RIGHT DANG ***SOON.***
OOOH, YES, LET ***ME*** OUT, TOO, I SIMPLY CAN'T ***ABIDE*** THE SERVICE HERE!
HAHAHAHA! BIG TOUGH ***EMOTICON,*** LOSING HIS ***GYROSCOPE*** THE THIRD NIGHT ***IN!***
GONNA ***CRY*** NOW, EMO? MAYBE SHE'LL BRING YOU A ***TISSUE!*** HAHAHAHA!
"HATE TO LEAVE YOU IN THE DARK."
YOU AND ME GO RAISE ***HELL.***

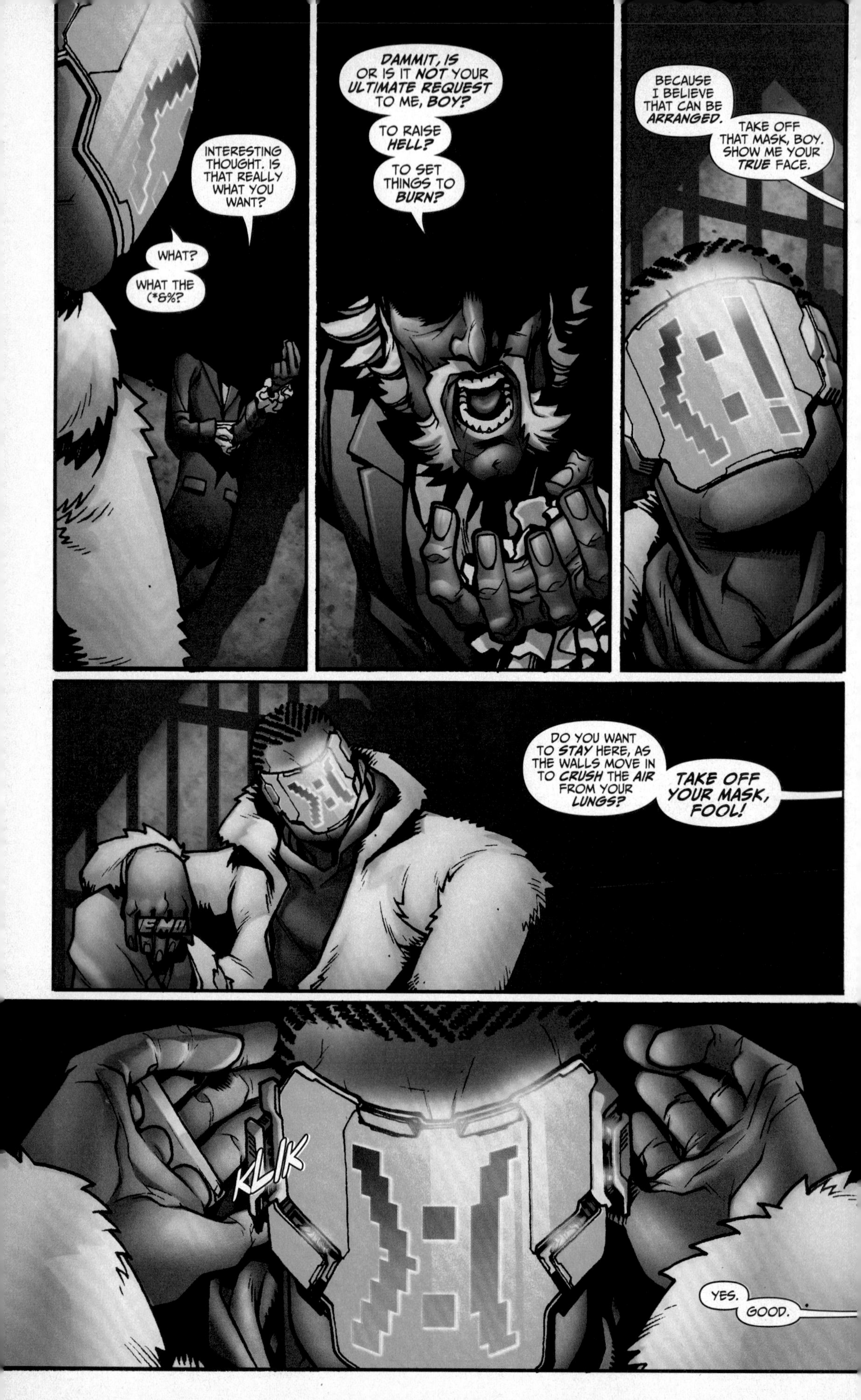
INTERESTING THOUGHT. IS THAT REALLY WHAT YOU WANT?
WHAT?
WHAT THE (*&%?
DAMMIT, IS OR IS IT NOT YOUR ULTIMATE REQUEST TO ME, BOY?
TO RAISE HELL?
TO SET THINGS TO BURN?
BECAUSE I BELIEVE THAT CAN BE ARRANGED.
TAKE OFF THAT MASK, BOY. SHOW ME YOUR TRUE FACE.
DO YOU WANT TO STAY HERE, AS THE WALLS MOVE IN TO CRUSH THE AIR FROM YOUR LUNGS?
TAKE OFF YOUR MASK, FOOL!
KLIK
YES.
GOOD.

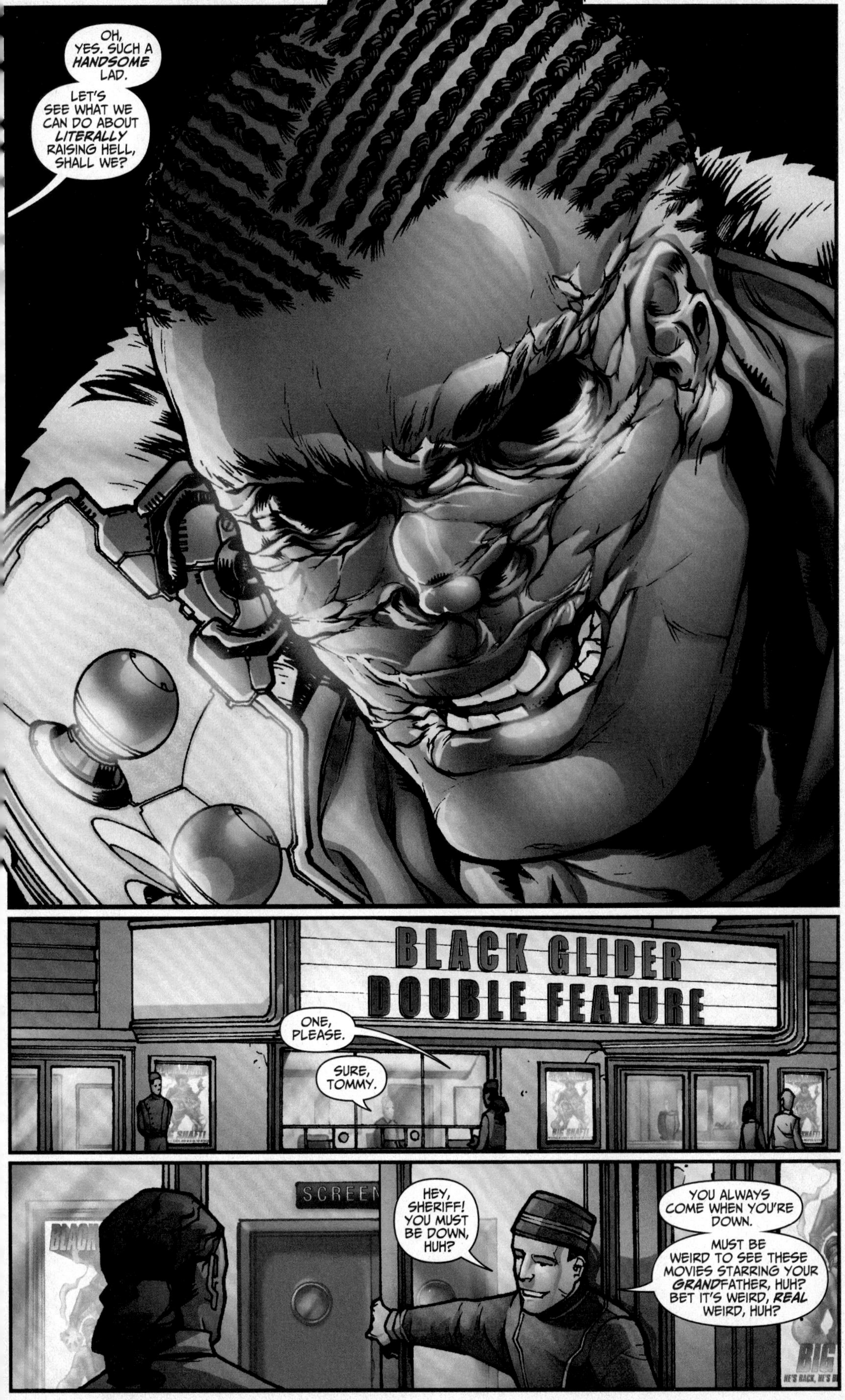
OH, YES. SUCH A ***HANDSOME*** LAD.
LET'S SEE WHAT WE CAN DO ABOUT ***LITERALLY*** RAISING HELL, SHALL WE?
BLACK GLIDER DOUBLE FEATURE
ONE, PLEASE.
SURE, TOMMY.
HEY, SHERIFF! YOU MUST BE DOWN, HUH?
YOU ALWAYS COME WHEN YOU'RE DOWN.
MUST BE WEIRD TO SEE THESE MOVIES STARRING YOUR ***GRAND***FATHER, HUH? BET IT'S WEIRD, ***REAL*** WEIRD, HUH?

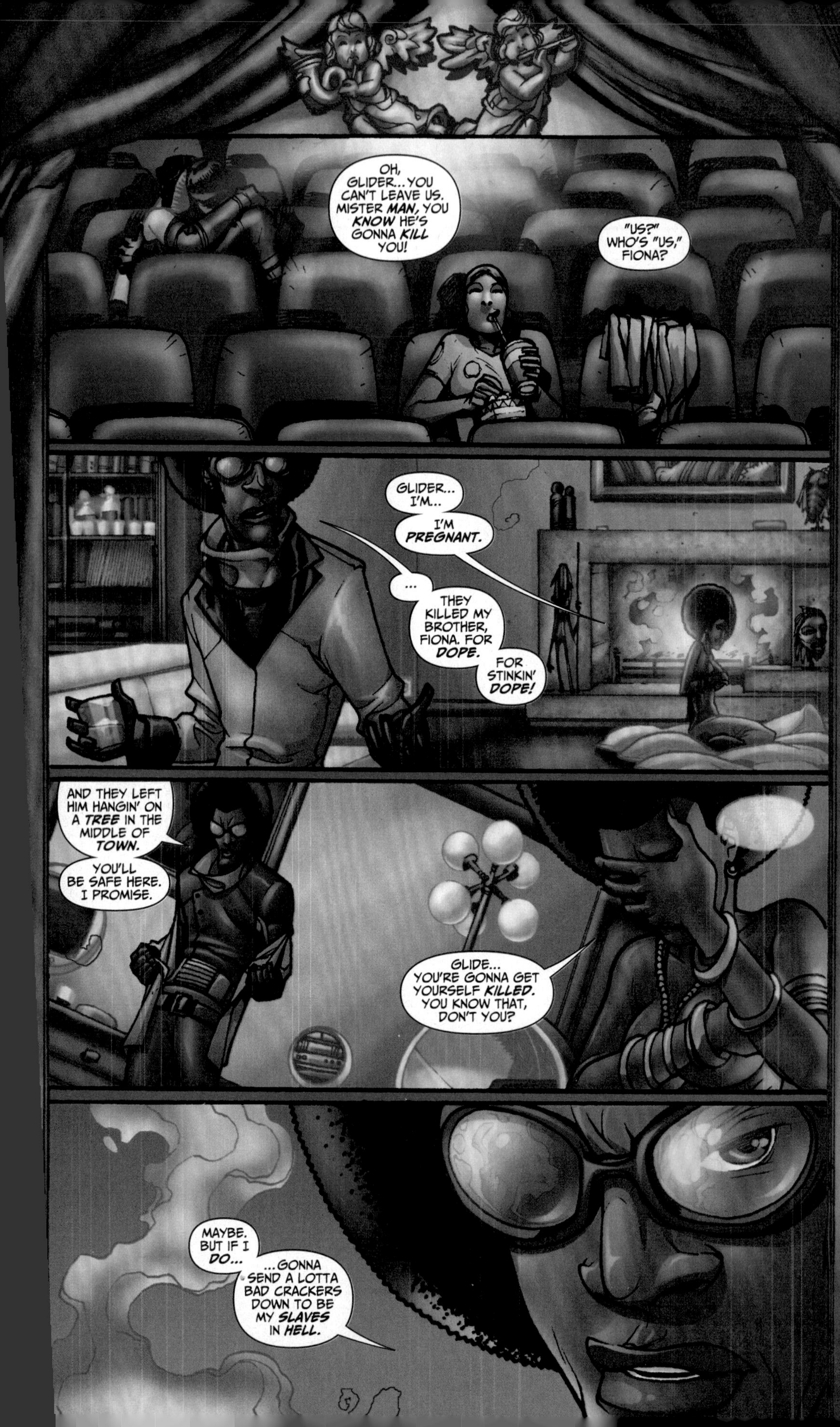
OH, GLIDER...YOU CAN'T LEAVE US. MISTER MAN, YOU KNOW HE'S GONNA KILL YOU!
"US?" WHO'S "US," FIONA?
GLIDER... I'M...
I'M PREGNANT.
...
THEY KILLED MY BROTHER, FIONA. FOR DOPE.
FOR STINKIN' DOPE!
AND THEY LEFT HIM HANGIN' ON A TREE IN THE MIDDLE OF TOWN.
YOU'LL BE SAFE HERE. I PROMISE.
GLIDE... YOU'RE GONNA GET YOURSELF KILLED. YOU KNOW THAT, DON'T YOU?
MAYBE. BUT IF I DO...
...GONNA SEND A LOTTA BAD CRACKERS DOWN TO BE MY SLAVES IN HELL.

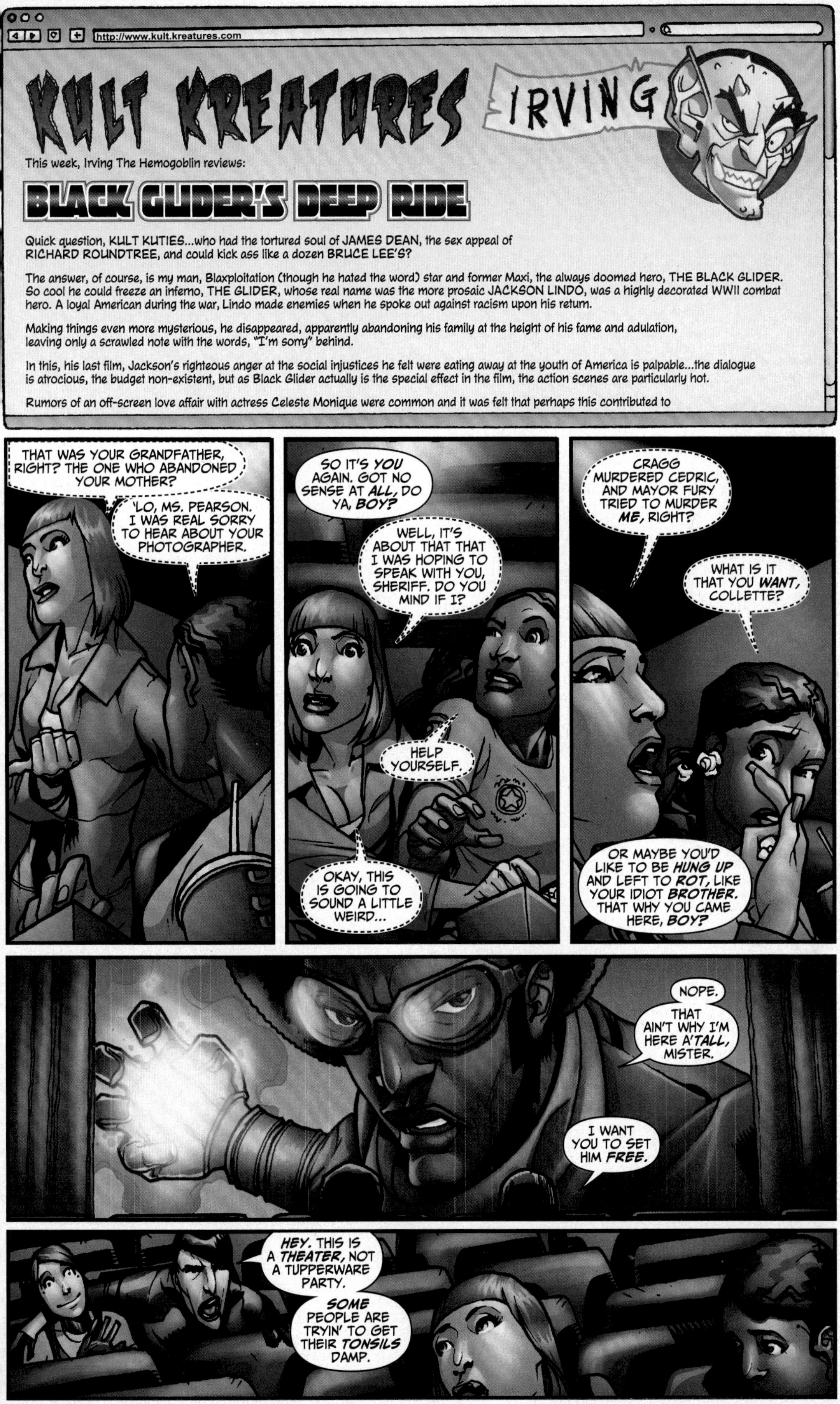
http://www.kult.kreatures.com
KULT KREATURES
IRVING
This week, Irving The Hemogoblin reviews:
BLACK GLIDER'S DEEP RIDE
Quick question, KULT KUTIES...who had the tortured soul of JAMES DEAN, the sex appeal of RICHARD ROUNDTREE, and could kick ass like a dozen BRUCE LEE'S?
The answer, of course, is my man, Blaxploitation (though he hated the word) star and former Maxi, the always doomed hero, THE BLACK GLIDER. So cool he could freeze an inferno, THE GLIDER, whose real name was the more prosaic JACKSON LINDO, was a highly decorated WWII combat hero. A loyal American during the war, Lindo made enemies when he spoke out against racism upon his return.
Making things even more mysterious, he disappeared, apparently abandoning his family at the height of his fame and adulation, leaving only a scrawled note with the words, "I'm sorry" behind.
In this, his last film, Jackson's righteous anger at the social injustices he felt were eating away at the youth of America is palpable...the dialogue is atrocious, the budget non-existent, but as Black Glider actually is the special effect in the film, the action scenes are particularly hot.
Rumors of an off-screen love affair with actress Celeste Monique were common and it was felt that perhaps this contributed to
THAT WAS YOUR GRANDFATHER, RIGHT? THE ONE WHO ABANDONED YOUR MOTHER?
'LO, MS. PEARSON. I WAS REAL SORRY TO HEAR ABOUT YOUR PHOTOGRAPHER.
SO IT'S YOU AGAIN. GOT NO SENSE AT ALL, DO YA, BOY?
WELL, IT'S ABOUT THAT THAT I WAS HOPING TO SPEAK WITH YOU, SHERIFF. DO YOU MIND IF I?
HELP YOURSELF.
OKAY, THIS IS GOING TO SOUND A LITTLE WEIRD...
CRAGG MURDERED CEDRIC, AND MAYOR FURY TRIED TO MURDER ME, RIGHT?
WHAT IS IT THAT YOU WANT, COLLETTE?
OR MAYBE YOU'D LIKE TO BE HUNG UP AND LEFT TO ROT, LIKE YOUR IDIOT BROTHER. THAT WHY YOU CAME HERE, BOY?
NOPE.
THAT AIN'T WHY I'M HERE A'TALL, MISTER.
I WANT YOU TO SET HIM FREE.
HEY. THIS IS A THEATER, NOT A TUPPERWARE PARTY.
SOME PEOPLE ARE TRYIN' TO GET THEIR TONSILS DAMP.

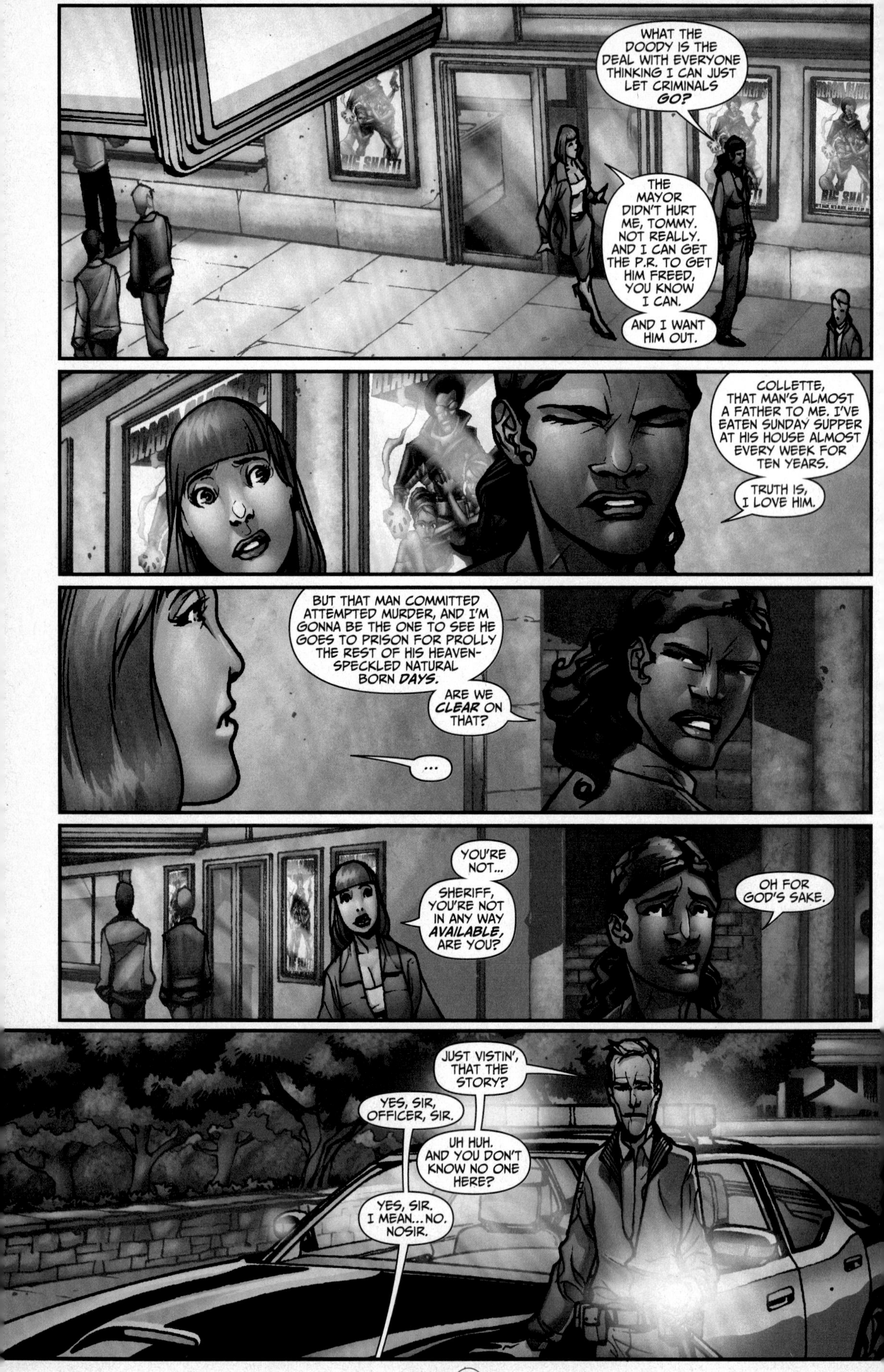
WHAT THE DOODY IS THE DEAL WITH EVERYONE THINKING I CAN JUST LET CRIMINALS GO?
THE MAYOR DIDN'T HURT ME, TOMMY. NOT REALLY. AND I CAN GET THE P.R. TO GET HIM FREED, YOU KNOW I CAN.
AND I WANT HIM OUT.
COLLETTE, THAT MAN'S ALMOST A FATHER TO ME. I'VE EATEN SUNDAY SUPPER AT HIS HOUSE ALMOST EVERY WEEK FOR TEN YEARS.
TRUTH IS, I LOVE HIM.
BUT THAT MAN COMMITTED ATTEMPTED MURDER, AND I'M GONNA BE THE ONE TO SEE HE GOES TO PRISON FOR PROLLY THE REST OF HIS HEAVEN-SPECKLED NATURAL BORN DAYS.
ARE WE CLEAR ON THAT?
...
YOU'RE NOT...
SHERIFF, YOU'RE NOT IN ANY WAY AVAILABLE, ARE YOU?
OH FOR GOD'S SAKE.
JUST VISTIN', THAT THE STORY?
YES, SIR, OFFICER, SIR.
UH HUH. AND YOU DON'T KNOW NO ONE HERE?
YES, SIR. I MEAN... NO. NOSIR.

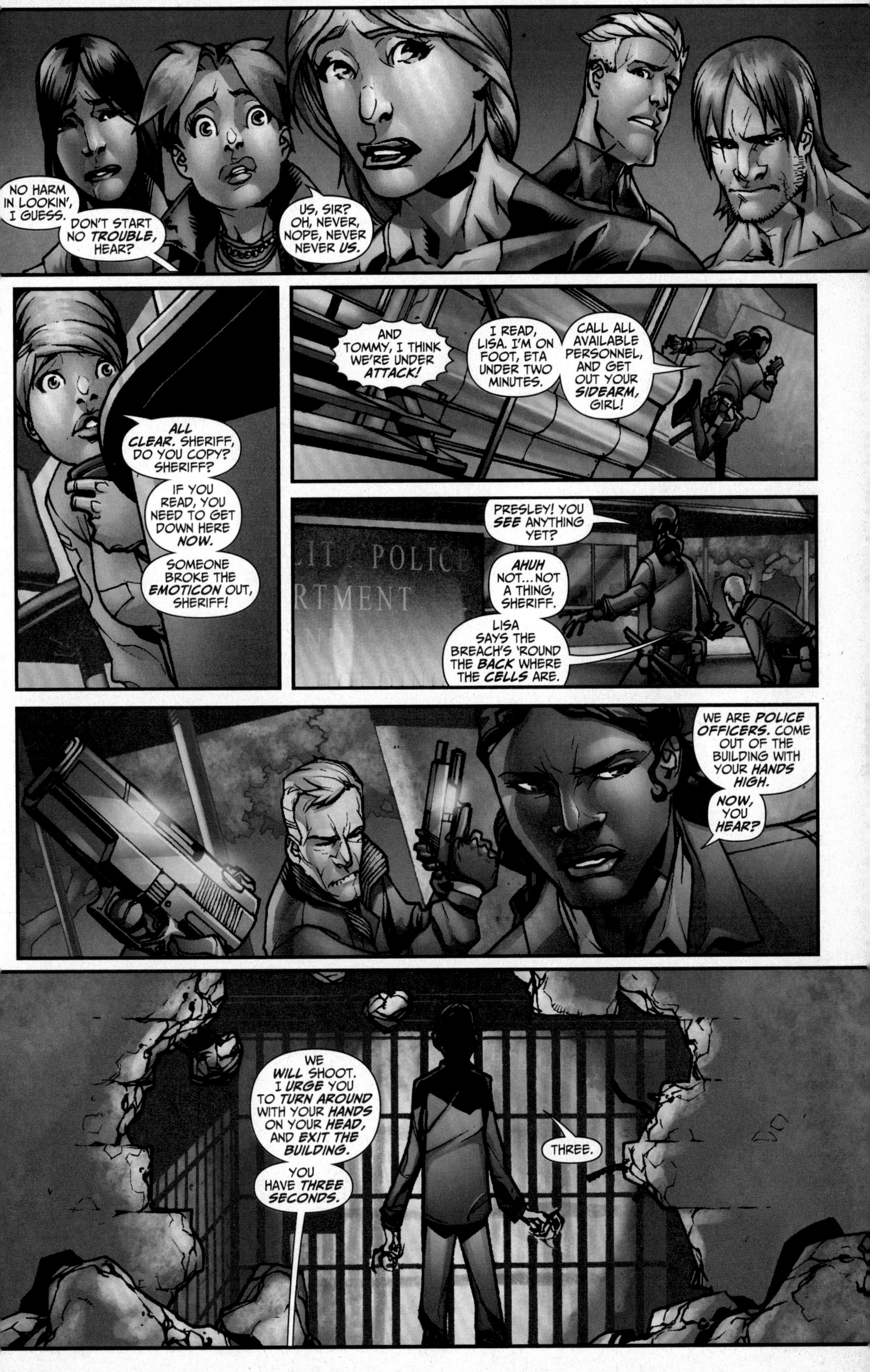
NO HARM IN LOOKIN', I GUESS.
DON'T START NO TROUBLE, HEAR?
US, SIR? OH, NEVER, NOPE, NEVER NEVER NEVER US.
ALL CLEAR. SHERIFF, DO YOU COPY? SHERIFF?
IF YOU READ, YOU NEED TO GET DOWN HERE NOW.
SOMEONE BROKE THE EMOTICON OUT, SHERIFF!
AND TOMMY, I THINK WE'RE UNDER ATTACK!
I READ, LISA. I'M ON FOOT, ETA UNDER TWO MINUTES.
CALL ALL AVAILABLE PERSONNEL, AND GET OUT YOUR SIDEARM, GIRL!
LIT POLICE
RTMENT
PRESLEY! YOU SEE ANYTHING YET?
AHUH NOT... NOT A THING, SHERIFF.
LISA SAYS THE BREACH'S 'ROUND THE BACK WHERE THE CELLS ARE.
WE ARE POLICE OFFICERS. COME OUT OF THE BUILDING WITH YOUR HANDS HIGH.
NOW, YOU HEAR?
WE WILL SHOOT. I URGE YOU TO TURN AROUND WITH YOUR HANDS ON YOUR HEAD, AND EXIT THE BUILDING.
YOU HAVE THREE SECONDS.
THREE.

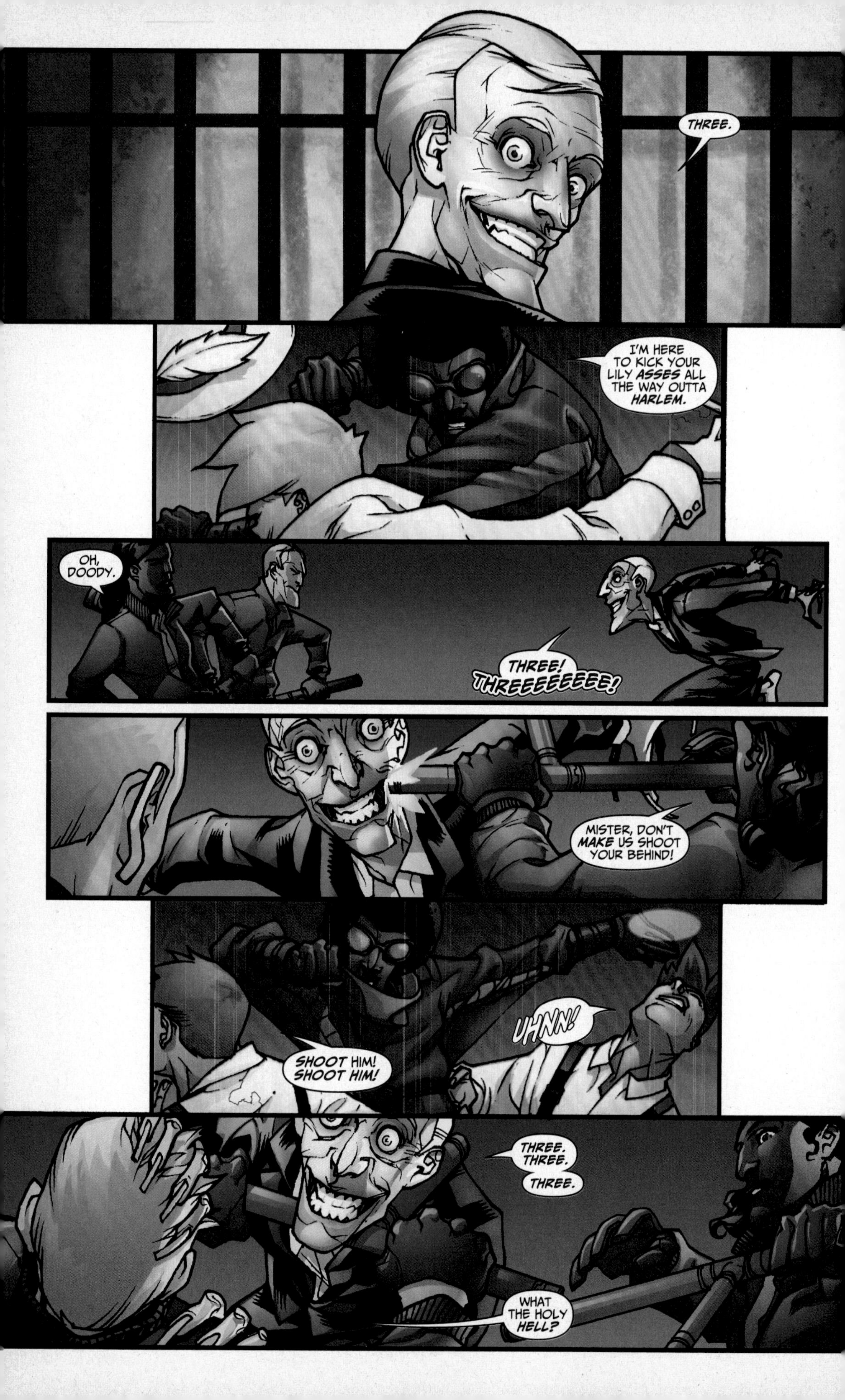
THREE.
I'M HERE TO KICK YOUR LILY ASSES ALL THE WAY OUTTA HARLEM.
OH, DOODY.
THREE! THREEEEEEEEE!
MISTER, DON'T MAKE US SHOOT YOUR BEHIND!
SHOOT HIM! SHOOT HIM!
UHNN!
THREE. THREE.
THREE.
WHAT THE HOLY HELL?

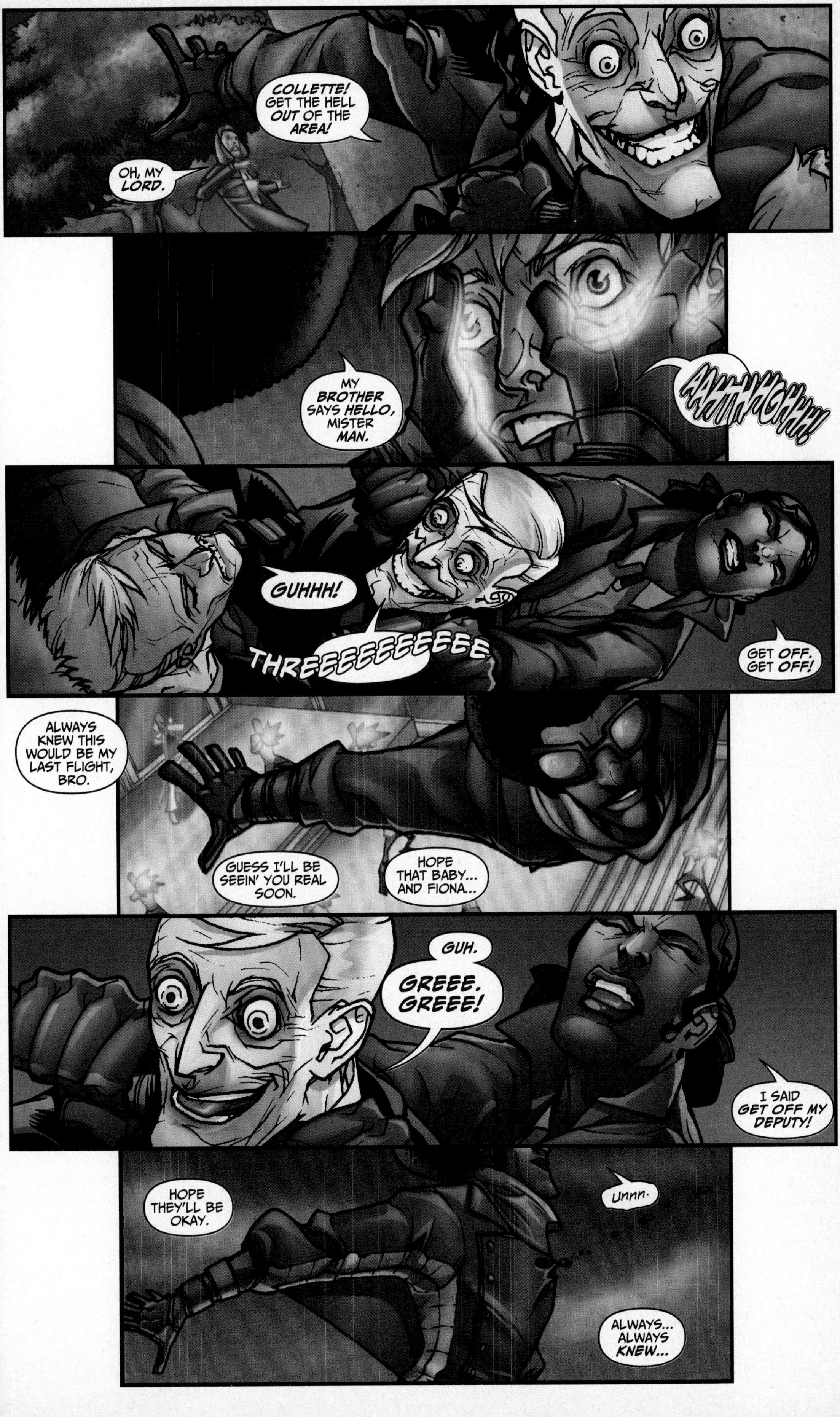
COLLETTE! GET THE HELL OUT OF THE AREA!
OH, MY LORD.
MY BROTHER SAYS HELLO, MISTER MAN.
AAAHHHGHHH!
GUHHH!
THREEEEEEEEEEE
GET OFF. GET OFF!
ALWAYS KNEW THIS WOULD BE MY LAST FLIGHT, BRO.
GUESS I'LL BE SEEIN' YOU REAL SOON.
HOPE THAT BABY... AND FIONA...
GUH.
GREEE. GREEE!
I SAID GET OFF MY DEPUTY!
HOPE THEY'LL BE OKAY.
Unnn.
ALWAYS... ALWAYS KNEW...

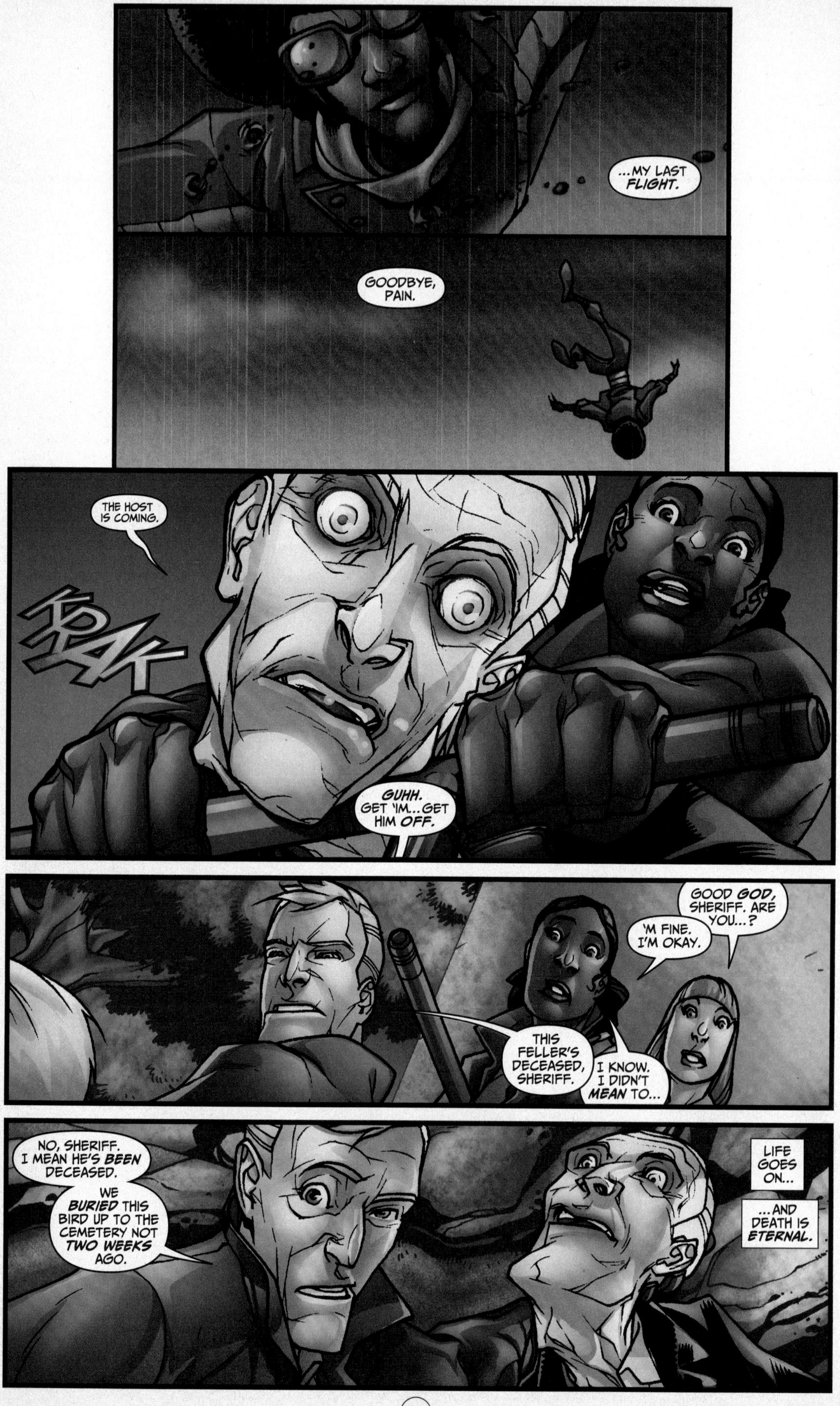
...MY LAST FLIGHT.
GOODBYE, PAIN.
THE HOST IS COMING.
KRAK
GUHH. GET 'IM...GET HIM OFF.
GOOD GOD, SHERIFF. ARE YOU...?
'M FINE. I'M OKAY.
THIS FELLER'S DECEASED, SHERIFF.
I KNOW. I DIDN'T MEAN TO...
NO, SHERIFF. I MEAN HE'S BEEN DECEASED.
WE BURIED THIS BIRD UP TO THE CEMETERY NOT TWO WEEKS AGO.
LIFE GOES ON...
...AND DEATH IS ETERNAL.

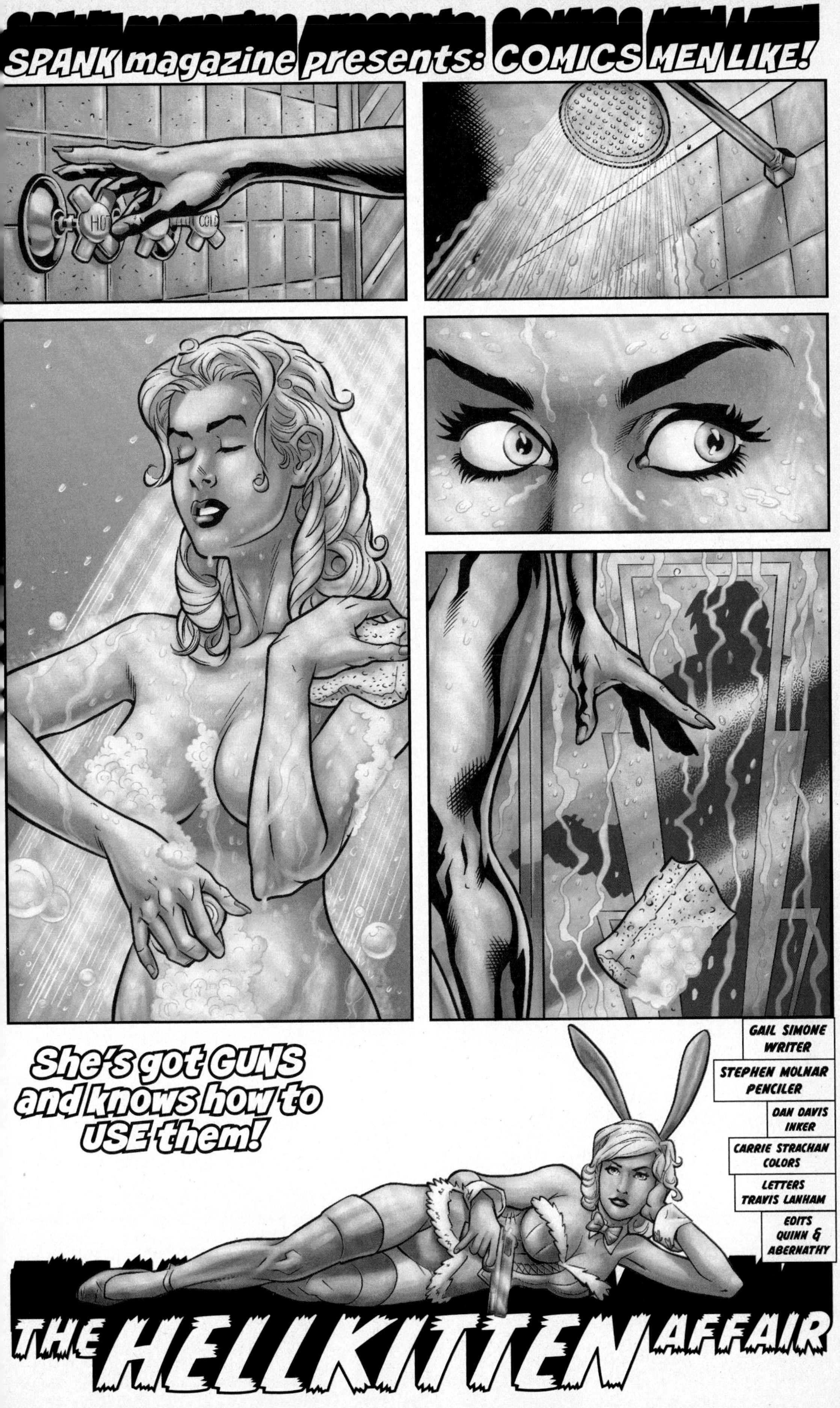
SPANK magazine presents: COMICS MEN LIKE!
She's got GUNS and knows how to USE them!
GAIL SIMONE WRITER
STEPHEN MOLNAR PENCILER
DAN DAVIS INKER
CARRIE STRACHAN COLORS
LETTERS TRAVIS LANHAM
EDITS QUINN & ABERNATHY
THE HELLKITTEN AFFAIR

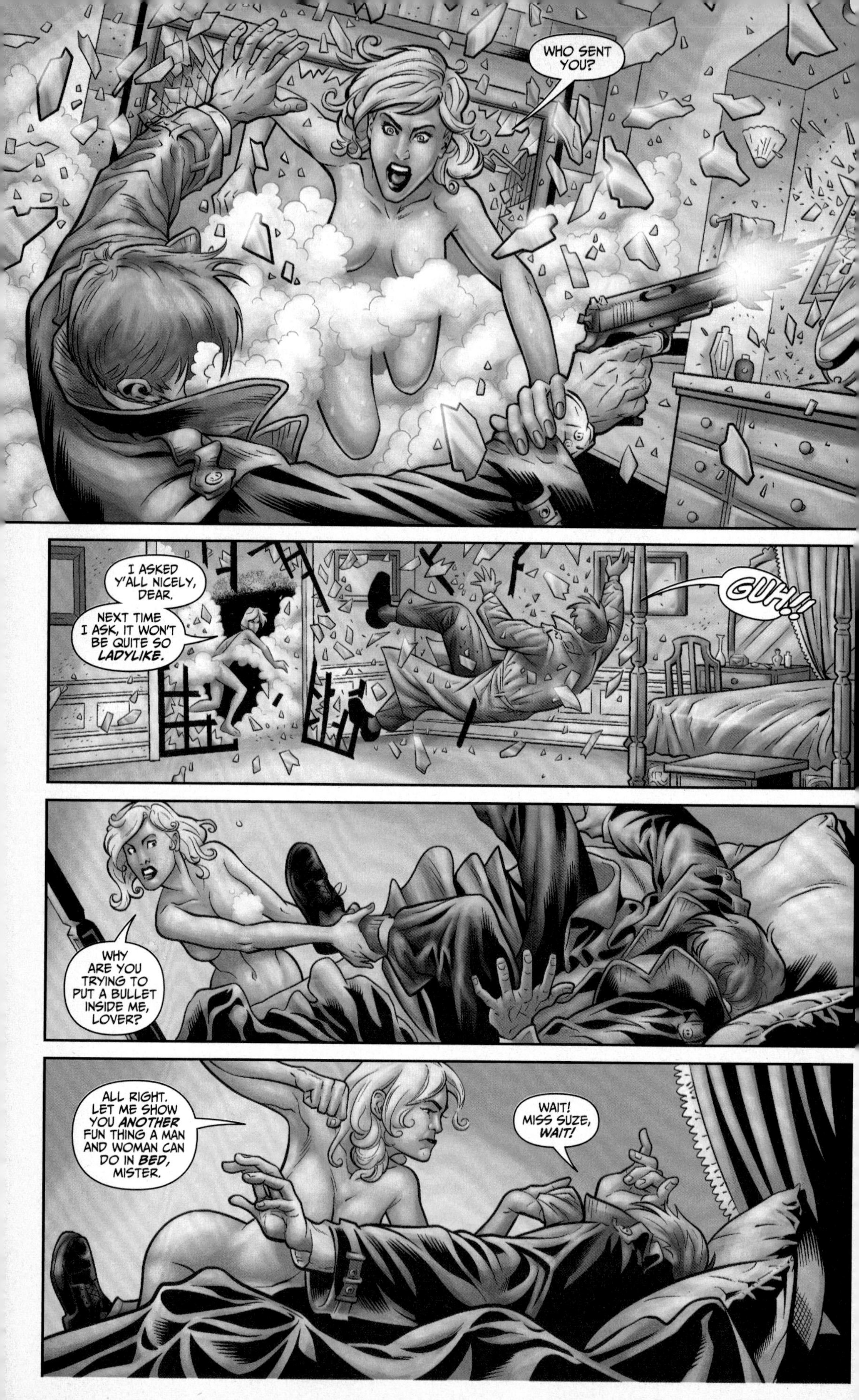
WHO SENT YOU?
I ASKED Y'ALL NICELY, DEAR.
NEXT TIME I ASK, IT WON'T BE QUITE SO LADYLIKE.
GUH!!
WHY ARE YOU TRYING TO PUT A BULLET INSIDE ME, LOVER?
ALL RIGHT. LET ME SHOW YOU ANOTHER FUN THING A MAN AND WOMAN CAN DO IN BED, MISTER.
WAIT! MISS SUZE, WAIT!

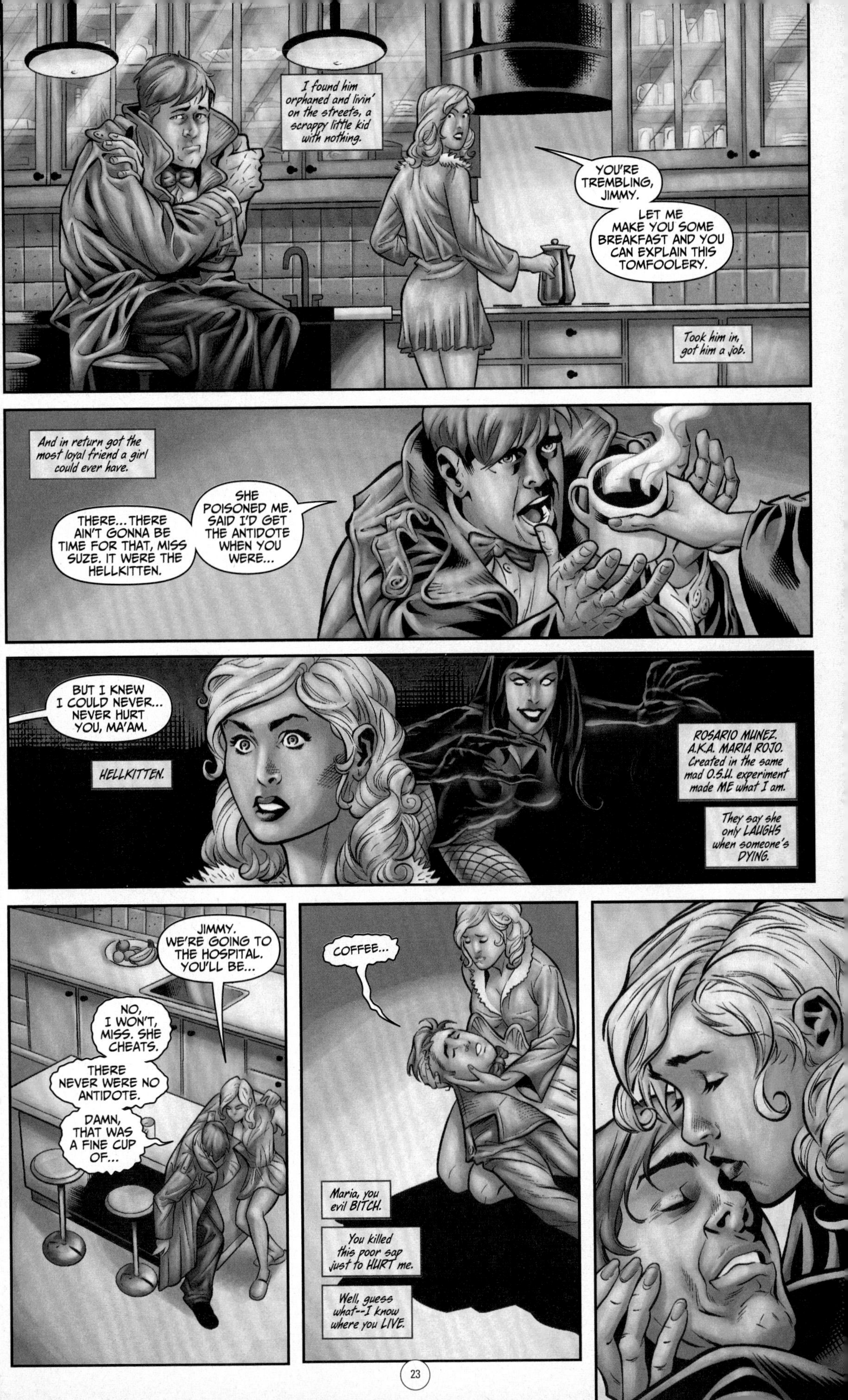
I found him orphaned and livin' on the streets, a scrappy little kid with nothing.
YOU'RE TREMBLING, JIMMY.
LET ME MAKE YOU SOME BREAKFAST AND YOU CAN EXPLAIN THIS TOMFOOLERY.
Took him in, got him a job.
And in return got the most loyal friend a girl could ever have.
THERE... THERE AIN'T GONNA BE TIME FOR THAT, MISS SUZE. IT WERE THE HELLKITTEN.
SHE POISONED ME. SAID I'D GET THE ANTIDOTE WHEN YOU WERE...
BUT I KNEW I COULD NEVER... NEVER HURT YOU, MA'AM.
HELLKITTEN.
ROSARIO MUNEZ. A.K.A. MARIA ROJO. Created in the same mad O.S.U. experiment made ME what I am.
They say she only LAUGHS when someone's DYING.
JIMMY. WE'RE GOING TO THE HOSPITAL. YOU'LL BE...
NO, I WON'T, MISS. SHE CHEATS.
THERE NEVER WERE NO ANTIDOTE.
DAMN, THAT WAS A FINE CUP OF...
COFFEE...
Maria, you evil BITCH.
You killed this poor sap just to HURT me.
Well, guess what--I know where you LIVE.

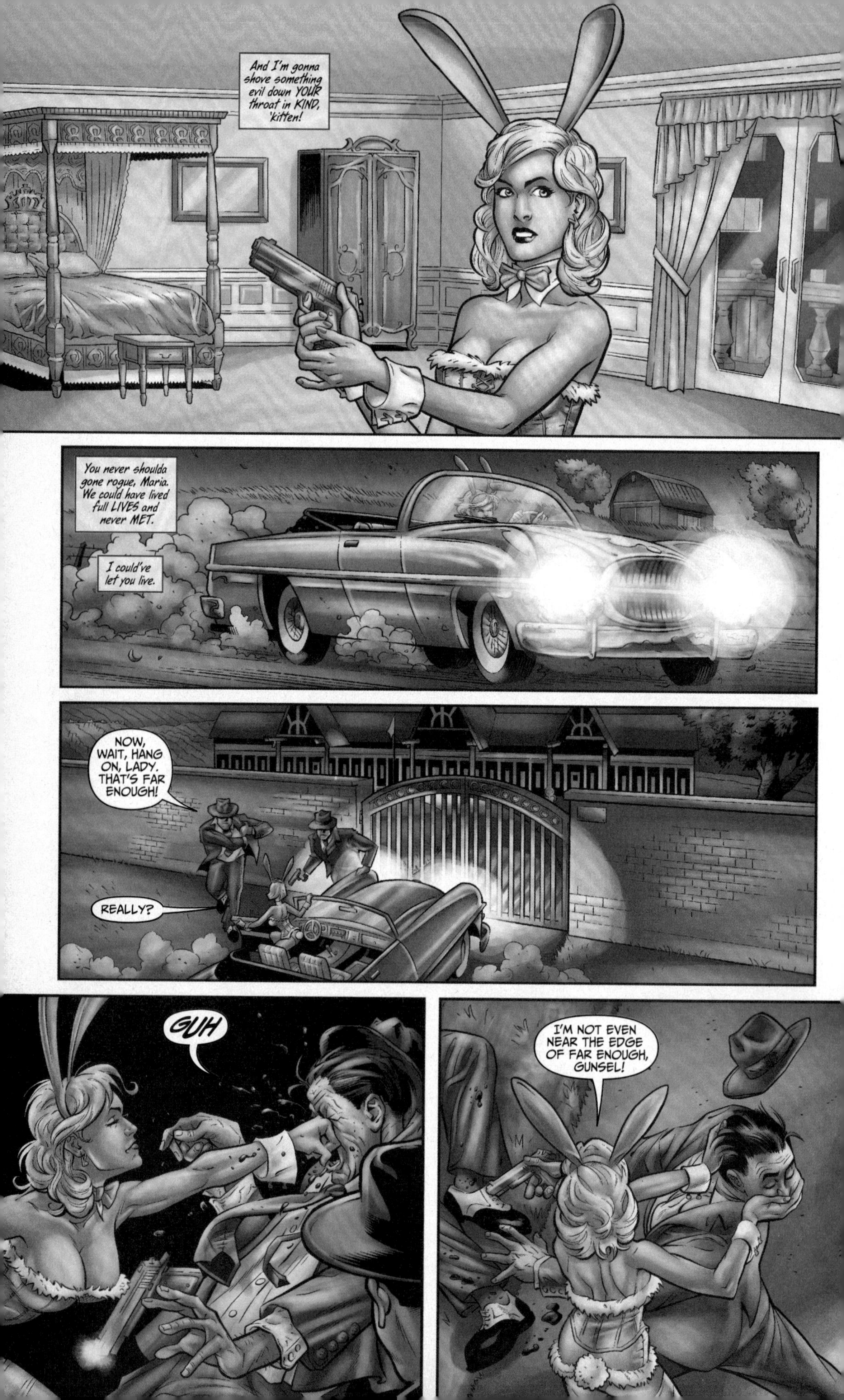
And I'm gonna shove something evil down YOUR throat in KIND, 'kitten!
You never shoulda gone rogue, Maria. We could have lived full LIVES and never MET.
I could've let you live.
NOW, WAIT, HANG ON, LADY. THAT'S FAR ENOUGH!
REALLY?
GUH
I'M NOT EVEN NEAR THE EDGE OF FAR ENOUGH, GUNSEL!

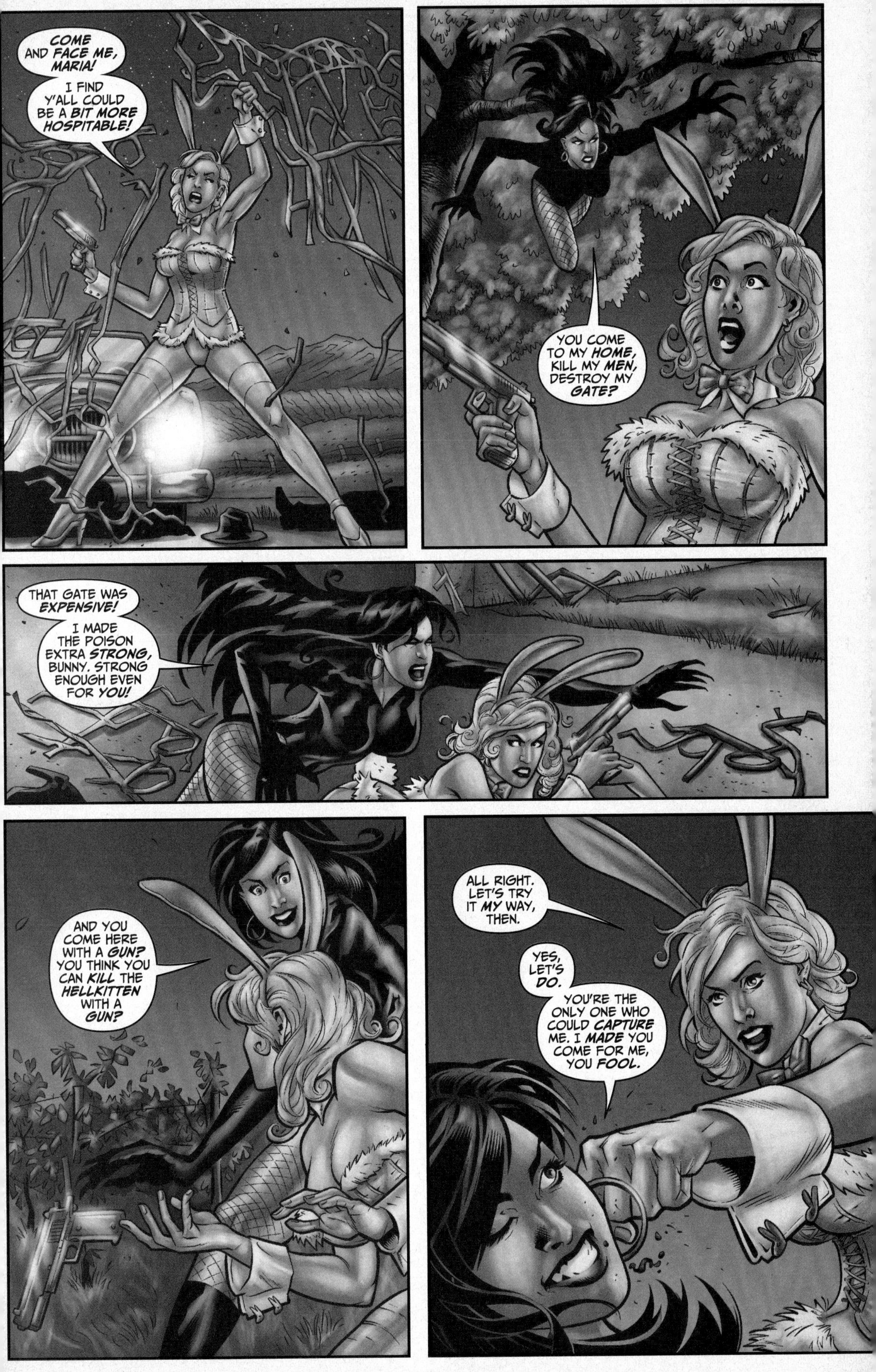
COME AND FACE ME, MARIA!
I FIND Y'ALL COULD BE A BIT MORE HOSPITABLE!
YOU COME TO MY HOME, KILL MY MEN, DESTROY MY GATE?
THAT GATE WAS EXPENSIVE!
I MADE THE POISON EXTRA STRONG, BUNNY. STRONG ENOUGH EVEN FOR YOU!
AND YOU COME HERE WITH A GUN? YOU THINK YOU CAN KILL THE HELLKITTEN WITH A GUN?
ALL RIGHT. LET'S TRY IT MY WAY, THEN.
YES, LET'S DO.
YOU'RE THE ONLY ONE WHO COULD CAPTURE ME. I MADE YOU COME FOR ME, YOU FOOL.

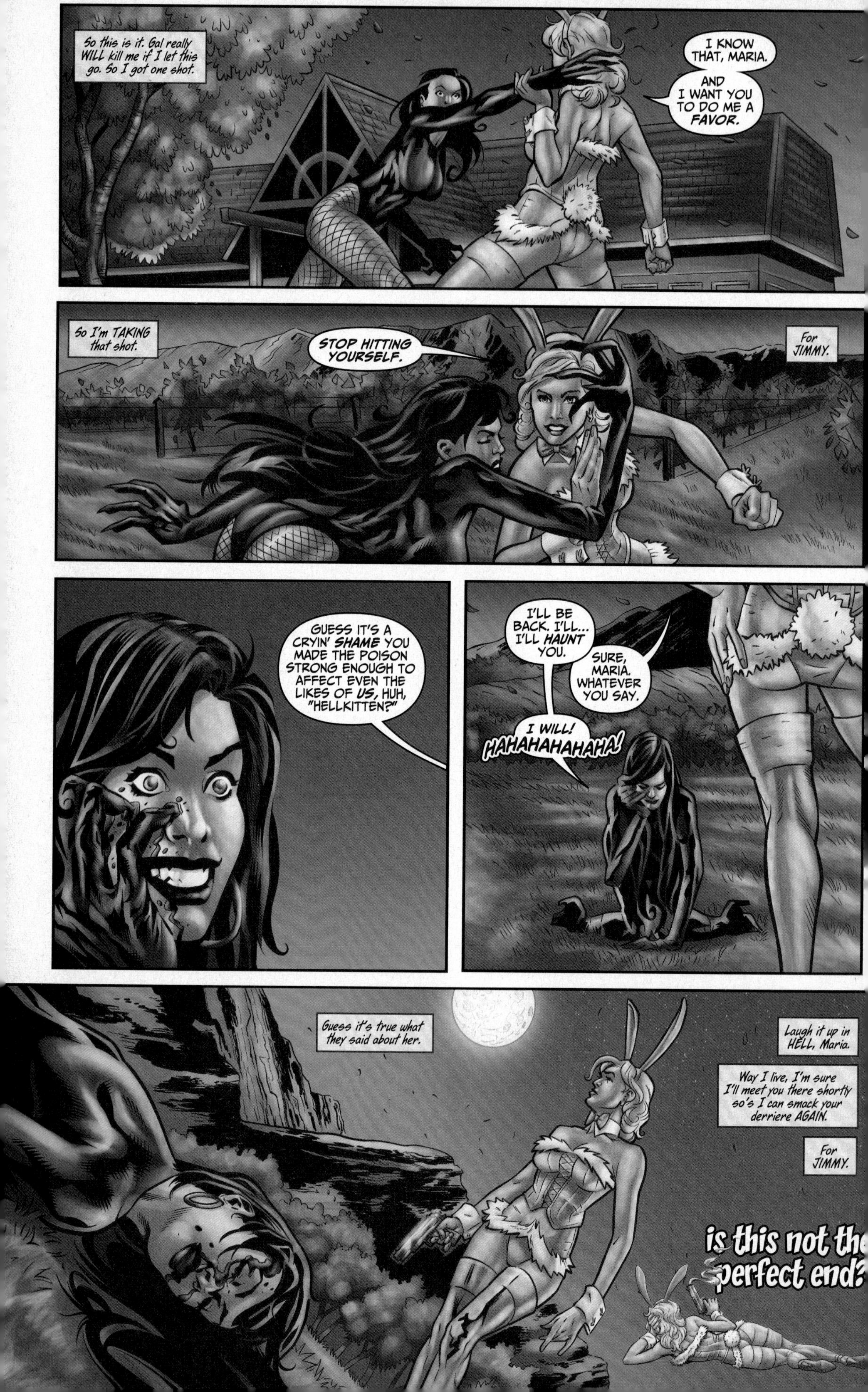
So this is it. Gal really WILL kill me if I let this go. So I got one shot.
I KNOW THAT, MARIA.
AND I WANT YOU TO DO ME A FAVOR.
So I'm TAKING that shot.
STOP HITTING YOURSELF.
For JIMMY.
GUESS IT'S A CRYIN' SHAME YOU MADE THE POISON STRONG ENOUGH TO AFFECT EVEN THE LIKES OF US, HUH, "HELLKITTEN?"
I'LL BE BACK. I'LL... I'LL HAUNT YOU.
SURE, MARIA. WHATEVER YOU SAY.
I WILL! HAHAHAHAHAHA!
Guess it's true what they said about her.
Laugh it up in HELL, Maria.
Way I live, I'm sure I'll meet you there shortly so's I can smack your derriere AGAIN.
For JIMMY.
is this not the perfect end?

CHAPTER TWO

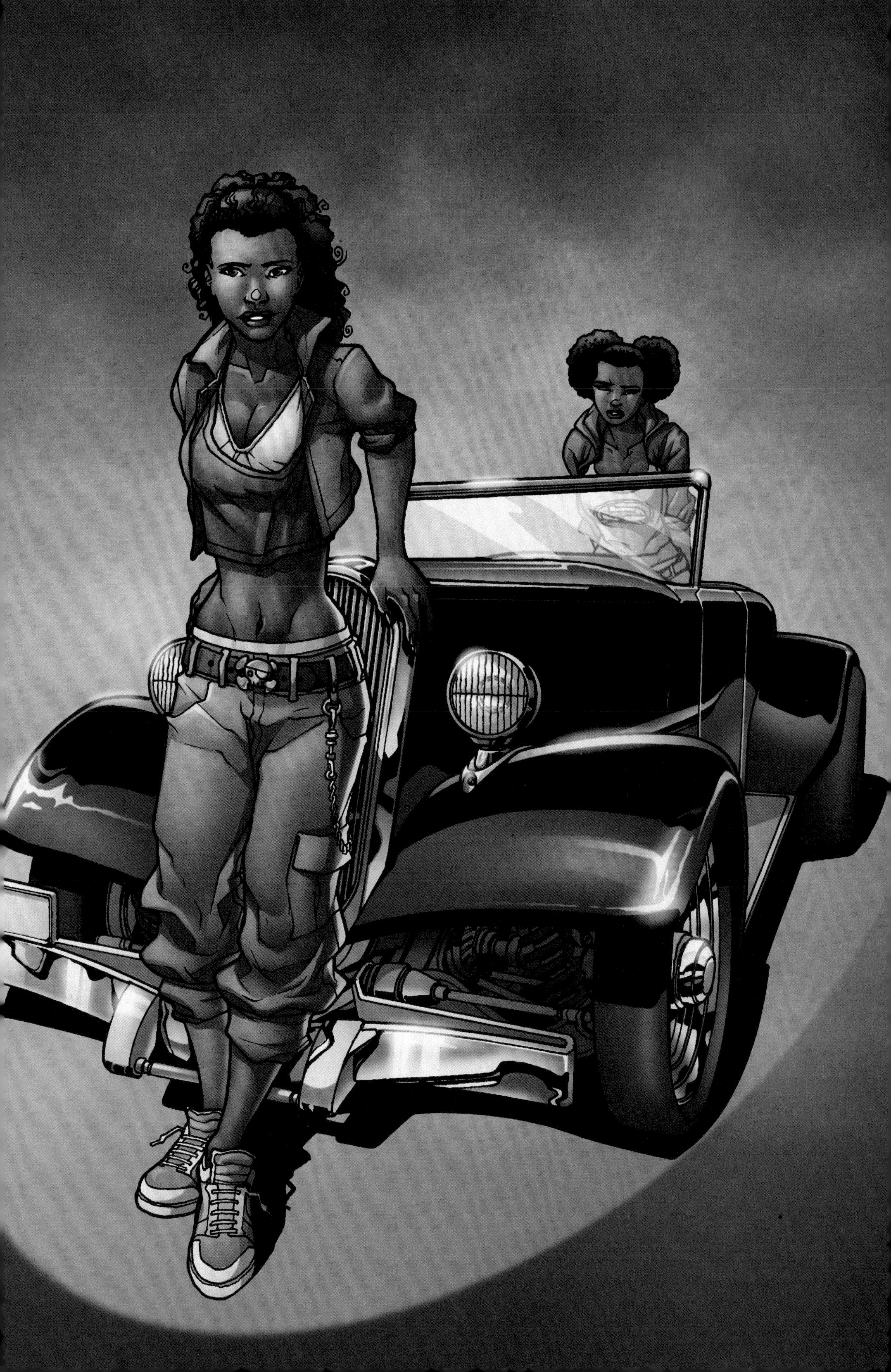

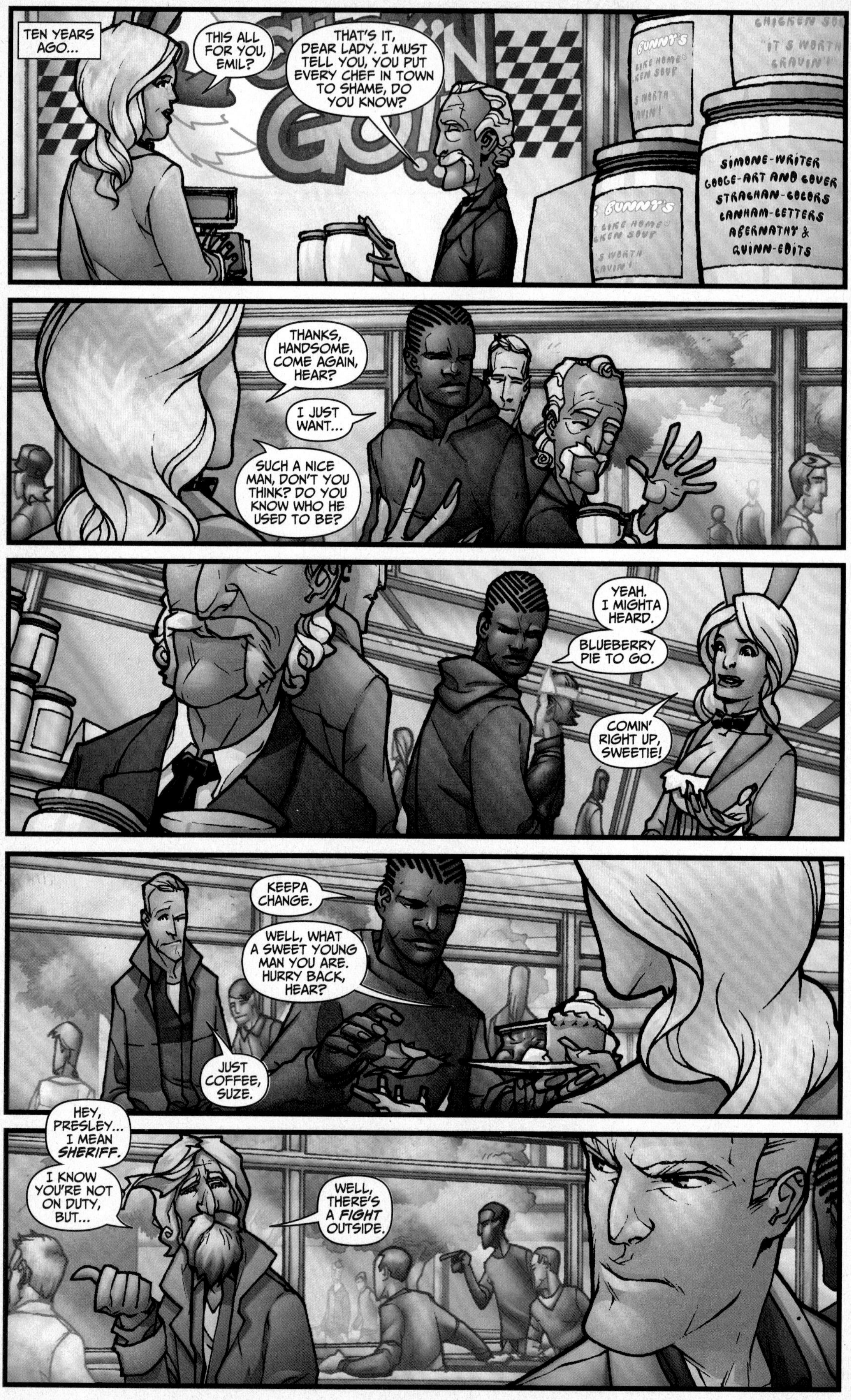
TEN YEARS AGO...
THIS ALL FOR YOU, EMIL?
THAT'S IT, DEAR LADY. I MUST TELL YOU, YOU PUT EVERY CHEF IN TOWN TO SHAME, DO YOU KNOW?
CHICKEN SOUP
"IT'S WORTH CRAVIN'!"
SIMONE-WRITER
GOOGE-ART AND COVER
STRAGHAN-COLORS
LANHAM-LETTERS
ABERNATHY & QUINN-EDITS
THANKS, HANDSOME, COME AGAIN, HEAR?
I JUST WANT...
SUCH A NICE MAN, DON'T YOU THINK? DO YOU KNOW WHO HE USED TO BE?
YEAH. I MIGHTA HEARD.
BLUEBERRY PIE TO GO.
COMIN' RIGHT UP, SWEETIE!
KEEPA CHANGE.
WELL, WHAT A SWEET YOUNG MAN YOU ARE. HURRY BACK, HEAR?
JUST COFFEE, SUZE.
HEY, PRESLEY... I MEAN *SHERIFF*.
I KNOW YOU'RE NOT ON DUTY, BUT...
WELL, THERE'S A *FIGHT* OUTSIDE.

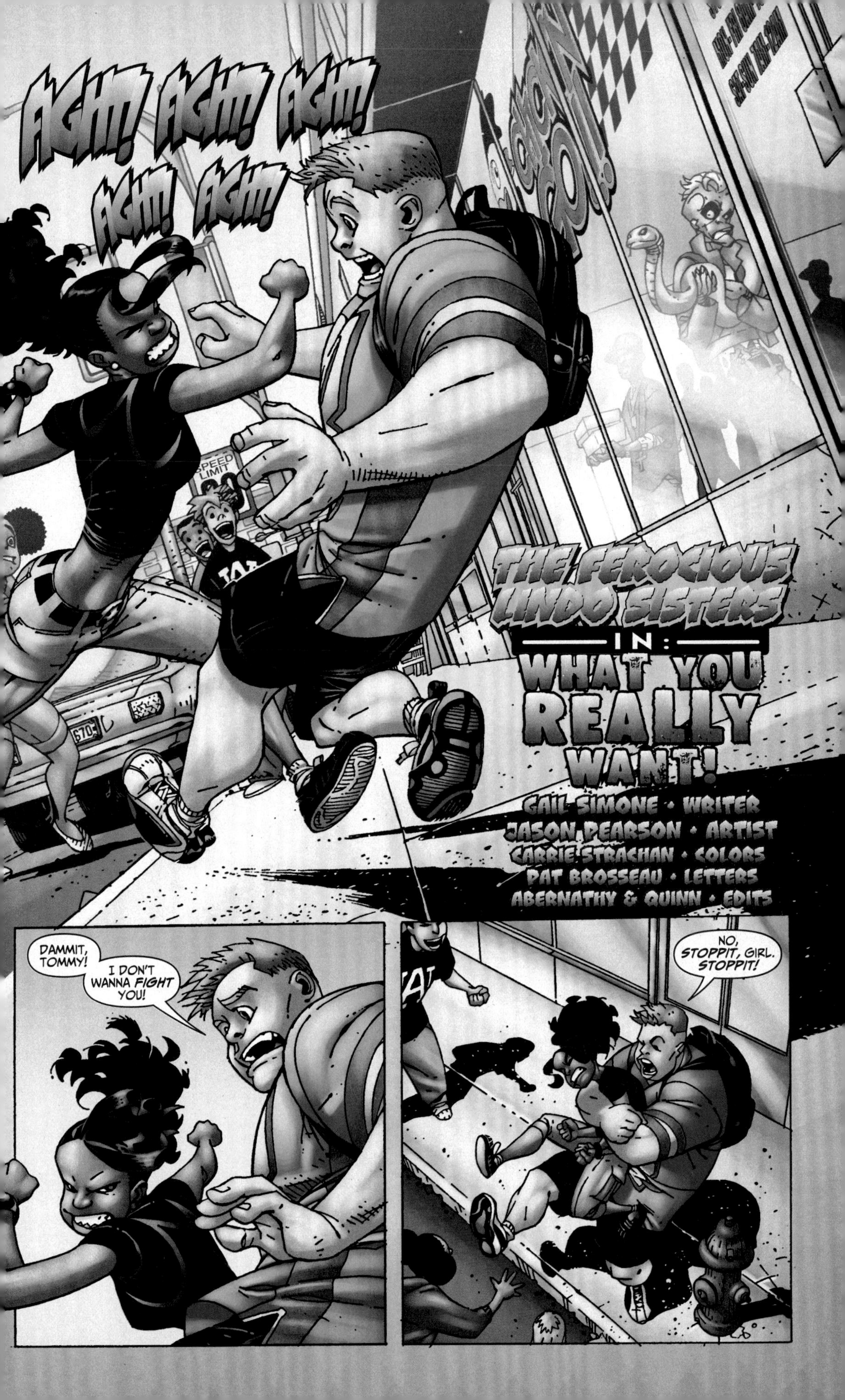
FIGHT! FIGHT! FIGHT!
FIGHT! FIGHT!
SPEED LIMIT
THE FEROCIOUS LINDO SISTERS
IN:
WHAT YOU REALLY WANT!
GAIL SIMONE • WRITER
JASON PEARSON • ARTIST
CARRIE STRACHAN • COLORS
PAT BROSSEAU • LETTERS
ABERNATHY & QUINN • EDITS
DAMMIT, TOMMY!
I DON'T WANNA FIGHT YOU!
NO, STOPPIT, GIRL. STOPPIT!

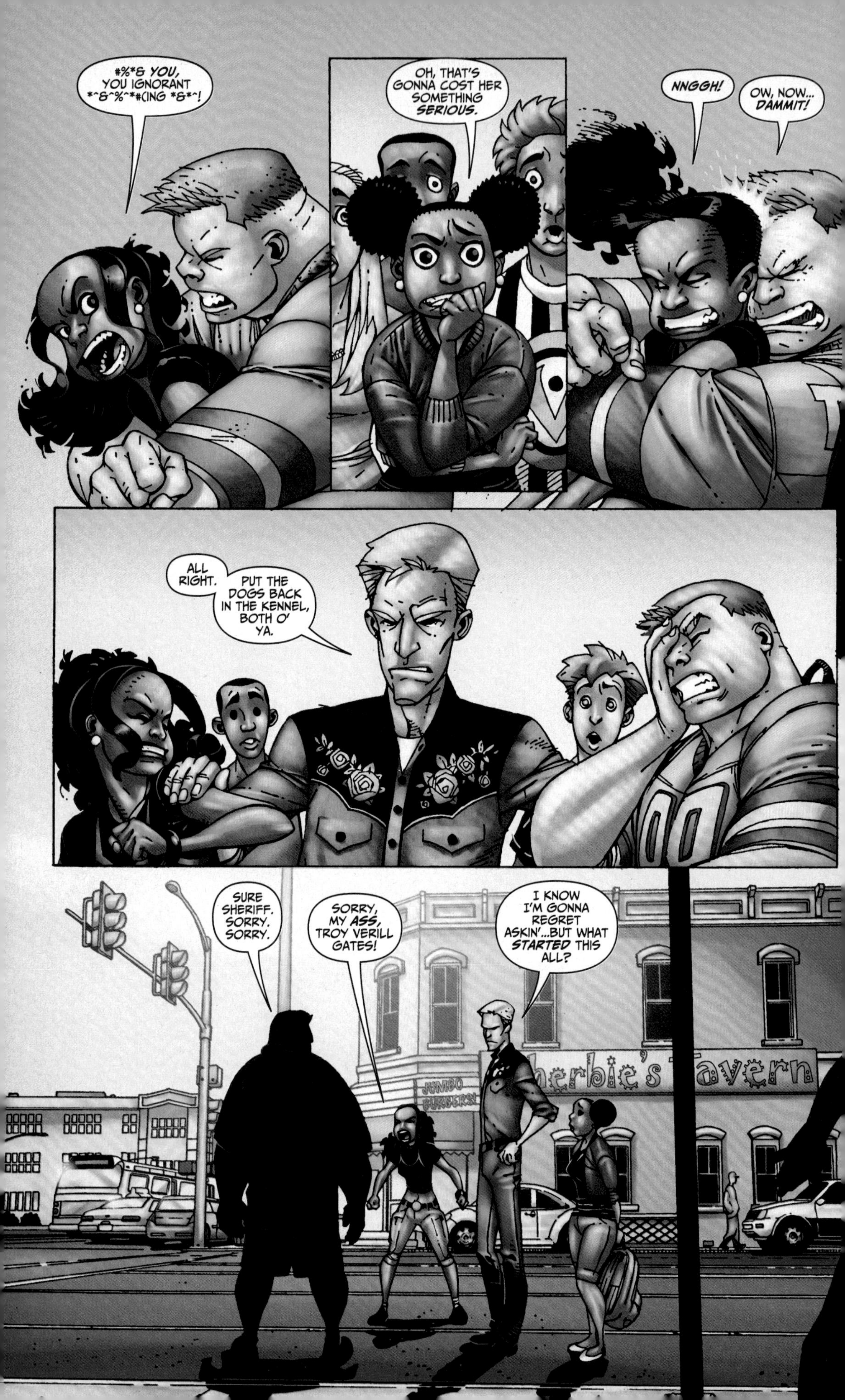
#%*& YOU, YOU IGNORANT *^&^%^*#CING *&*^!
OH, THAT'S GONNA COST HER SOMETHING SERIOUS.
NNGGH!
OW, NOW... DAMMIT!
ALL RIGHT.
PUT THE DOGS BACK IN THE KENNEL, BOTH O' YA.
SURE SHERIFF. SORRY. SORRY.
SORRY, MY ASS, TROY VERILL GATES!
I KNOW I'M GONNA REGRET ASKIN'...BUT WHAT STARTED THIS ALL?
JUMBO BURGERS!
Herbie's Tavern

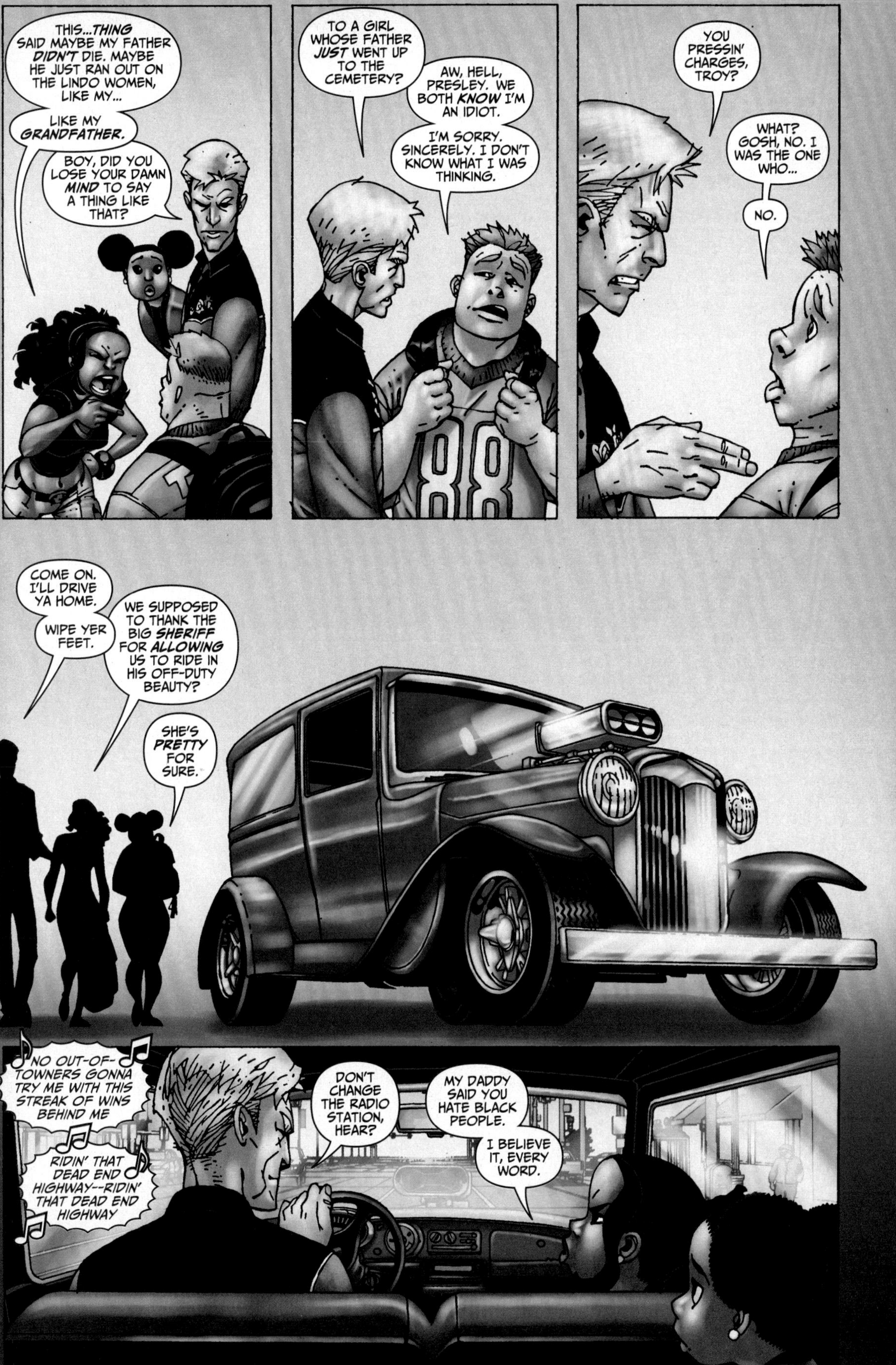
THIS...THING SAID MAYBE MY FATHER DIDN'T DIE. MAYBE HE JUST RAN OUT ON THE LINDO WOMEN, LIKE MY...
LIKE MY GRANDFATHER.
BOY, DID YOU LOSE YOUR DAMN MIND TO SAY A THING LIKE THAT?
TO A GIRL WHOSE FATHER JUST WENT UP TO THE CEMETERY?
AW, HELL, PRESLEY. WE BOTH KNOW I'M AN IDIOT.
I'M SORRY. SINCERELY. I DON'T KNOW WHAT I WAS THINKING.
88
YOU PRESSIN' CHARGES, TROY?
WHAT? GOSH, NO. I WAS THE ONE WHO...
NO.
COME ON. I'LL DRIVE YA HOME.
WIPE YER FEET.
WE SUPPOSED TO THANK THE BIG SHERIFF FOR ALLOWING US TO RIDE IN HIS OFF-DUTY BEAUTY?
SHE'S PRETTY FOR SURE.
NO OUT-OF-TOWNERS GONNA TRY ME WITH THIS STREAK OF WINS BEHIND ME
RIDIN' THAT DEAD END HIGHWAY--RIDIN' THAT DEAD END HIGHWAY
DON'T CHANGE THE RADIO STATION, HEAR?
MY DADDY SAID YOU HATE BLACK PEOPLE.
I BELIEVE IT, EVERY WORD.

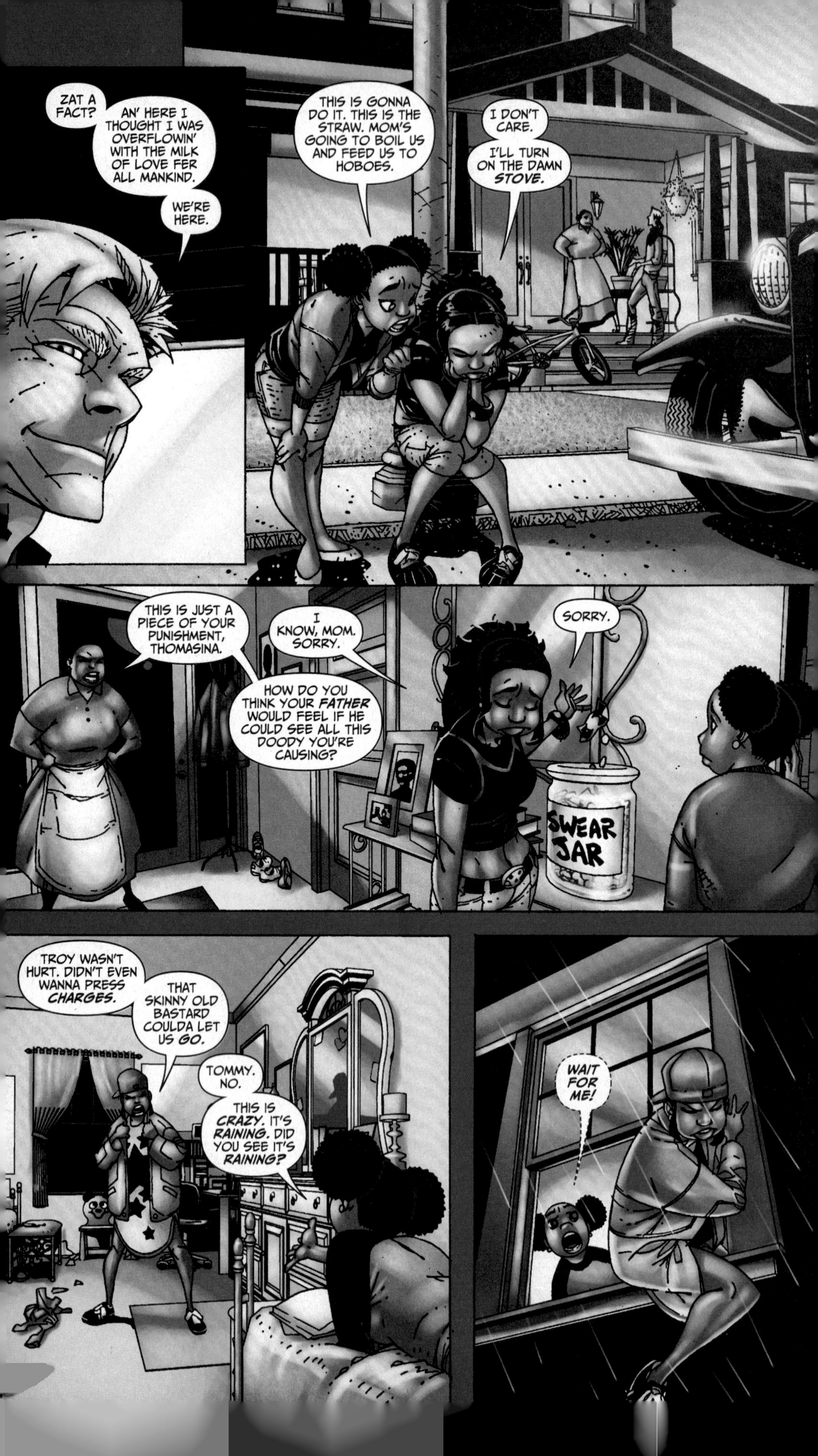
ZAT A FACT?
AN' HERE I THOUGHT I WAS OVERFLOWIN' WITH THE MILK OF LOVE FER ALL MANKIND.
WE'RE HERE.
THIS IS GONNA DO IT. THIS IS THE STRAW. MOM'S GOING TO BOIL US AND FEED US TO HOBOES.
I DON'T CARE.
I'LL TURN ON THE DAMN STOVE.
THIS IS JUST A PIECE OF YOUR PUNISHMENT, THOMASINA.
I KNOW, MOM. SORRY.
HOW DO YOU THINK YOUR FATHER WOULD FEEL IF HE COULD SEE ALL THIS DOODY YOU'RE CAUSING?
SORRY.
SWEAR JAR
TROY WASN'T HURT. DIDN'T EVEN WANNA PRESS CHARGES.
THAT SKINNY OLD BASTARD COULDA LET US GO.
TOMMY. NO.
THIS IS CRAZY. IT'S RAINING. DID YOU SEE IT'S RAINING?
WAIT FOR ME!

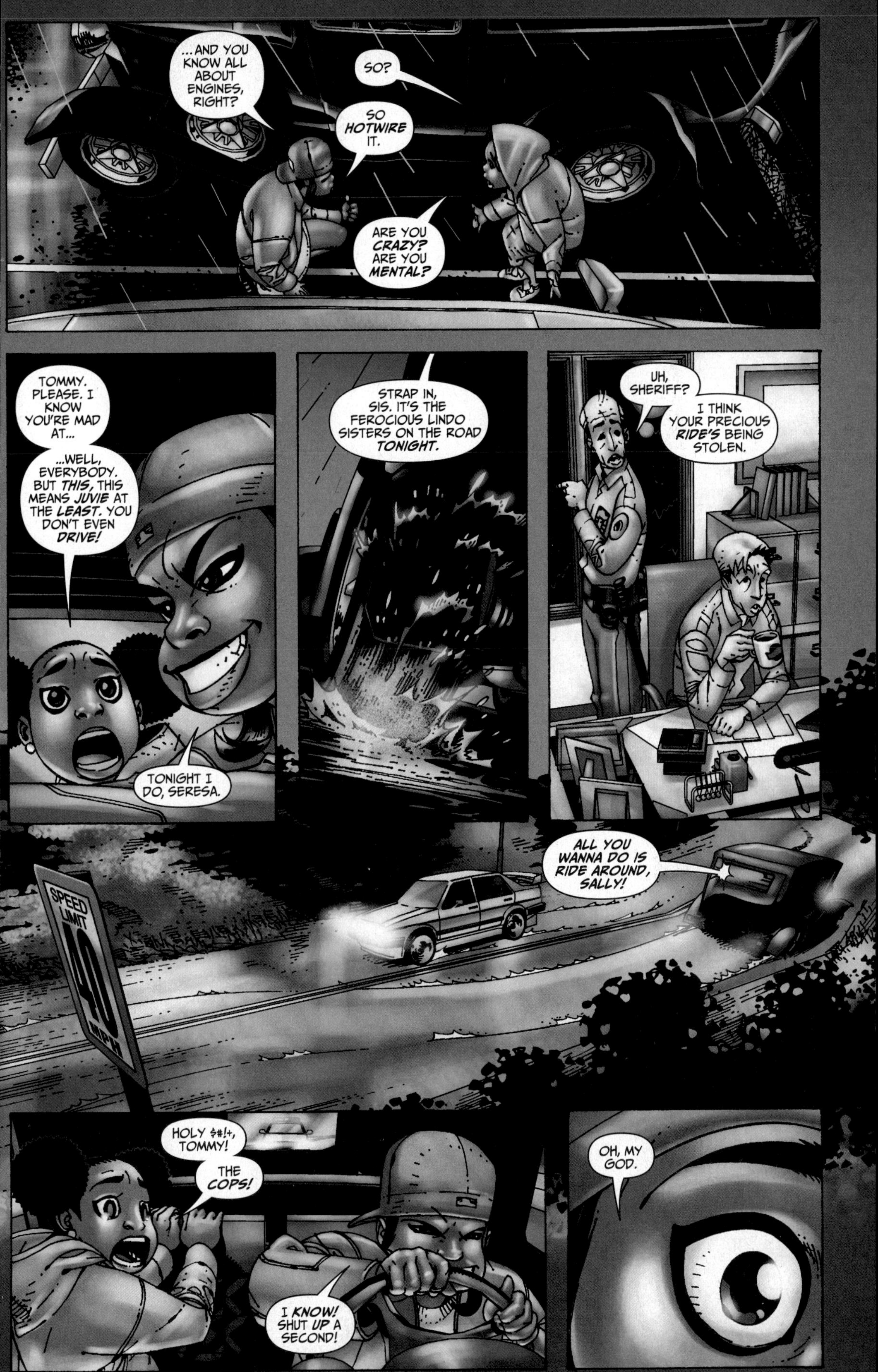
...AND YOU KNOW ALL ABOUT ENGINES, RIGHT?
SO?
SO *HOTWIRE* IT.
ARE YOU *CRAZY?* ARE YOU *MENTAL?*
TOMMY. PLEASE. I KNOW YOU'RE MAD AT...
...WELL, EVERYBODY. BUT *THIS*, THIS MEANS *JUVIE* AT THE *LEAST*. YOU DON'T EVEN *DRIVE!*
TONIGHT I DO, SERESA.
STRAP IN, SIS. IT'S THE FEROCIOUS LINDO SISTERS ON THE ROAD *TONIGHT.*
UH, SHERIFF?
I THINK YOUR PRECIOUS *RIDE'S* BEING STOLEN.
SPEED LIMIT 40 MPH
ALL YOU WANNA DO IS RIDE AROUND, SALLY!
HOLY $#!+, TOMMY!
THE *COPS!*
I *KNOW!* SHUT *UP* A SECOND!
OH, MY GOD.

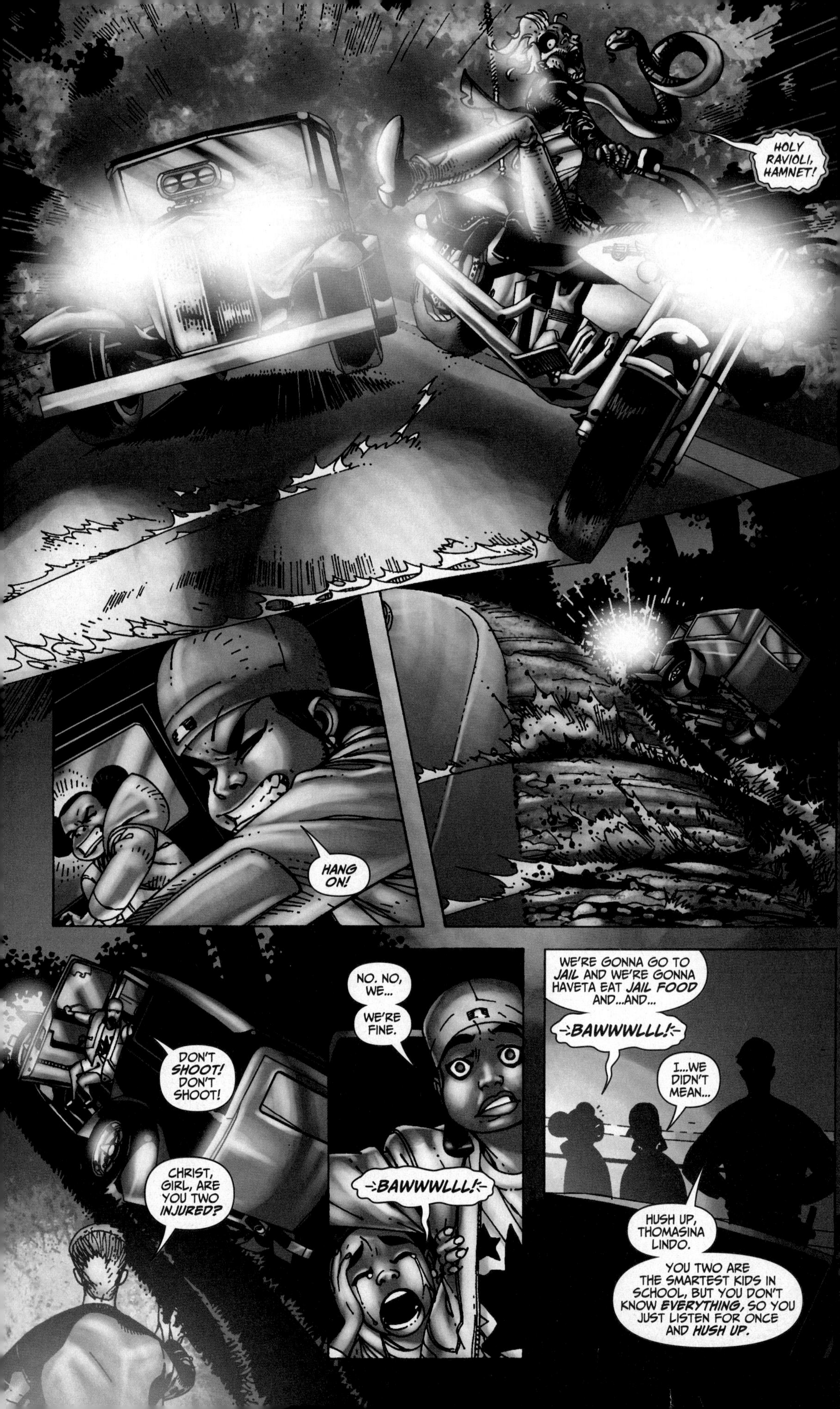
HOLY RAVIOLI, HAMNET!
HANG ON!
DON'T SHOOT! DON'T SHOOT!
CHRIST, GIRL, ARE YOU TWO INJURED?
NO. NO, WE...
WE'RE FINE.
-BAWWWLLL!-
WE'RE GONNA GO TO JAIL AND WE'RE GONNA HAVETA EAT JAIL FOOD AND...AND...
-BAWWWLLL!-
I...WE DIDN'T MEAN...
HUSH UP, THOMASINA LINDO.
YOU TWO ARE THE SMARTEST KIDS IN SCHOOL, BUT YOU DON'T KNOW EVERYTHING, SO YOU JUST LISTEN FOR ONCE AND HUSH UP.

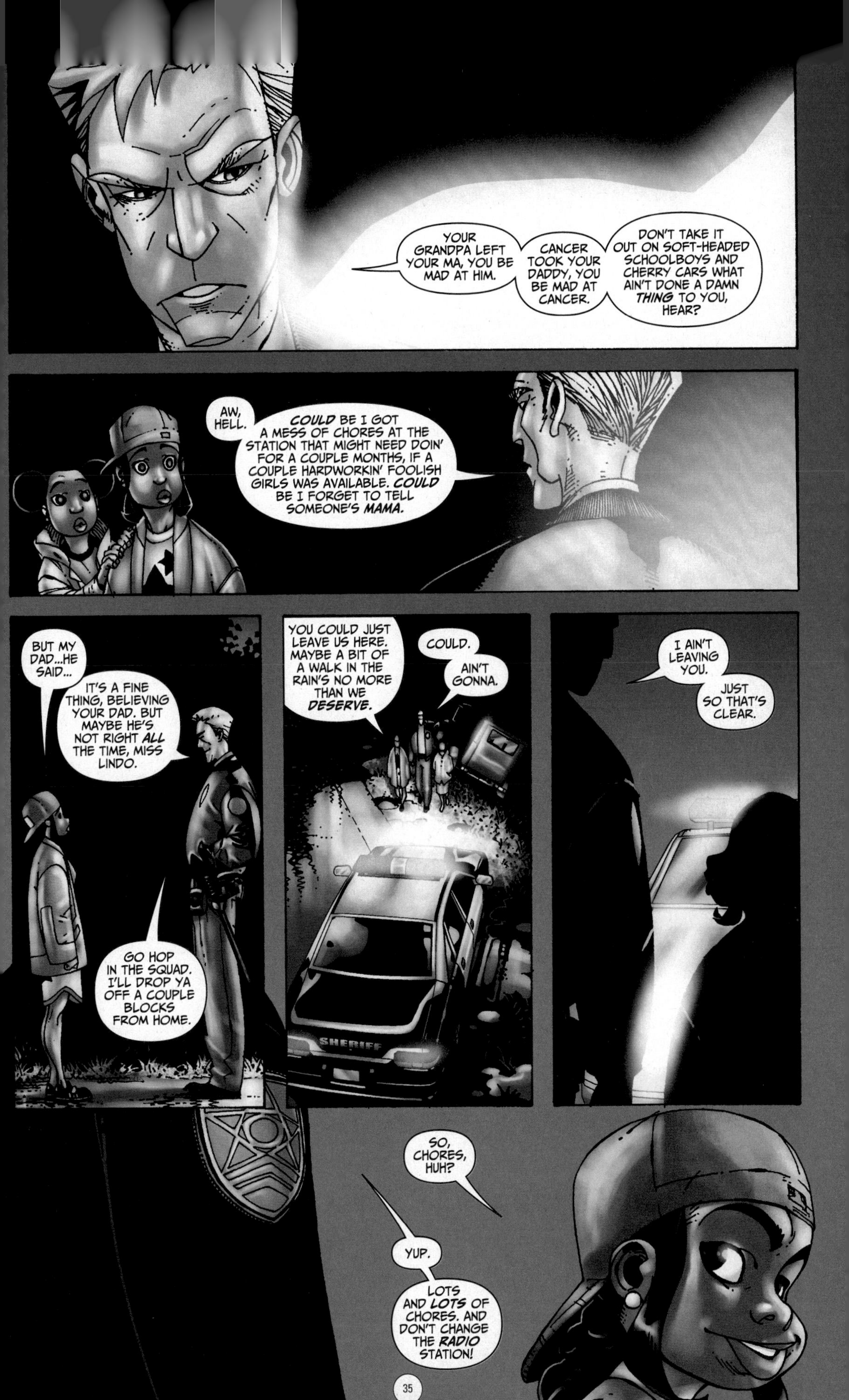
YOUR GRANDPA LEFT YOUR MA, YOU BE MAD AT HIM.
CANCER TOOK YOUR DADDY, YOU BE MAD AT CANCER.
DON'T TAKE IT OUT ON SOFT-HEADED SCHOOLBOYS AND CHERRY CARS WHAT AIN'T DONE A DAMN THING TO YOU, HEAR?
AW, HELL.
COULD BE I GOT A MESS OF CHORES AT THE STATION THAT MIGHT NEED DOIN' FOR A COUPLE MONTHS, IF A COUPLE HARDWORKIN' FOOLISH GIRLS WAS AVAILABLE. COULD BE I FORGET TO TELL SOMEONE'S MAMA.
BUT MY DAD...HE SAID...
IT'S A FINE THING, BELIEVING YOUR DAD. BUT MAYBE HE'S NOT RIGHT ALL THE TIME, MISS LINDO.
GO HOP IN THE SQUAD. I'LL DROP YA OFF A COUPLE BLOCKS FROM HOME.
YOU COULD JUST LEAVE US HERE. MAYBE A BIT OF A WALK IN THE RAIN'S NO MORE THAN WE DESERVE.
COULD.
AIN'T GONNA.
SHERIFF
I AIN'T LEAVING YOU.
JUST SO THAT'S CLEAR.
SO, CHORES, HUH?
YUP.
LOTS AND LOTS OF CHORES. AND DON'T CHANGE THE RADIO STATION!

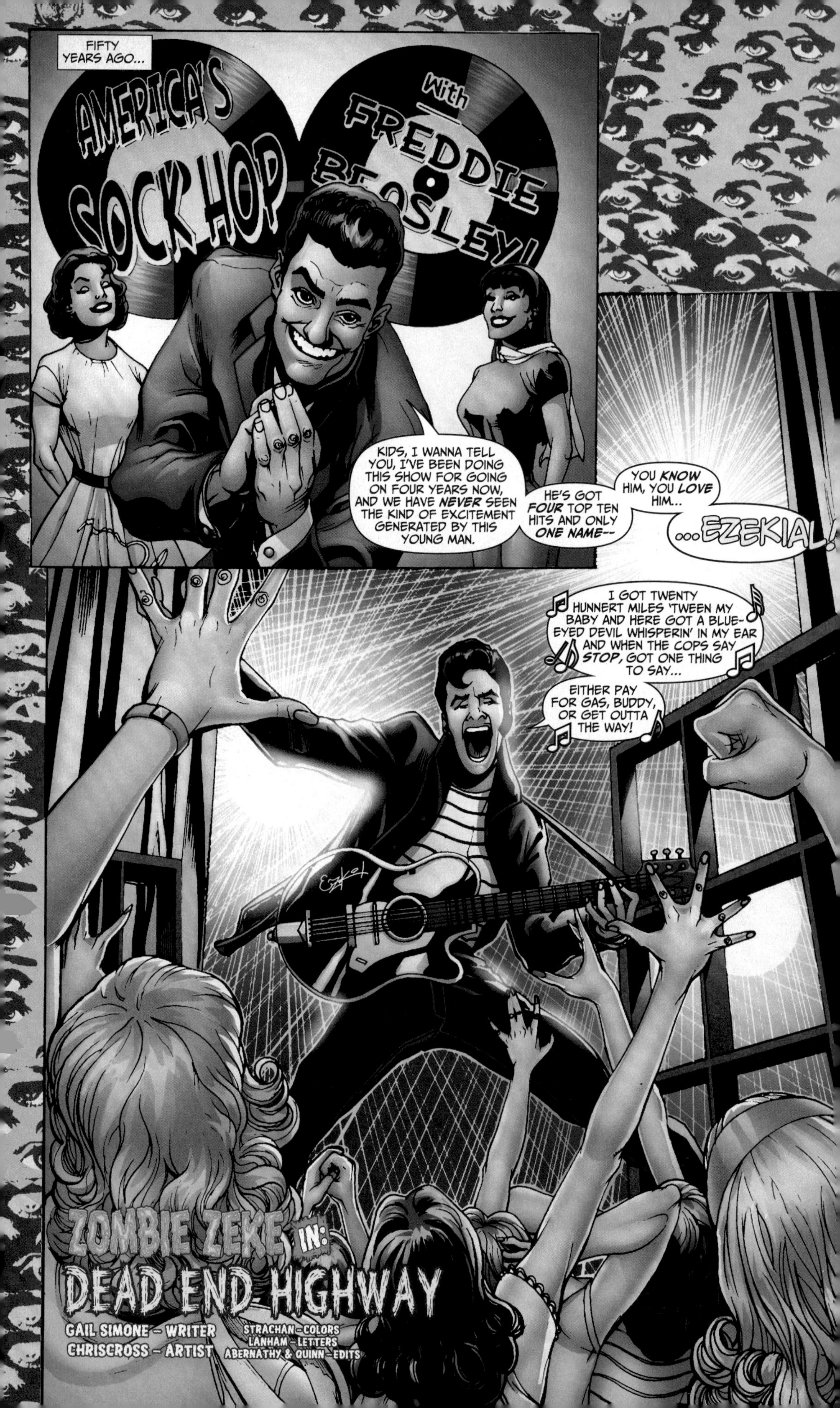
FIFTY YEARS AGO...
AMERICA'S SOCK HOP
With FREDDIE
KIDS, I WANNA TELL YOU, I'VE BEEN DOING THIS SHOW FOR GOING ON FOUR YEARS NOW, AND WE HAVE NEVER SEEN THE KIND OF EXCITEMENT GENERATED BY THIS YOUNG MAN.
HE'S GOT FOUR TOP TEN HITS AND ONLY ONE NAME--
YOU KNOW HIM, YOU LOVE HIM...
...EZEKIAL!
I GOT TWENTY HUNNERT MILES 'TWEEN MY BABY AND HERE GOT A BLUE-EYED DEVIL WHISPERIN' IN MY EAR AND WHEN THE COPS SAY STOP, GOT ONE THING TO SAY...
EITHER PAY FOR GAS, BUDDY, OR GET OUTTA THE WAY!
ZOMBIE ZEKE IN:
DEAD END HIGHWAY
GAIL SIMONE – WRITER
CHRISCROSS – ARTIST
STRACHAN – COLORS
LANHAM – LETTERS
ABERNATHY & QUINN – EDITS

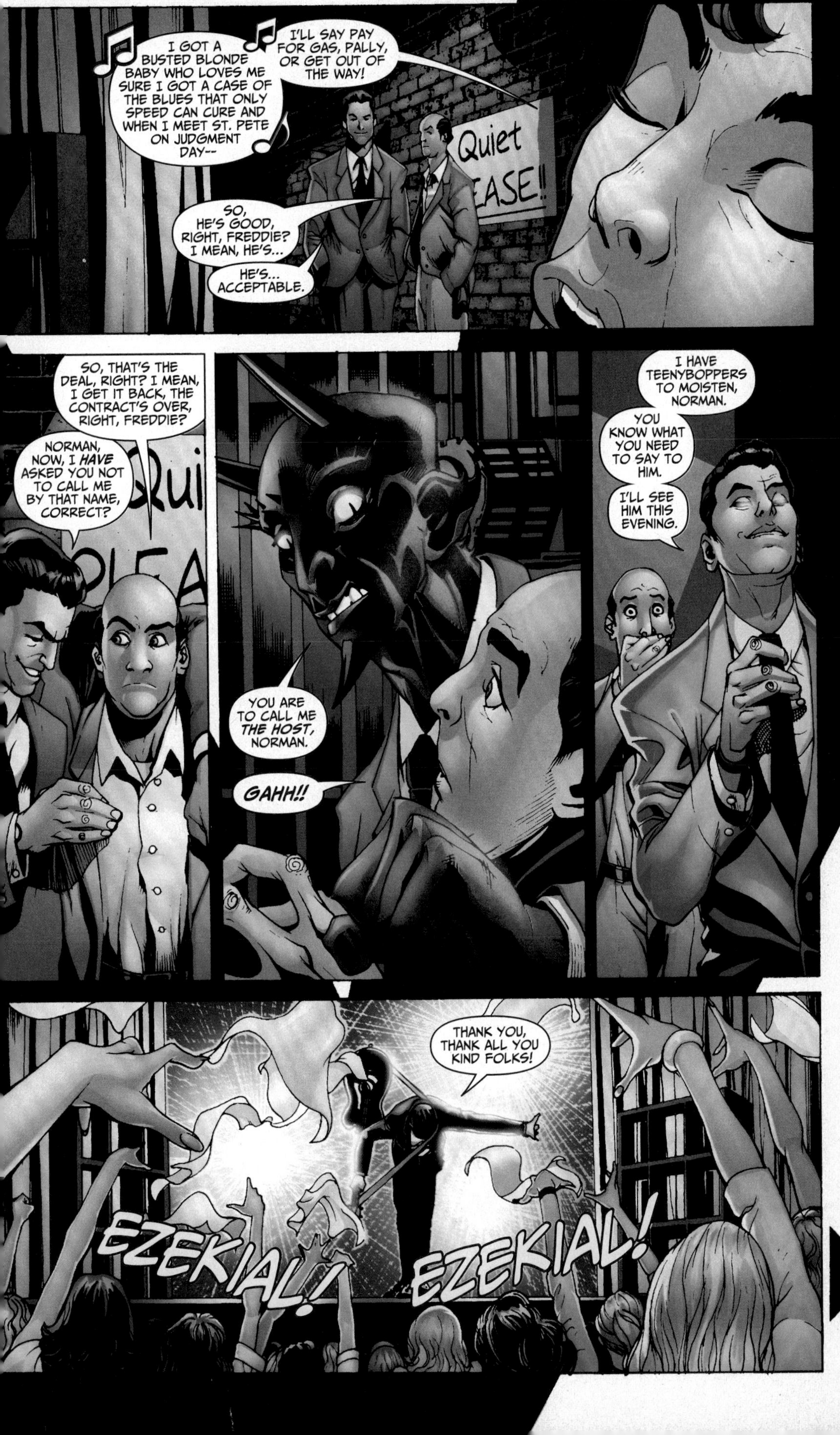
I GOT A BUSTED BLONDE BABY WHO LOVES ME SURE I GOT A CASE OF THE BLUES THAT ONLY SPEED CAN CURE AND WHEN I MEET ST. PETE ON JUDGMENT DAY--
I'LL SAY PAY FOR GAS, PALLY, OR GET OUT OF THE WAY!
Quiet
EASE!!
SO, HE'S GOOD, RIGHT, FREDDIE? I MEAN, HE'S...
HE'S... ACCEPTABLE.
SO, THAT'S THE DEAL, RIGHT? I MEAN, I GET IT BACK, THE CONTRACT'S OVER, RIGHT, FREDDIE?
NORMAN, NOW, I *HAVE* ASKED YOU NOT TO CALL ME BY THAT NAME, CORRECT?
YOU ARE TO CALL ME *THE HOST*, NORMAN.
GAHH!!
I HAVE TEENYBOPPERS TO MOISTEN, NORMAN.
YOU KNOW WHAT YOU NEED TO SAY TO HIM.
I'LL SEE HIM THIS EVENING.
THANK YOU, THANK ALL YOU KIND FOLKS!
EZEKIAL! EZEKIAL!

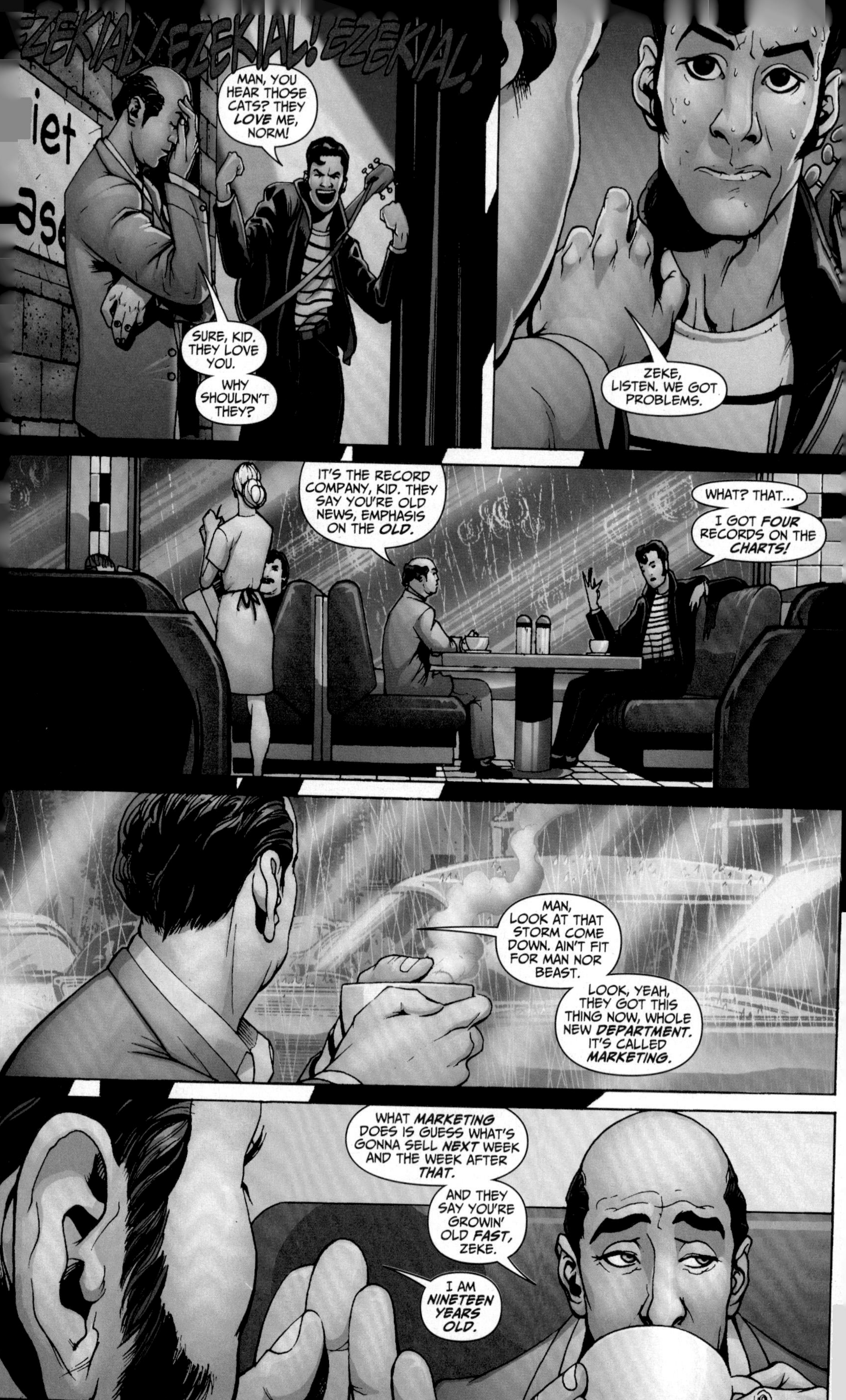
EZEKIAL! EZEKIAL! EZEKIAL!
iet
ase
MAN, YOU HEAR THOSE CATS? THEY LOVE ME, NORM!
SURE, KID. THEY LOVE YOU.
WHY SHOULDN'T THEY?
ZEKE, LISTEN. WE GOT PROBLEMS.
IT'S THE RECORD COMPANY, KID. THEY SAY YOU'RE OLD NEWS, EMPHASIS ON THE OLD.
WHAT? THAT...
I GOT FOUR RECORDS ON THE CHARTS!
MAN, LOOK AT THAT STORM COME DOWN. AIN'T FIT FOR MAN NOR BEAST.
LOOK, YEAH, THEY GOT THIS THING NOW, WHOLE NEW DEPARTMENT. IT'S CALLED MARKETING.
WHAT MARKETING DOES IS GUESS WHAT'S GONNA SELL NEXT WEEK AND THE WEEK AFTER THAT.
AND THEY SAY YOU'RE GROWIN' OLD FAST, ZEKE.
I AM NINETEEN YEARS OLD.

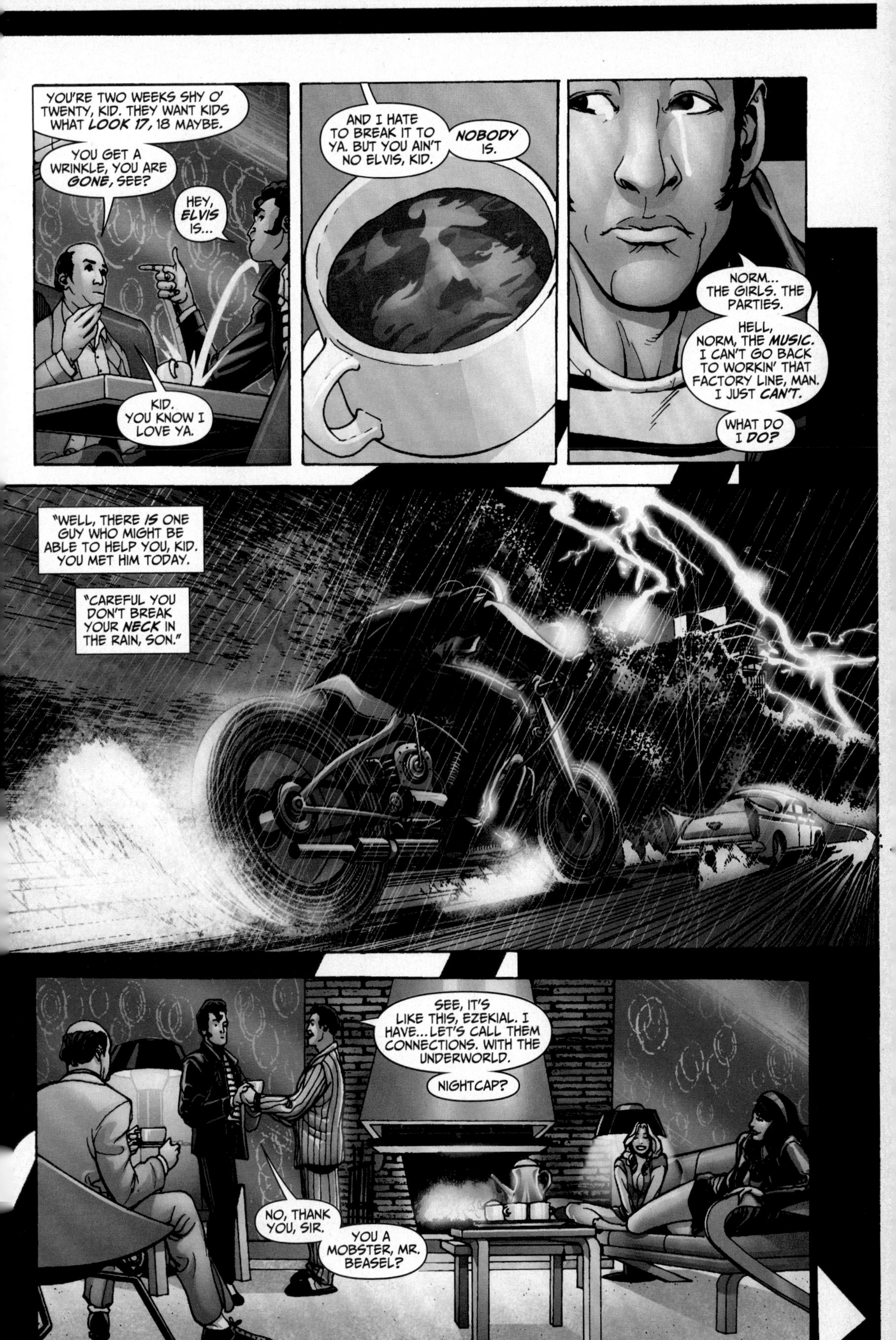
YOU'RE TWO WEEKS SHY O' TWENTY, KID. THEY WANT KIDS WHAT LOOK 17, 18 MAYBE.
YOU GET A WRINKLE, YOU ARE GONE, SEE?
HEY, ELVIS IS...
KID. YOU KNOW I LOVE YA.
AND I HATE TO BREAK IT TO YA. BUT YOU AIN'T NO ELVIS, KID.
NOBODY IS.
NORM... THE GIRLS. THE PARTIES.
HELL, NORM, THE MUSIC. I CAN'T GO BACK TO WORKIN' THAT FACTORY LINE, MAN. I JUST CAN'T.
WHAT DO I DO?
"WELL, THERE IS ONE GUY WHO MIGHT BE ABLE TO HELP YOU, KID. YOU MET HIM TODAY.
"CAREFUL YOU DON'T BREAK YOUR NECK IN THE RAIN, SON."
SEE, IT'S LIKE THIS, EZEKIAL. I HAVE...LET'S CALL THEM CONNECTIONS. WITH THE UNDERWORLD.
NIGHTCAP?
NO, THANK YOU, SIR.
YOU A MOBSTER, MR. BEASEL?

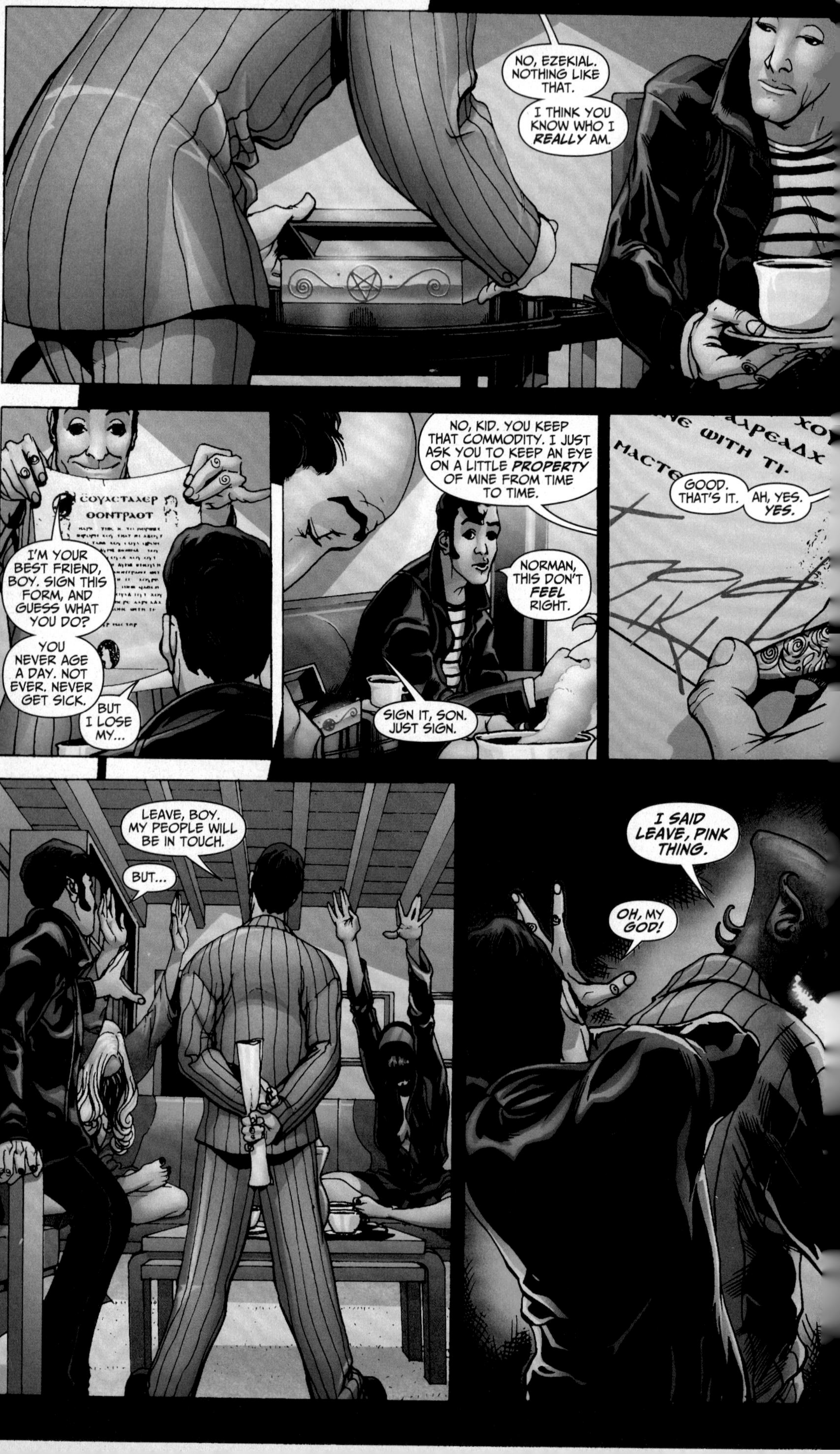
NO, EZEKIAL. NOTHING LIKE THAT.
I THINK YOU KNOW WHO I *REALLY* AM.
I'M YOUR BEST FRIEND, BOY. SIGN THIS FORM, AND GUESS WHAT YOU DO?
YOU NEVER AGE A DAY. NOT EVER. NEVER GET SICK.
BUT I LOSE MY...
NO, KID. YOU KEEP THAT COMMODITY. I JUST ASK YOU TO KEEP AN EYE ON A LITTLE *PROPERTY* OF MINE FROM TIME TO TIME.
NORMAN, THIS DON'T *FEEL* RIGHT.
SIGN IT, SON. JUST SIGN.
GOOD. THAT'S IT.
AH, YES. *YES.*
LEAVE, BOY. MY PEOPLE WILL BE IN TOUCH.
BUT...
I SAID LEAVE, PINK THING.
OH, MY GOD!

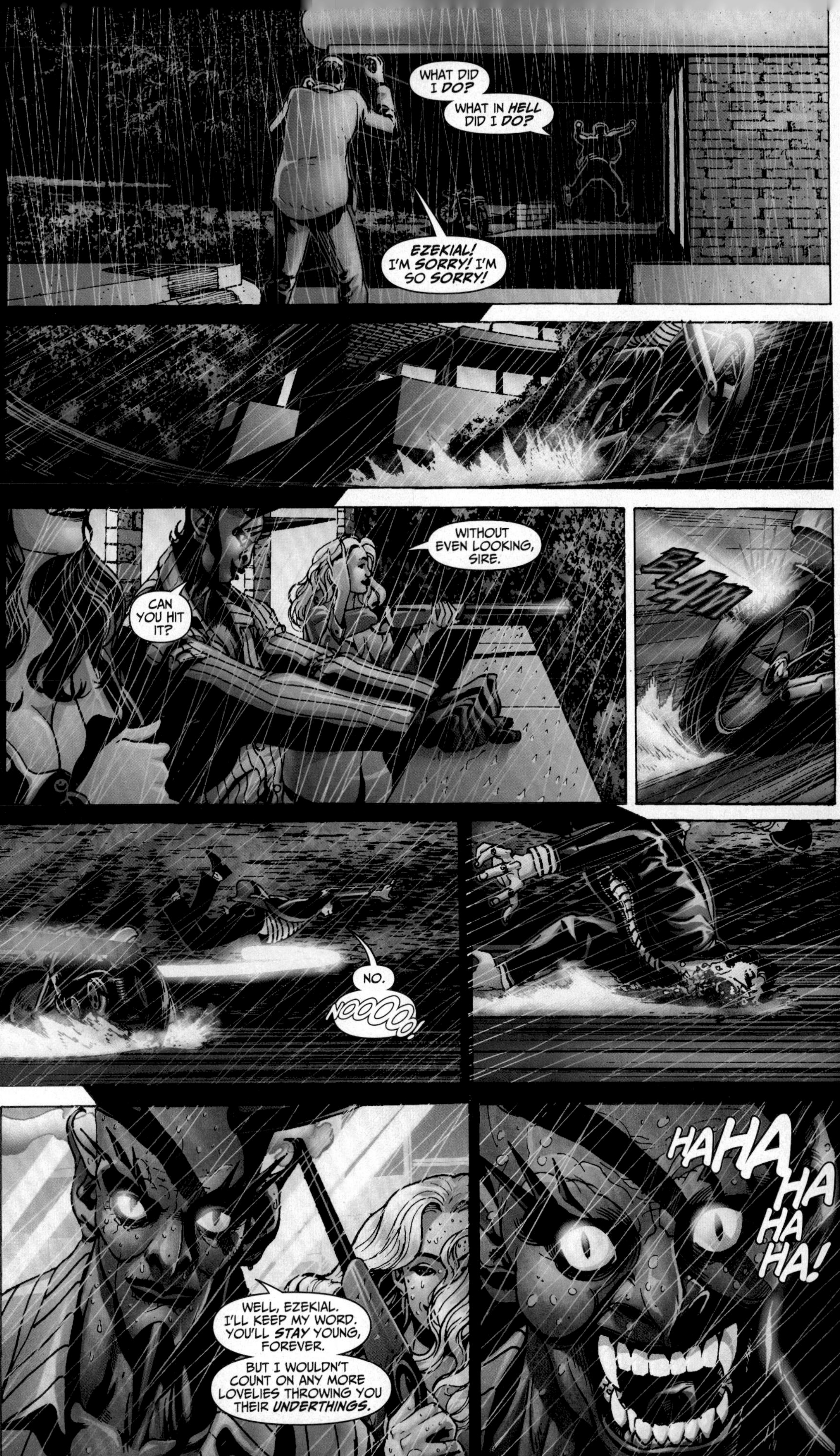
WHAT DID I DO?
WHAT IN HELL DID I DO?
EZEKIAL! I'M SORRY! I'M SO SORRY!
CAN YOU HIT IT?
WITHOUT EVEN LOOKING, SIRE.
BLAM
NO.
NOOOOO!
WELL, EZEKIAL. I'LL KEEP MY WORD. YOU'LL STAY YOUNG, FOREVER.
BUT I WOULDN'T COUNT ON ANY MORE LOVELIES THROWING YOU THEIR UNDERTHINGS.
HAHAHAHAHA!

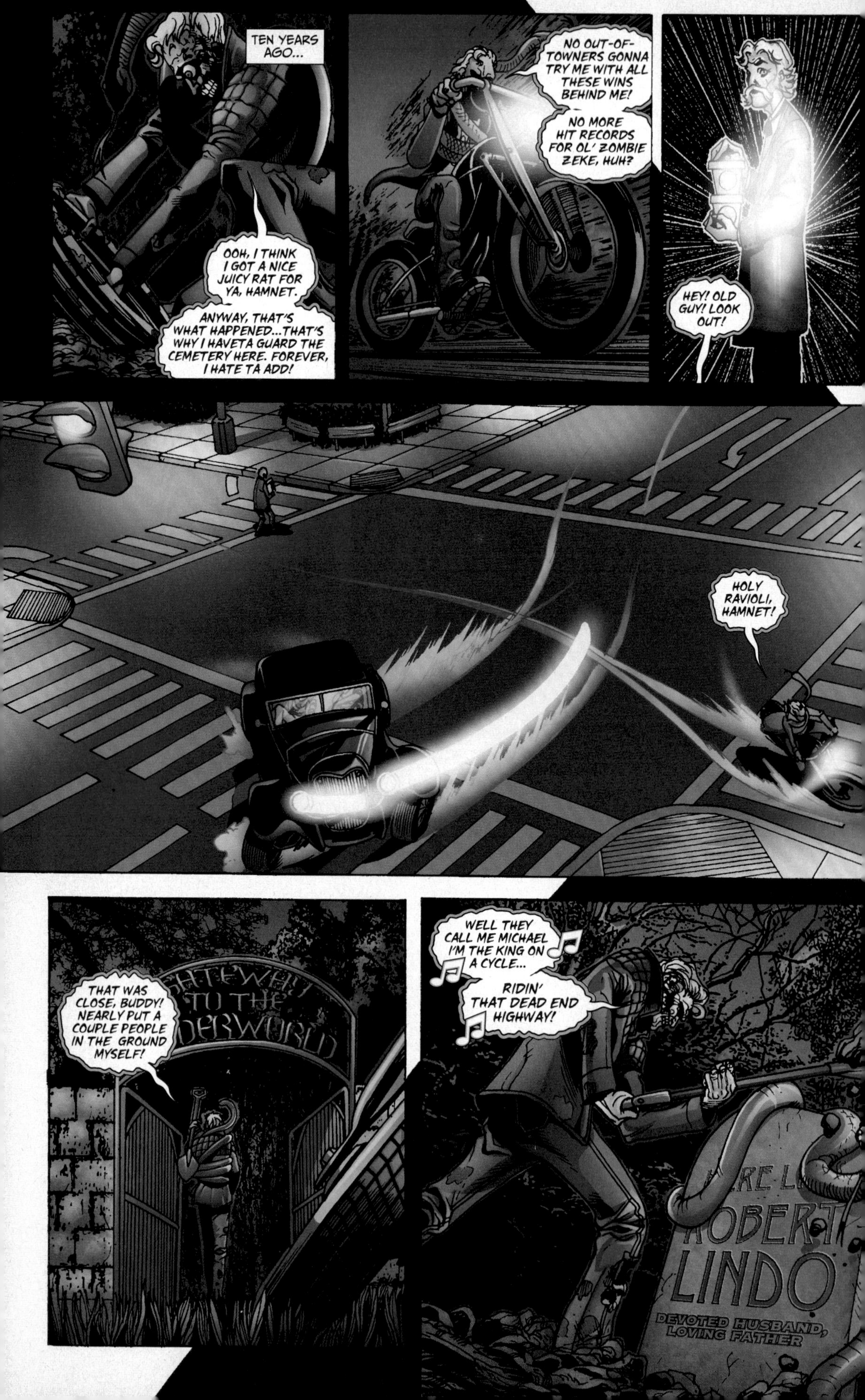
TEN YEARS AGO...
OOH, I THINK I GOT A NICE JUICY RAT FOR YA, HAMNET.
ANYWAY, THAT'S WHAT HAPPENED...THAT'S WHY I HAVETA GUARD THE CEMETERY HERE. FOREVER, I HATE TA ADD!
NO OUT-OF-TOWNERS GONNA TRY ME WITH ALL THESE WINS BEHIND ME!
NO MORE HIT RECORDS FOR OL' ZOMBIE ZEKE, HUH?
HEY! OLD GUY! LOOK OUT!
HOLY RAVIOLI, HAMNET!
THAT WAS CLOSE, BUDDY! NEARLY PUT A COUPLE PEOPLE IN THE GROUND MYSELF!
WELL THEY CALL ME MICHAEL I'M THE KING ON A CYCLE...
RIDIN' THAT DEAD END HIGHWAY!
ROBERT LINDO
DEVOTED HUSBAND, LOVING FATHER

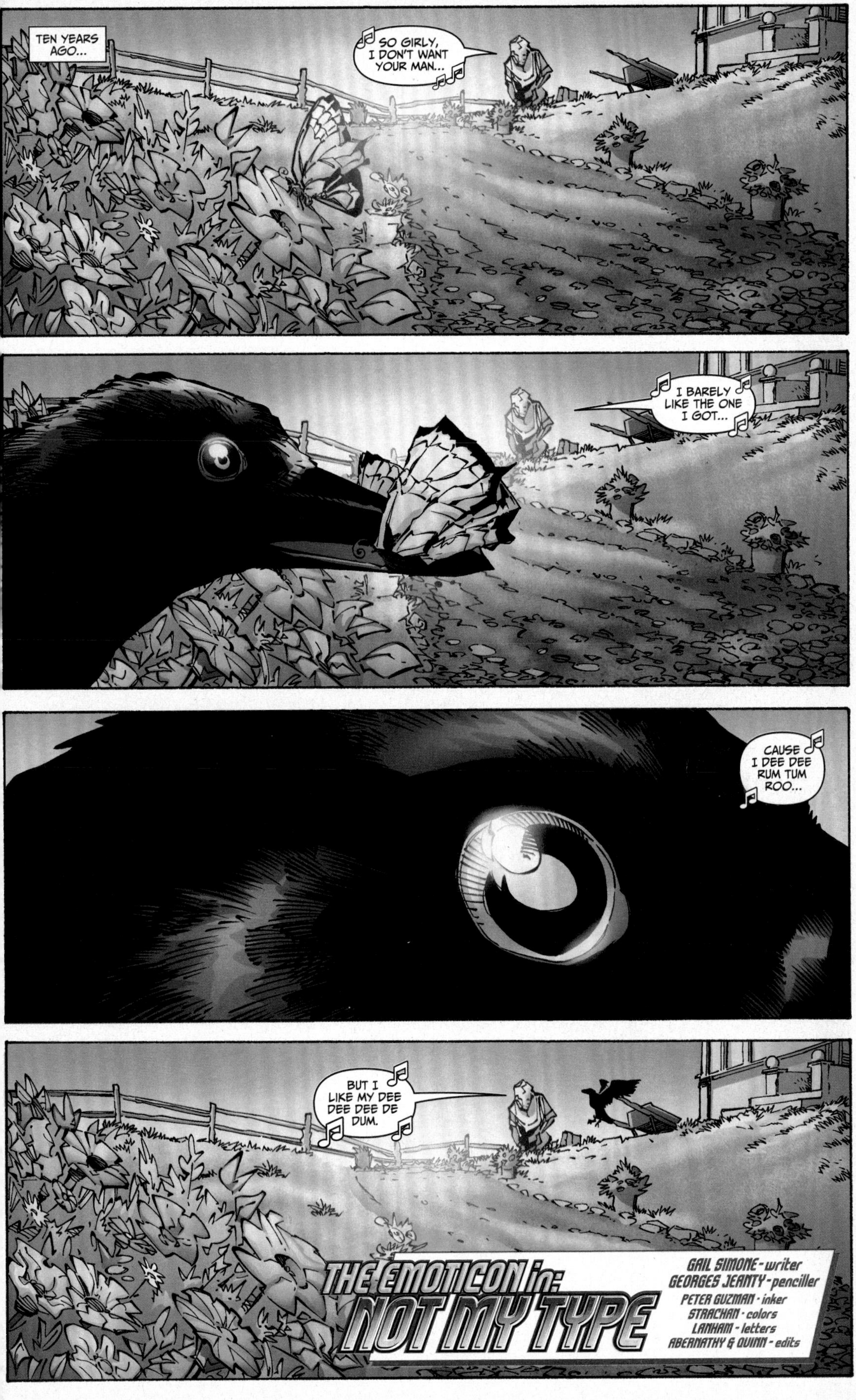
TEN YEARS AGO...
SO GIRLY, I DON'T WANT YOUR MAN...
I BARELY LIKE THE ONE I GOT...
CAUSE I DEE DEE RUM TUM ROO...
BUT I LIKE MY DEE DEE DEE DE DUM.
THE EMOTICON in:
NOT MY TYPE
GAIL SIMONE - writer
GEORGES JEANTY - penciller
PETER GUZMAN - inker
STRACHAN - colors
LANHAM - letters
ABERNATHY & QUINN - edits

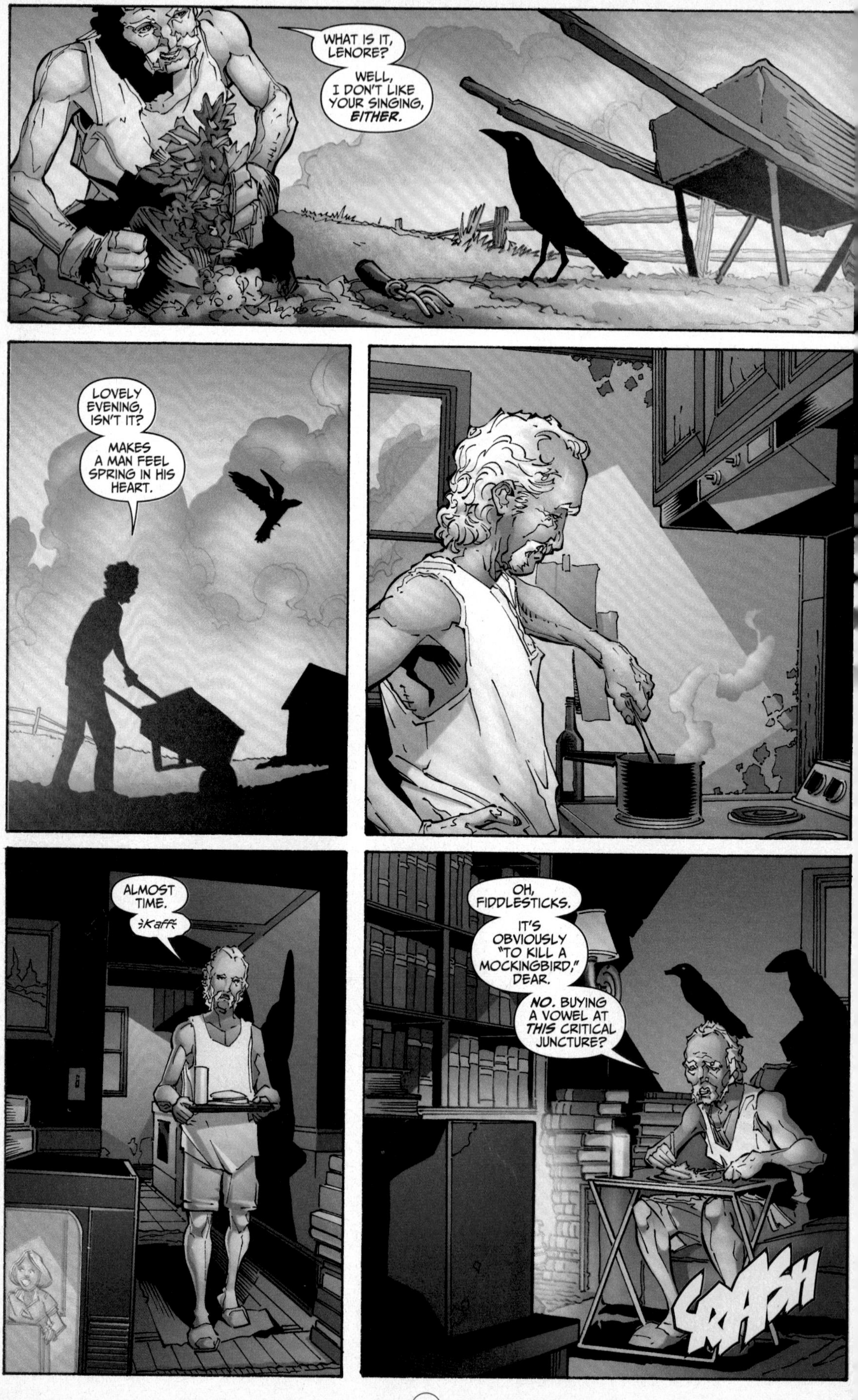
WHAT IS IT, LENORE?
WELL, I DON'T LIKE YOUR SINGING, *EITHER.*
LOVELY EVENING, ISN'T IT?
MAKES A MAN FEEL SPRING IN HIS HEART.
ALMOST TIME.
Kaff
OH, FIDDLESTICKS.
IT'S OBVIOUSLY "TO KILL A MOCKINGBIRD," DEAR.
NO. BUYING A VOWEL AT *THIS* CRITICAL JUNCTURE?
CRASH

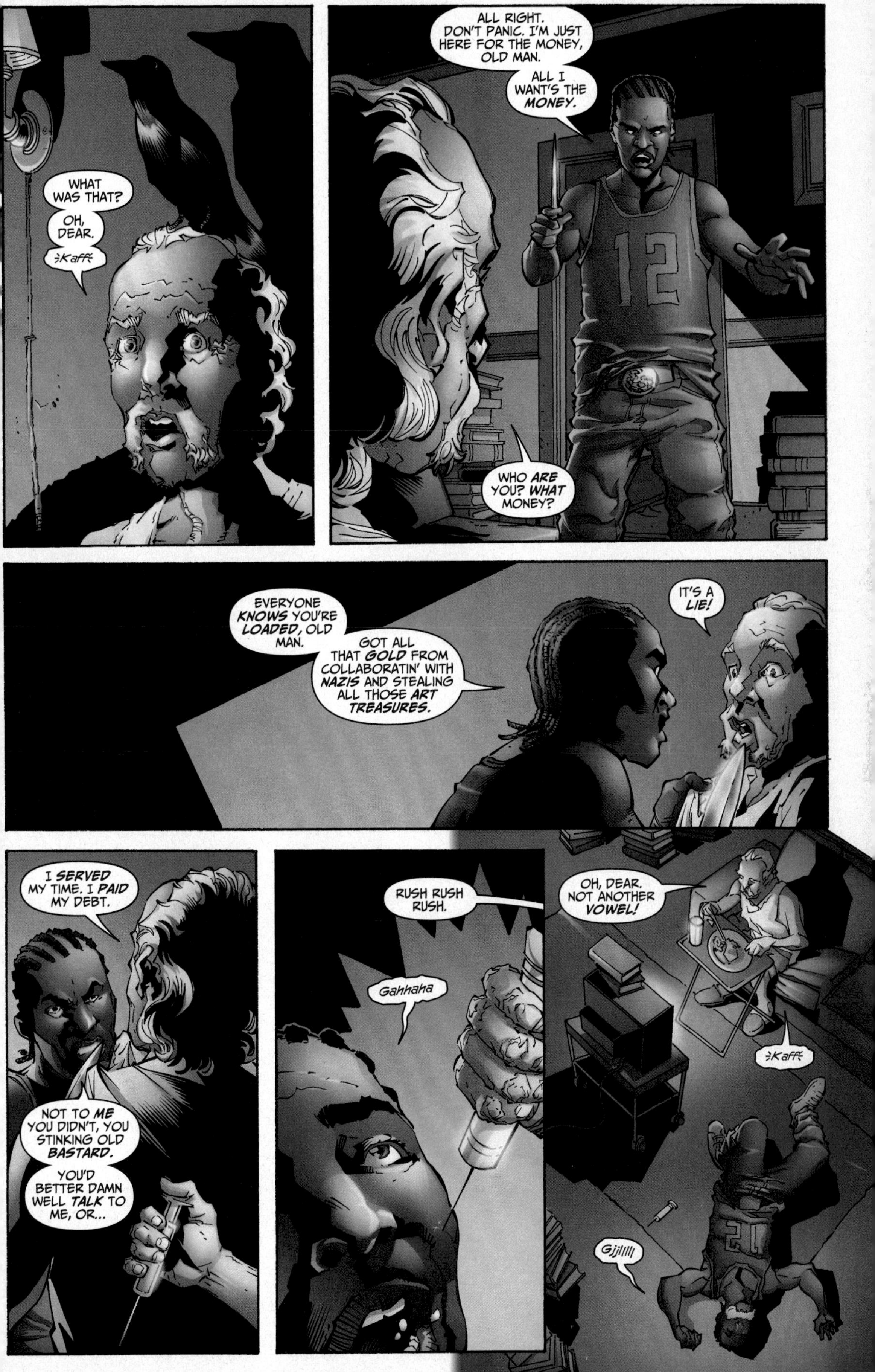
WHAT WAS THAT?
OH, DEAR.
KAFF
ALL RIGHT. DON'T PANIC. I'M JUST HERE FOR THE MONEY, OLD MAN.
ALL I WANT'S THE MONEY.
WHO ARE YOU? WHAT MONEY?
EVERYONE KNOWS YOU'RE LOADED, OLD MAN.
GOT ALL THAT GOLD FROM COLLABORATIN' WITH NAZIS AND STEALING ALL THOSE ART TREASURES.
IT'S A LIE!
I SERVED MY TIME. I PAID MY DEBT.
NOT TO ME YOU DIDN'T, YOU STINKING OLD BASTARD.
YOU'D BETTER DAMN WELL TALK TO ME, OR...
RUSH RUSH RUSH.
Gahhaha
OH, DEAR. NOT ANOTHER VOWEL!
Kaff
Gjjllll

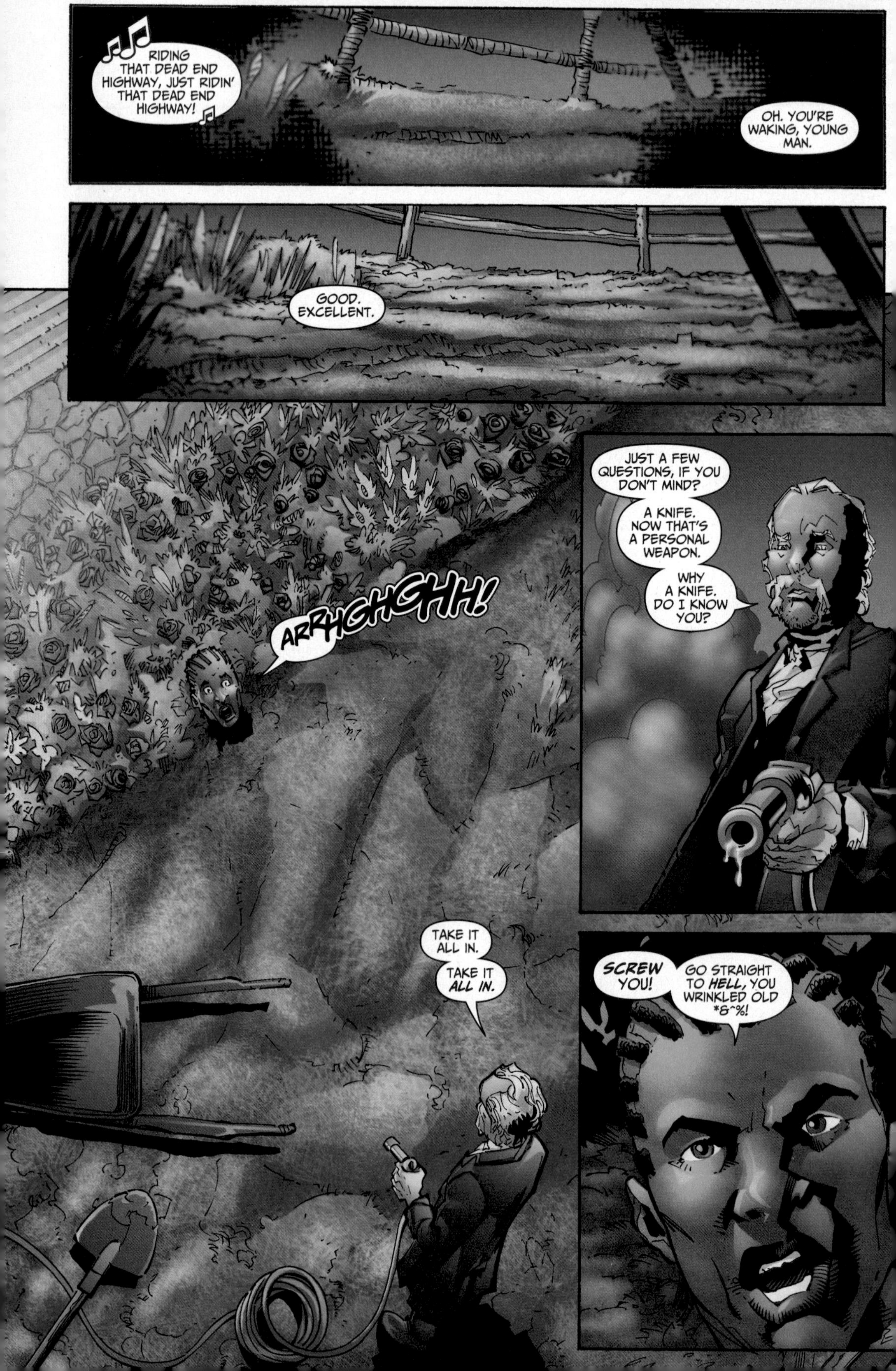
RIDING THAT DEAD END HIGHWAY, JUST RIDIN' THAT DEAD END HIGHWAY!
OH. YOU'RE WAKING, YOUNG MAN.
GOOD. EXCELLENT.
ARRHGHGHH!
JUST A FEW QUESTIONS, IF YOU DON'T MIND?
A KNIFE. NOW THAT'S A PERSONAL WEAPON.
WHY A KNIFE. DO I KNOW YOU?
TAKE IT ALL IN.
TAKE IT ALL IN.
SCREW YOU!
GO STRAIGHT TO HELL, YOU WRINKLED OLD *&^%!

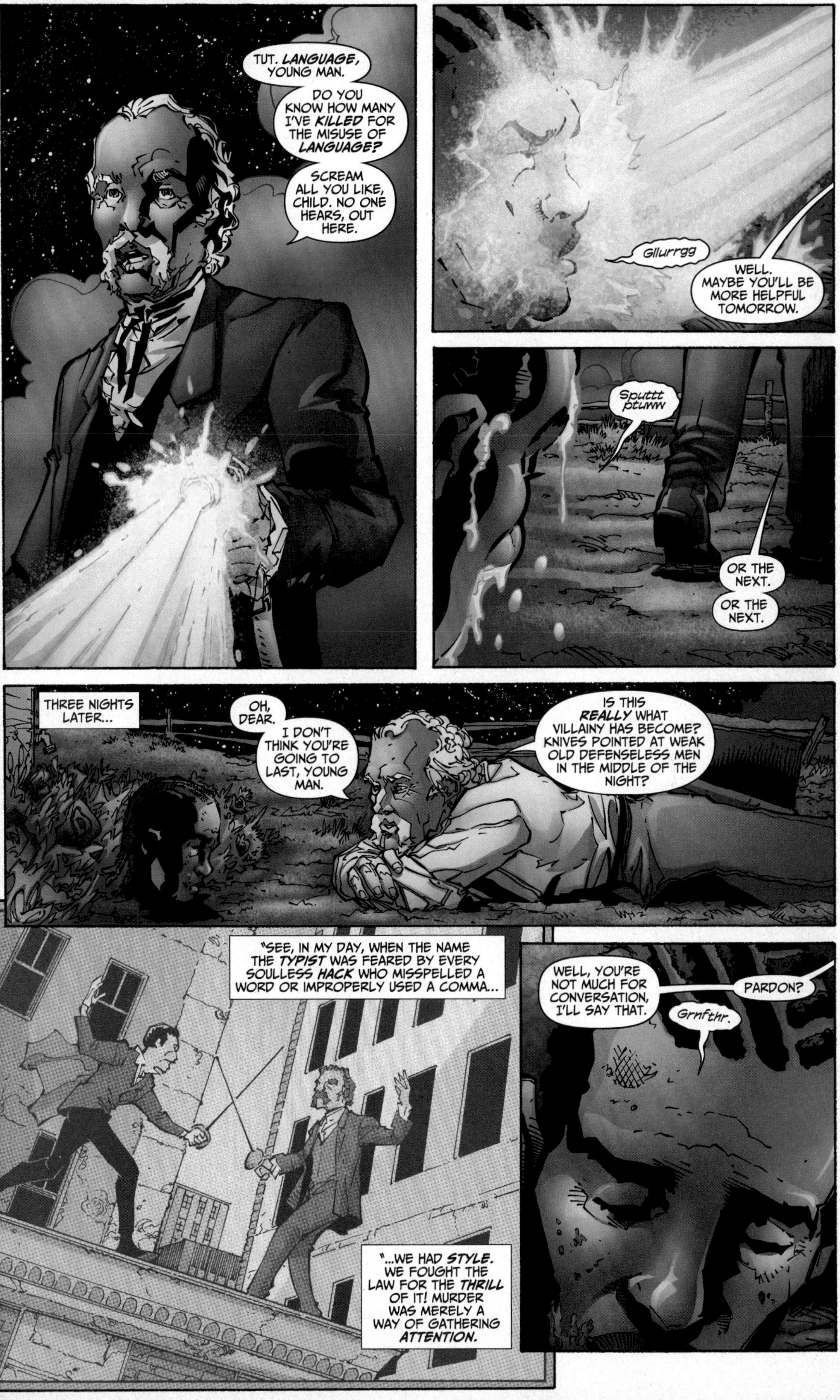
TUT. LANGUAGE, YOUNG MAN.
DO YOU KNOW HOW MANY I'VE KILLED FOR THE MISUSE OF LANGUAGE?
SCREAM ALL YOU LIKE, CHILD. NO ONE HEARS, OUT HERE.
Gllurrgg
WELL. MAYBE YOU'LL BE MORE HELPFUL TOMORROW.
Sputtt ptuww
OR THE NEXT.
OR THE NEXT.
THREE NIGHTS LATER...
OH, DEAR.
I DON'T THINK YOU'RE GOING TO LAST, YOUNG MAN.
IS THIS REALLY WHAT VILLAINY HAS BECOME? KNIVES POINTED AT WEAK OLD DEFENSELESS MEN IN THE MIDDLE OF THE NIGHT?
"SEE, IN MY DAY, WHEN THE NAME THE TYPIST WAS FEARED BY EVERY SOULLESS HACK WHO MISSPELLED A WORD OR IMPROPERLY USED A COMMA...
"...WE HAD STYLE. WE FOUGHT THE LAW FOR THE THRILL OF IT! MURDER WAS MERELY A WAY OF GATHERING ATTENTION.
WELL, YOU'RE NOT MUCH FOR CONVERSATION, I'LL SAY THAT.
PARDON?
Grnfthr.

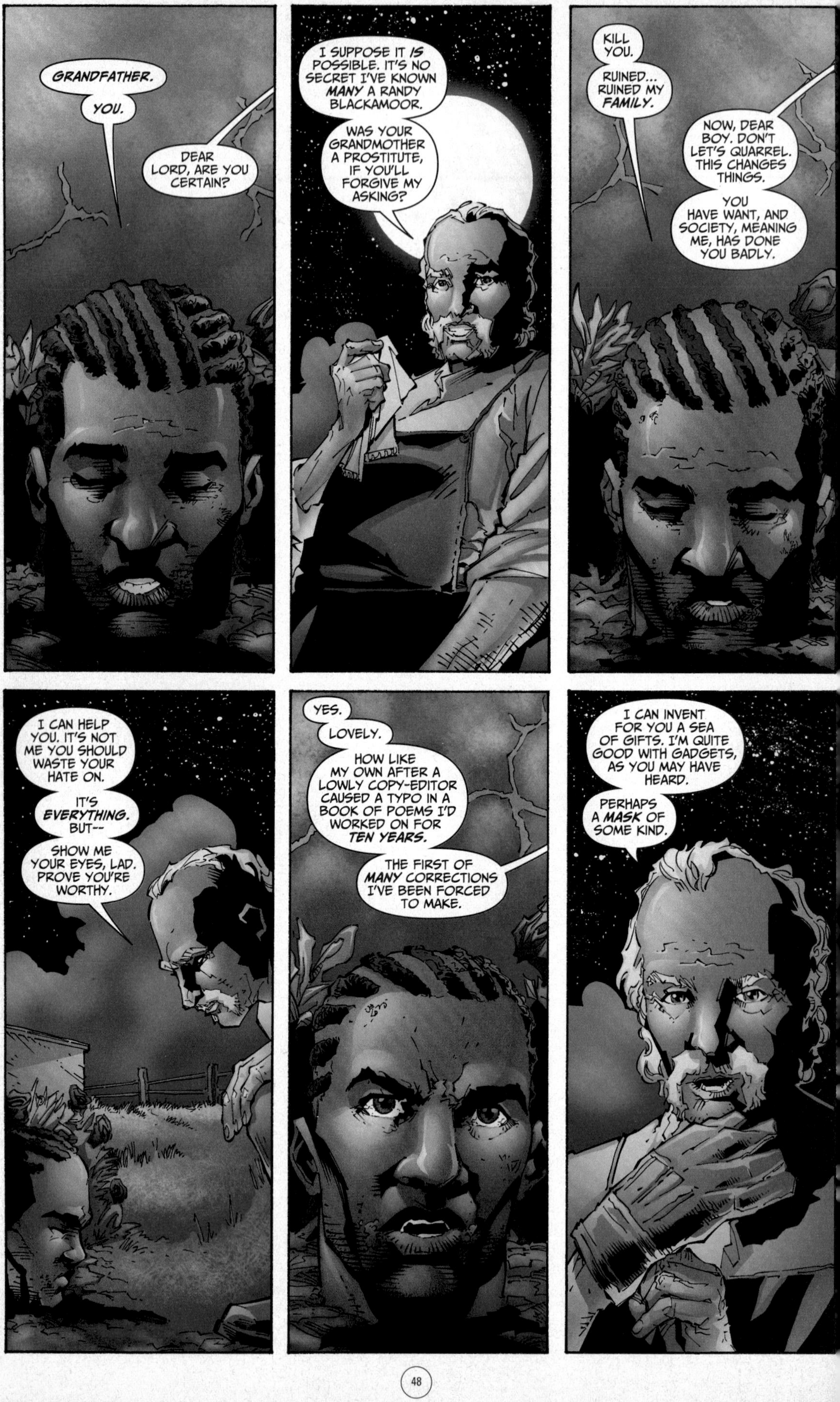
GRANDFATHER.
YOU.
DEAR LORD, ARE YOU CERTAIN?
I SUPPOSE IT IS POSSIBLE. IT'S NO SECRET I'VE KNOWN MANY A RANDY BLACKAMOOR.
WAS YOUR GRANDMOTHER A PROSTITUTE, IF YOU'LL FORGIVE MY ASKING?
KILL YOU.
RUINED... RUINED MY FAMILY.
NOW, DEAR BOY. DON'T LET'S QUARREL. THIS CHANGES THINGS.
YOU HAVE WANT, AND SOCIETY, MEANING ME, HAS DONE YOU BADLY.
I CAN HELP YOU. IT'S NOT ME YOU SHOULD WASTE YOUR HATE ON.
IT'S EVERYTHING. BUT--
SHOW ME YOUR EYES, LAD. PROVE YOU'RE WORTHY.
YES.
LOVELY.
HOW LIKE MY OWN AFTER A LOWLY COPY-EDITOR CAUSED A TYPO IN A BOOK OF POEMS I'D WORKED ON FOR TEN YEARS.
THE FIRST OF MANY CORRECTIONS I'VE BEEN FORCED TO MAKE.
I CAN INVENT FOR YOU A SEA OF GIFTS. I'M QUITE GOOD WITH GADGETS, AS YOU MAY HAVE HEARD.
PERHAPS A MASK OF SOME KIND.

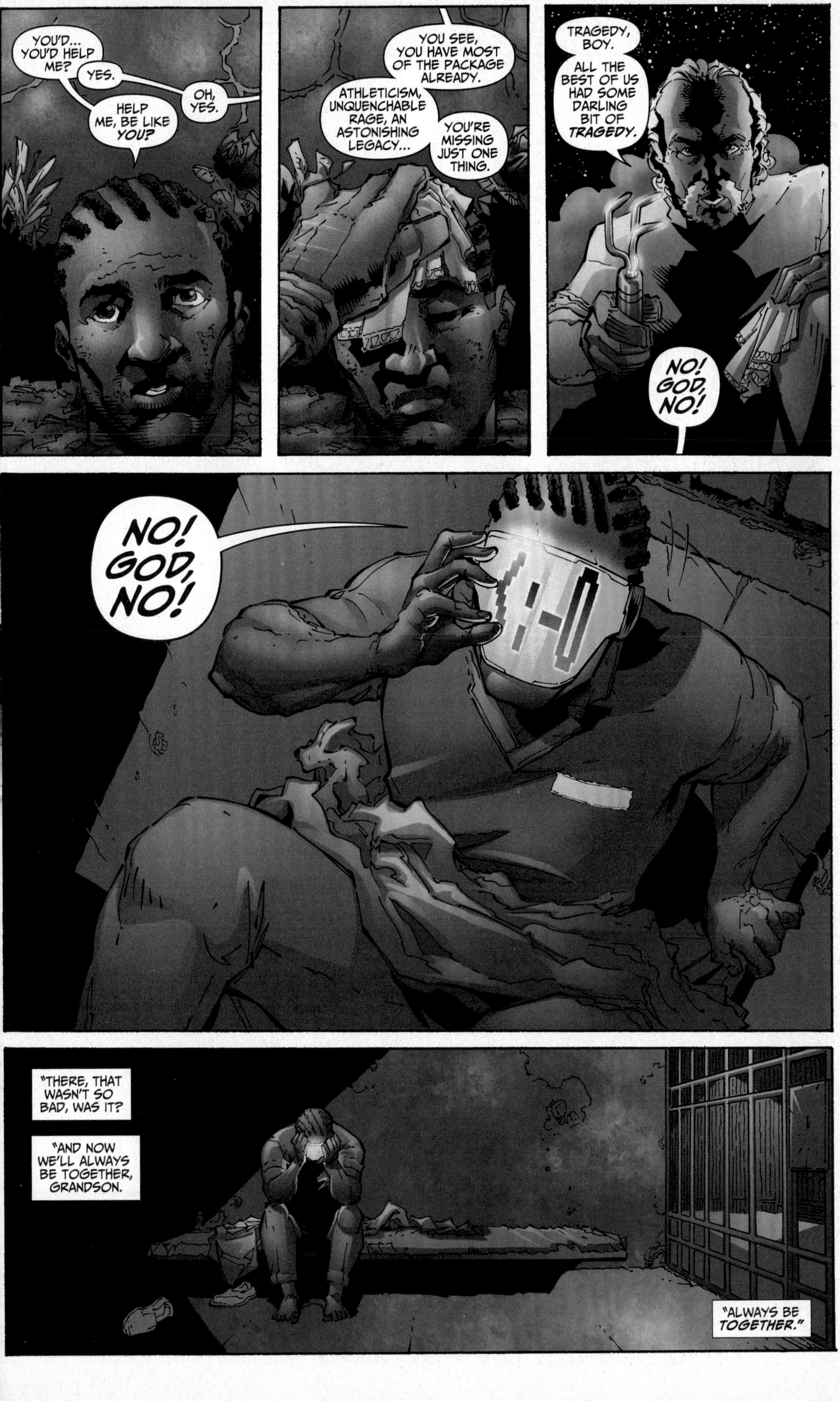
YOU'D... YOU'D HELP ME?
YES.
OH, YES.
HELP ME, BE LIKE *YOU?*
YOU SEE, YOU HAVE MOST OF THE PACKAGE ALREADY.
ATHLETICISM, UNQUENCHABLE RAGE, AN ASTONISHING LEGACY...
YOU'RE MISSING JUST ONE THING.
TRAGEDY, BOY.
ALL THE BEST OF US HAD SOME DARLING BIT OF *TRAGEDY.*
NO! GOD, NO!
NO! GOD, NO!
"THERE, THAT WASN'T SO BAD, WAS IT?
"AND NOW WE'LL ALWAYS BE TOGETHER, GRANDSON.
"ALWAYS BE *TOGETHER.*"

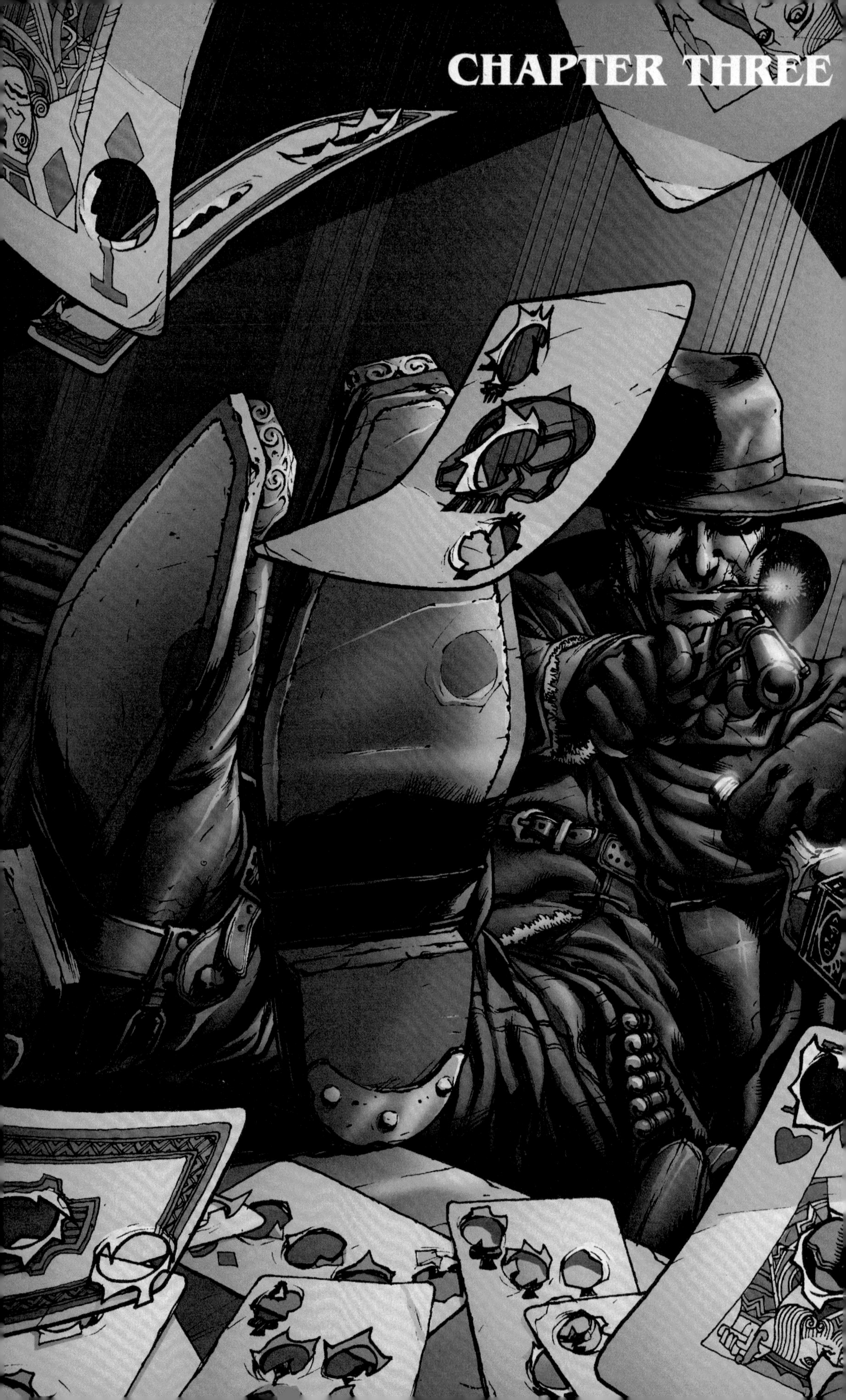
CHAPTER THREE

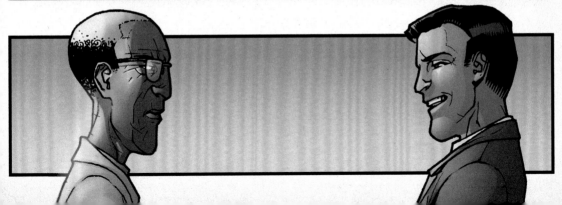

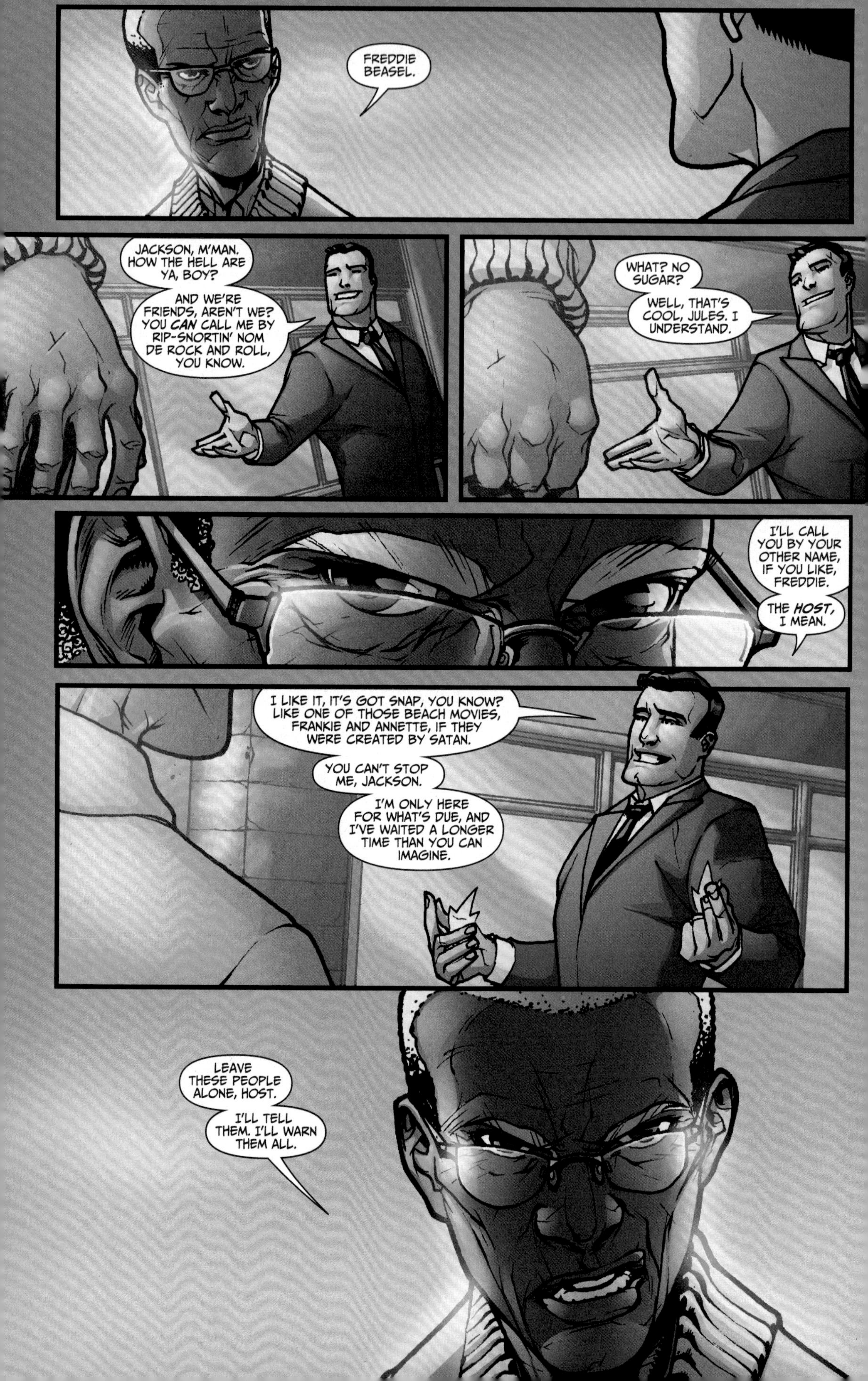
FREDDIE BEASEL.
JACKSON, M'MAN. HOW THE HELL ARE YA, BOY?
AND WE'RE FRIENDS, AREN'T WE? YOU CAN CALL ME BY RIP-SNORTIN' NOM DE ROCK AND ROLL, YOU KNOW.
WHAT? NO SUGAR?
WELL, THAT'S COOL, JULES. I UNDERSTAND.
I'LL CALL YOU BY YOUR OTHER NAME, IF YOU LIKE, FREDDIE.
THE HOST, I MEAN.
I LIKE IT, IT'S GOT SNAP, YOU KNOW? LIKE ONE OF THOSE BEACH MOVIES, FRANKIE AND ANNETTE, IF THEY WERE CREATED BY SATAN.
YOU CAN'T STOP ME, JACKSON.
I'M ONLY HERE FOR WHAT'S DUE, AND I'VE WAITED A LONGER TIME THAN YOU CAN IMAGINE.
LEAVE THESE PEOPLE ALONE, HOST.
I'LL TELL THEM. I'LL WARN THEM ALL.

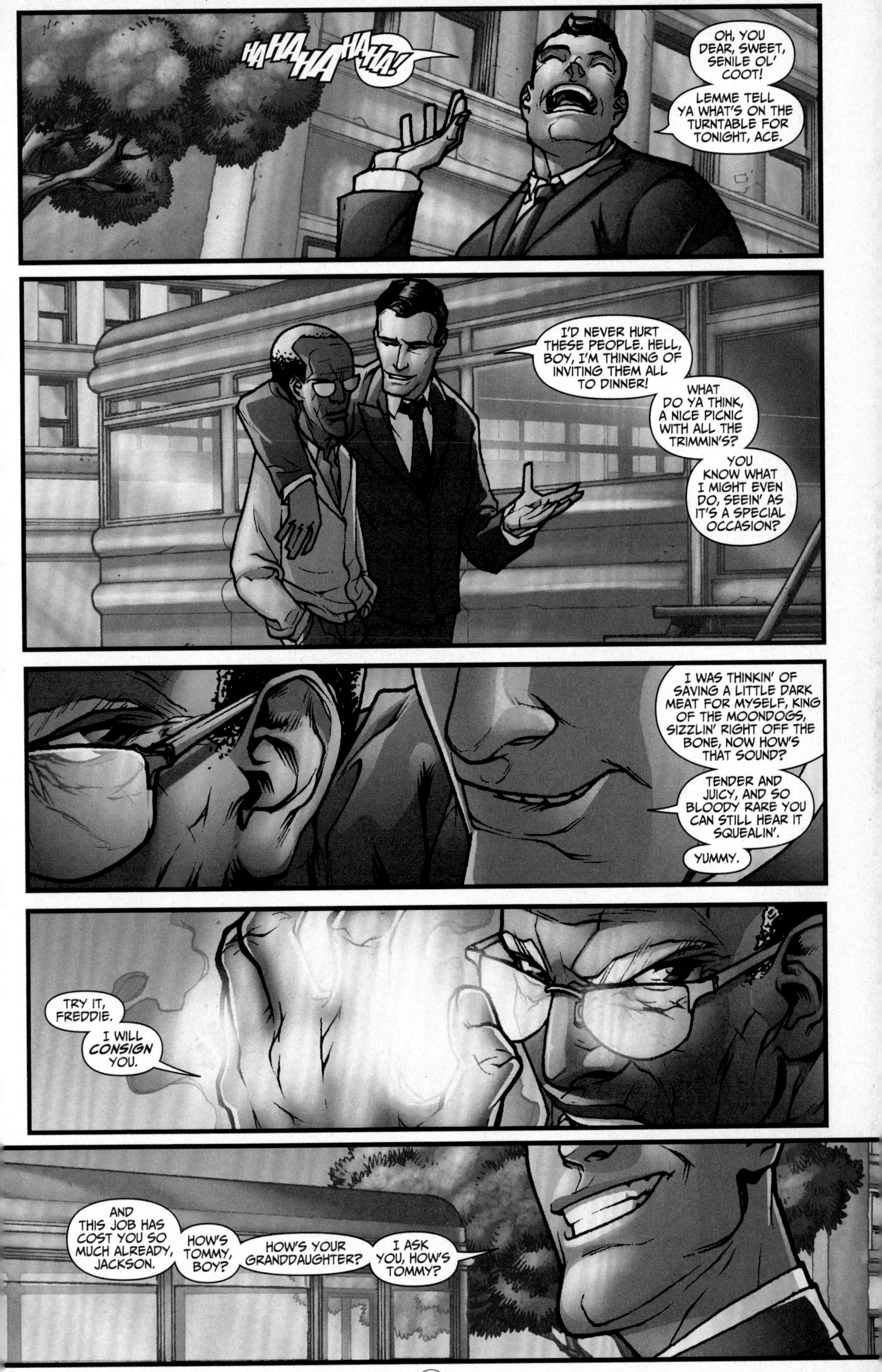
HAHAHAHAHA!
OH, YOU DEAR, SWEET, SENILE OL' COOT!
LEMME TELL YA WHAT'S ON THE TURNTABLE FOR TONIGHT, ACE.
I'D NEVER HURT THESE PEOPLE. HELL, BOY, I'M THINKING OF INVITING THEM ALL TO DINNER!
WHAT DO YA THINK, A NICE PICNIC WITH ALL THE TRIMMIN'S?
YOU KNOW WHAT I MIGHT EVEN DO, SEEIN' AS IT'S A SPECIAL OCCASION?
I WAS THINKIN' OF SAVING A LITTLE DARK MEAT FOR MYSELF, KING OF THE MOONDOGS, SIZZLIN' RIGHT OFF THE BONE, NOW HOW'S THAT SOUND?
TENDER AND JUICY, AND SO BLOODY RARE YOU CAN STILL HEAR IT SQUEALIN'.
YUMMY.
TRY IT, FREDDIE.
I WILL CONSIGN YOU.
AND THIS JOB HAS COST YOU SO MUCH ALREADY, JACKSON.
HOW'S TOMMY, BOY?
HOW'S YOUR GRANDDAUGHTER?
I ASK YOU, HOW'S TOMMY?

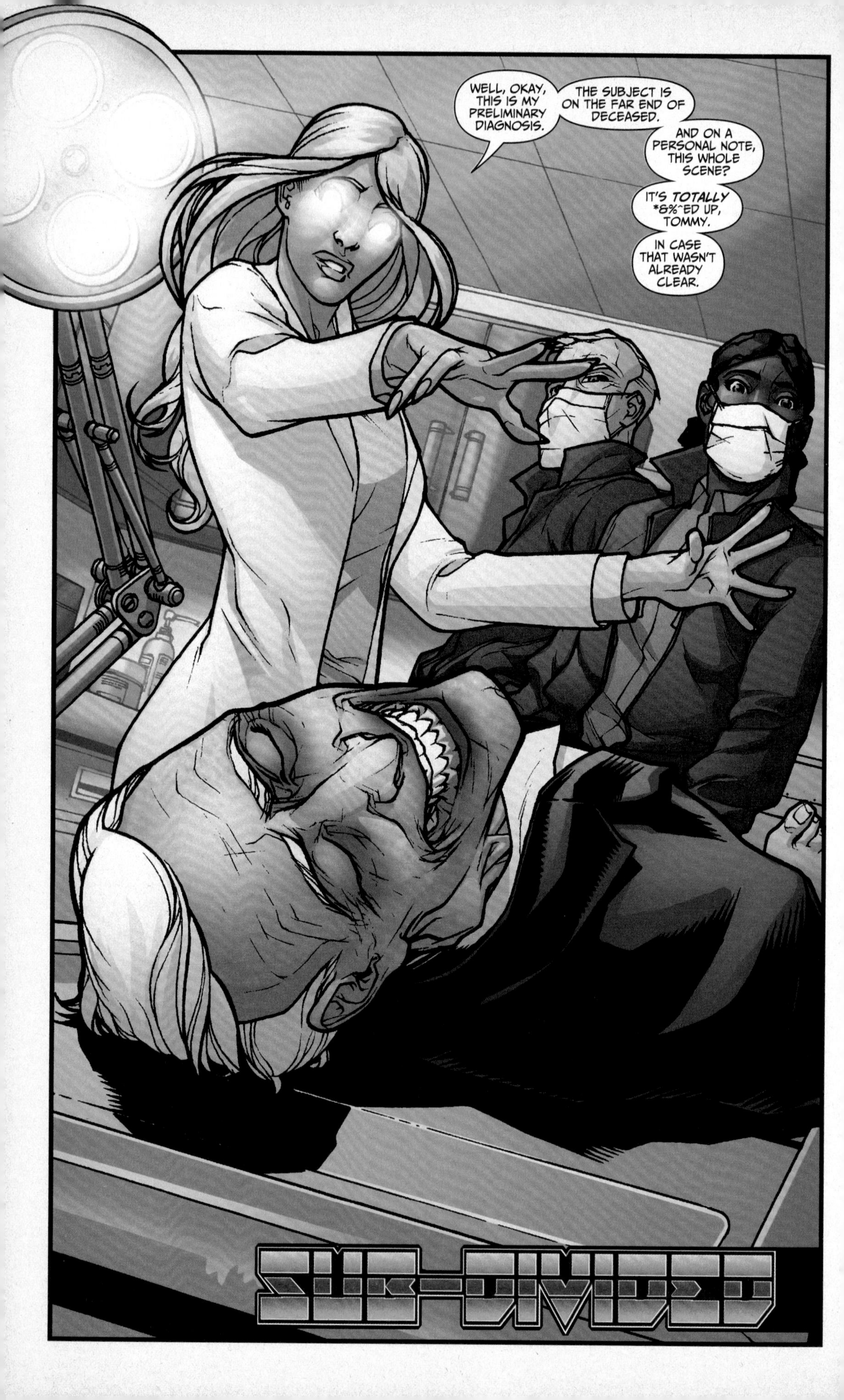
WELL, OKAY, THIS IS MY PRELIMINARY DIAGNOSIS.
THE SUBJECT IS ON THE FAR END OF DECEASED.
AND ON A PERSONAL NOTE, THIS WHOLE SCENE?
IT'S *TOTALLY* *&%^ED UP, TOMMY.
IN CASE THAT WASN'T ALREADY CLEAR.
SUB-DIVIDED

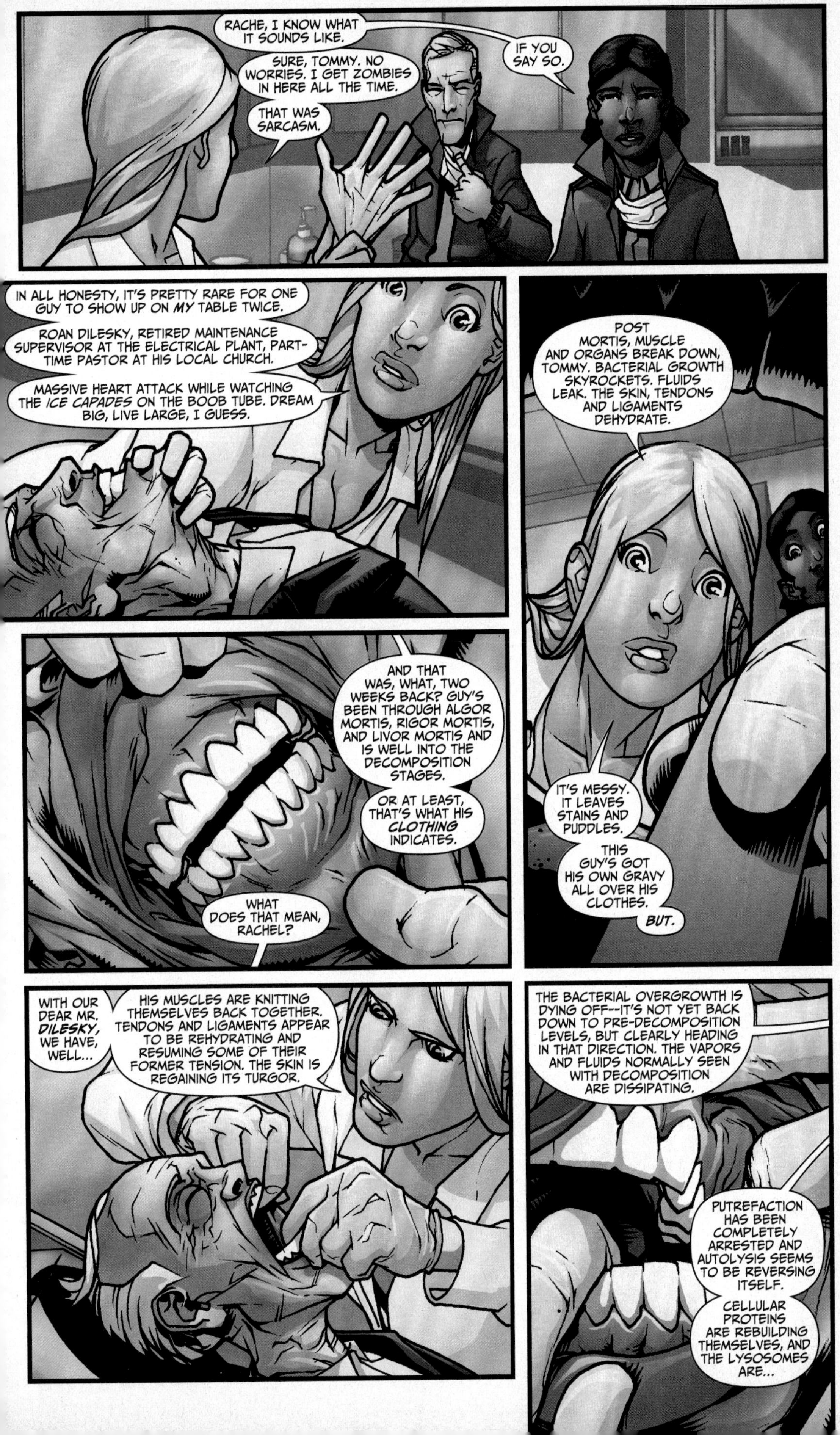
RACHE, I KNOW WHAT IT SOUNDS LIKE.
SURE, TOMMY. NO WORRIES. I GET ZOMBIES IN HERE ALL THE TIME.
THAT WAS SARCASM.
IF YOU SAY SO.
IN ALL HONESTY, IT'S PRETTY RARE FOR ONE GUY TO SHOW UP ON *MY* TABLE TWICE.
ROAN DILESKY, RETIRED MAINTENANCE SUPERVISOR AT THE ELECTRICAL PLANT, PART-TIME PASTOR AT HIS LOCAL CHURCH.
MASSIVE HEART ATTACK WHILE WATCHING THE *ICE CAPADES* ON THE BOOB TUBE. DREAM BIG, LIVE LARGE, I GUESS.
AND THAT WAS, WHAT, TWO WEEKS BACK? GUY'S BEEN THROUGH ALGOR MORTIS, RIGOR MORTIS, AND LIVOR MORTIS AND IS WELL INTO THE DECOMPOSITION STAGES.
OR AT LEAST, THAT'S WHAT HIS ***CLOTHING*** INDICATES.
WHAT DOES THAT MEAN, RACHEL?
POST MORTIS, MUSCLE AND ORGANS BREAK DOWN, TOMMY. BACTERIAL GROWTH SKYROCKETS. FLUIDS LEAK. THE SKIN, TENDONS AND LIGAMENTS DEHYDRATE.
IT'S MESSY. IT LEAVES STAINS AND PUDDLES.
THIS GUY'S GOT HIS OWN GRAVY ALL OVER HIS CLOTHES.
BUT.
WITH OUR DEAR MR. ***DILESKY,*** WE HAVE, WELL...
HIS MUSCLES ARE KNITTING THEMSELVES BACK TOGETHER. TENDONS AND LIGAMENTS APPEAR TO BE REHYDRATING AND RESUMING SOME OF THEIR FORMER TENSION. THE SKIN IS REGAINING ITS TURGOR.
THE BACTERIAL OVERGROWTH IS DYING OFF--IT'S NOT YET BACK DOWN TO PRE-DECOMPOSITION LEVELS, BUT CLEARLY HEADING IN THAT DIRECTION. THE VAPORS AND FLUIDS NORMALLY SEEN WITH DECOMPOSITION ARE DISSIPATING.
PUTREFACTION HAS BEEN COMPLETELY ARRESTED AND AUTOLYSIS SEEMS TO BE REVERSING ITSELF.
CELLULAR PROTEINS ARE REBUILDING THEMSELVES, AND THE LYSOSOMES ARE...

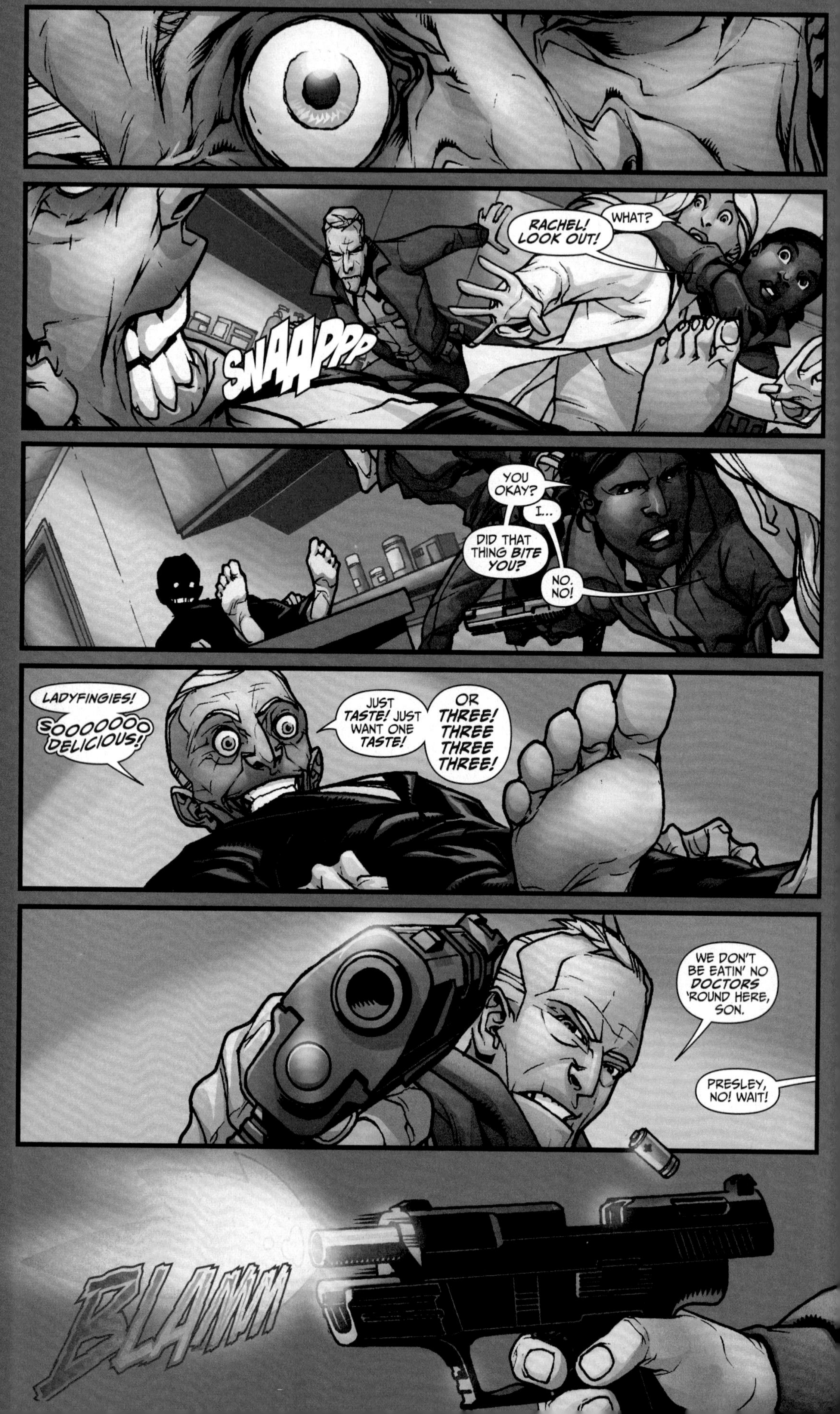
RACHEL! LOOK OUT!
WHAT?
SNAAPPP
YOU OKAY?
I...
DID THAT THING *BITE* YOU?
NO. NO!
LADYFINGIES!
SOOOOOOO DELICIOUS!
JUST *TASTE!* JUST WANT ONE *TASTE!*
OR *THREE! THREE THREE THREE!*
WE DON'T BE EATIN' NO *DOCTORS* 'ROUND HERE, SON.
PRESLEY, NO! WAIT!
BLAMM

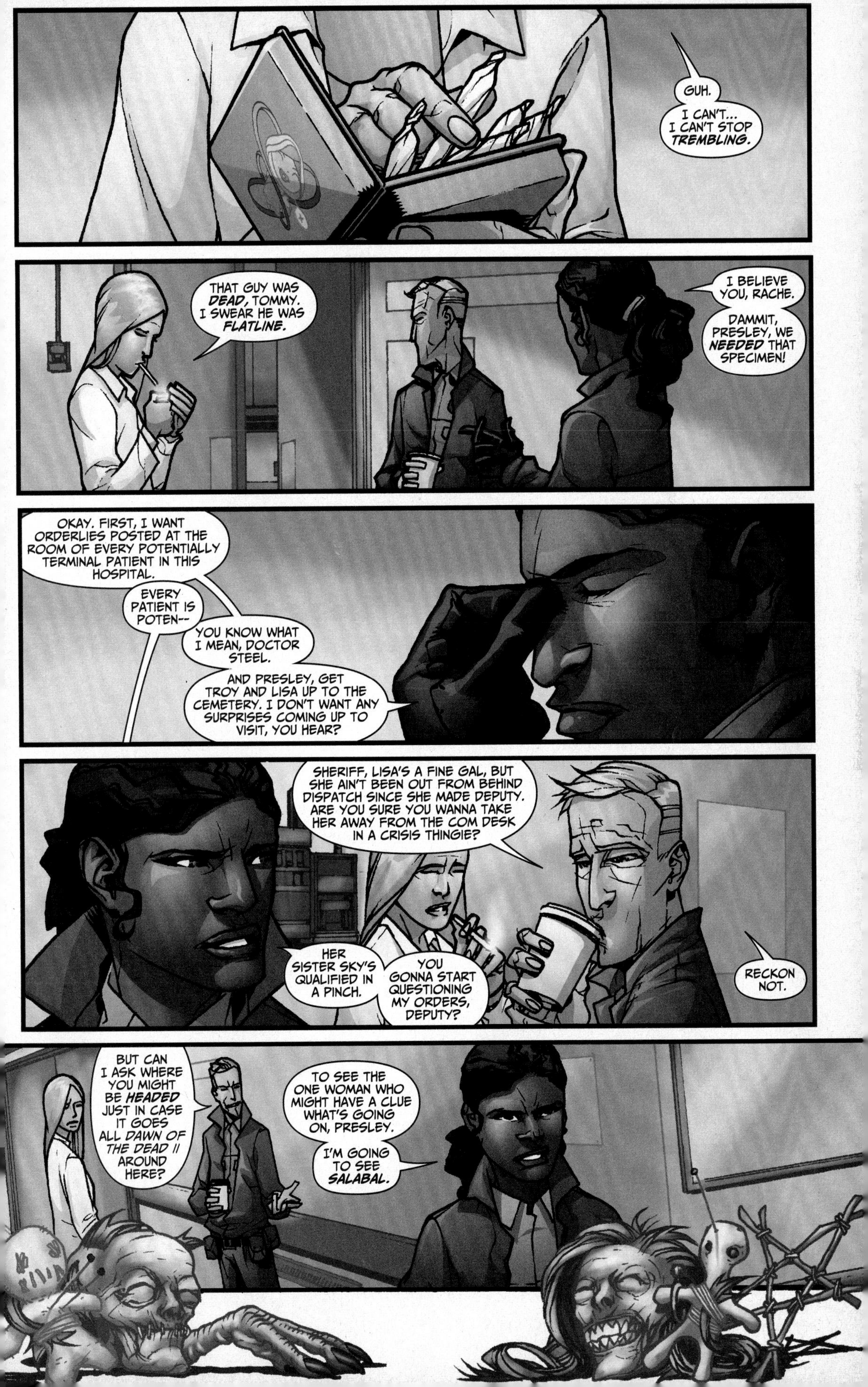
GUH.
I CAN'T... I CAN'T STOP TREMBLING.
THAT GUY WAS DEAD, TOMMY. I SWEAR HE WAS FLATLINE.
I BELIEVE YOU, RACHE.
DAMMIT, PRESLEY, WE NEEDED THAT SPECIMEN!
OKAY. FIRST, I WANT ORDERLIES POSTED AT THE ROOM OF EVERY POTENTIALLY TERMINAL PATIENT IN THIS HOSPITAL.
EVERY PATIENT IS POTEN--
YOU KNOW WHAT I MEAN, DOCTOR STEEL.
AND PRESLEY, GET TROY AND LISA UP TO THE CEMETERY. I DON'T WANT ANY SURPRISES COMING UP TO VISIT, YOU HEAR?
SHERIFF, LISA'S A FINE GAL, BUT SHE AIN'T BEEN OUT FROM BEHIND DISPATCH SINCE SHE MADE DEPUTY. ARE YOU SURE YOU WANNA TAKE HER AWAY FROM THE COM DESK IN A CRISIS THINGIE?
HER SISTER SKY'S QUALIFIED IN A PINCH.
YOU GONNA START QUESTIONING MY ORDERS, DEPUTY?
RECKON NOT.
BUT CAN I ASK WHERE YOU MIGHT BE HEADED JUST IN CASE IT GOES ALL DAWN OF THE DEAD II AROUND HERE?
TO SEE THE ONE WOMAN WHO MIGHT HAVE A CLUE WHAT'S GOING ON, PRESLEY.
I'M GOING TO SEE SALABAL.

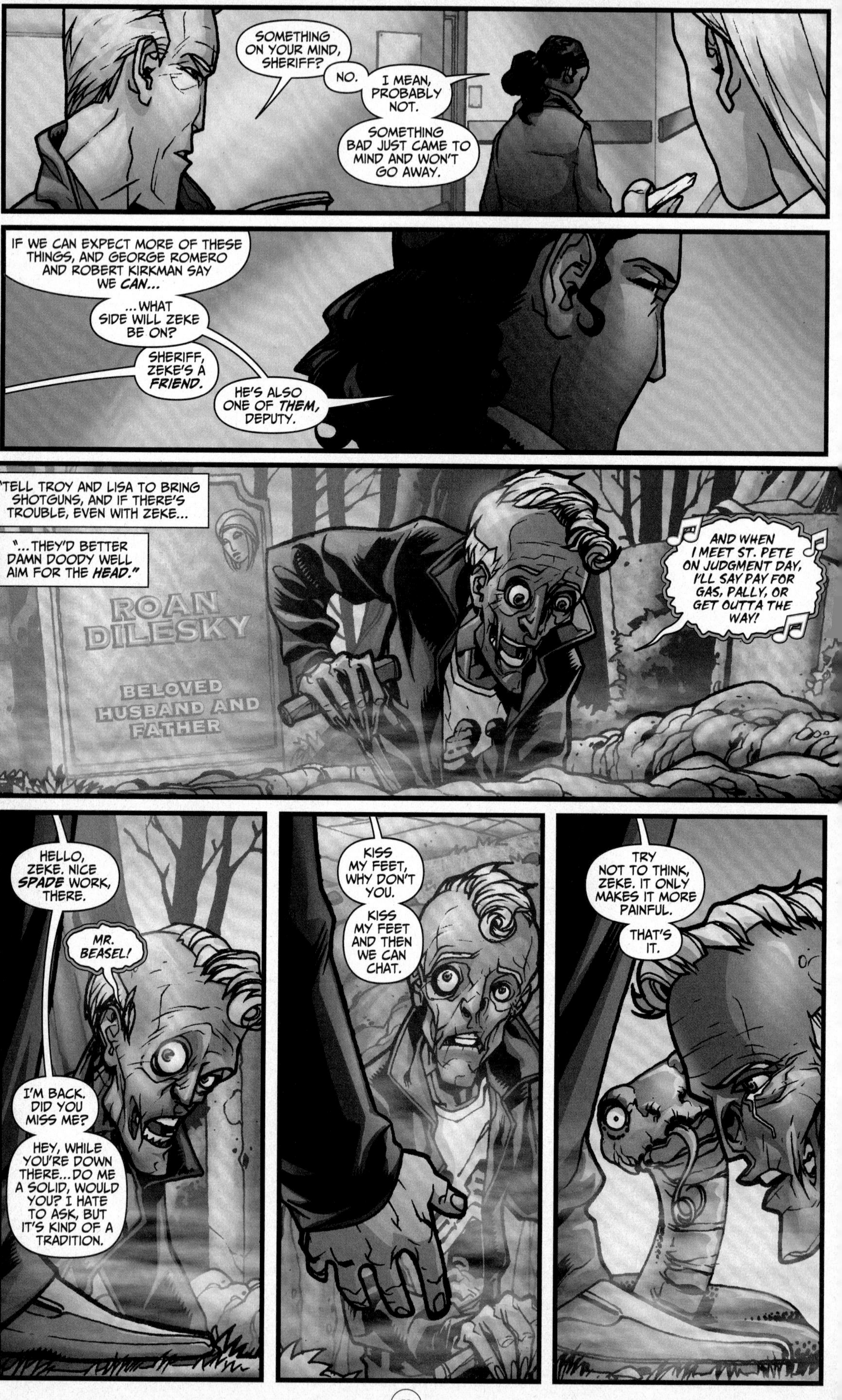
SOMETHING ON YOUR MIND, SHERIFF?
NO.
I MEAN, PROBABLY NOT.
SOMETHING BAD JUST CAME TO MIND AND WON'T GO AWAY.
IF WE CAN EXPECT MORE OF THESE THINGS, AND GEORGE ROMERO AND ROBERT KIRKMAN SAY WE *CAN*...
...WHAT SIDE WILL ZEKE BE ON?
SHERIFF, ZEKE'S A *FRIEND.*
HE'S ALSO ONE OF *THEM,* DEPUTY.
"TELL TROY AND LISA TO BRING SHOTGUNS, AND IF THERE'S TROUBLE, EVEN WITH ZEKE...
"...THEY'D BETTER DAMN DOODY WELL AIM FOR THE *HEAD.*"
ROAN DILESKY
BELOVED HUSBAND AND FATHER
AND WHEN I MEET ST. PETE ON JUDGMENT DAY, I'LL SAY PAY FOR GAS, PALLY, OR GET OUTTA THE WAY!
HELLO, ZEKE. NICE *SPADE* WORK, THERE.
MR. BEASEL!
I'M BACK. DID YOU MISS ME?
HEY, WHILE YOU'RE DOWN THERE...DO ME A SOLID, WOULD YOU? I HATE TO ASK, BUT IT'S KIND OF A TRADITION.
KISS MY FEET, WHY DON'T YOU.
KISS MY FEET AND THEN WE CAN CHAT.
TRY NOT TO THINK, ZEKE. IT ONLY MAKES IT MORE PAINFUL.
THAT'S IT.

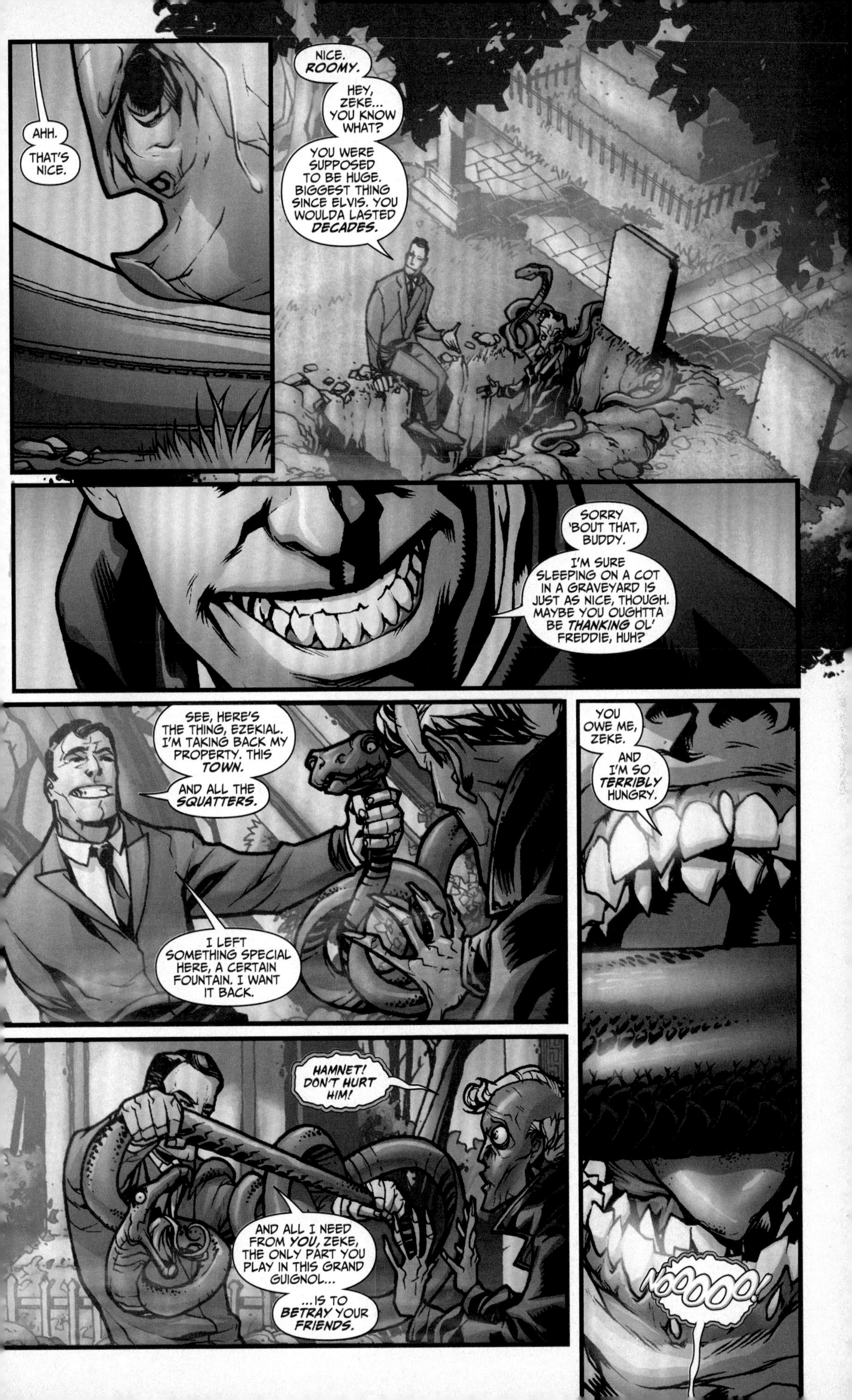
AHH. THAT'S NICE.
NICE. ROOMY.
HEY, ZEKE... YOU KNOW WHAT?
YOU WERE SUPPOSED TO BE HUGE. BIGGEST THING SINCE ELVIS. YOU WOULDA LASTED DECADES.
SORRY 'BOUT THAT, BUDDY.
I'M SURE SLEEPING ON A COT IN A GRAVEYARD IS JUST AS NICE, THOUGH. MAYBE YOU OUGHTTA BE THANKING OL' FREDDIE, HUH?
SEE, HERE'S THE THING, EZEKIAL. I'M TAKING BACK MY PROPERTY. THIS TOWN.
AND ALL THE SQUATTERS.
I LEFT SOMETHING SPECIAL HERE, A CERTAIN FOUNTAIN. I WANT IT BACK.
HAMNET! DON'T HURT HIM!
AND ALL I NEED FROM YOU, ZEKE, THE ONLY PART YOU PLAY IN THIS GRAND GUIGNOL...
...IS TO BETRAY YOUR FRIENDS.
YOU OWE ME, ZEKE.
AND I'M SO TERRIBLY HUNGRY.
NOOOOO!

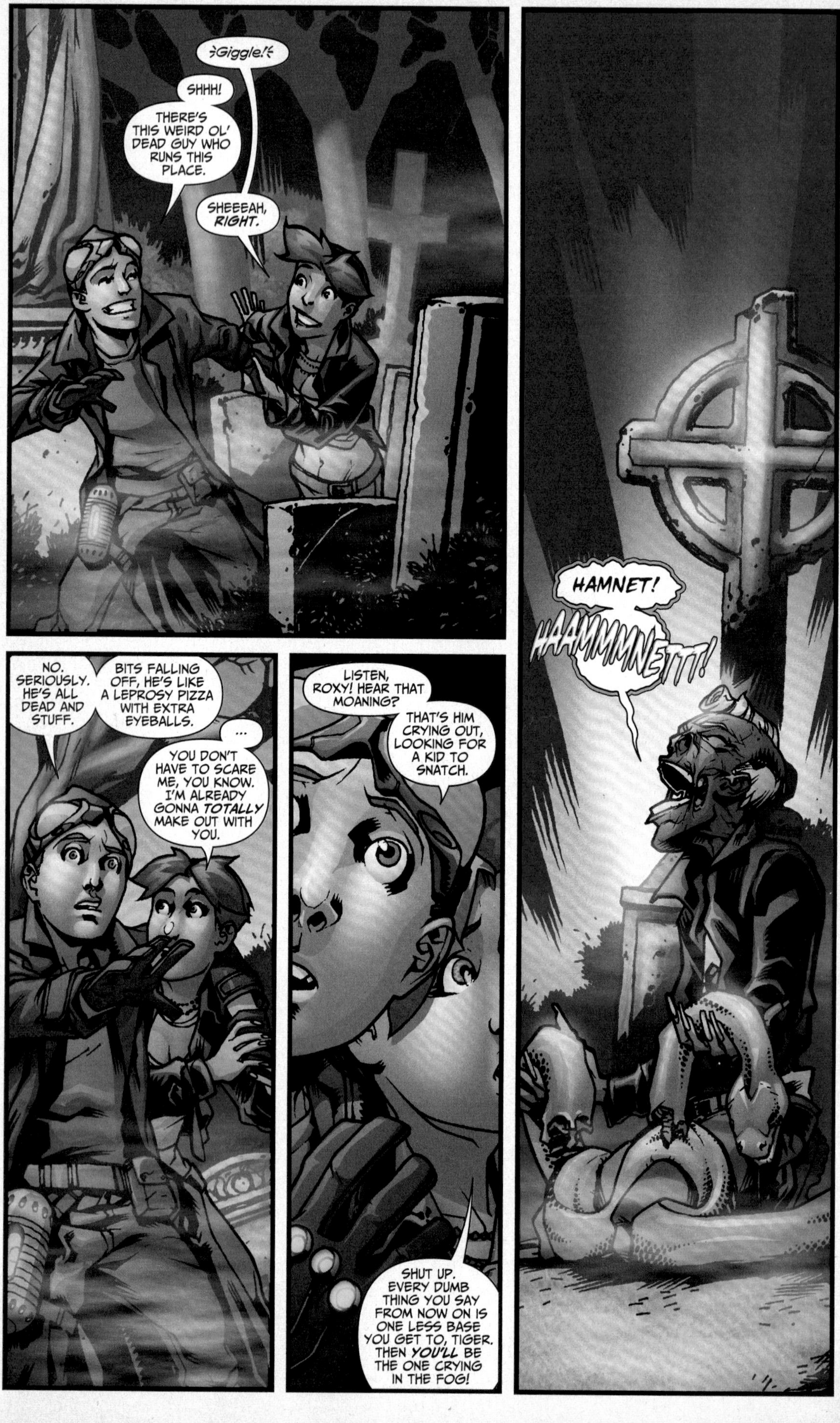

SHHH!
THERE'S THIS WEIRD OL' DEAD GUY WHO RUNS THIS PLACE.
⊰Giggle!⊱
SHEEEAH, *RIGHT*.
NO. SERIOUSLY. HE'S ALL DEAD AND STUFF.
BITS FALLING OFF, HE'S LIKE A LEPROSY PIZZA WITH EXTRA EYEBALLS.
...
YOU DON'T HAVE TO SCARE ME, YOU KNOW. I'M ALREADY GONNA *TOTALLY* MAKE OUT WITH YOU.
LISTEN, ROXY! HEAR THAT MOANING?
THAT'S HIM CRYING OUT, LOOKING FOR A KID TO SNATCH.
SHUT UP. EVERY DUMB THING YOU SAY FROM NOW ON IS ONE LESS BASE YOU GET TO, TIGER. THEN *YOU'LL* BE THE ONE CRYING IN THE FOG!
HAMNET!
HAAMMMNETTT!

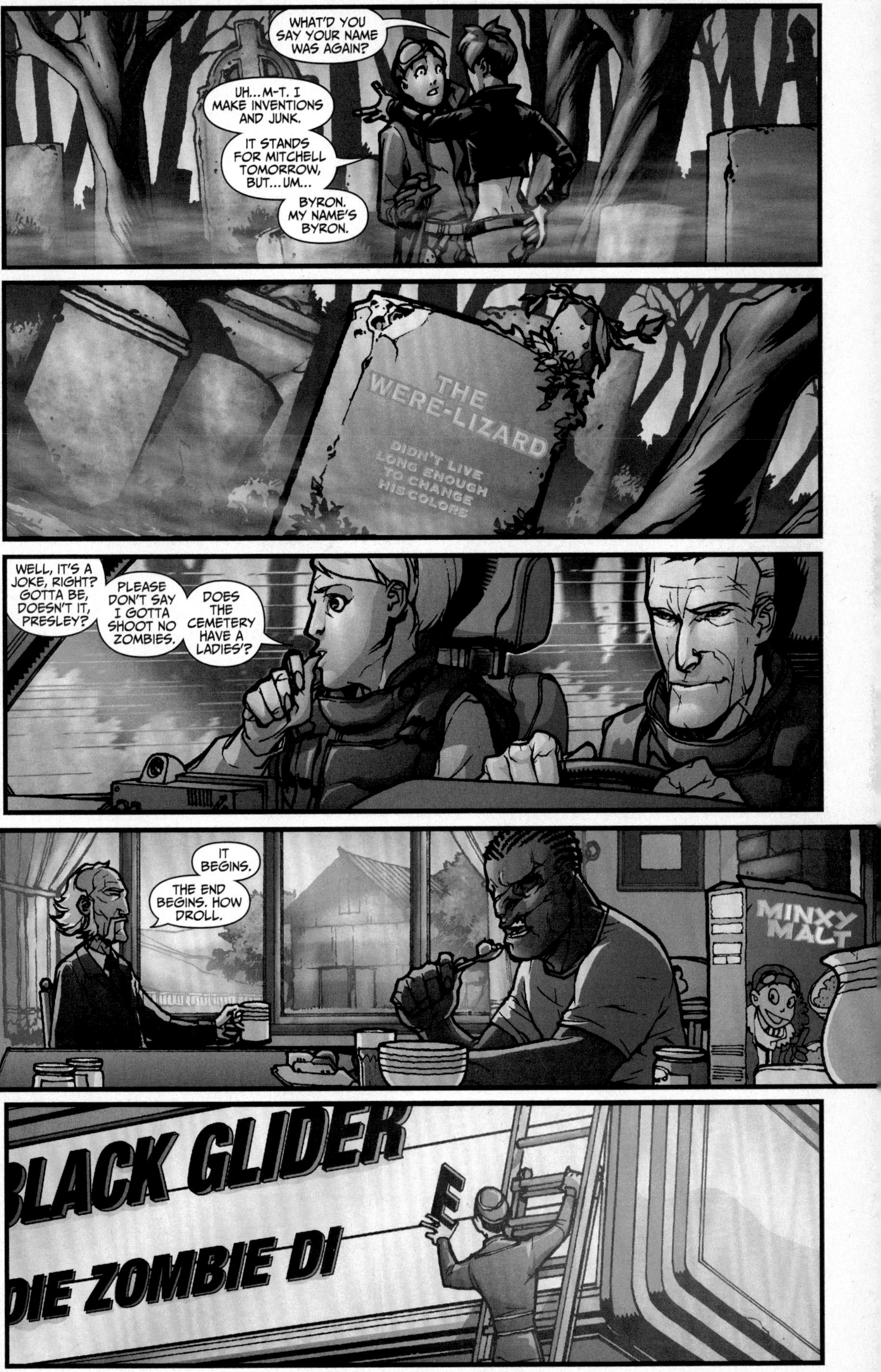
WHAT'D YOU SAY YOUR NAME WAS AGAIN?
UH...M-T. I MAKE INVENTIONS AND JUNK.
IT STANDS FOR MITCHELL TOMORROW, BUT...UM...
BYRON. MY NAME'S BYRON.
THE WERE-LIZARD
DIDN'T LIVE LONG ENOUGH TO CHANGE HIS COLORS
WELL, IT'S A JOKE, RIGHT? GOTTA BE, DOESN'T IT, PRESLEY?
PLEASE DON'T SAY I GOTTA SHOOT NO ZOMBIES.
DOES THE CEMETERY HAVE A LADIES'?
IT BEGINS.
THE END BEGINS. HOW DROLL.
MINXY MALT
BLACK GLIDER
E
DIE ZOMBIE DI

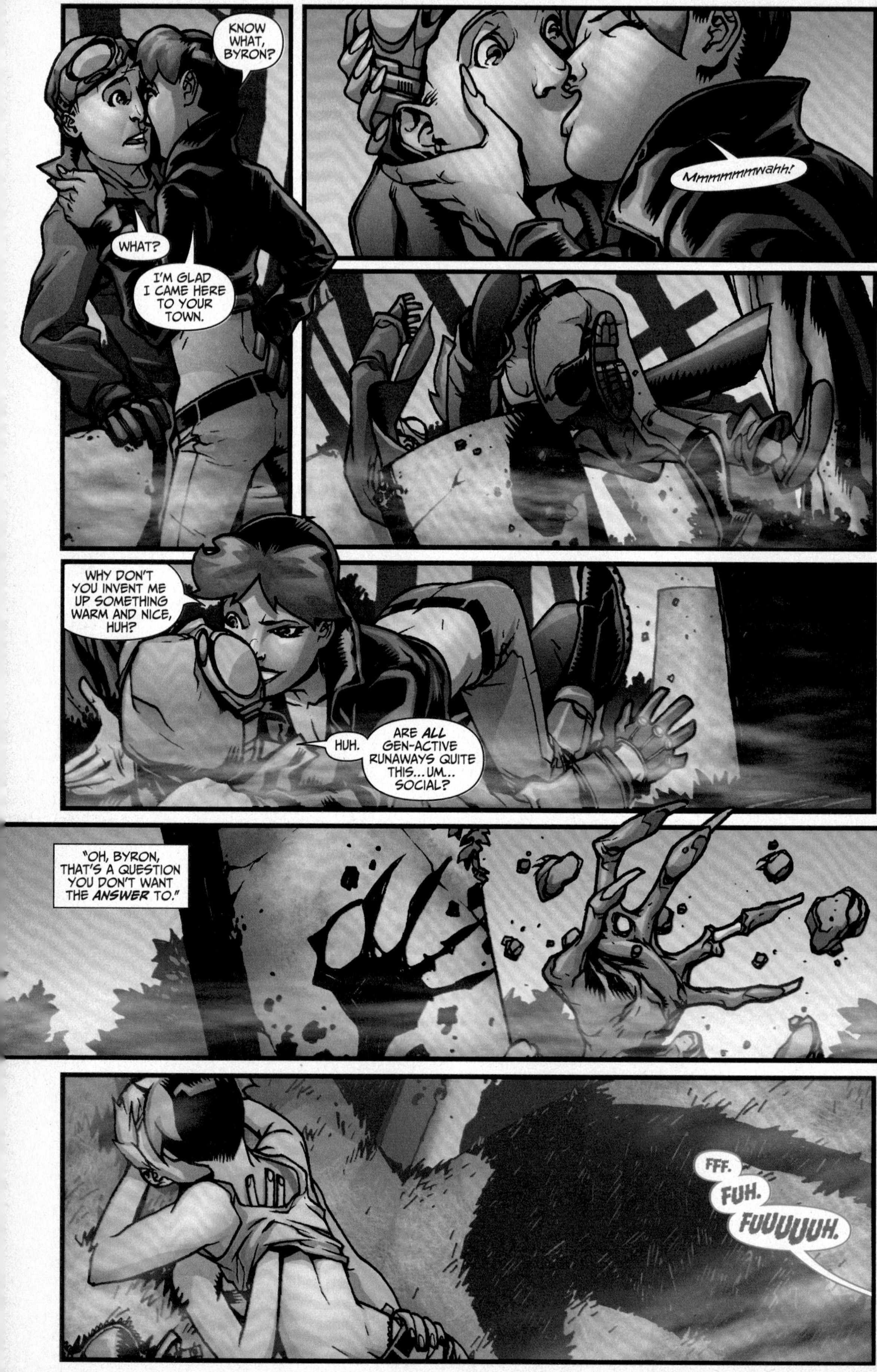
KNOW WHAT, BYRON?
WHAT?
I'M GLAD I CAME HERE TO YOUR TOWN.
Mmmmmmmwahh!
WHY DON'T YOU INVENT ME UP SOMETHING WARM AND NICE, HUH?
HUH.
ARE *ALL* GEN-ACTIVE RUNAWAYS QUITE THIS...UM... SOCIAL?
"OH, BYRON, THAT'S A QUESTION YOU DON'T WANT THE *ANSWER* TO."
FFF.
FUH.
FUUUUUH.

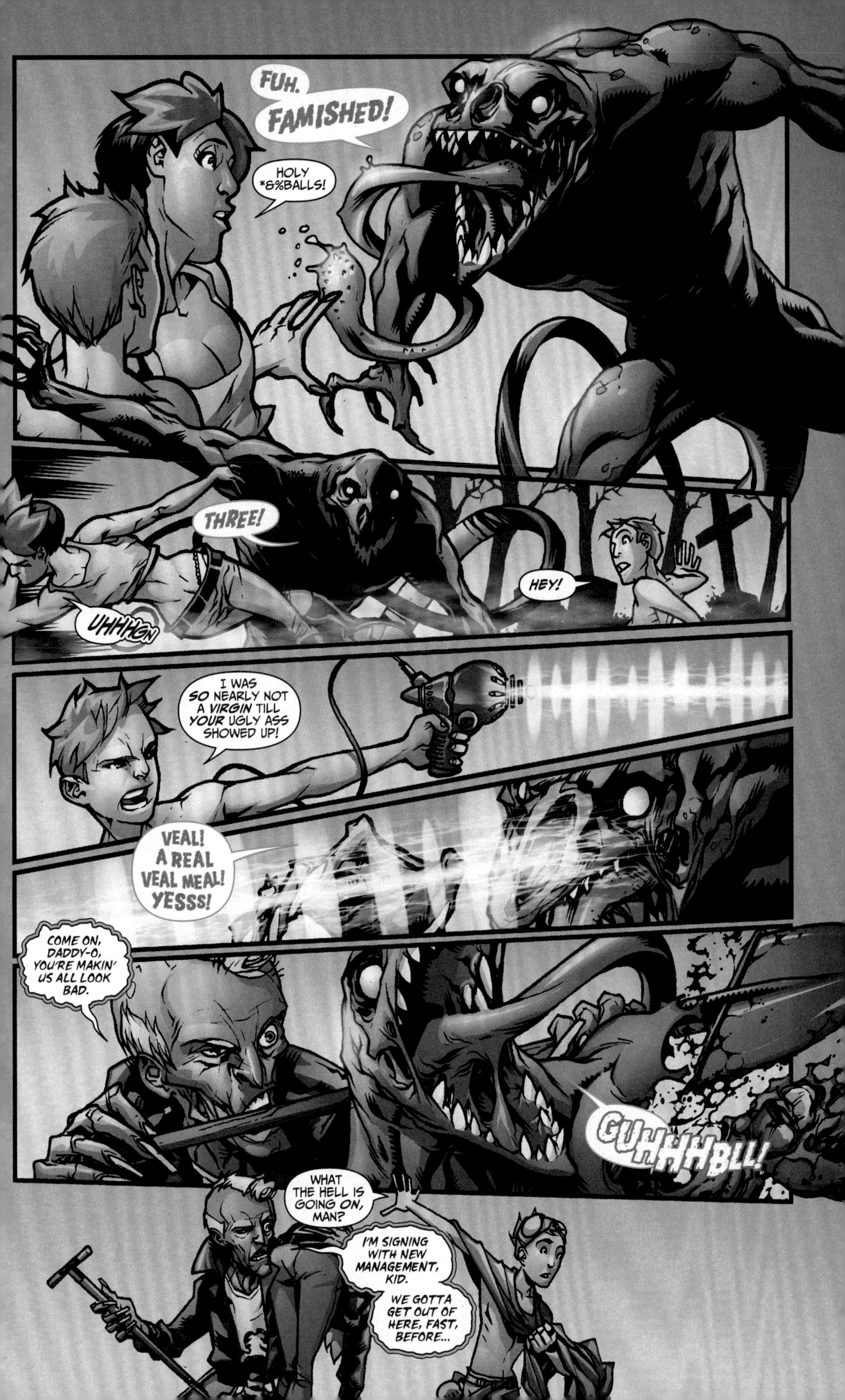
FUH.
FAMISHED!
HOLY *&%BALLS!
THREE!
UHHHGN
HEY!
I WAS SO NEARLY NOT A VIRGIN TILL YOUR UGLY ASS SHOWED UP!
VEAL! A REAL VEAL MEAL! YESSS!
COME ON, DADDY-O, YOU'RE MAKIN' US ALL LOOK BAD.
GUHHHHBLL!
WHAT THE HELL IS GOING ON, MAN?
I'M SIGNING WITH NEW MANAGEMENT, KID.
WE GOTTA GET OUT OF HERE, FAST, BEFORE...

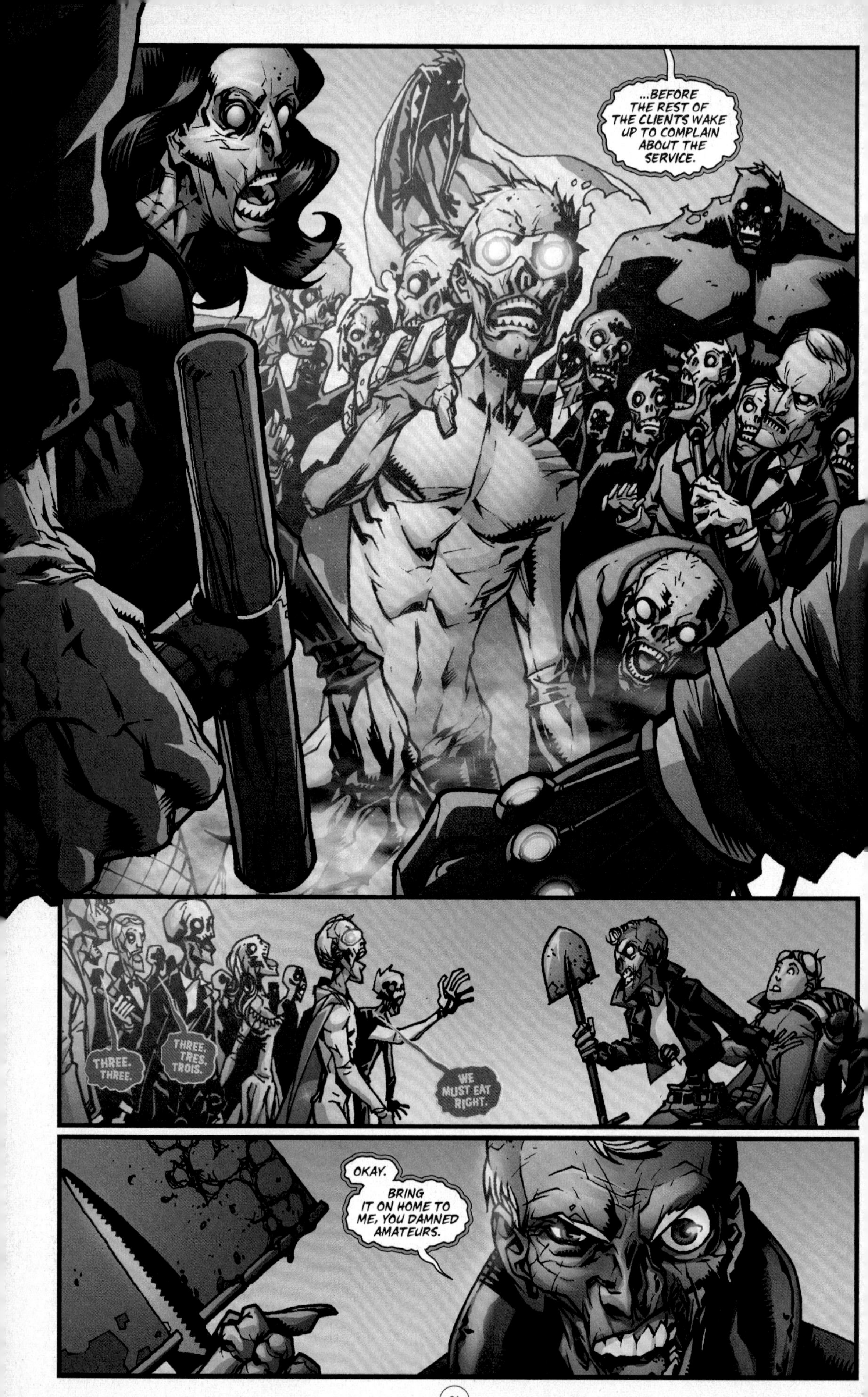

...BEFORE THE REST OF THE CLIENTS WAKE UP TO COMPLAIN ABOUT THE SERVICE.
THREE. THREE.
THREE, TRES, TROIS.
WE MUST EAT RIGHT.
OKAY.
BRING IT ON HOME TO ME, YOU DAMNED AMATEURS.

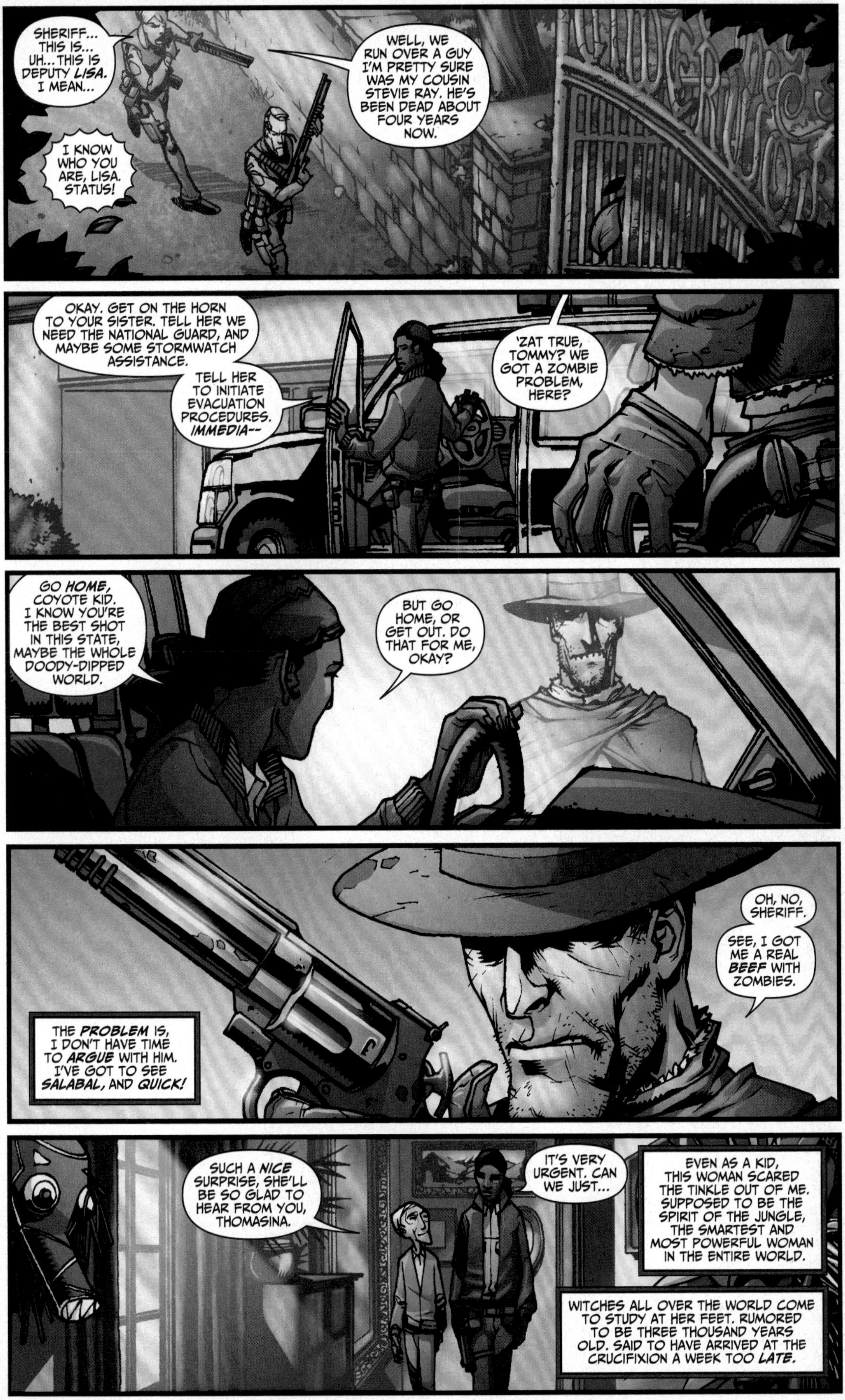

SHERIFF... THIS IS... UH...THIS IS DEPUTY *LISA.* I MEAN...
I KNOW WHO YOU ARE, LISA. STATUS!
WELL, WE RUN OVER A GUY I'M PRETTY SURE WAS MY COUSIN STEVIE RAY. HE'S BEEN DEAD ABOUT FOUR YEARS NOW.
OKAY. GET ON THE HORN TO YOUR SISTER. TELL HER WE NEED THE NATIONAL GUARD, AND MAYBE SOME STORMWATCH ASSISTANCE.
TELL HER TO INITIATE EVACUATION PROCEDURES. *IMMEDIA--*
'ZAT TRUE, TOMMY? WE GOT A ZOMBIE PROBLEM, HERE?
GO *HOME,* COYOTE KID. I KNOW YOU'RE THE BEST SHOT IN THIS STATE, MAYBE THE WHOLE DOODY-DIPPED WORLD.
BUT GO HOME, OR GET OUT. DO THAT FOR ME, OKAY?
THE *PROBLEM* IS, I DON'T HAVE TIME TO *ARGUE* WITH HIM. I'VE GOT TO SEE *SALABAL,* AND *QUICK!*
OH, NO, SHERIFF.
SEE, I GOT ME A REAL *BEEF* WITH ZOMBIES.
SUCH A *NICE* SURPRISE, SHE'LL BE SO GLAD TO HEAR FROM YOU, THOMASINA.
IT'S VERY URGENT. CAN WE JUST...
EVEN AS A KID, THIS WOMAN SCARED THE TINKLE OUT OF ME. SUPPOSED TO BE THE SPIRIT OF THE JUNGLE, THE SMARTEST AND MOST POWERFUL WOMAN IN THE ENTIRE WORLD.
WITCHES ALL OVER THE WORLD COME TO STUDY AT HER FEET. RUMORED TO BE THREE THOUSAND YEARS OLD. SAID TO HAVE ARRIVED AT THE CRUCIFIXION A WEEK TOO *LATE.*

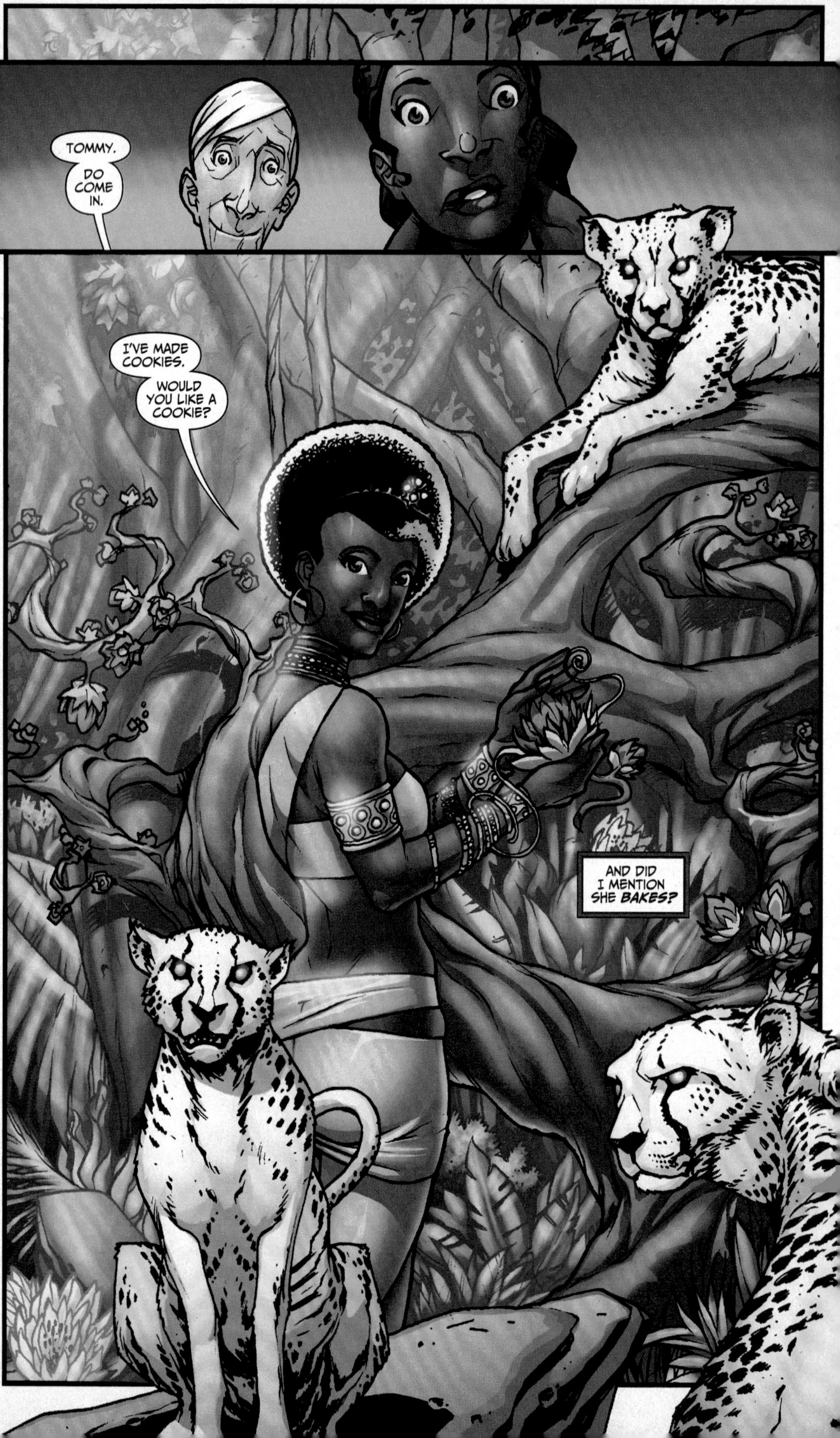
TOMMY.
DO COME IN.
I'VE MADE COOKIES.
WOULD YOU LIKE A COOKIE?
AND DID I MENTION SHE *BAKES?*

♣♥ COYOTE KID IN ♦♠
FOUR OF A KIND

WRITER • GAIL SIMONE
PENCILER • LEANDRO FERNÃNDEZ
INKER • FRANCISCO PARONZINI

COLORIST • CARRIE STRACHAN
LETTERER • TRAVIS LANHAM
EDITS • ABERNATHY & QUINN

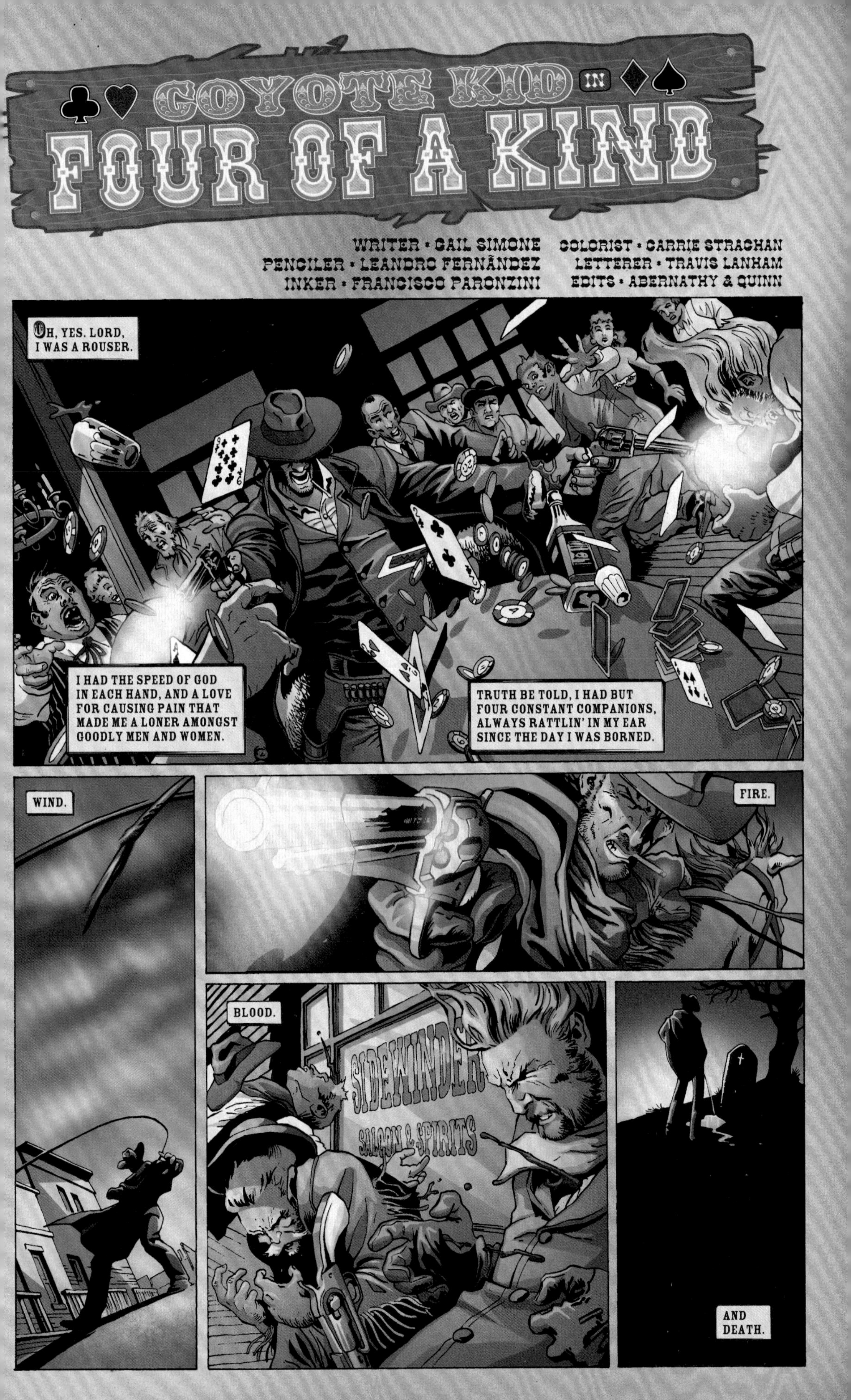
OH, YES. LORD, I WAS A ROUSER.
I HAD THE SPEED OF GOD IN EACH HAND, AND A LOVE FOR CAUSING PAIN THAT MADE ME A LONER AMONGST GOODLY MEN AND WOMEN.
TRUTH BE TOLD, I HAD BUT FOUR CONSTANT COMPANIONS, ALWAYS RATTLIN' IN MY EAR SINCE THE DAY I WAS BORNED.
WIND.
FIRE.
BLOOD.
SIDEWINDER
SALOON & SPIRITS
AND DEATH.

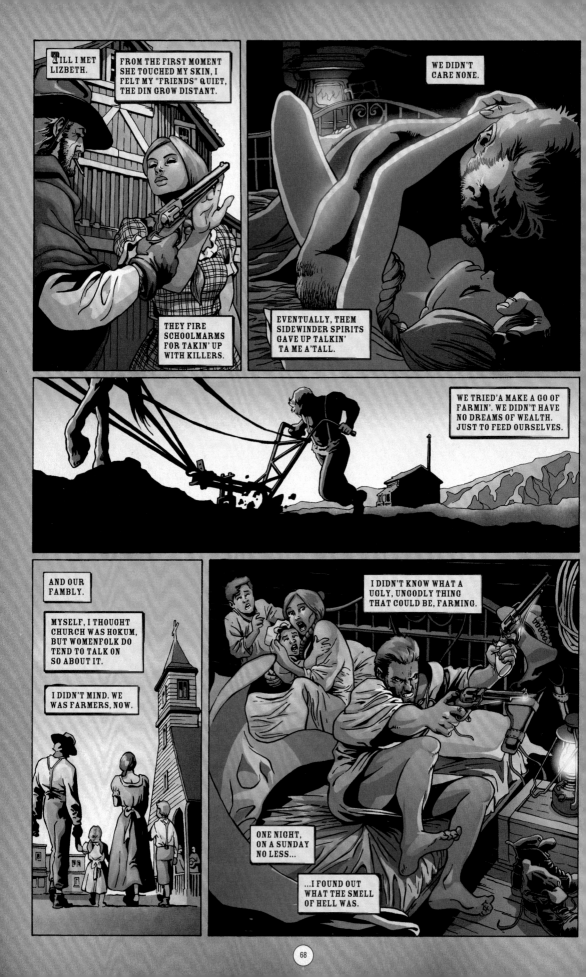

TILL I MET LIZBETH.

FROM THE FIRST MOMENT SHE TOUCHED MY SKIN, I FELT MY "FRIENDS" QUIET, THE DIN GROW DISTANT.

THEY FIRE SCHOOLMARMS FOR TAKIN' UP WITH KILLERS.

WE DIDN'T CARE NONE.

EVENTUALLY, THEM SIDEWINDER SPIRITS GAVE UP TALKIN' TA ME A'TALL.

WE TRIED'A MAKE A GO OF FARMIN'. WE DIDN'T HAVE NO DREAMS OF WEALTH. JUST TO FEED OURSELVES.

AND OUR FAMBLY.

MYSELF, I THOUGHT CHURCH WAS HOKUM, BUT WOMENFOLK DO TEND TO TALK ON SO ABOUT IT.

I DIDN'T MIND. WE WAS FARMERS, NOW.

I DIDN'T KNOW WHAT A UGLY, UNGODLY THING THAT COULD BE, FARMING.

ONE NIGHT, ON A SUNDAY NO LESS...

...I FOUND OUT WHAT THE SMELL OF HELL WAS.

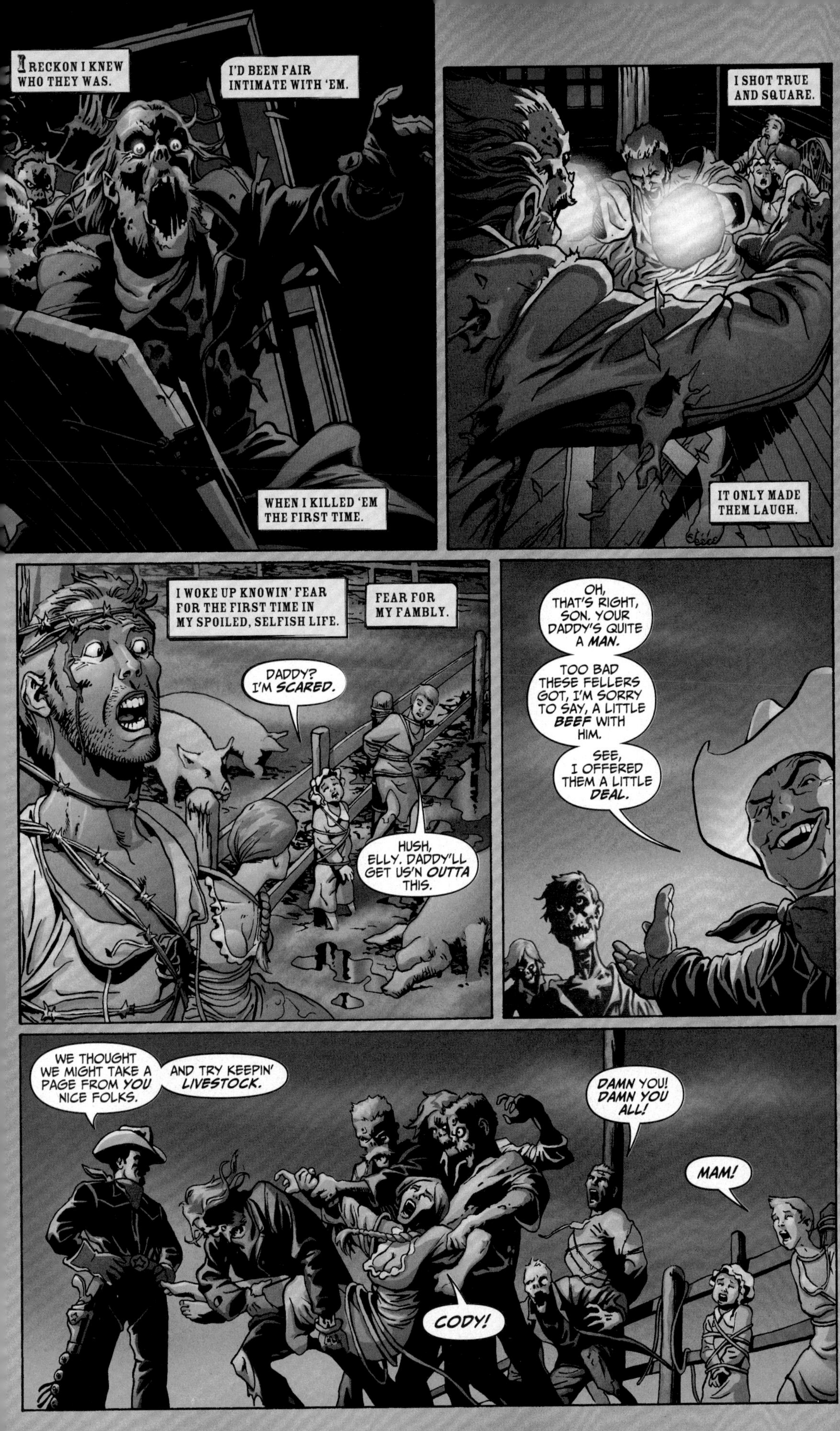
I RECKON I KNEW WHO THEY WAS.
I'D BEEN FAIR INTIMATE WITH 'EM.
WHEN I KILLED 'EM THE FIRST TIME.
I SHOT TRUE AND SQUARE.
IT ONLY MADE THEM LAUGH.
I WOKE UP KNOWIN' FEAR FOR THE FIRST TIME IN MY SPOILED, SELFISH LIFE.
FEAR FOR MY FAMBLY.
DADDY? I'M SCARED.
HUSH, ELLY. DADDY'LL GET US'N OUTTA THIS.
OH, THAT'S RIGHT, SON. YOUR DADDY'S QUITE A MAN.
TOO BAD THESE FELLERS GOT, I'M SORRY TO SAY, A LITTLE BEEF WITH HIM.
SEE, I OFFERED THEM A LITTLE DEAL.
WE THOUGHT WE MIGHT TAKE A PAGE FROM YOU NICE FOLKS.
AND TRY KEEPIN' LIVESTOCK.
DAMN YOU! DAMN YOU ALL!
MAM!
CODY!

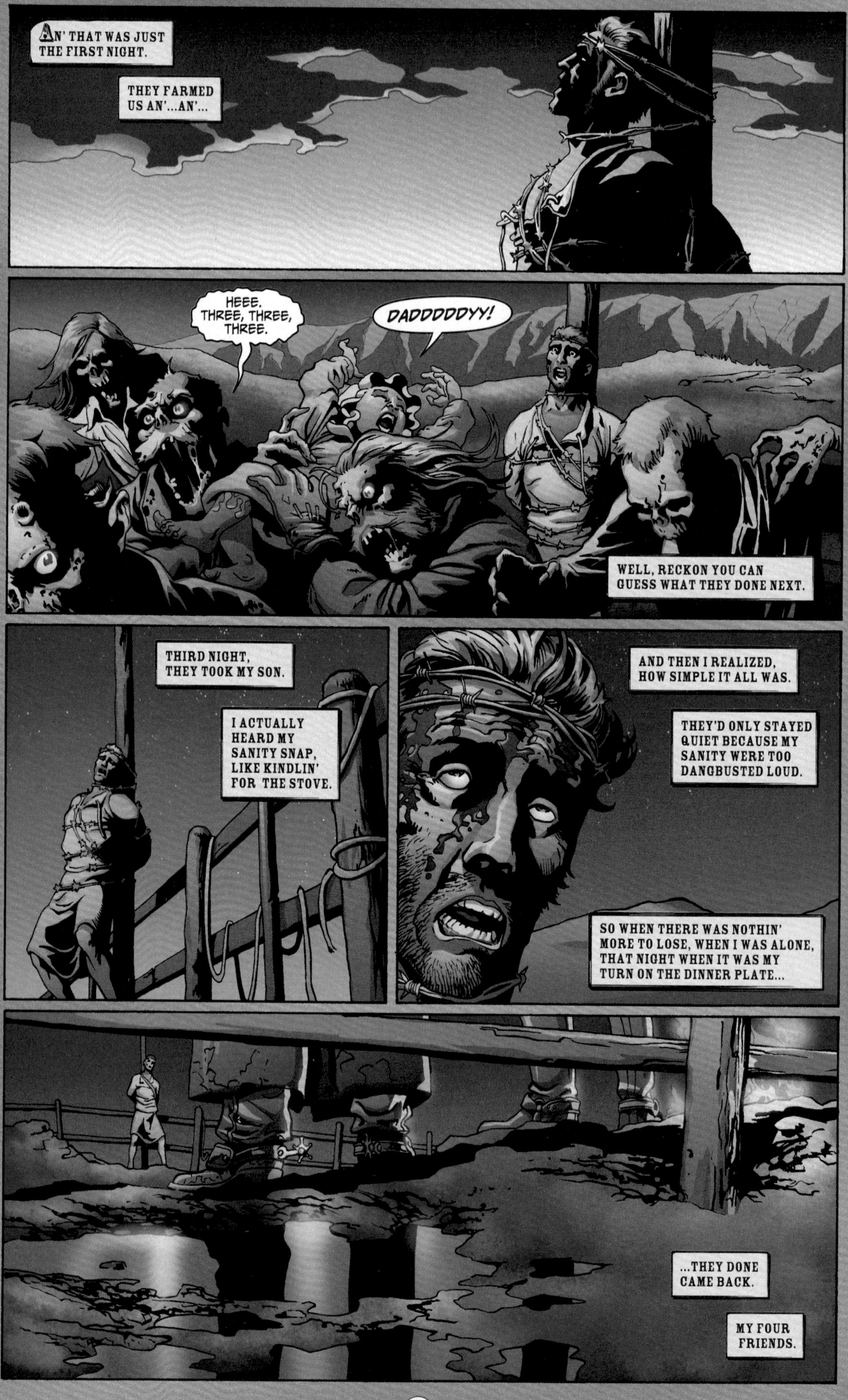
AN' THAT WAS JUST THE FIRST NIGHT.
THEY FARMED US AN'...AN'...
HEEE. THREE, THREE, THREE.
DADDDDDYY!
WELL, RECKON YOU CAN GUESS WHAT THEY DONE NEXT.
THIRD NIGHT, THEY TOOK MY SON.
I ACTUALLY HEARD MY SANITY SNAP, LIKE KINDLIN' FOR THE STOVE.
AND THEN I REALIZED, HOW SIMPLE IT ALL WAS.
THEY'D ONLY STAYED QUIET BECAUSE MY SANITY WERE TOO DANGBUSTED LOUD.
SO WHEN THERE WAS NOTHIN' MORE TO LOSE, WHEN I WAS ALONE, THAT NIGHT WHEN IT WAS MY TURN ON THE DINNER PLATE...
...THEY DONE CAME BACK.
MY FOUR FRIENDS.

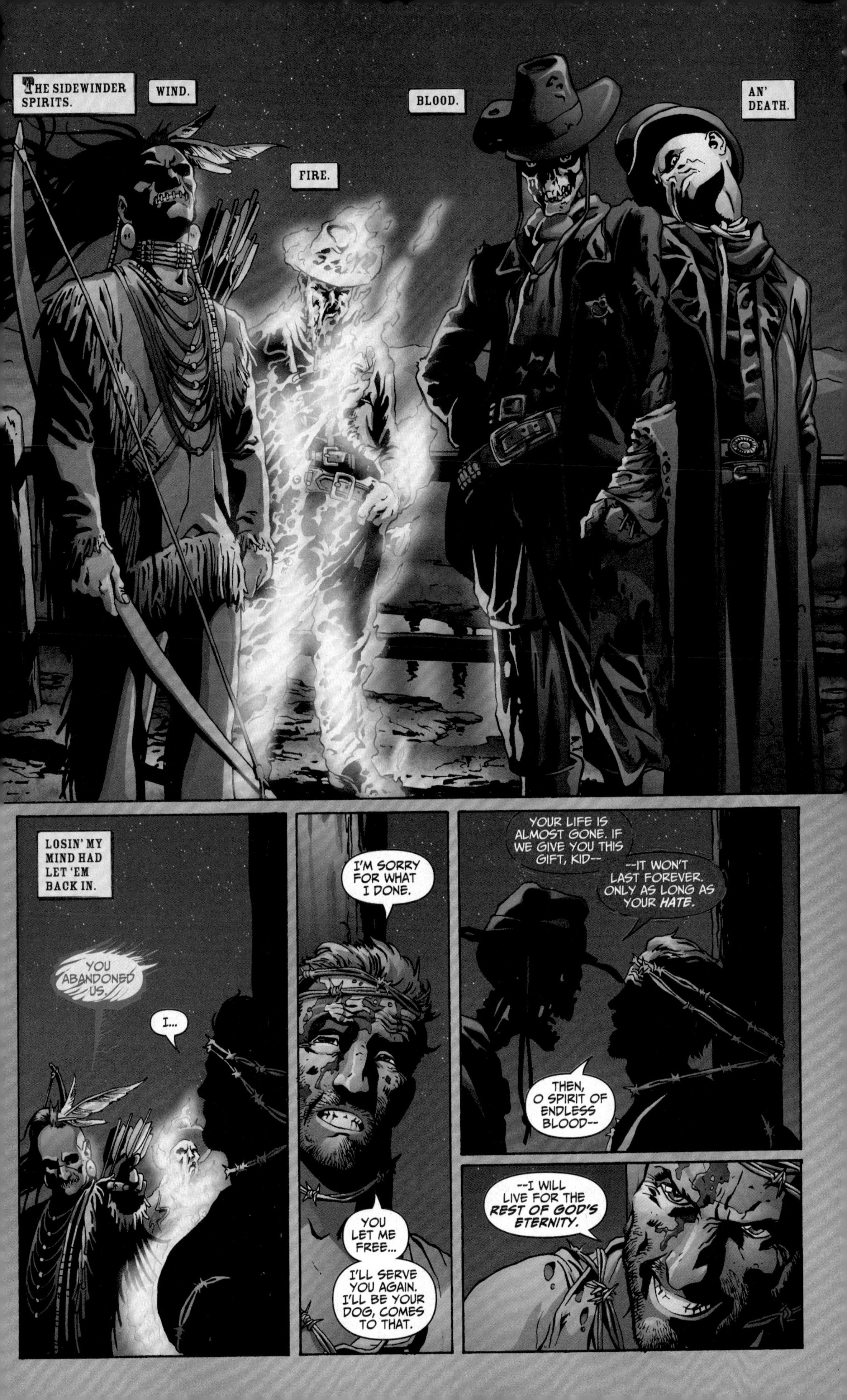
THE SIDEWINDER SPIRITS.
WIND.
FIRE.
BLOOD.
AN' DEATH.
LOSIN' MY MIND HAD LET 'EM BACK IN.
YOU ABANDONED US.
I...
I'M SORRY FOR WHAT I DONE.
YOU LET ME FREE...
I'LL SERVE YOU AGAIN. I'LL BE YOUR DOG, COMES TO THAT.
YOUR LIFE IS ALMOST GONE. IF WE GIVE YOU THIS GIFT, KID--
--IT WON'T LAST FOREVER. ONLY AS LONG AS YOUR HATE.
THEN, O SPIRIT OF ENDLESS BLOOD--
--I WILL LIVE FOR THE REST OF GOD'S ETERNITY.

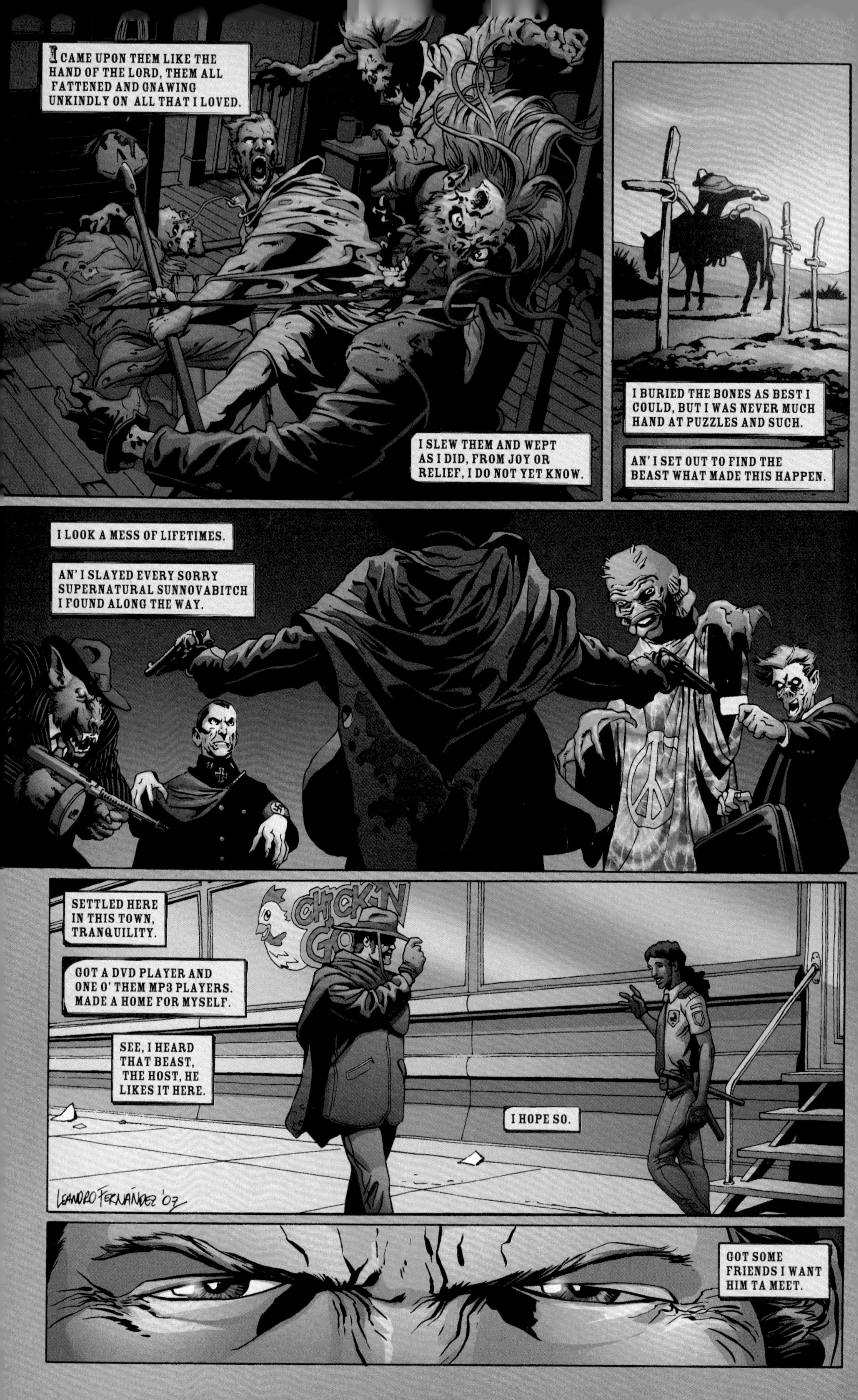
I CAME UPON THEM LIKE THE HAND OF THE LORD, THEM ALL FATTENED AND GNAWING UNKINDLY ON ALL THAT I LOVED.
I SLEW THEM AND WEPT AS I DID, FROM JOY OR RELIEF, I DO NOT YET KNOW.
I BURIED THE BONES AS BEST I COULD, BUT I WAS NEVER MUCH HAND AT PUZZLES AND SUCH.
AN' I SET OUT TO FIND THE BEAST WHAT MADE THIS HAPPEN.
I LOOK A MESS OF LIFETIMES.
AN' I SLAYED EVERY SORRY SUPERNATURAL SUNNOVABITCH I FOUND ALONG THE WAY.
SETTLED HERE IN THIS TOWN, TRANQUILITY.
CHICK'N GO
GOT A DVD PLAYER AND ONE O' THEM MP3 PLAYERS. MADE A HOME FOR MYSELF.
SEE, I HEARD THAT BEAST, THE HOST, HE LIKES IT HERE.
I HOPE SO.
LEANDRO FERNÁNDEZ '07
GOT SOME FRIENDS I WANT HIM TA MEET.

CHAPTER FOUR

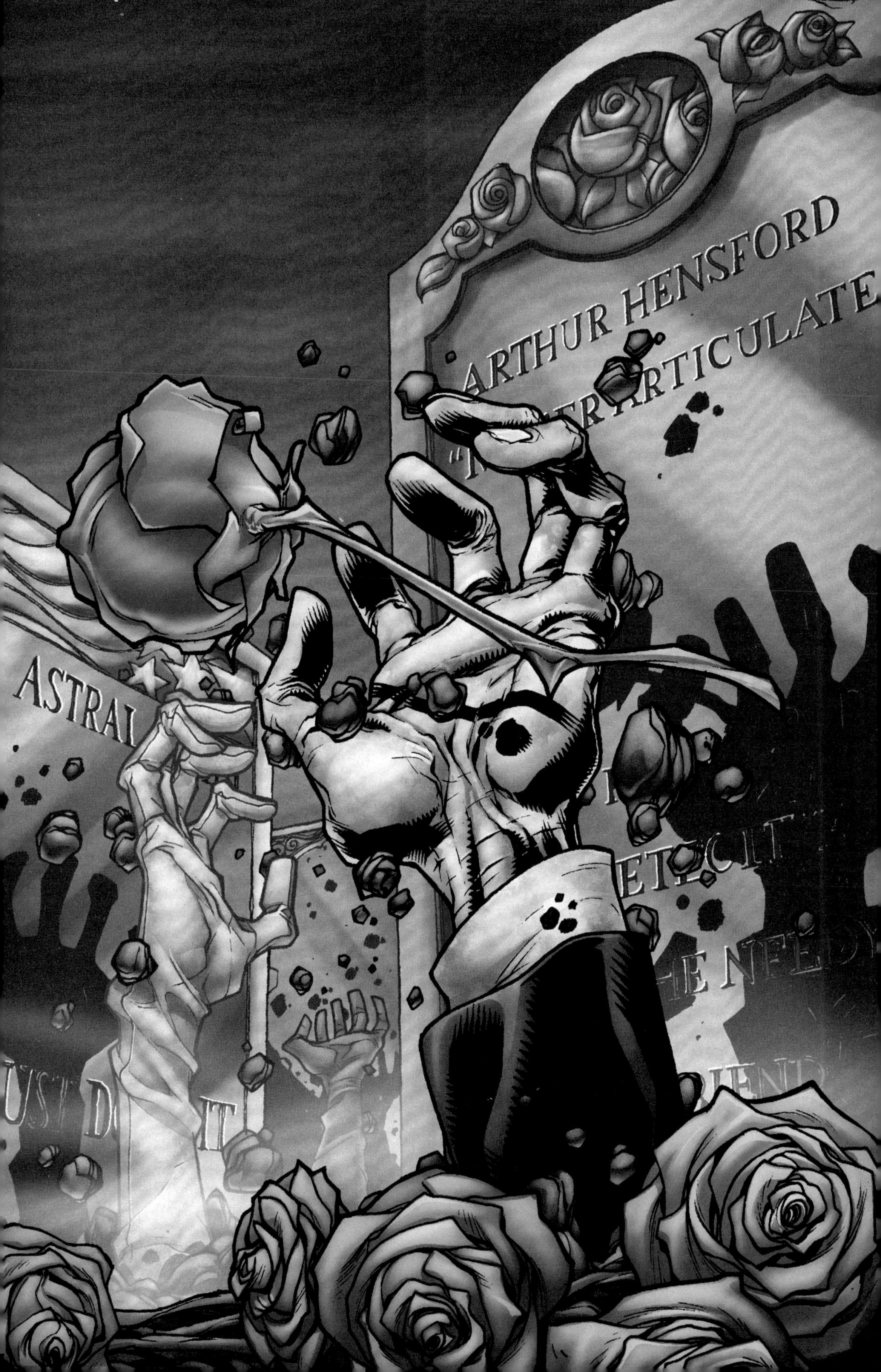
ARTHUR HENSFORD
ARTICULATE

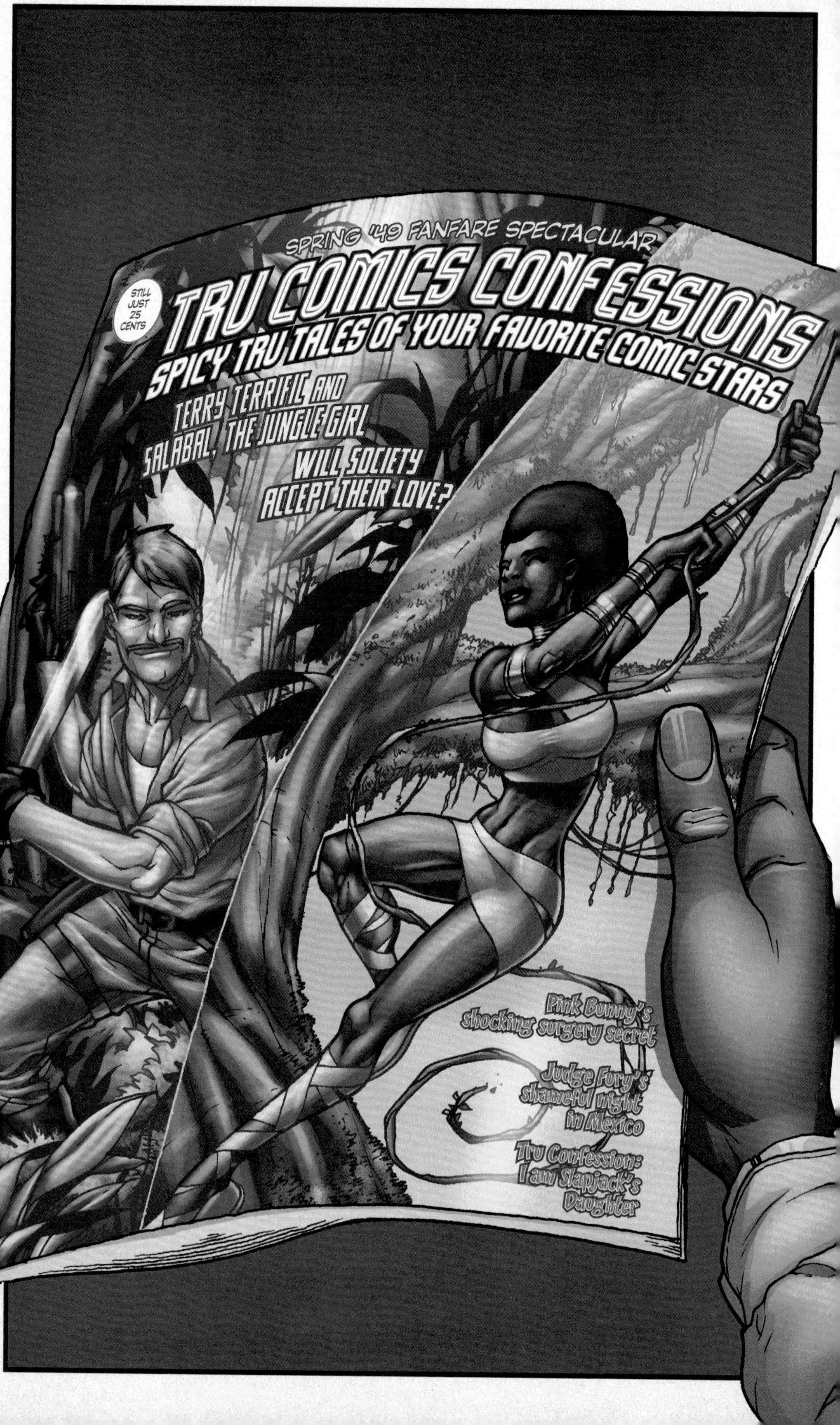

SPRING '49 FANFARE SPECTACULAR
STILL JUST 25 CENTS
TRU COMICS CONFESSIONS
SPICY TRU TALES OF YOUR FAVORITE COMIC STARS
TERRY TERRIFIC AND SALABAL, THE JUNGLE GIRL
WILL SOCIETY ACCEPT THEIR LOVE?
Pink Bunny's shocking surgery secret
Judge Fury's shameful night in Mexico
Tru Confession: I am Slapjack's Daughter

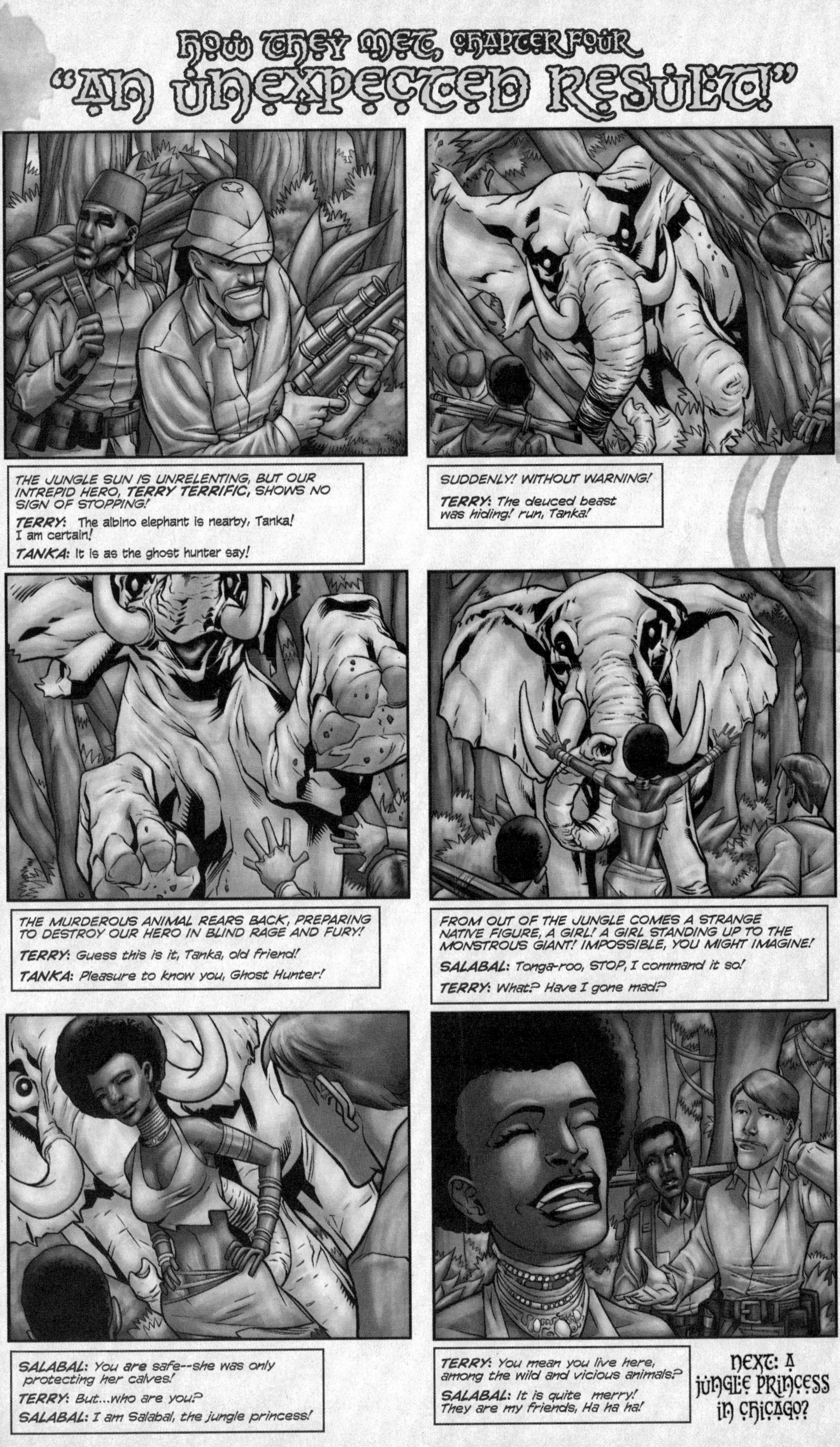

HOW THEY MET, CHAPTER FOUR
"AN UNEXPECTED RESULT!"
THE JUNGLE SUN IS UNRELENTING, BUT OUR INTREPID HERO, TERRY TERRIFIC, SHOWS NO SIGN OF STOPPING!
TERRY: The albino elephant is nearby, Tanka! I am certain!
TANKA: It is as the ghost hunter say!
SUDDENLY! WITHOUT WARNING!
TERRY: The deuced beast was hiding! run, Tanka!
THE MURDEROUS ANIMAL REARS BACK, PREPARING TO DESTROY OUR HERO IN BLIND RAGE AND FURY!
TERRY: Guess this is it, Tanka, old friend!
TANKA: Pleasure to know you, Ghost Hunter!
FROM OUT OF THE JUNGLE COMES A STRANGE NATIVE FIGURE, A GIRL! A GIRL STANDING UP TO THE MONSTROUS GIANT! IMPOSSIBLE, YOU MIGHT IMAGINE!
SALABAL: Tonga-roo, STOP, I command it so!
TERRY: What? Have I gone mad?
SALABAL: You are safe--she was only protecting her calves!
TERRY: But...who are you?
SALABAL: I am Salabal, the jungle princess!
TERRY: You mean you live here, among the wild and vicious animals?
SALABAL: It is quite merry! They are my friends, Ha ha ha!
NEXT: A JUNGLE PRINCESS IN CHICAGO?

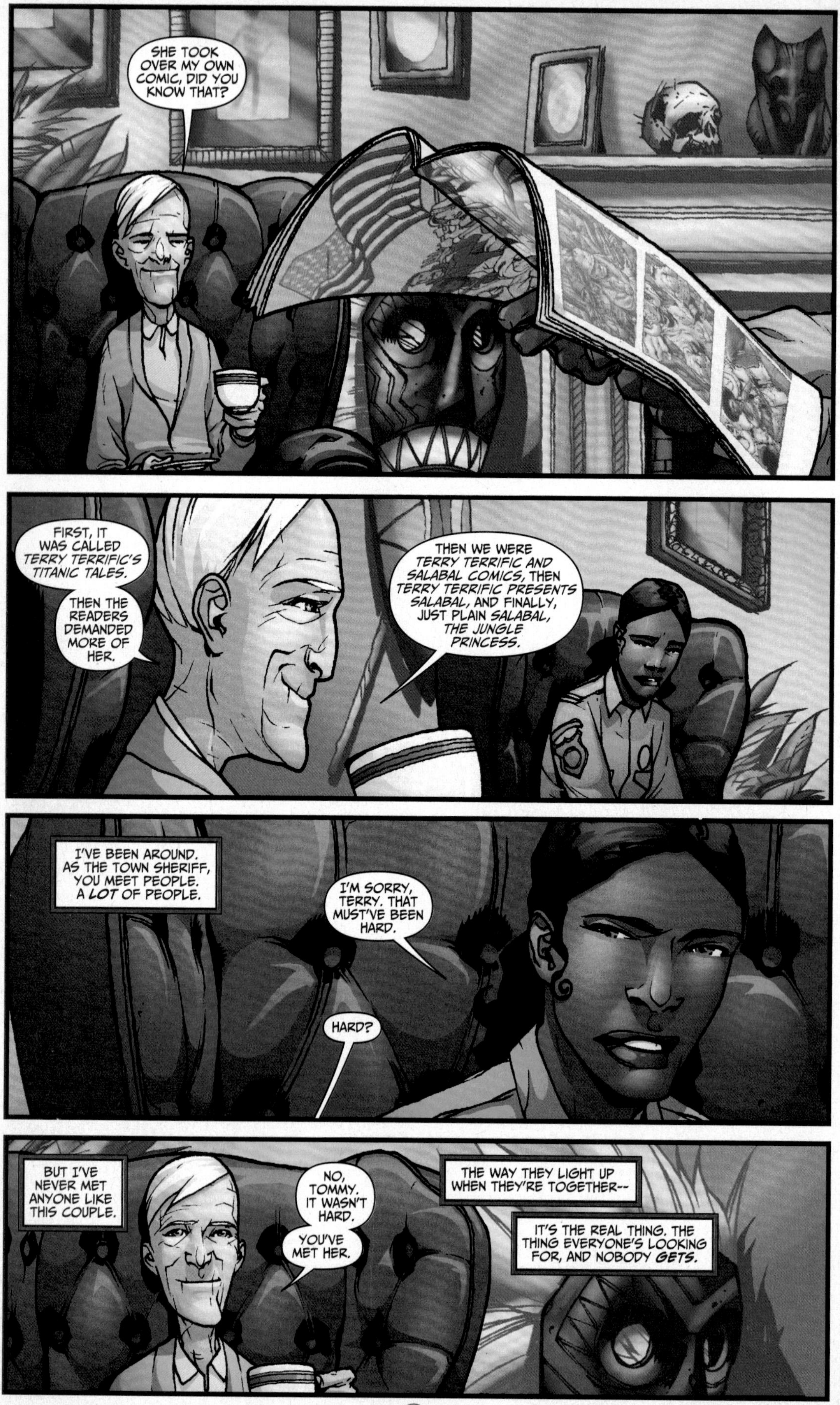
SHE TOOK OVER MY OWN COMIC, DID YOU KNOW THAT?
FIRST, IT WAS CALLED *TERRY TERRIFIC'S TITANIC TALES.*
THEN THE READERS DEMANDED MORE OF HER.
THEN WE WERE *TERRY TERRIFIC AND SALABAL COMICS,* THEN *TERRY TERRIFIC PRESENTS SALABAL,* AND FINALLY, JUST PLAIN *SALABAL, THE JUNGLE PRINCESS.*
I'VE BEEN AROUND. AS THE TOWN SHERIFF, YOU MEET PEOPLE. A ***LOT*** OF PEOPLE.
I'M SORRY, TERRY. THAT MUST'VE BEEN HARD.
HARD?
BUT I'VE NEVER MET ANYONE LIKE THIS COUPLE.
NO, TOMMY. IT WASN'T HARD.
YOU'VE MET HER.
THE WAY THEY LIGHT UP WHEN THEY'RE TOGETHER--
IT'S THE REAL THING. THE THING EVERYONE'S LOOKING FOR, AND NOBODY ***GETS.***

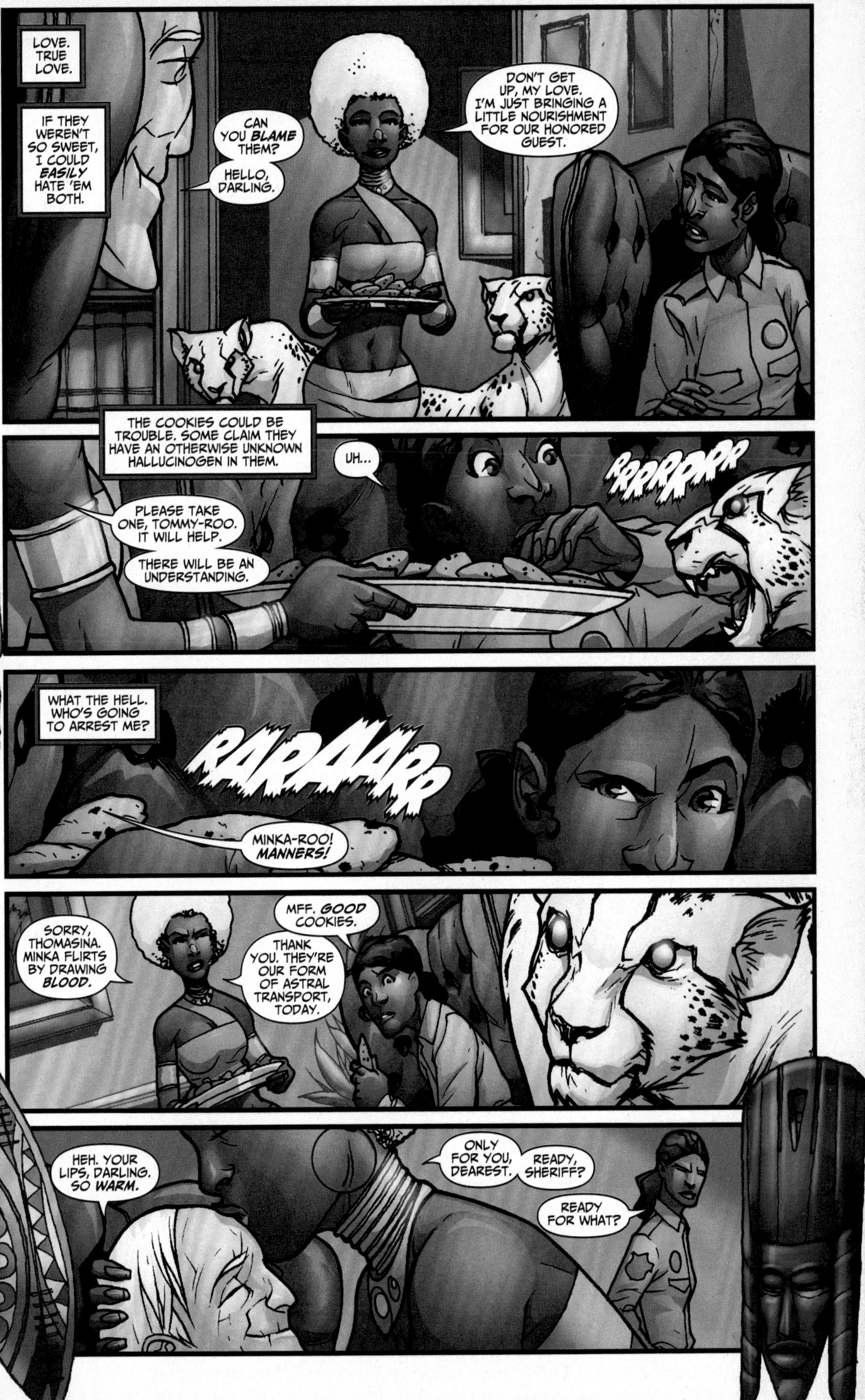

LOVE. TRUE LOVE.
IF THEY WEREN'T SO SWEET, I COULD EASILY HATE 'EM BOTH.
CAN YOU BLAME THEM?
HELLO, DARLING.
DON'T GET UP, MY LOVE. I'M JUST BRINGING A LITTLE NOURISHMENT FOR OUR HONORED GUEST.
THE COOKIES COULD BE TROUBLE. SOME CLAIM THEY HAVE AN OTHERWISE UNKNOWN HALLUCINOGEN IN THEM.
PLEASE TAKE ONE, TOMMY-ROO. IT WILL HELP.
THERE WILL BE AN UNDERSTANDING.
UH...
RRRRRRR
WHAT THE HELL. WHO'S GOING TO ARREST ME?
RARAARR
MINKA-ROO! MANNERS!
SORRY, THOMASINA. MINKA FLIRTS BY DRAWING BLOOD.
MFF. GOOD COOKIES.
THANK YOU. THEY'RE OUR FORM OF ASTRAL TRANSPORT, TODAY.
HEH. YOUR LIPS, DARLING. SO WARM.
ONLY FOR YOU, DEAREST.
READY, SHERIFF?
READY FOR WHAT?

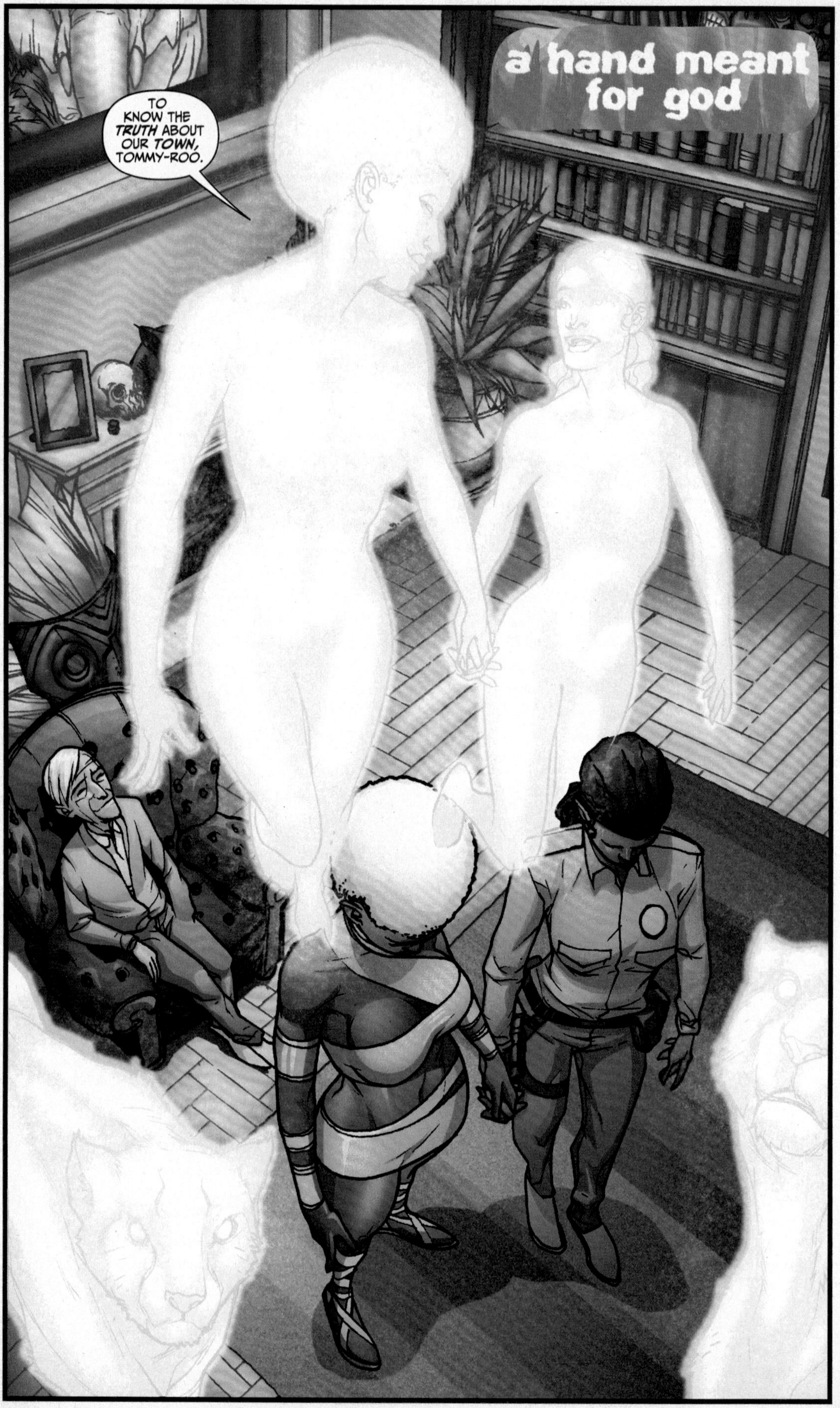
TO KNOW THE *TRUTH* ABOUT OUR *TOWN*, TOMMY-ROO.
a hand meant for god

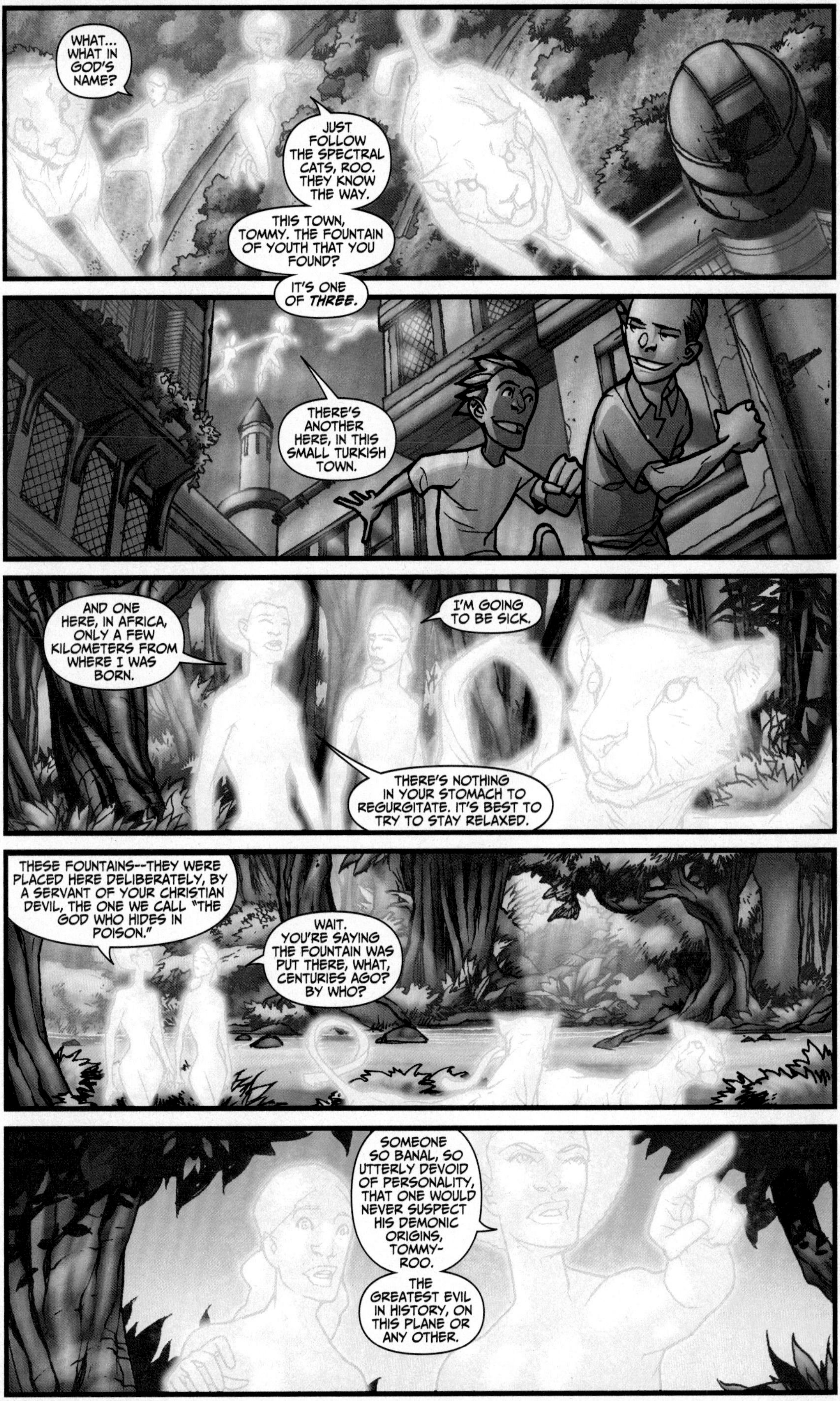
WHAT... WHAT IN GOD'S NAME?
JUST FOLLOW THE SPECTRAL CATS, ROO. THEY KNOW THE WAY.
THIS TOWN, TOMMY. THE FOUNTAIN OF YOUTH THAT YOU FOUND?
IT'S ONE OF THREE.
THERE'S ANOTHER HERE, IN THIS SMALL TURKISH TOWN.
AND ONE HERE, IN AFRICA, ONLY A FEW KILOMETERS FROM WHERE I WAS BORN.
I'M GOING TO BE SICK.
THERE'S NOTHING IN YOUR STOMACH TO REGURGITATE. IT'S BEST TO TRY TO STAY RELAXED.
THESE FOUNTAINS--THEY WERE PLACED HERE DELIBERATELY, BY A SERVANT OF YOUR CHRISTIAN DEVIL, THE ONE WE CALL "THE GOD WHO HIDES IN POISON."
WAIT. YOU'RE SAYING THE FOUNTAIN WAS PUT THERE, WHAT, CENTURIES AGO? BY WHO?
SOMEONE SO BANAL, SO UTTERLY DEVOID OF PERSONALITY, THAT ONE WOULD NEVER SUSPECT HIS DEMONIC ORIGINS, TOMMY-ROO.
THE GREATEST EVIL IN HISTORY, ON THIS PLANE OR ANY OTHER.

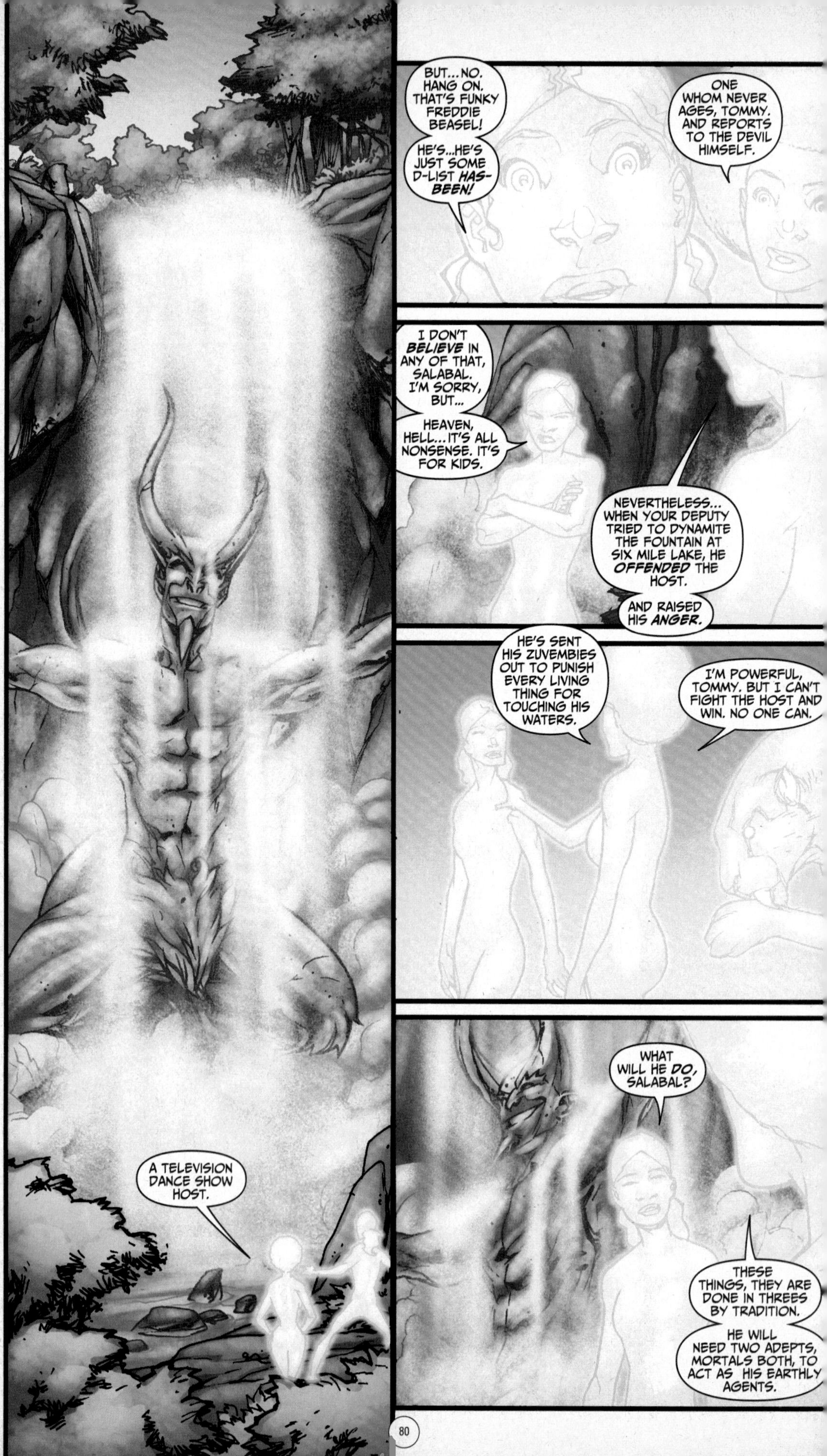
A TELEVISION DANCE SHOW HOST.
BUT...NO. HANG ON. THAT'S FUNKY FREDDIE BEASEL!
HE'S...HE'S JUST SOME D-LIST *HAS-BEEN!*
ONE WHOM NEVER AGES, TOMMY. AND REPORTS TO THE DEVIL HIMSELF.
I DON'T *BELIEVE* IN ANY OF THAT, SALABAL. I'M SORRY, BUT...
HEAVEN, HELL...IT'S ALL NONSENSE. IT'S FOR KIDS.
NEVERTHELESS... WHEN YOUR DEPUTY TRIED TO DYNAMITE THE FOUNTAIN AT SIX MILE LAKE, HE *OFFENDED* THE HOST.
AND RAISED HIS *ANGER.*
HE'S SENT HIS ZUVEMBIES OUT TO PUNISH EVERY LIVING THING FOR TOUCHING HIS WATERS.
I'M POWERFUL, TOMMY. BUT I CAN'T FIGHT THE HOST AND WIN. NO ONE CAN.
WHAT WILL HE *DO,* SALABAL?
THESE THINGS, THEY ARE DONE IN THREES BY TRADITION.
HE WILL NEED TWO ADEPTS, MORTALS BOTH, TO ACT AS HIS EARTHLY AGENTS.

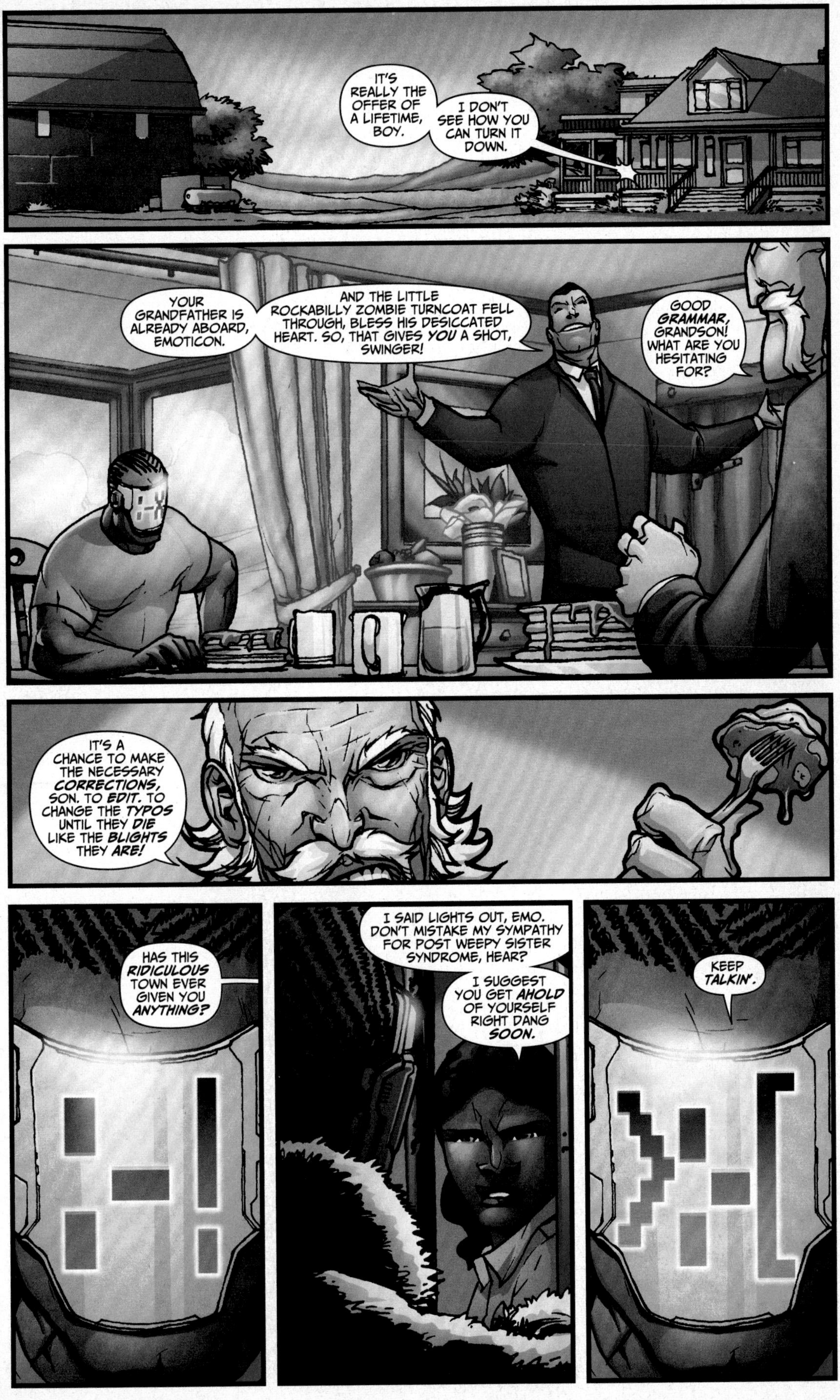
IT'S REALLY THE OFFER OF A LIFETIME, BOY.
I DON'T SEE HOW YOU CAN TURN IT DOWN.
YOUR GRANDFATHER IS ALREADY ABOARD, EMOTICON.
AND THE LITTLE ROCKABILLY ZOMBIE TURNCOAT FELL THROUGH, BLESS HIS DESICCATED HEART. SO, THAT GIVES *YOU* A SHOT, SWINGER!
GOOD *GRAMMAR*, GRANDSON! WHAT ARE YOU HESITATING FOR?
IT'S A CHANCE TO MAKE THE NECESSARY *CORRECTIONS*, SON. TO *EDIT*. TO CHANGE THE *TYPOS* UNTIL THEY *DIE* LIKE THE *BLIGHTS* THEY *ARE!*
HAS THIS *RIDICULOUS* TOWN EVER GIVEN YOU *ANYTHING?*
I SAID LIGHTS OUT, EMO. DON'T MISTAKE MY SYMPATHY FOR POST WEEPY SISTER SYNDROME, HEAR?
I SUGGEST YOU GET *AHOLD* OF YOURSELF RIGHT DANG *SOON*.
KEEP *TALKIN'*.

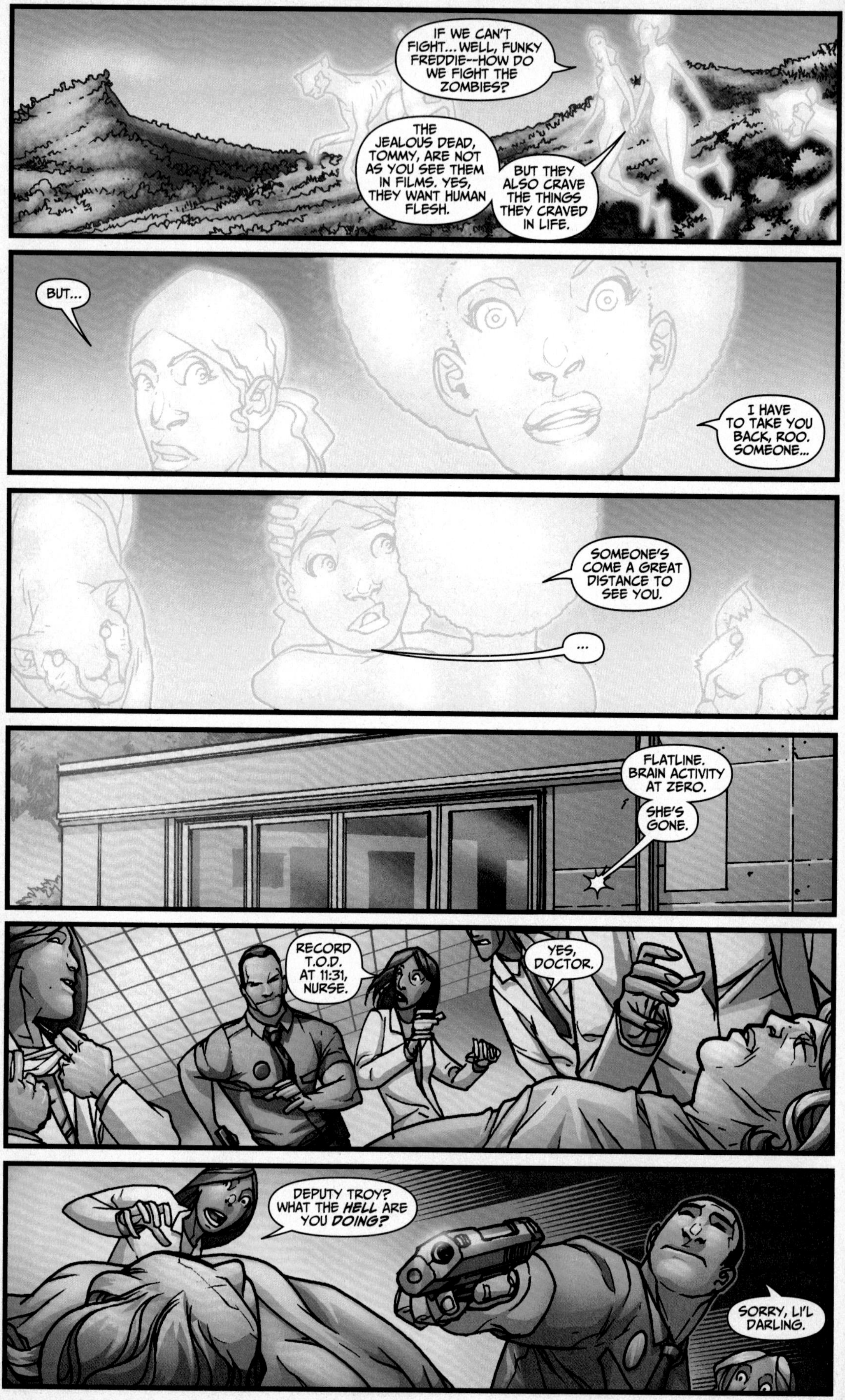
IF WE CAN'T FIGHT... WELL, FUNKY FREDDIE--HOW DO WE FIGHT THE ZOMBIES?
THE JEALOUS DEAD, TOMMY, ARE NOT AS YOU SEE THEM IN FILMS. YES, THEY WANT HUMAN FLESH.
BUT THEY ALSO CRAVE THE THINGS THEY CRAVED IN LIFE.
BUT...
I HAVE TO TAKE YOU BACK, ROO. SOMEONE...
SOMEONE'S COME A GREAT DISTANCE TO SEE YOU.
...
FLATLINE. BRAIN ACTIVITY AT ZERO.
SHE'S GONE.
RECORD T.O.D. AT 11:31, NURSE.
YES, DOCTOR.
DEPUTY TROY? WHAT THE HELL ARE YOU DOING?
SORRY, LI'L DARLING.

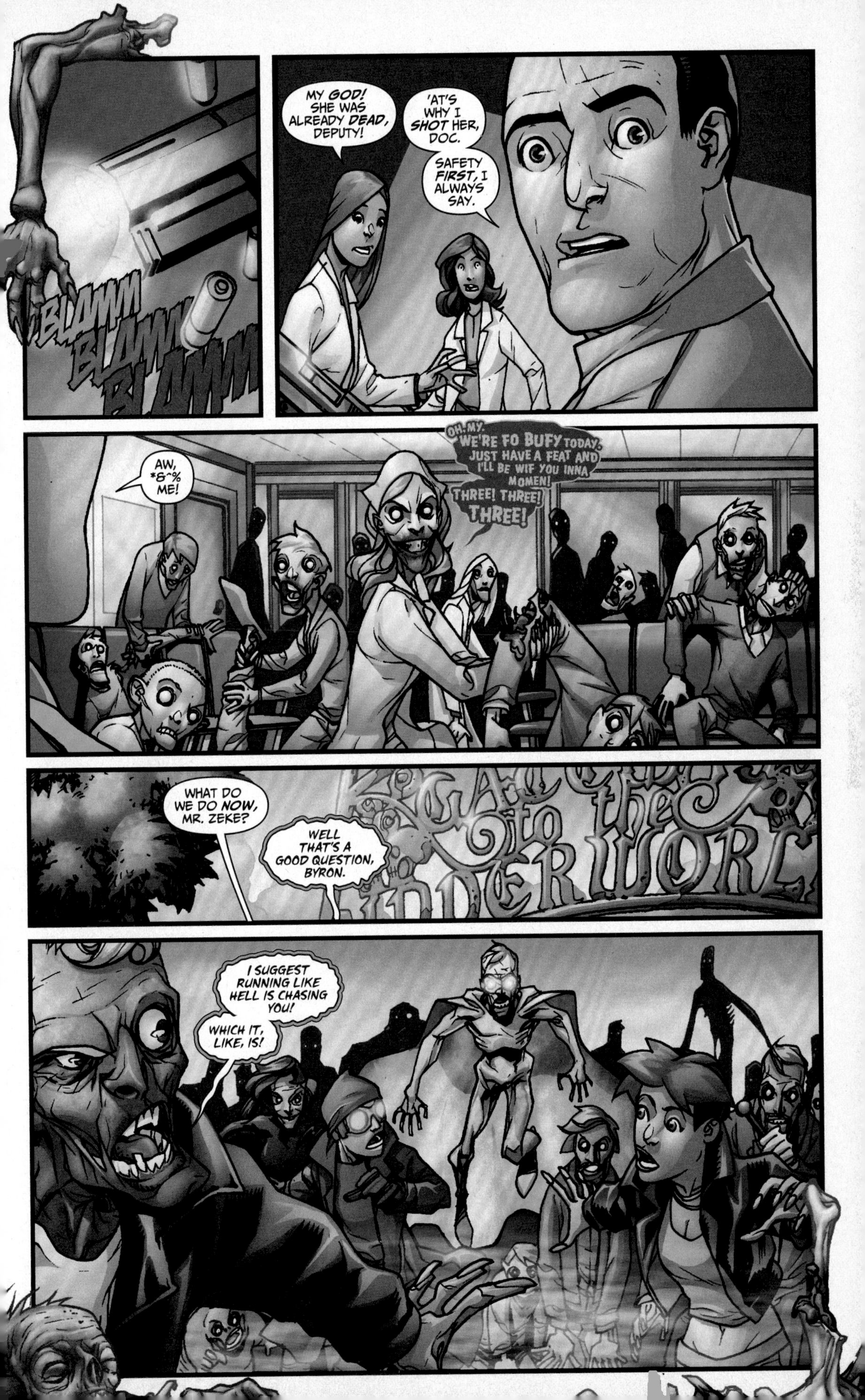
BLAMM BLAMM BLAMM
MY GOD! SHE WAS ALREADY DEAD, DEPUTY!
'AT'S WHY I SHOT HER, DOC.
SAFETY FIRST, I ALWAYS SAY.
AW, *&^% ME!
OH, MY. WE'RE FO BUFY TODAY. JUST HAVE A FEAT AND I'LL BE WIF YOU INNA MOMEN!
THREE! THREE! THREE!
WHAT DO WE DO NOW, MR. ZEKE?
to the
WELL THAT'S A GOOD QUESTION, BYRON.
I SUGGEST RUNNING LIKE HELL IS CHASING YOU!
WHICH IT, LIKE, IS!

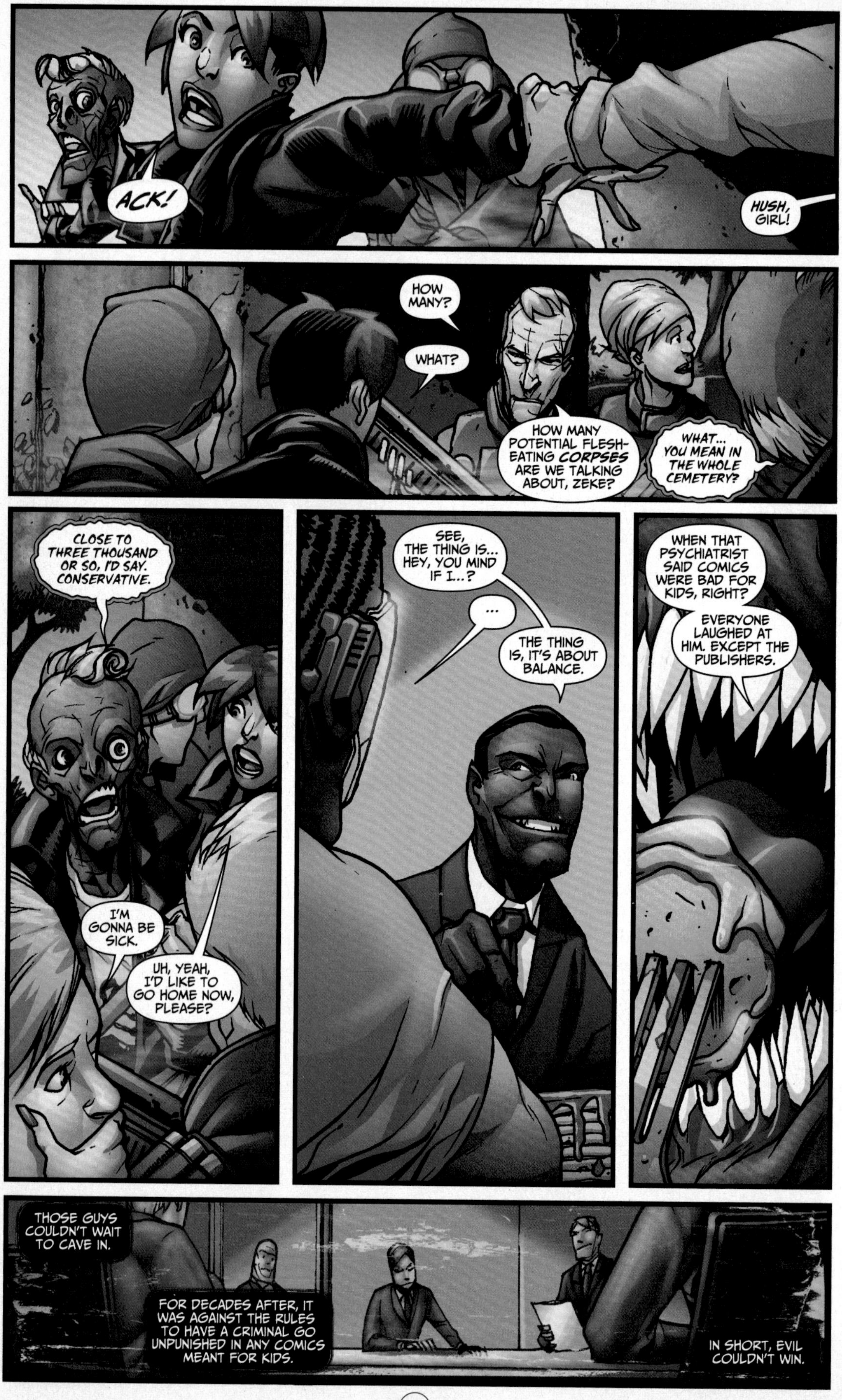
ACK!
HUSH, GIRL!
HOW MANY?
WHAT?
HOW MANY POTENTIAL FLESH-EATING CORPSES ARE WE TALKING ABOUT, ZEKE?
WHAT... YOU MEAN IN THE WHOLE CEMETERY?
CLOSE TO THREE THOUSAND OR SO, I'D SAY. CONSERVATIVE.
I'M GONNA BE SICK.
UH, YEAH, I'D LIKE TO GO HOME NOW, PLEASE?
SEE, THE THING IS... HEY, YOU MIND IF I...?
...
THE THING IS, IT'S ABOUT BALANCE.
WHEN THAT PSYCHIATRIST SAID COMICS WERE BAD FOR KIDS, RIGHT?
EVERYONE LAUGHED AT HIM. EXCEPT THE PUBLISHERS.
THOSE GUYS COULDN'T WAIT TO CAVE IN.
FOR DECADES AFTER, IT WAS AGAINST THE RULES TO HAVE A CRIMINAL GO UNPUNISHED IN ANY COMICS MEANT FOR KIDS.
IN SHORT, EVIL COULDN'T WIN.

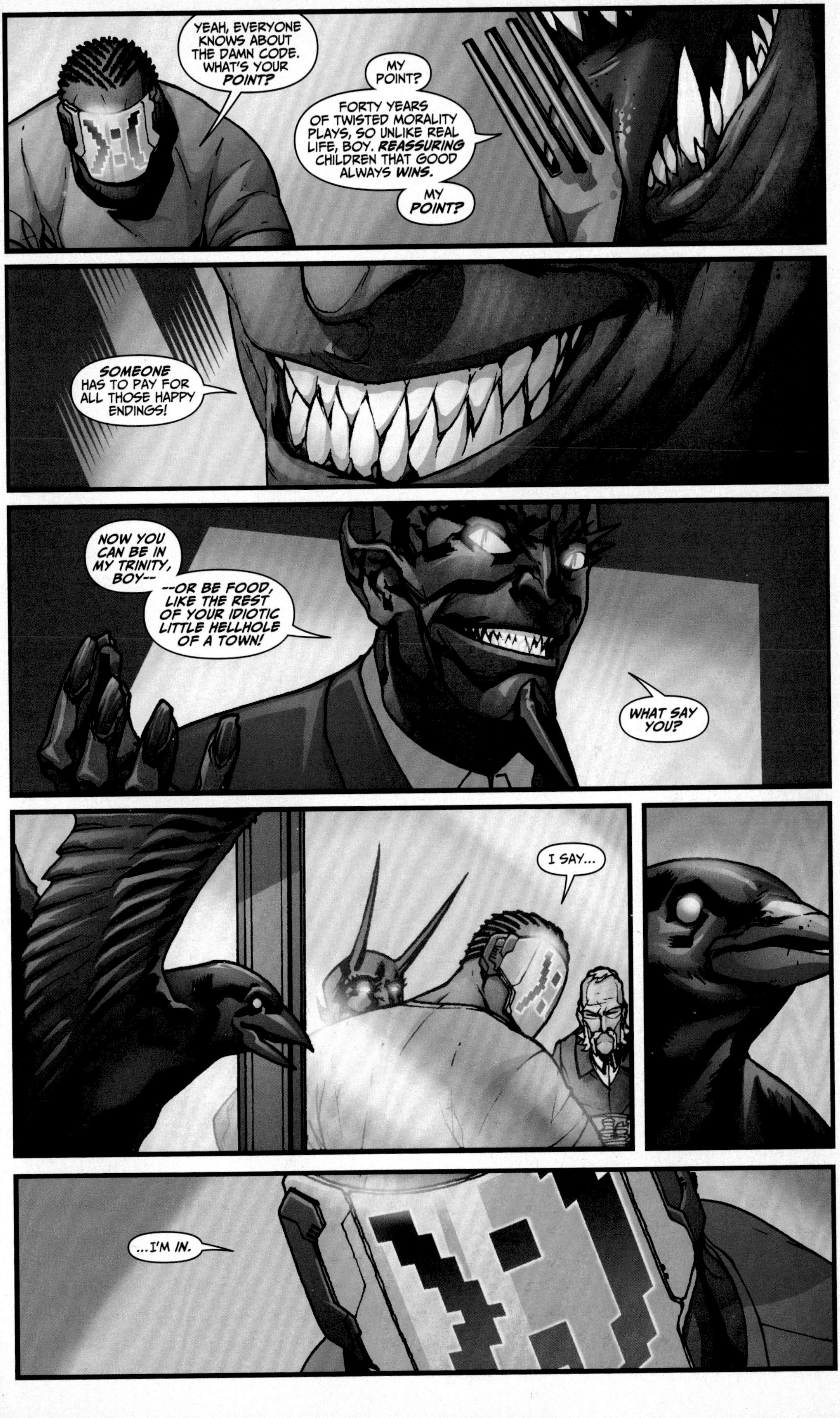
YEAH, EVERYONE KNOWS ABOUT THE DAMN CODE. WHAT'S YOUR POINT?
MY POINT?
FORTY YEARS OF TWISTED MORALITY PLAYS, SO UNLIKE REAL LIFE, BOY. REASSURING CHILDREN THAT GOOD ALWAYS WINS.
MY POINT?
SOMEONE HAS TO PAY FOR ALL THOSE HAPPY ENDINGS!
NOW YOU CAN BE IN MY TRINITY, BOY--
--OR BE FOOD, LIKE THE REST OF YOUR IDIOTIC LITTLE HELLHOLE OF A TOWN!
WHAT SAY YOU?
I SAY...
...I'M IN.

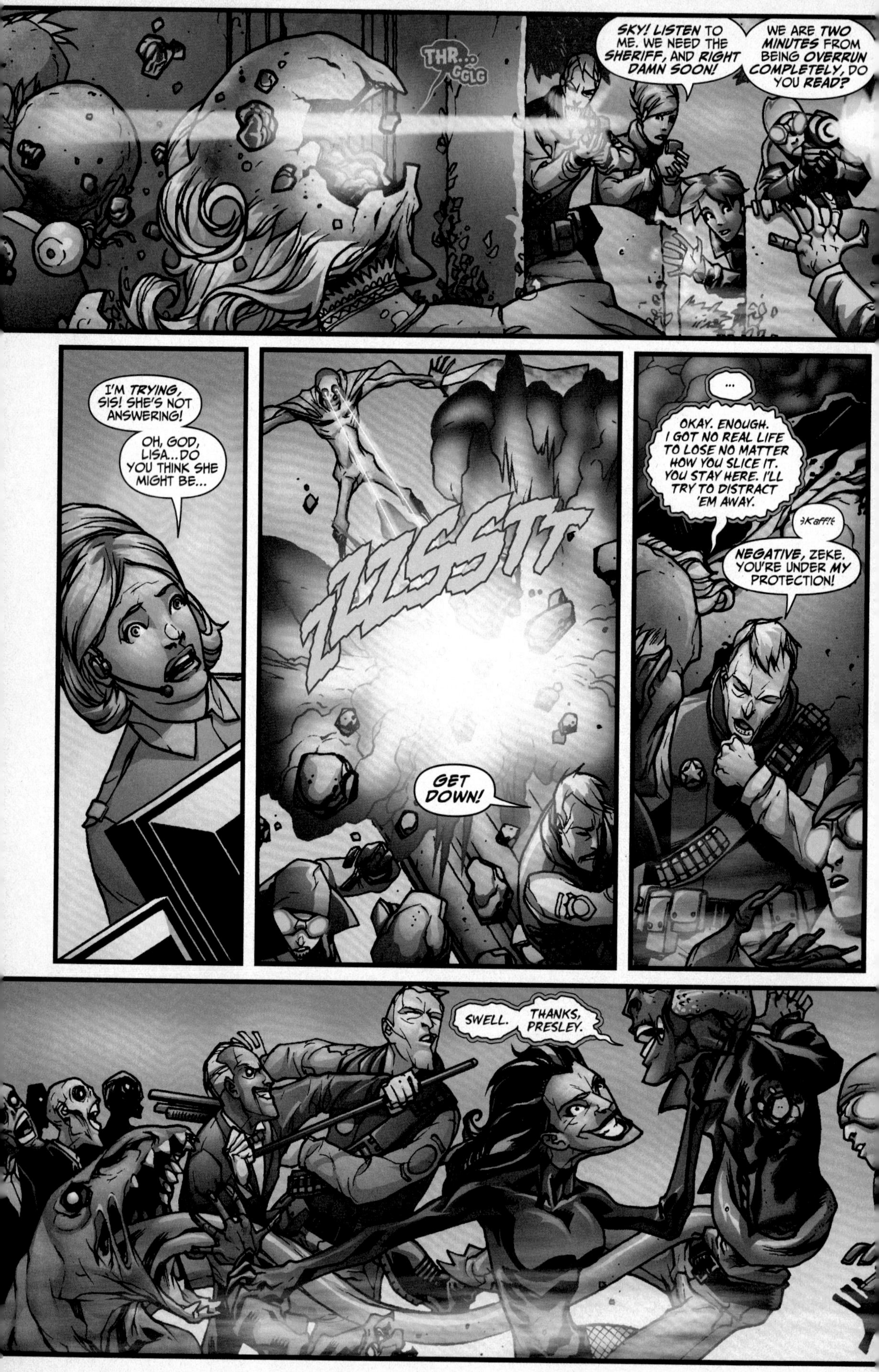
THR...
GGLG
SKY! LISTEN TO ME. WE NEED THE SHERIFF, AND RIGHT DAMN SOON!
WE ARE TWO MINUTES FROM BEING OVERRUN COMPLETELY, DO YOU READ?
I'M TRYING, SIS! SHE'S NOT ANSWERING!
OH, GOD, LISA...DO YOU THINK SHE MIGHT BE...
ZZZSSTT
GET DOWN!
...
OKAY. ENOUGH. I GOT NO REAL LIFE TO LOSE NO MATTER HOW YOU SLICE IT. YOU STAY HERE. I'LL TRY TO DISTRACT 'EM AWAY.
Kaff!
NEGATIVE, ZEKE. YOU'RE UNDER MY PROTECTION!
SWELL.
THANKS, PRESLEY.

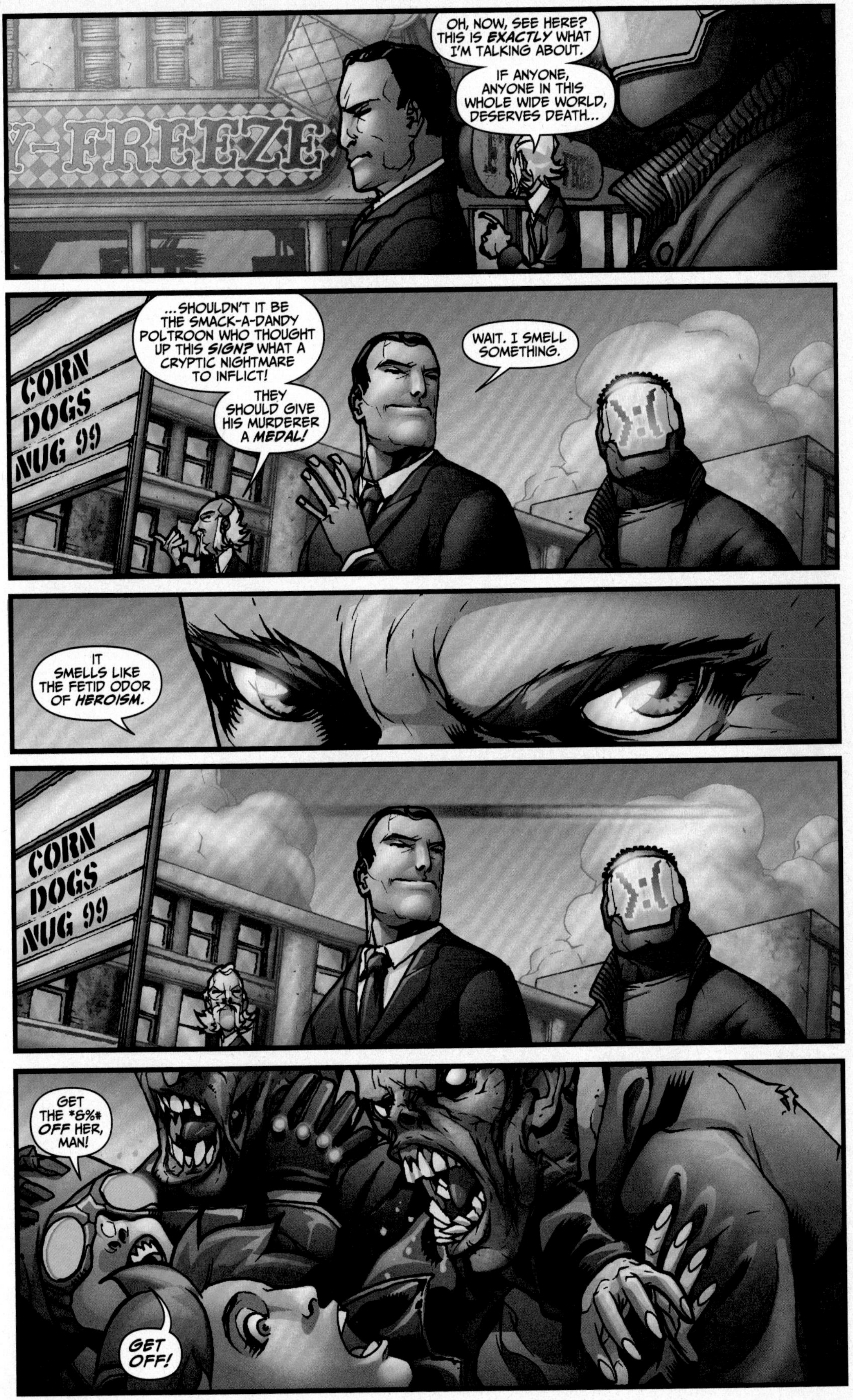
Y-FREEZE
OH, NOW, SEE HERE? THIS IS *EXACTLY* WHAT I'M TALKING ABOUT.
IF ANYONE, ANYONE IN THIS WHOLE WIDE WORLD, DESERVES DEATH...
...SHOULDN'T IT BE THE SMACK-A-DANDY POLTROON WHO THOUGHT UP THIS *SIGN?* WHAT A CRYPTIC NIGHTMARE TO INFLICT!
THEY SHOULD GIVE HIS MURDERER A *MEDAL!*
CORN DOGS NUG 99
WAIT. I SMELL SOMETHING.
IT SMELLS LIKE THE FETID ODOR OF *HEROISM.*
CORN DOGS NUG 99
GET THE *&%# *OFF* HER, MAN!
GET OFF!

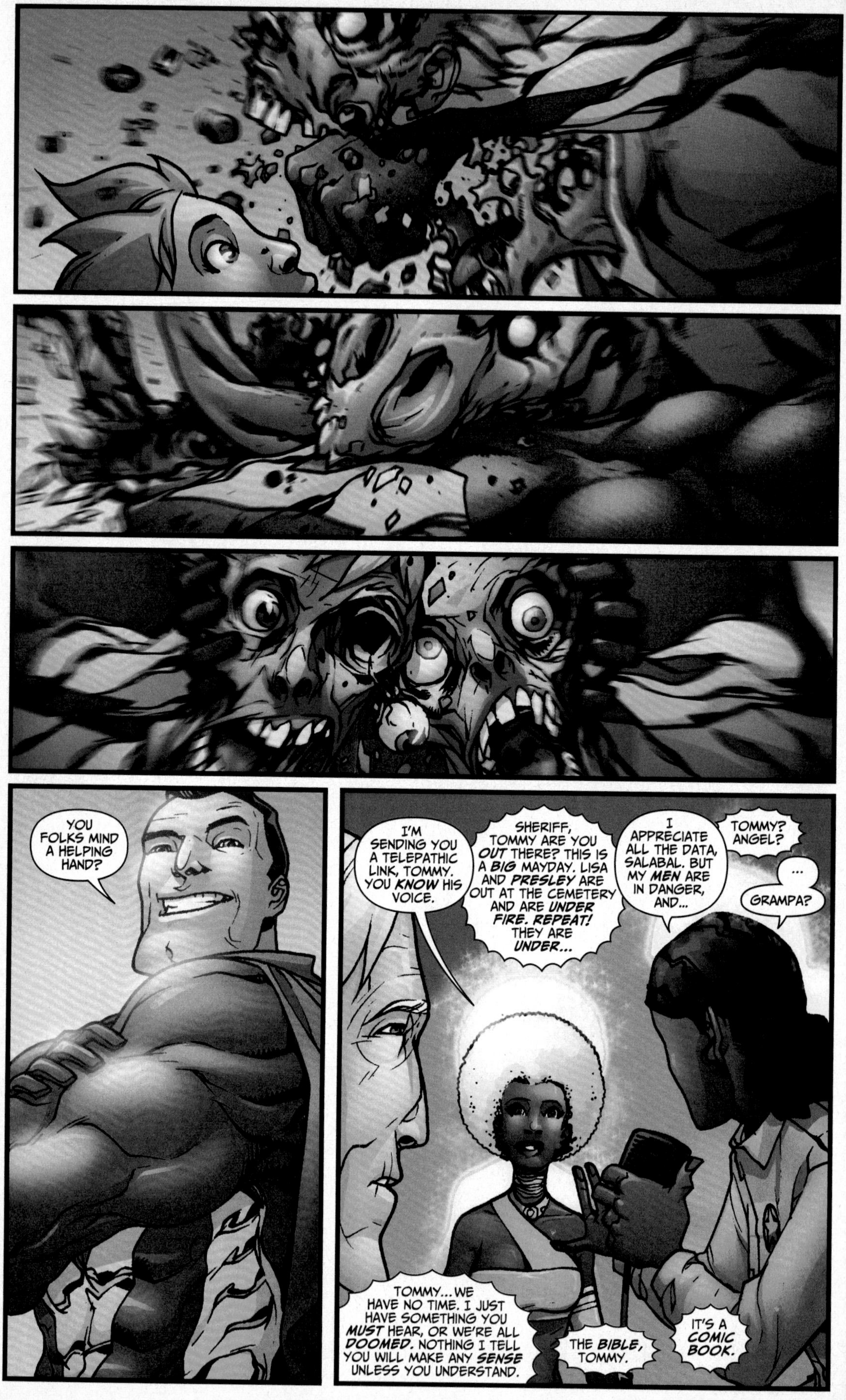

YOU FOLKS MIND A HELPING HAND?
I'M SENDING YOU A TELEPATHIC LINK, TOMMY. YOU **KNOW** HIS VOICE.
SHERIFF, TOMMY ARE YOU **OUT** THERE? THIS IS A **BIG** MAYDAY. LISA AND **PRESLEY** ARE OUT AT THE CEMETERY AND ARE **UNDER FIRE. REPEAT!** THEY ARE **UNDER...**
I APPRECIATE ALL THE DATA, SALABAL. BUT MY **MEN** ARE IN DANGER, AND...
TOMMY? ANGEL?
...
GRAMPA?
TOMMY... WE HAVE NO TIME. I JUST HAVE SOMETHING YOU **MUST** HEAR, OR WE'RE ALL **DOOMED.** NOTHING I TELL YOU WILL MAKE ANY **SENSE** UNLESS YOU UNDERSTAND.
THE **BIBLE,** TOMMY.
IT'S A **COMIC BOOK.**

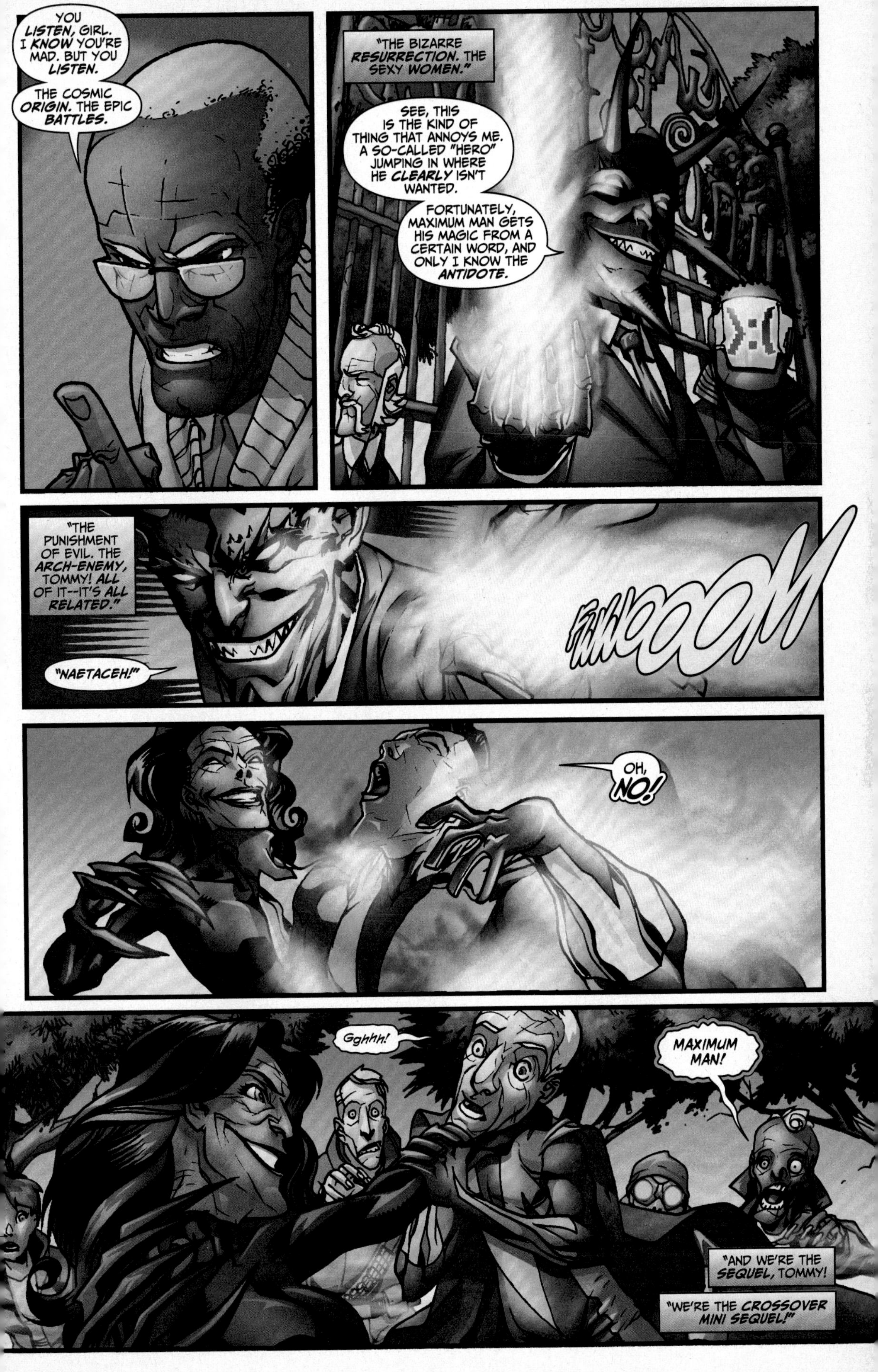
YOU LISTEN, GIRL. I KNOW YOU'RE MAD. BUT YOU LISTEN.
THE COSMIC ORIGIN. THE EPIC BATTLES.
"THE BIZARRE RESURRECTION. THE SEXY WOMEN."
SEE, THIS IS THE KIND OF THING THAT ANNOYS ME. A SO-CALLED "HERO" JUMPING IN WHERE HE CLEARLY ISN'T WANTED.
FORTUNATELY, MAXIMUM MAN GETS HIS MAGIC FROM A CERTAIN WORD, AND ONLY I KNOW THE ANTIDOTE.
"THE PUNISHMENT OF EVIL. THE ARCH-ENEMY, TOMMY! ALL OF IT--IT'S ALL RELATED."
"NAETACEH!"
FWWOOOOM
OH, NO!
Gghhh!
MAXIMUM MAN!
"AND WE'RE THE SEQUEL, TOMMY!
"WE'RE THE CROSSOVER MINI SEQUEL!"

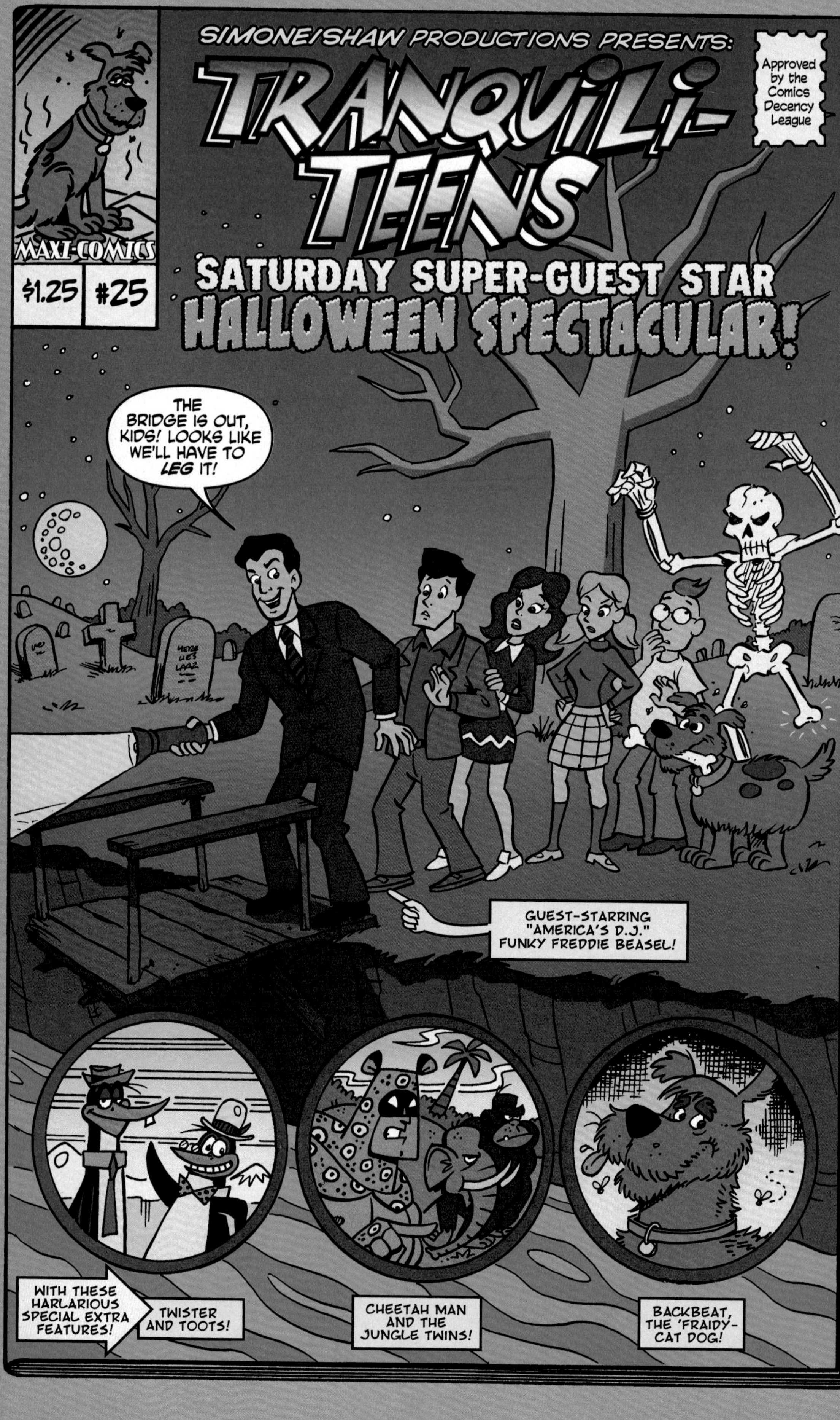
MAXI-COMICS
$1.25
#25
SIMONE/SHAW PRODUCTIONS PRESENTS:
TRANQUILI-TEENS
Approved by the Comics Decency League
SATURDAY SUPER-GUEST STAR
HALLOWEEN SPECTACULAR!
THE BRIDGE IS OUT, KIDS! LOOKS LIKE WE'LL HAVE TO LEG IT!
GUEST-STARRING "AMERICA'S D.J." FUNKY FREDDIE BEASEL!
WITH THESE HARLARIOUS SPECIAL EXTRA FEATURES!
TWISTER AND TOOTS!
CHEETAH MAN AND THE JUNGLE TWINS!
BACKBEAT, THE 'FRAIDY-CAT DOG!

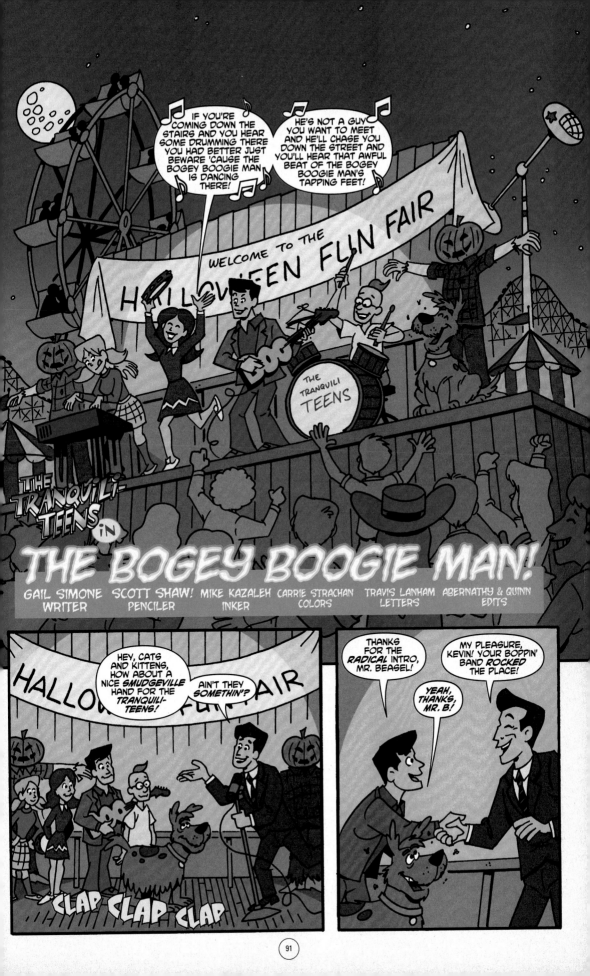

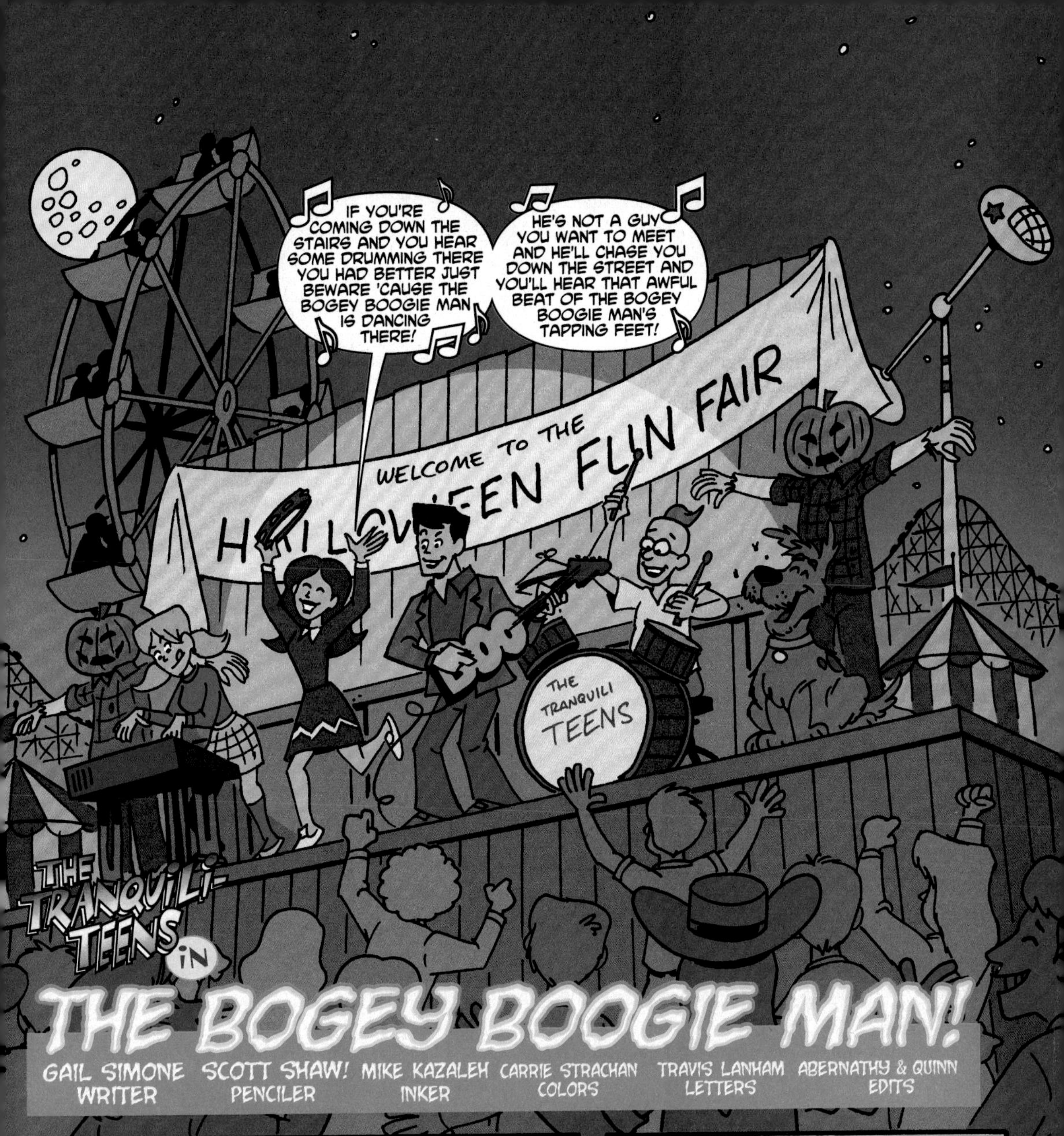
IF YOU'RE COMING DOWN THE STAIRS AND YOU HEAR SOME DRUMMING THERE YOU HAD BETTER JUST BEWARE 'CAUSE THE BOGEY BOOGIE MAN IS DANCING THERE!
HE'S NOT A GUY YOU WANT TO MEET AND HE'LL CHASE YOU DOWN THE STREET AND YOU'LL HEAR THAT AWFUL BEAT OF THE BOGEY BOOGIE MAN'S TAPPING FEET!
WELCOME TO THE HALLOWEEN FUN FAIR
THE TRANQUILI TEENS
THE TRANQUILI-TEENS iN
THE BOGEY BOOGIE MAN!
GAIL SIMONE WRITER
SCOTT SHAW! PENCILER
MIKE KAZALEH INKER
CARRIE STRACHAN COLORS
TRAVIS LANHAM LETTERS
ABERNATHY & QUINN EDITS

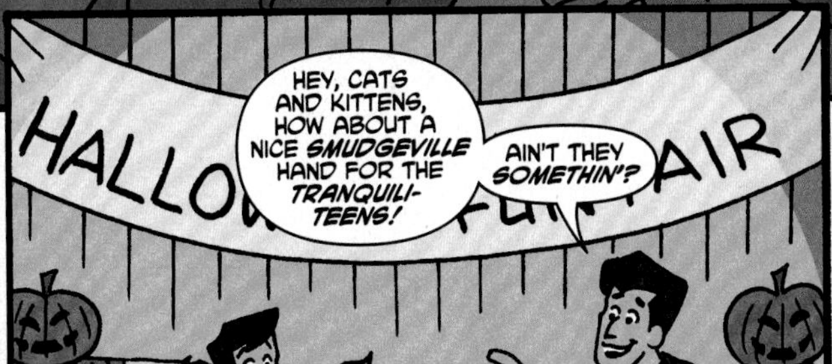
HEY, CATS AND KITTENS, HOW ABOUT A NICE *SMUDGEVILLE* HAND FOR THE *TRANQUILI-TEENS!*
AIN'T THEY *SOMETHIN'?*
CLAP CLAP CLAP

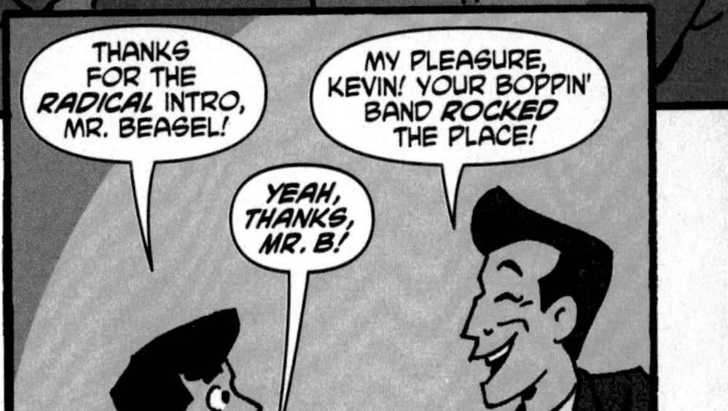
THANKS FOR THE *RADICAL* INTRO, MR. BEASEL!
MY PLEASURE, KEVIN! YOUR BOPPIN' BAND *ROCKED* THE PLACE!
YEAH, THANKS, MR. B!

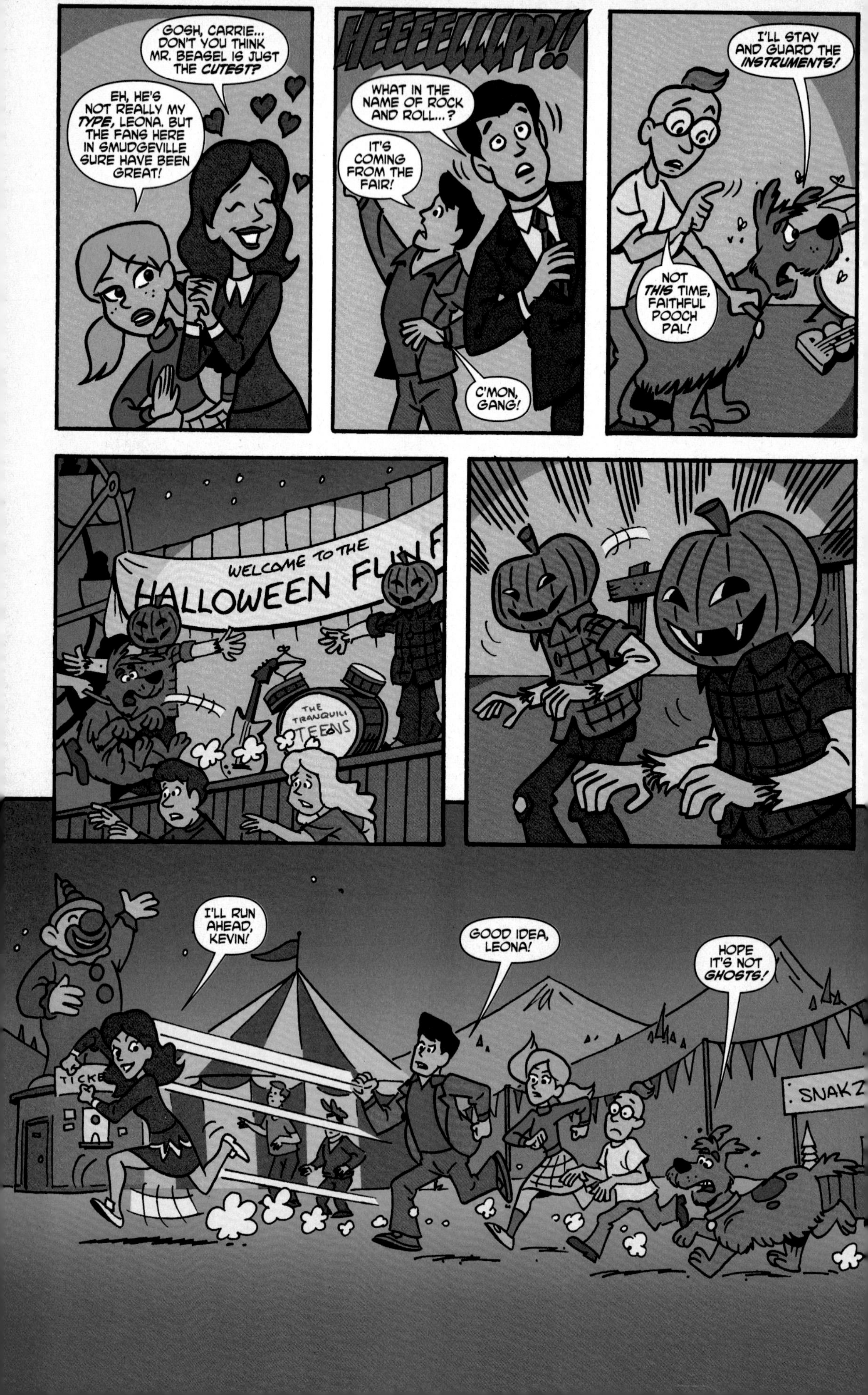

GOSH, CARRIE... DON'T YOU THINK MR. BEASEL IS JUST THE *CUTEST?*
EH, HE'S NOT REALLY MY *TYPE,* LEONA. BUT THE FANS HERE IN SMUDGEVILLE SURE HAVE BEEN GREAT!
HEEEEELLLLPP!!
WHAT IN THE NAME OF ROCK AND ROLL...?
IT'S COMING FROM THE FAIR!
C'MON, GANG!
I'LL STAY AND GUARD THE *INSTRUMENTS!*
NOT *THIS* TIME, FAITHFUL POOCH PAL!
WELCOME TO THE HALLOWEEN FUN F
THE TRANQUILI TEENS
I'LL RUN AHEAD, KEVIN!
TICKE
GOOD IDEA, LEONA!
HOPE IT'S NOT *GHOSTS!*
SNAKZ

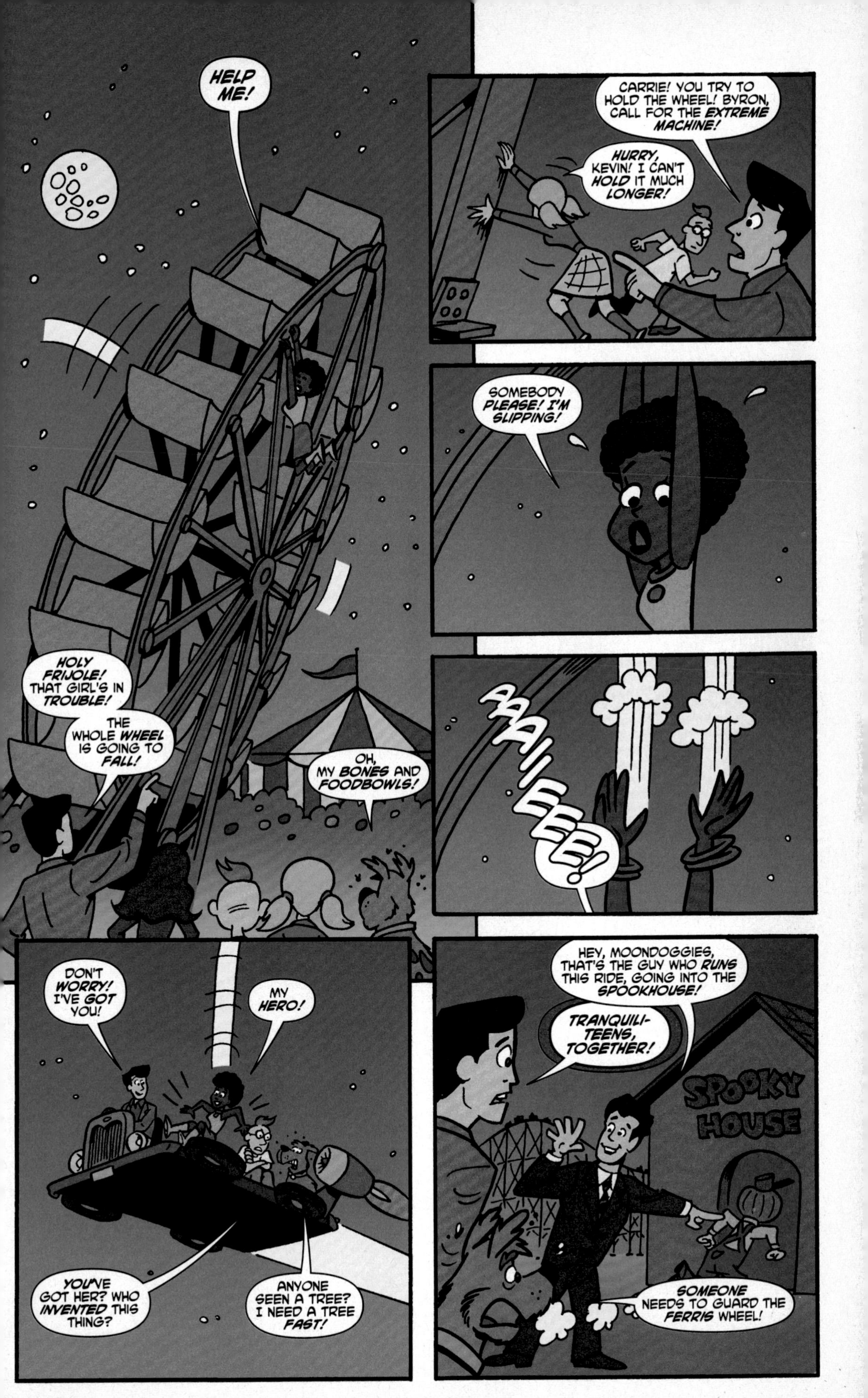
HELP ME!
HOLY FRIJOLE! THAT GIRL'S IN TROUBLE!
THE WHOLE WHEEL IS GOING TO FALL!
OH, MY BONES AND FOODBOWLS!
CARRIE! YOU TRY TO HOLD THE WHEEL! BYRON, CALL FOR THE EXTREME MACHINE!
HURRY, KEVIN! I CAN'T HOLD IT MUCH LONGER!
SOMEBODY PLEASE! I'M SLIPPING!
AAAIIEEEE!
DON'T WORRY! I'VE GOT YOU!
MY HERO!
YOU'VE GOT HER? WHO INVENTED THIS THING?
ANYONE SEEN A TREE? I NEED A TREE FAST!
HEY, MOONDOGGIES, THAT'S THE GUY WHO RUNS THIS RIDE, GOING INTO THE SPOOKHOUSE!
TRANQUILI-TEENS, TOGETHER!
SPOOKY HOUSE
SOMEONE NEEDS TO GUARD THE FERRIS WHEEL!

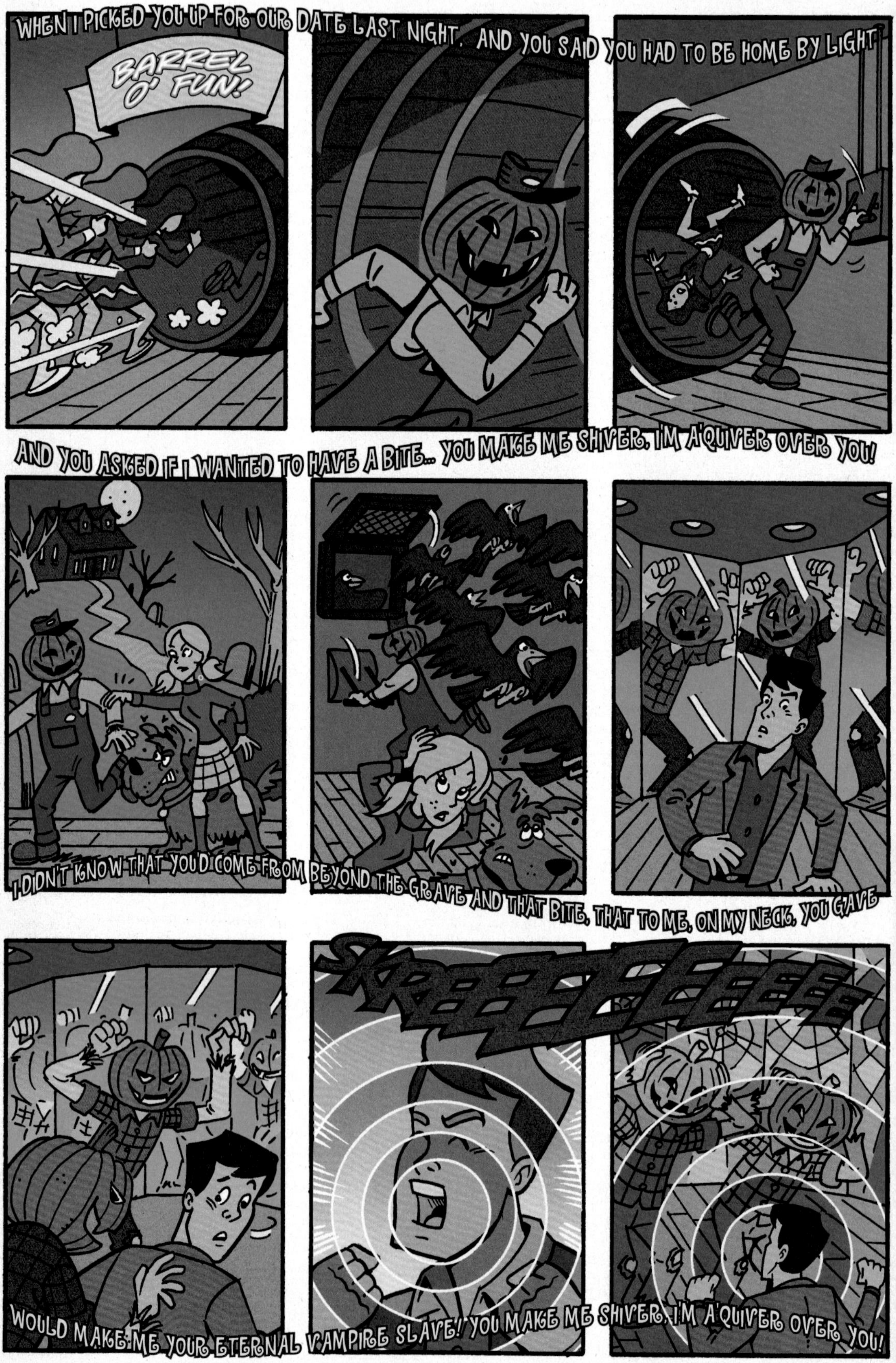
WHEN I PICKED YOU UP FOR OUR DATE LAST NIGHT, AND YOU SAID YOU HAD TO BE HOME BY LIGHT
BARREL O' FUN!
AND YOU ASKED IF I WANTED TO HAVE A BITE... YOU MAKE ME SHIVER, I'M A'QUIVER OVER YOU!
I DIDN'T KNOW THAT YOU'D COME FROM BEYOND THE GRAVE AND THAT BITE, THAT TO ME, ON MY NECK, YOU GAVE
SKREEEEEEEEE!
WOULD MAKE ME YOUR ETERNAL VAMPIRE SLAVE! YOU MAKE ME SHIVER, I'M A'QUIVER OVER YOU!

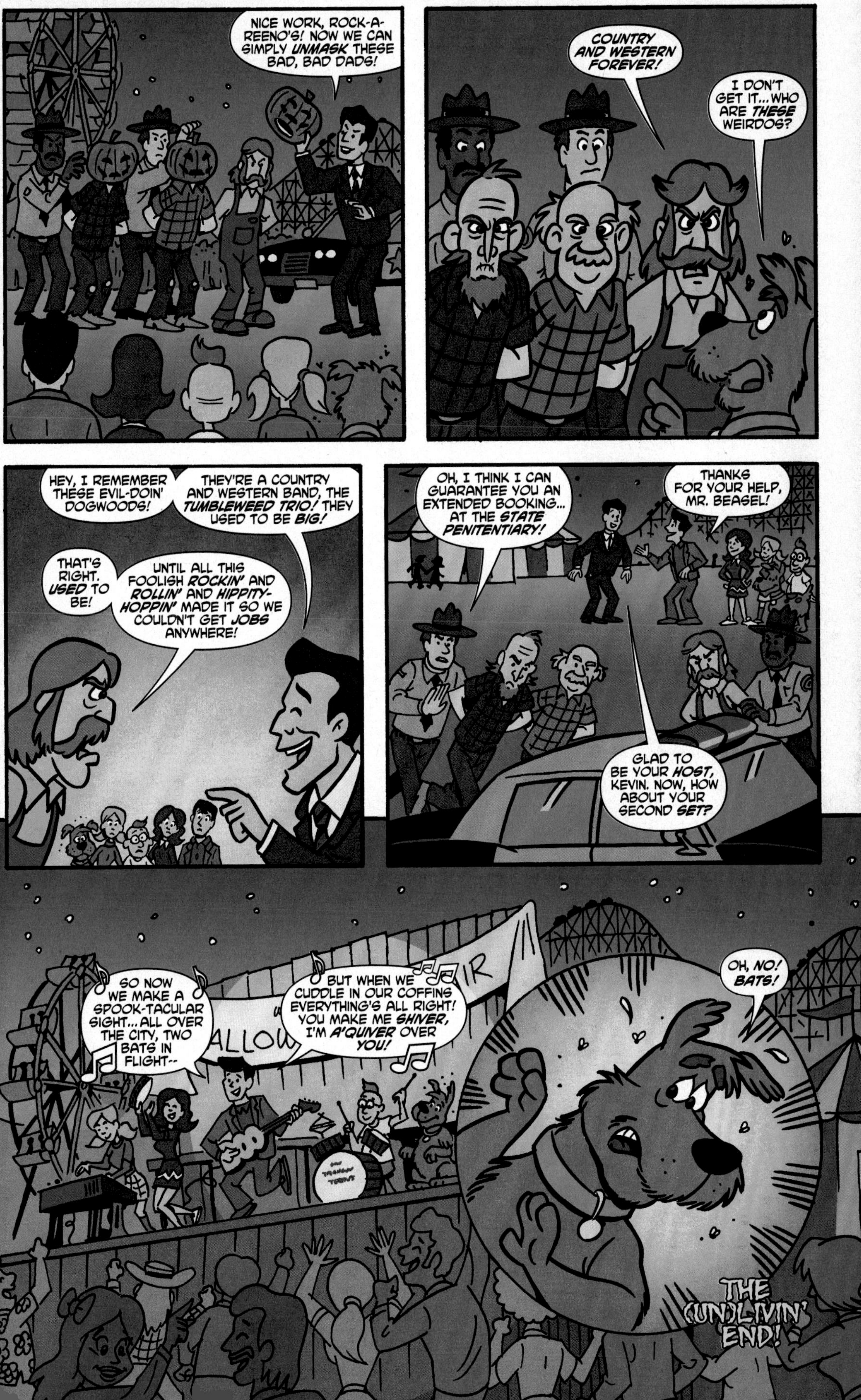
NICE WORK, ROCK-A-REENO'S! NOW WE CAN SIMPLY UNMASK THESE BAD, BAD DADS!
COUNTRY AND WESTERN FOREVER!
I DON'T GET IT... WHO ARE THESE WEIRDOS?
HEY, I REMEMBER THESE EVIL-DOIN' DOGWOODS!
THEY'RE A COUNTRY AND WESTERN BAND, THE TUMBLEWEED TRIO! THEY USED TO BE BIG!
THAT'S RIGHT. USED TO BE!
UNTIL ALL THIS FOOLISH ROCKIN' AND ROLLIN' AND HIPPITY-HOPPIN' MADE IT SO WE COULDN'T GET JOBS ANYWHERE!
OH, I THINK I CAN GUARANTEE YOU AN EXTENDED BOOKING... AT THE STATE PENITENTIARY!
THANKS FOR YOUR HELP, MR. BEASEL!
GLAD TO BE YOUR HOST, KEVIN. NOW, HOW ABOUT YOUR SECOND SET?
SO NOW WE MAKE A SPOOK-TACULAR SIGHT... ALL OVER THE CITY, TWO BATS IN FLIGHT--
BUT WHEN WE CUDDLE IN OUR COFFINS EVERYTHING'S ALL RIGHT! YOU MAKE ME SHIVER, I'M A'QUIVER OVER YOU!
OH, NO! BATS!
THE (UN)LIVIN' END!

CHAPTER FIVE

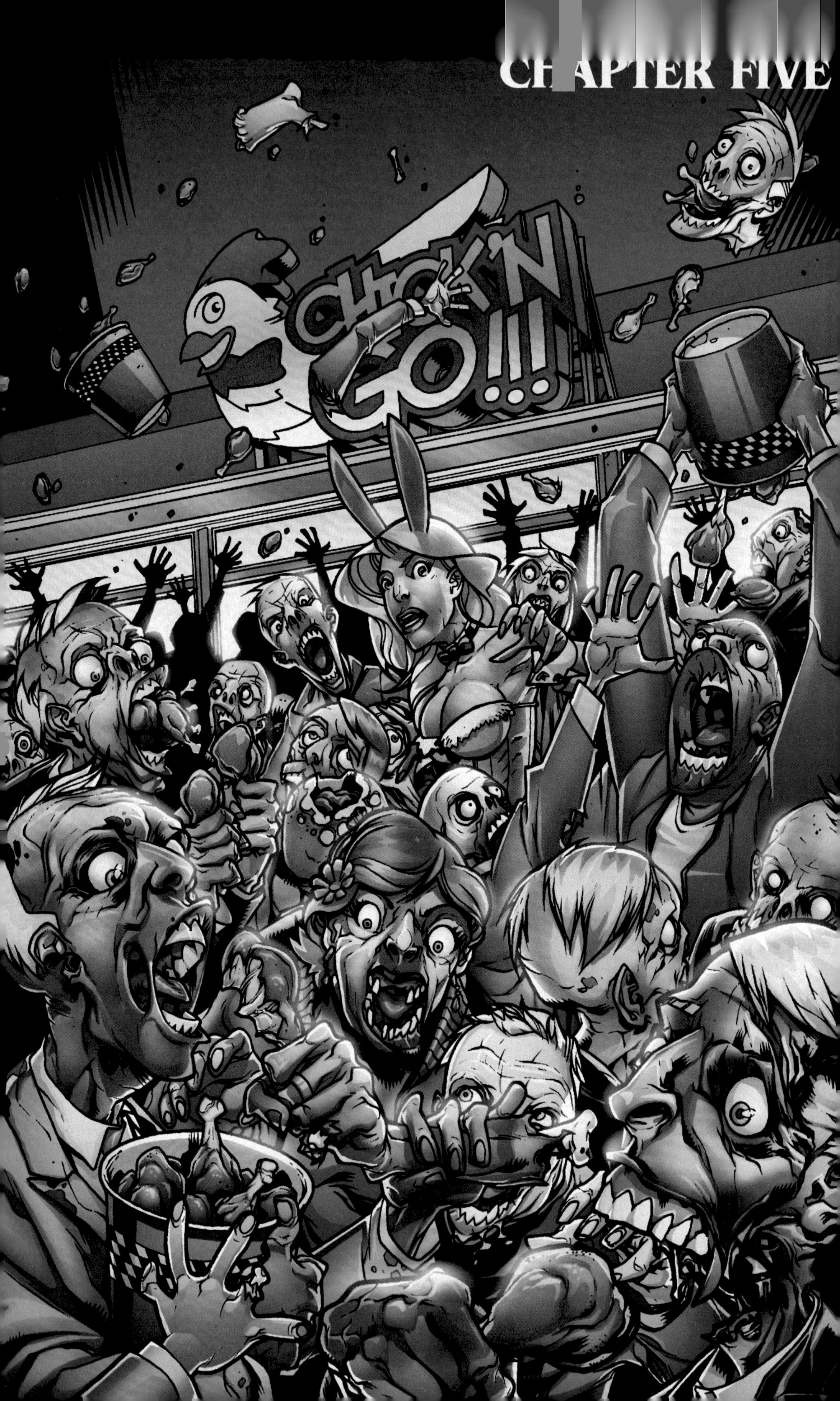
CHICK'N GO!!!

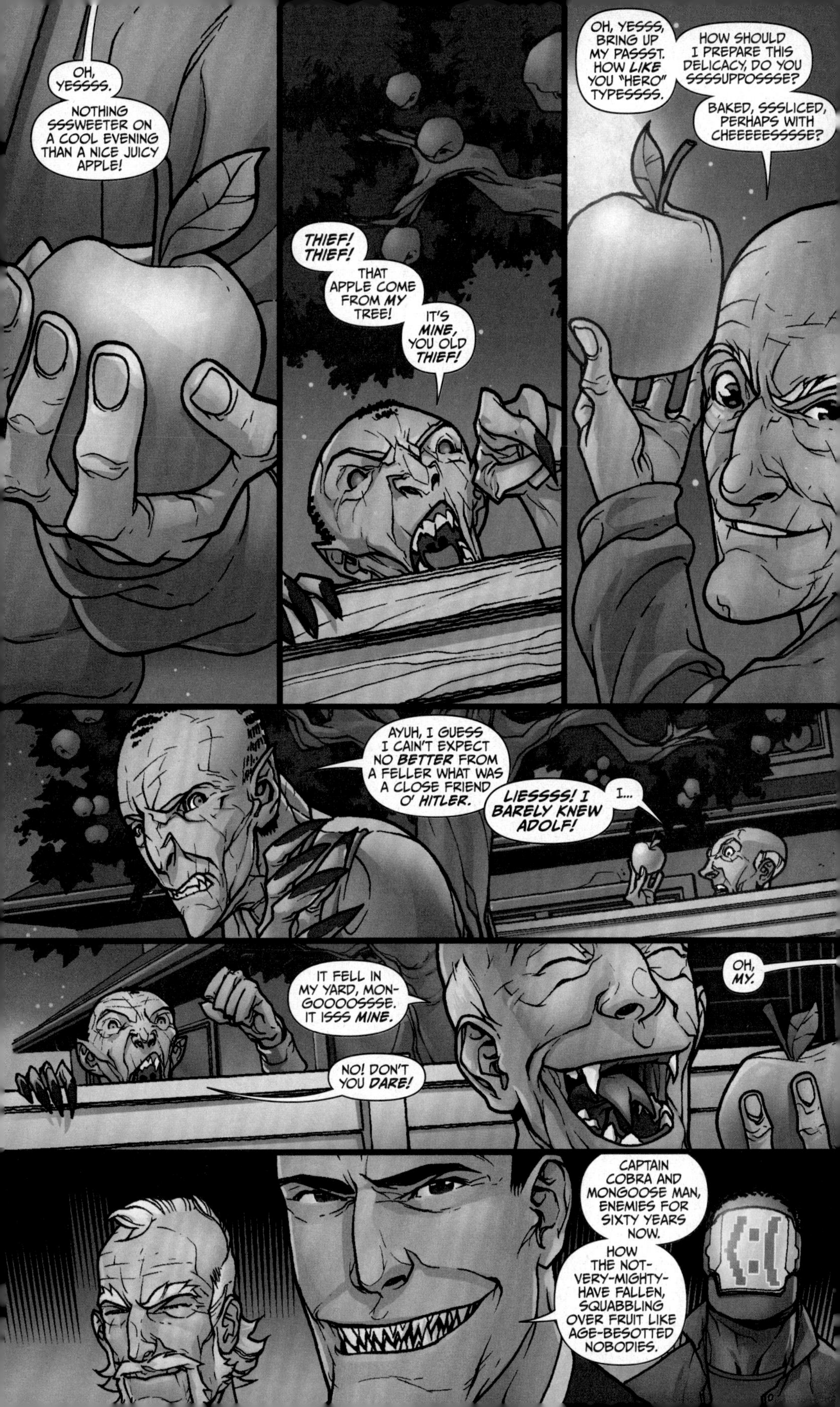
OH, YESSSS.
NOTHING SSSWEETER ON A COOL EVENING THAN A NICE JUICY APPLE!
THIEF! THIEF!
THAT APPLE COME FROM MY TREE!
IT'S MINE, YOU OLD THIEF!
OH, YESSS, BRING UP MY PASSST. HOW LIKE YOU "HERO" TYPESSSS.
HOW SHOULD I PREPARE THIS DELICACY, DO YOU SSSSUPPOSSSE?
BAKED, SSSLICED, PERHAPS WITH CHEEEEESSSSE?
AYUH, I GUESS I CAIN'T EXPECT NO BETTER FROM A FELLER WHAT WAS A CLOSE FRIEND O' HITLER.
I...
LIESSSS! I BARELY KNEW ADOLF!
IT FELL IN MY YARD, MON-GOOOOSSSE. IT ISSS MINE.
NO! DON'T YOU DARE!
OH, MY.
CAPTAIN COBRA AND MONGOOSE MAN, ENEMIES FOR SIXTY YEARS NOW.
HOW THE NOT-VERY-MIGHTY-HAVE FALLEN, SQUABBLING OVER FRUIT LIKE AGE-BESOTTED NOBODIES.

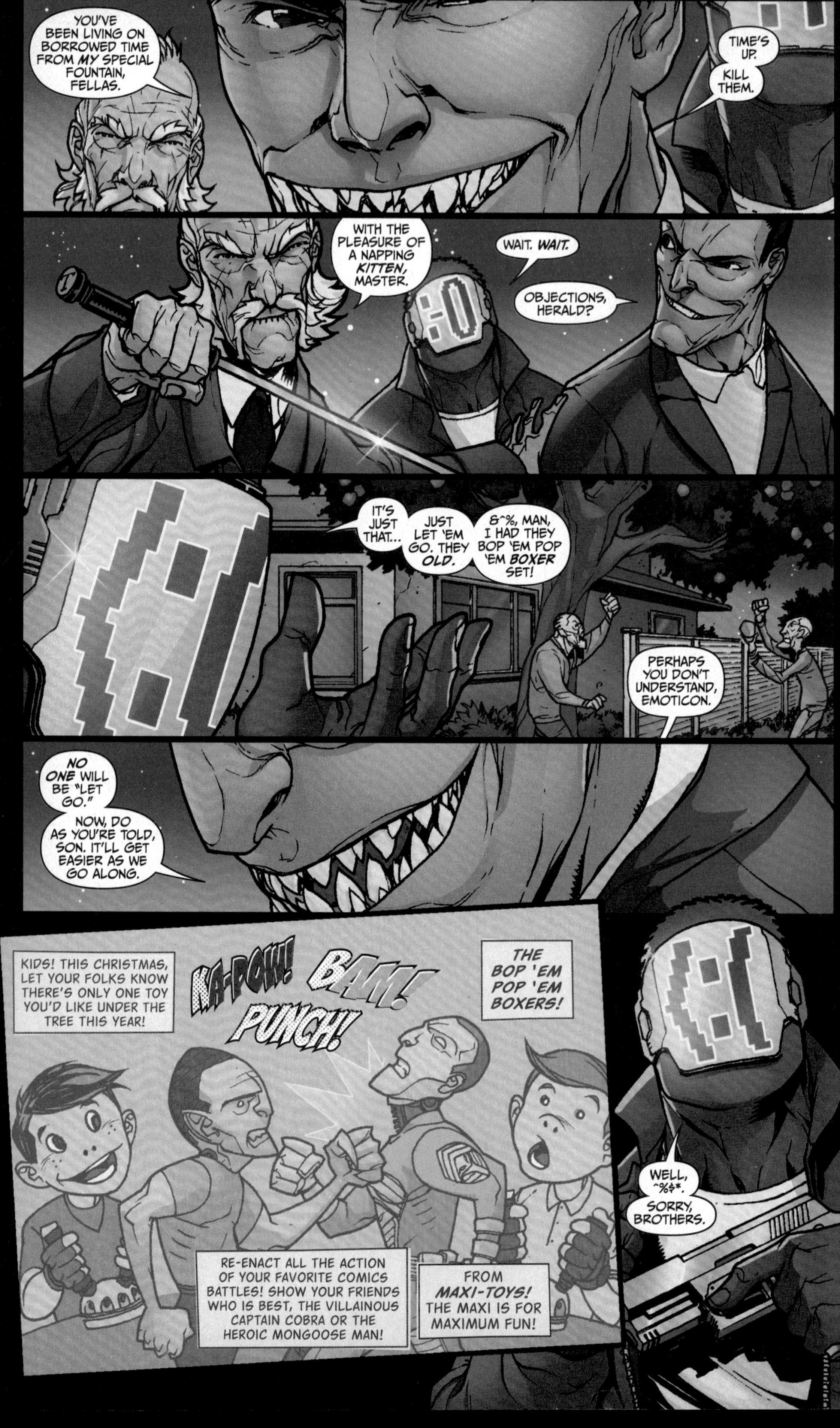
YOU'VE BEEN LIVING ON BORROWED TIME FROM MY SPECIAL FOUNTAIN, FELLAS.
TIME'S UP.
KILL THEM.
WITH THE PLEASURE OF A NAPPING KITTEN, MASTER.
WAIT. WAIT.
OBJECTIONS, HERALD?
IT'S JUST THAT...
JUST LET 'EM GO. THEY OLD.
&^%, MAN, I HAD THEY BOP 'EM POP 'EM BOXER SET!
PERHAPS YOU DON'T UNDERSTAND, EMOTICON.
NO ONE WILL BE "LET GO."
NOW, DO AS YOU'RE TOLD, SON. IT'LL GET EASIER AS WE GO ALONG.
KIDS! THIS CHRISTMAS, LET YOUR FOLKS KNOW THERE'S ONLY ONE TOY YOU'D LIKE UNDER THE TREE THIS YEAR!
KA-POW!
BAM!
PUNCH!
THE BOP 'EM POP 'EM BOXERS!
RE-ENACT ALL THE ACTION OF YOUR FAVORITE COMICS BATTLES! SHOW YOUR FRIENDS WHO IS BEST, THE VILLAINOUS CAPTAIN COBRA OR THE HEROIC MONGOOSE MAN!
FROM MAXI-TOYS! THE MAXI IS FOR MAXIMUM FUN!
WELL, ^%$*.
SORRY, BROTHERS.

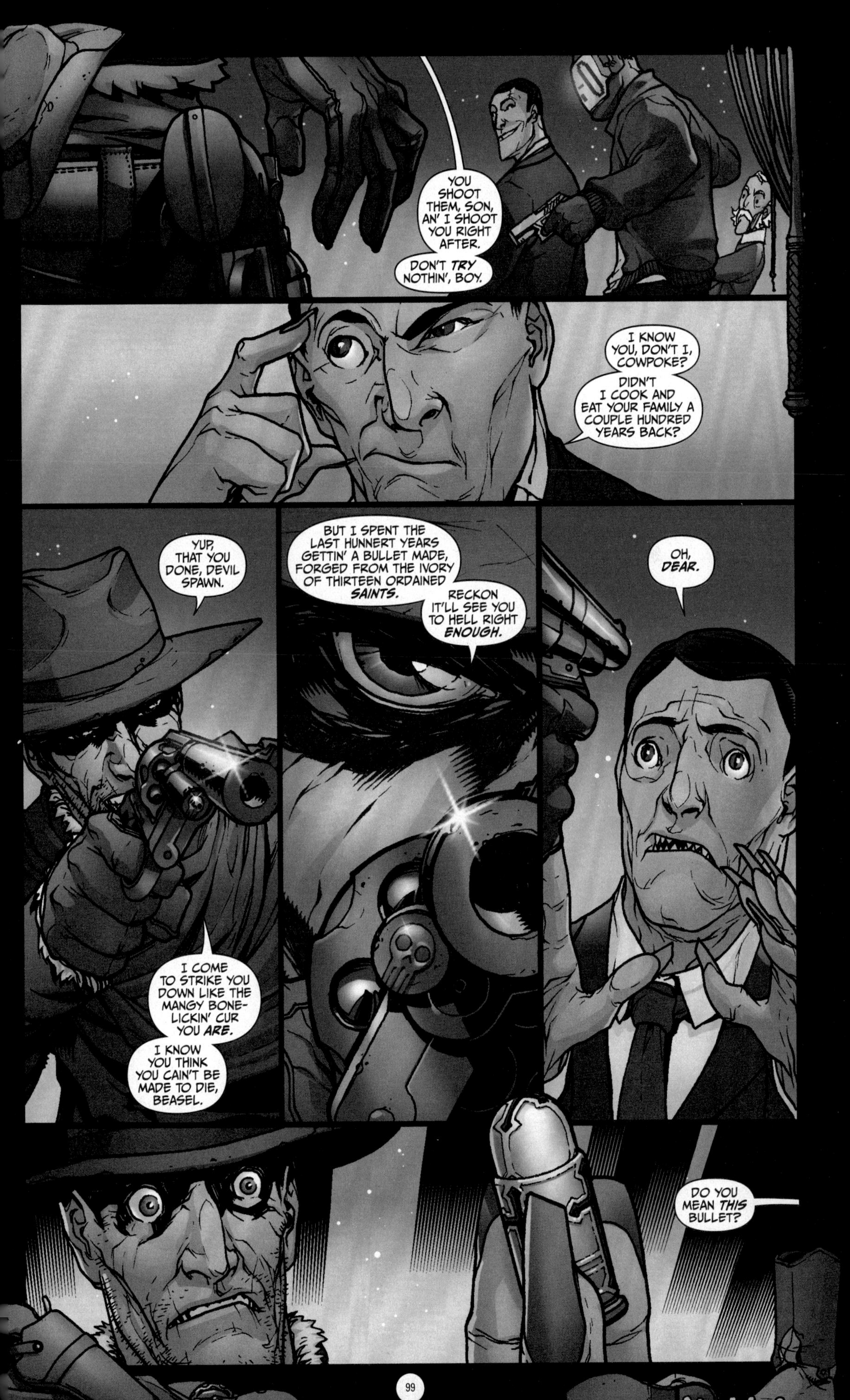

YOU SHOOT THEM, SON, AN' I SHOOT YOU RIGHT AFTER.
DON'T *TRY* NOTHIN', BOY.
I KNOW YOU, DON'T I, COWPOKE?
DIDN'T I COOK AND EAT YOUR FAMILY A COUPLE HUNDRED YEARS BACK?
YUP, THAT YOU DONE, DEVIL SPAWN.
I COME TO STRIKE YOU DOWN LIKE THE MANGY BONE-LICKIN' CUR YOU *ARE.*
I KNOW YOU THINK YOU CAIN'T BE MADE TO DIE, BEASEL.
BUT I SPENT THE LAST HUNNERT YEARS GETTIN' A BULLET MADE, FORGED FROM THE IVORY OF THIRTEEN ORDAINED *SAINTS.*
RECKON IT'LL SEE YOU TO HELL RIGHT *ENOUGH.*
OH, *DEAR.*
DO YOU MEAN *THIS* BULLET?

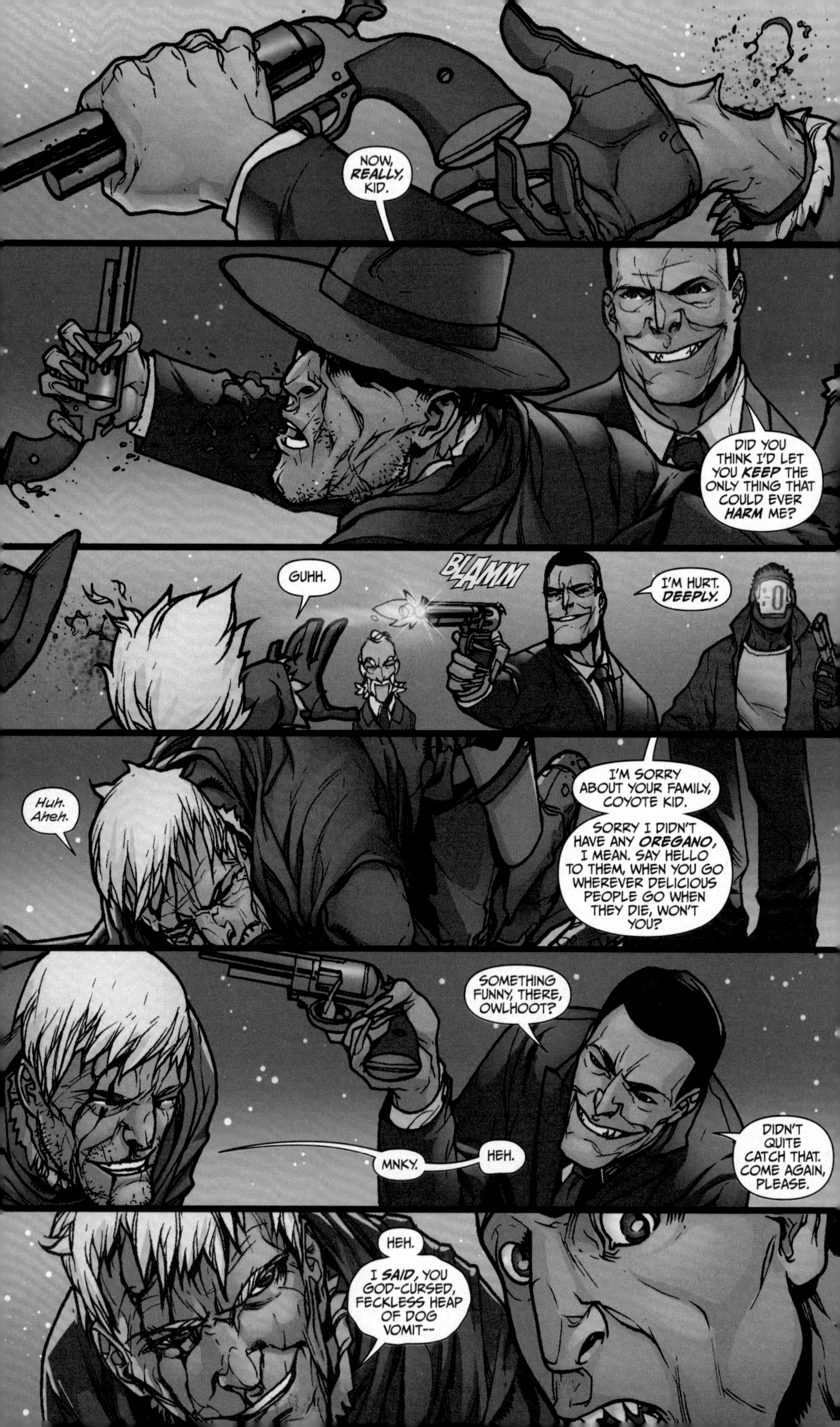
NOW, *REALLY,* KID.
DID YOU THINK I'D LET YOU *KEEP* THE ONLY THING THAT COULD EVER *HARM* ME?
GUHH.
BLAMM
I'M HURT. *DEEPLY.*
Huh. Aheh.
I'M SORRY ABOUT YOUR FAMILY, COYOTE KID.
SORRY I DIDN'T HAVE ANY *OREGANO,* I MEAN. SAY HELLO TO THEM, WHEN YOU GO WHEREVER DELICIOUS PEOPLE GO WHEN THEY DIE, WON'T YOU?
SOMETHING FUNNY, THERE, OWLHOOT?
MNKY.
HEH.
DIDN'T QUITE CATCH THAT. COME AGAIN, PLEASE.
HEH.
I *SAID,* YOU GOD-CURSED, FECKLESS HEAP OF DOG VOMIT--

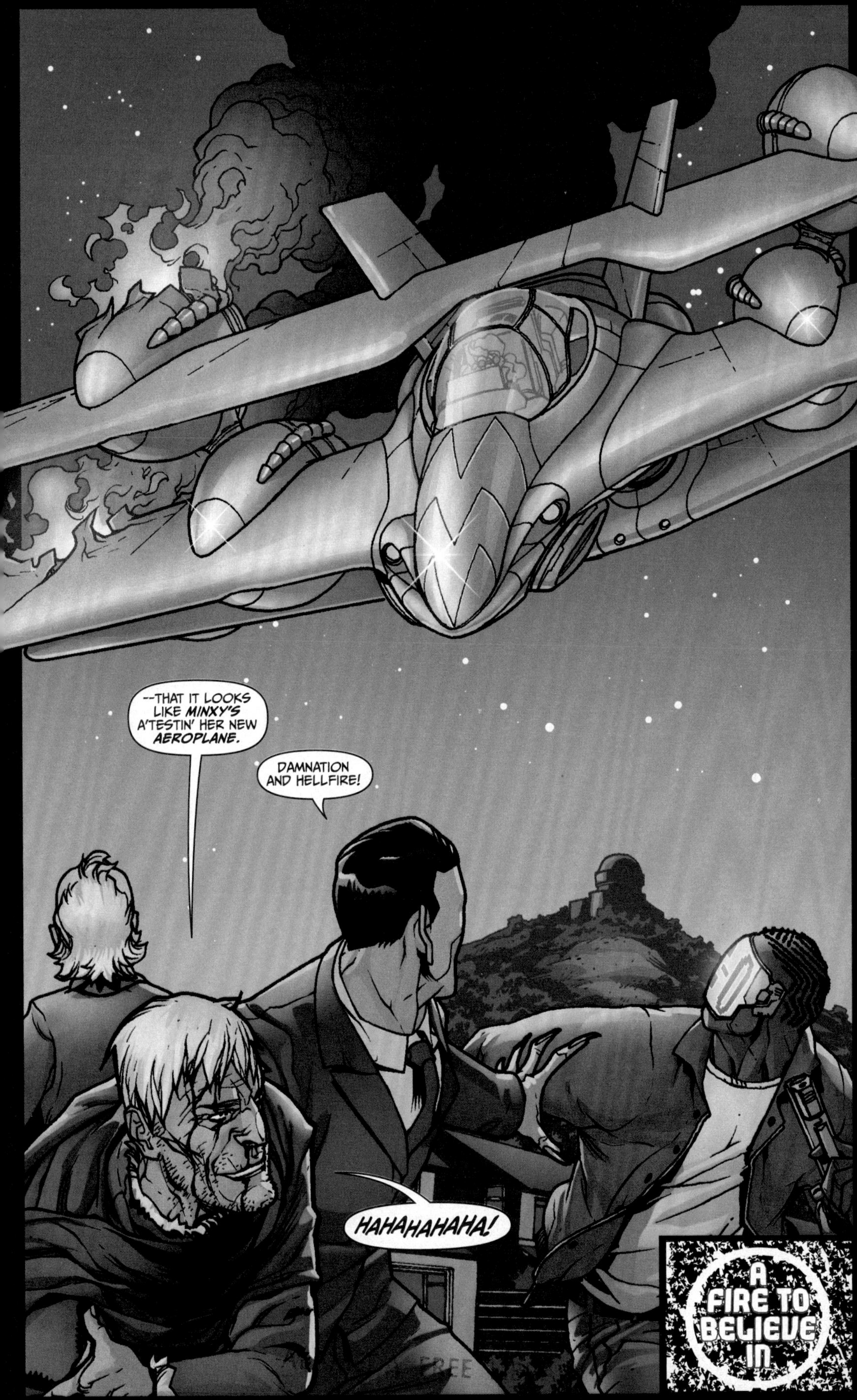
--THAT IT LOOKS LIKE MINXY'S A'TESTIN' HER NEW AEROPLANE.
DAMNATION AND HELLFIRE!
HAHAHAHAHA!
A FIRE TO BELIEVE IN

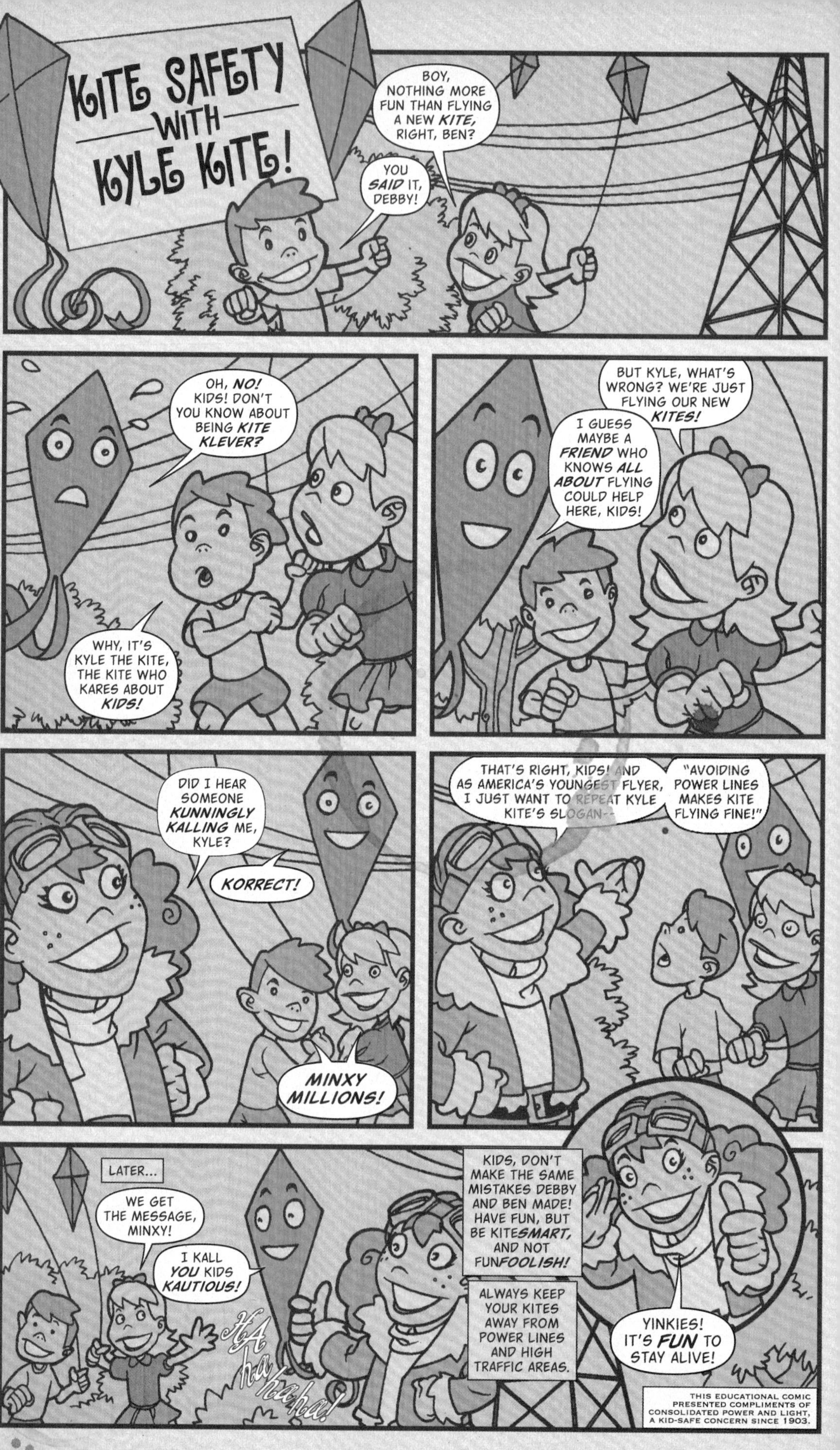
KITE SAFETY WITH KYLE KITE!
BOY, NOTHING MORE FUN THAN FLYING A NEW KITE, RIGHT, BEN?
YOU SAID IT, DEBBY!
OH, NO! KIDS! DON'T YOU KNOW ABOUT BEING KITE KLEVER?
WHY, IT'S KYLE THE KITE, THE KITE WHO KARES ABOUT KIDS!
BUT KYLE, WHAT'S WRONG? WE'RE JUST FLYING OUR NEW KITES!
I GUESS MAYBE A FRIEND WHO KNOWS ALL ABOUT FLYING COULD HELP HERE, KIDS!
DID I HEAR SOMEONE KUNNINGLY KALLING ME, KYLE?
KORRECT!
MINXY MILLIONS!
THAT'S RIGHT, KIDS! AND AS AMERICA'S YOUNGEST FLYER, I JUST WANT TO REPEAT KYLE KITE'S SLOGAN--
"AVOIDING POWER LINES MAKES KITE FLYING FINE!"
LATER...
WE GET THE MESSAGE, MINXY!
I KALL YOU KIDS KAUTIOUS!
HA ha ha ha!
KIDS, DON'T MAKE THE SAME MISTAKES DEBBY AND BEN MADE! HAVE FUN, BUT BE KITESMART, AND NOT FUNFOOLISH!
ALWAYS KEEP YOUR KITES AWAY FROM POWER LINES AND HIGH TRAFFIC AREAS.
YINKIES! IT'S FUN TO STAY ALIVE!
THIS EDUCATIONAL COMIC PRESENTED COMPLIMENTS OF CONSOLIDATED POWER AND LIGHT, A KID-SAFE CONCERN SINCE 1903.

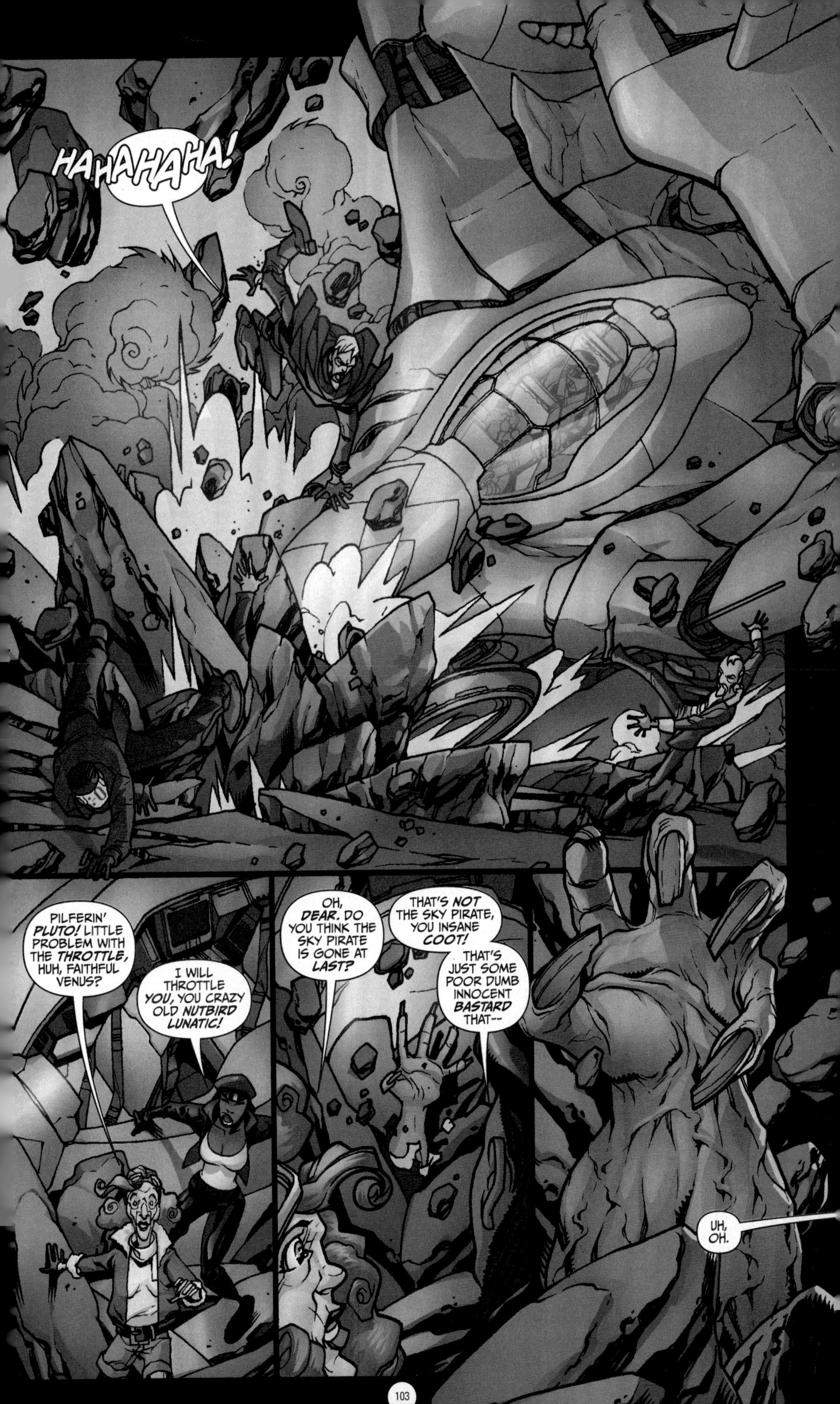
HAHAHAHA!
PILFERIN' PLUTO! LITTLE PROBLEM WITH THE THROTTLE, HUH, FAITHFUL VENUS?
I WILL THROTTLE YOU, YOU CRAZY OLD NUTBIRD LUNATIC!
OH, DEAR. DO YOU THINK THE SKY PIRATE IS GONE AT LAST?
THAT'S NOT THE SKY PIRATE, YOU INSANE COOT!
THAT'S JUST SOME POOR DUMB INNOCENT BASTARD THAT--
UH, OH.

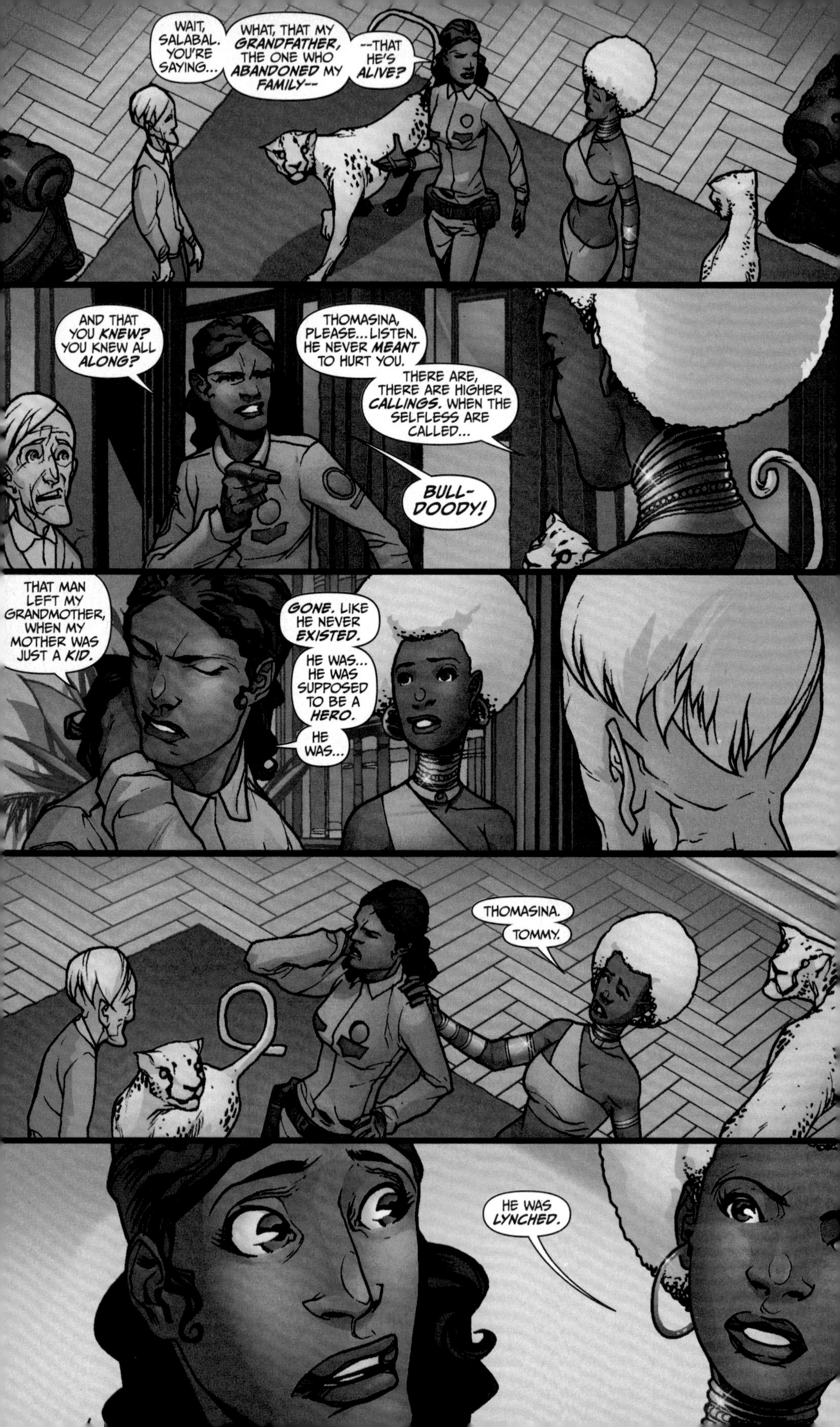
WAIT, SALABAL. YOU'RE SAYING...
WHAT, THAT MY GRANDFATHER, THE ONE WHO ABANDONED MY FAMILY--
--THAT HE'S ALIVE?
AND THAT YOU KNEW? YOU KNEW ALL ALONG?
THOMASINA, PLEASE...LISTEN. HE NEVER MEANT TO HURT YOU.
THERE ARE, THERE ARE HIGHER CALLINGS. WHEN THE SELFLESS ARE CALLED...
BULL-DOODY!
THAT MAN LEFT MY GRANDMOTHER, WHEN MY MOTHER WAS JUST A KID.
GONE. LIKE HE NEVER EXISTED.
HE WAS... HE WAS SUPPOSED TO BE A HERO.
HE WAS...
THOMASINA.
TOMMY.
HE WAS LYNCHED.

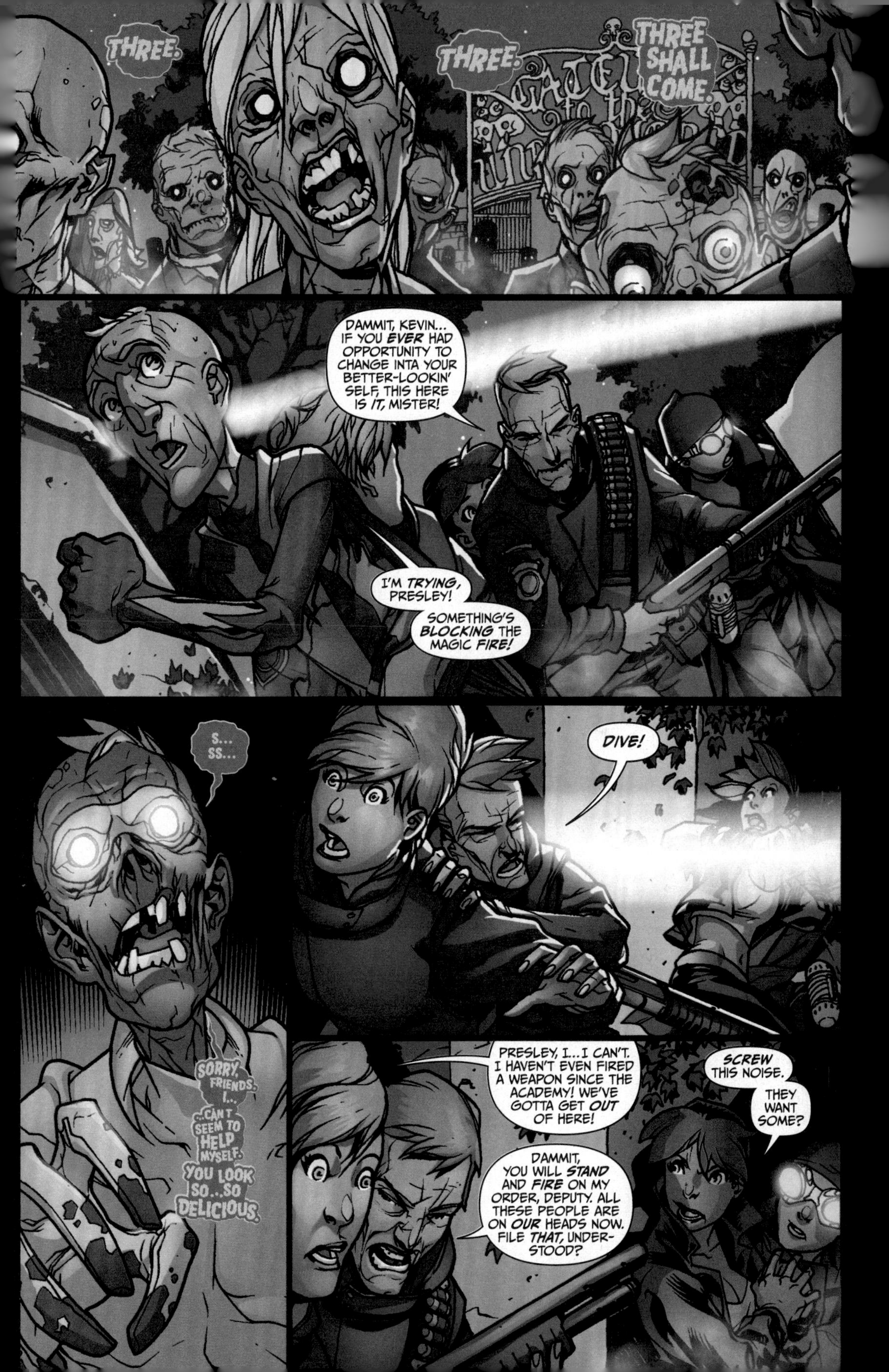
THREE.
THREE.
THREE SHALL COME.
DAMMIT, KEVIN... IF YOU EVER HAD OPPORTUNITY TO CHANGE INTA YOUR BETTER-LOOKIN' SELF, THIS HERE IS IT, MISTER!
I'M TRYING, PRESLEY!
SOMETHING'S BLOCKING THE MAGIC FIRE!
S... SS...
SORRY, FRIENDS. I...
...CAN'T SEEM TO HELP MYSELF.
YOU LOOK SO...SO DELICIOUS.
DIVE!
PRESLEY, I...I CAN'T. I HAVEN'T EVEN FIRED A WEAPON SINCE THE ACADEMY! WE'VE GOTTA GET OUT OF HERE!
DAMMIT, YOU WILL STAND AND FIRE ON MY ORDER, DEPUTY. ALL THESE PEOPLE ARE ON OUR HEADS NOW. FILE THAT, UNDERSTOOD?
SCREW THIS NOISE.
THEY WANT SOME?

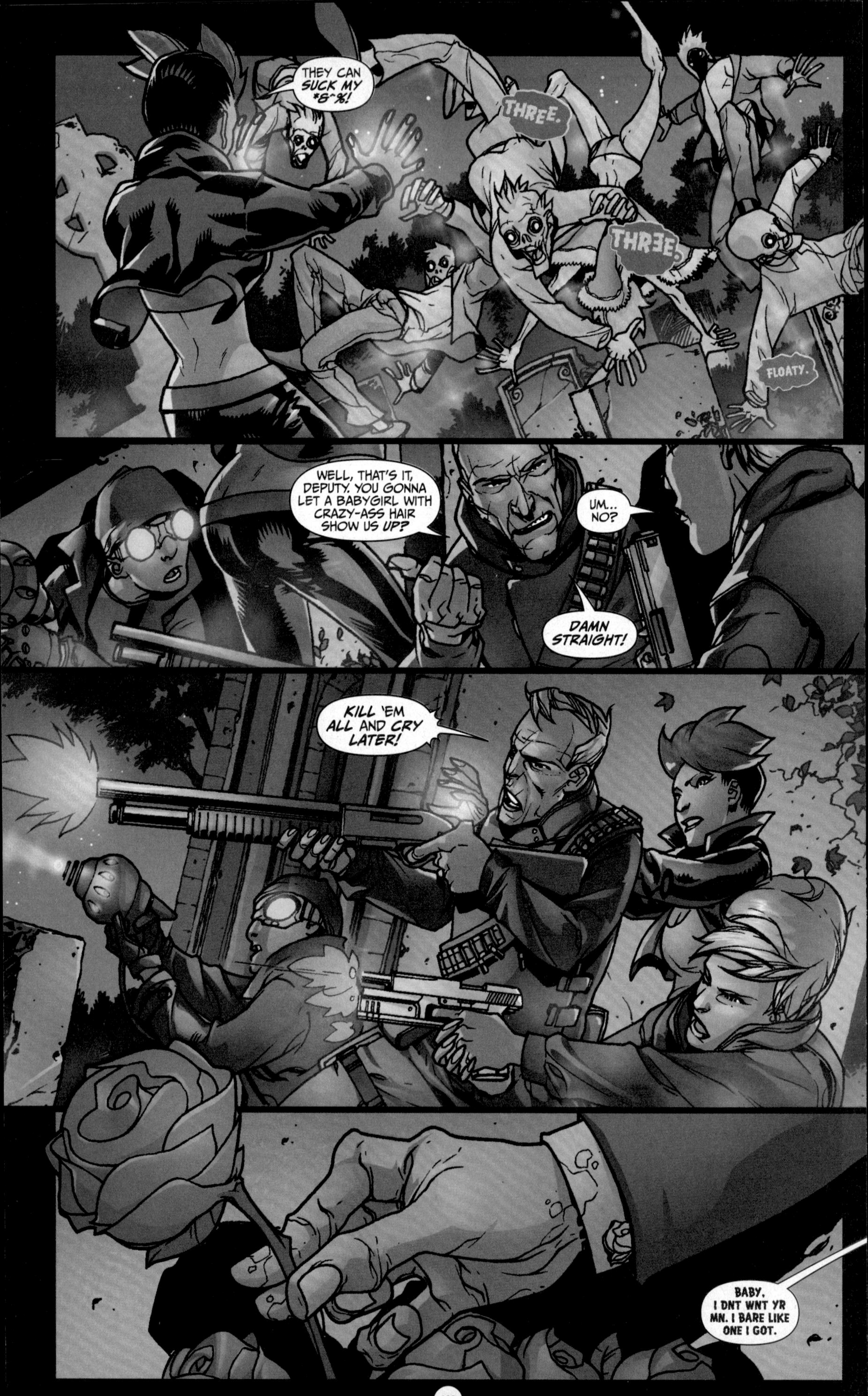

THEY CAN SUCK MY *&^%!
THREE.
THREE.
FLOATY.
WELL, THAT'S IT, DEPUTY. YOU GONNA LET A BABYGIRL WITH CRAZY-ASS HAIR SHOW US UP?
UM... NO?
DAMN STRAIGHT!
KILL 'EM ALL AND CRY LATER!
BABY. I DNT WNT YR MN. I BARE LIKE ONE I GOT.

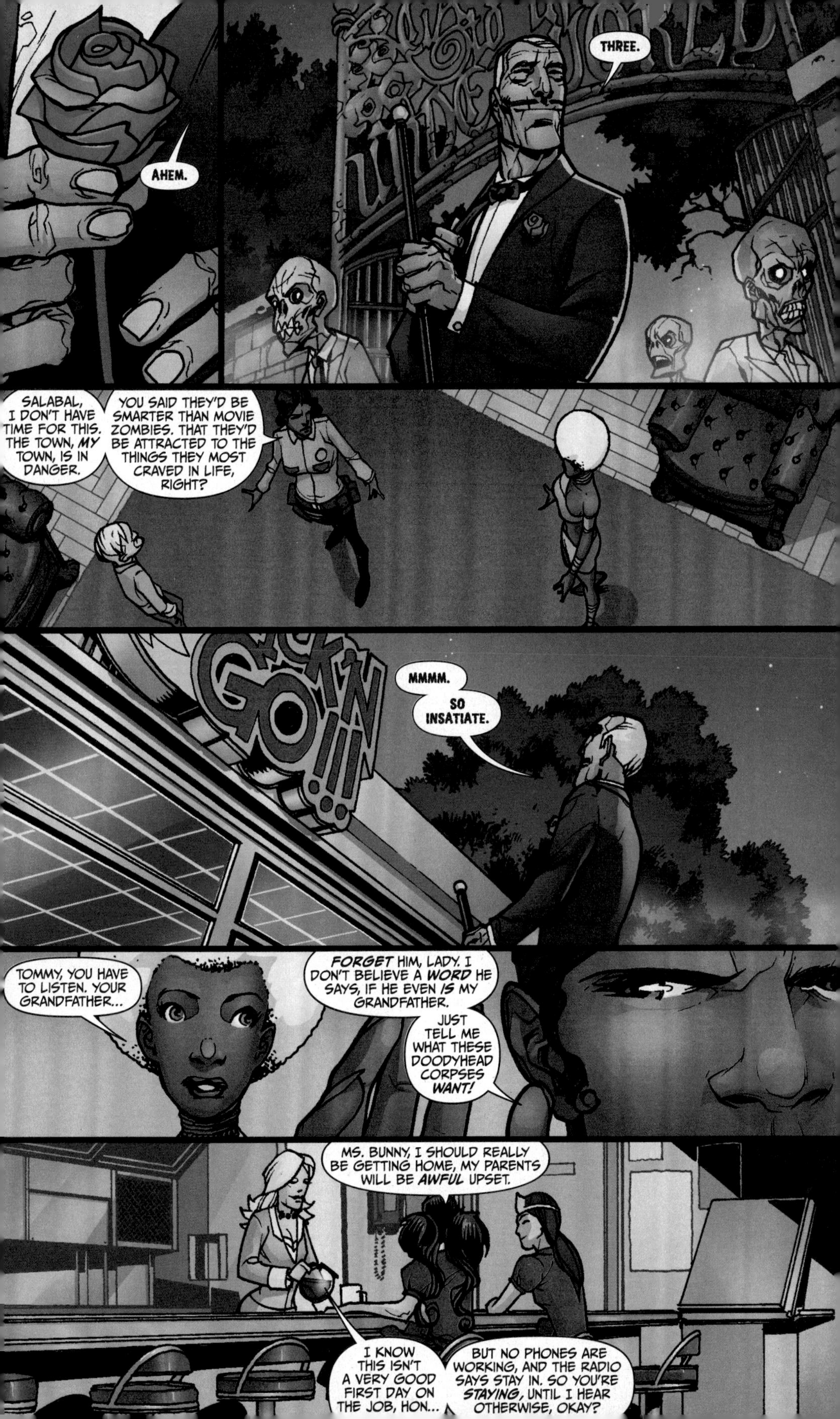
AHEM.
THREE.
SALABAL, I DON'T HAVE TIME FOR THIS. THE TOWN, *MY* TOWN, IS IN DANGER.
YOU SAID THEY'D BE SMARTER THAN MOVIE ZOMBIES. THAT THEY'D BE ATTRACTED TO THE THINGS THEY MOST CRAVED IN LIFE, RIGHT?
MMMM.
SO INSATIATE.
TOMMY, YOU HAVE TO LISTEN. YOUR GRANDFATHER...
FORGET HIM, LADY. I DON'T BELIEVE A *WORD* HE SAYS, IF HE EVEN *IS* MY GRANDFATHER.
JUST TELL ME WHAT THESE DOODYHEAD CORPSES *WANT!*
MS. BUNNY, I SHOULD REALLY BE GETTING HOME, MY PARENTS WILL BE *AWFUL* UPSET.
I KNOW THIS ISN'T A VERY GOOD FIRST DAY ON THE JOB, HON...
BUT NO PHONES ARE WORKING, AND THE RADIO SAYS STAY IN. SO YOU'RE *STAYING,* UNTIL I HEAR OTHERWISE, OKAY?

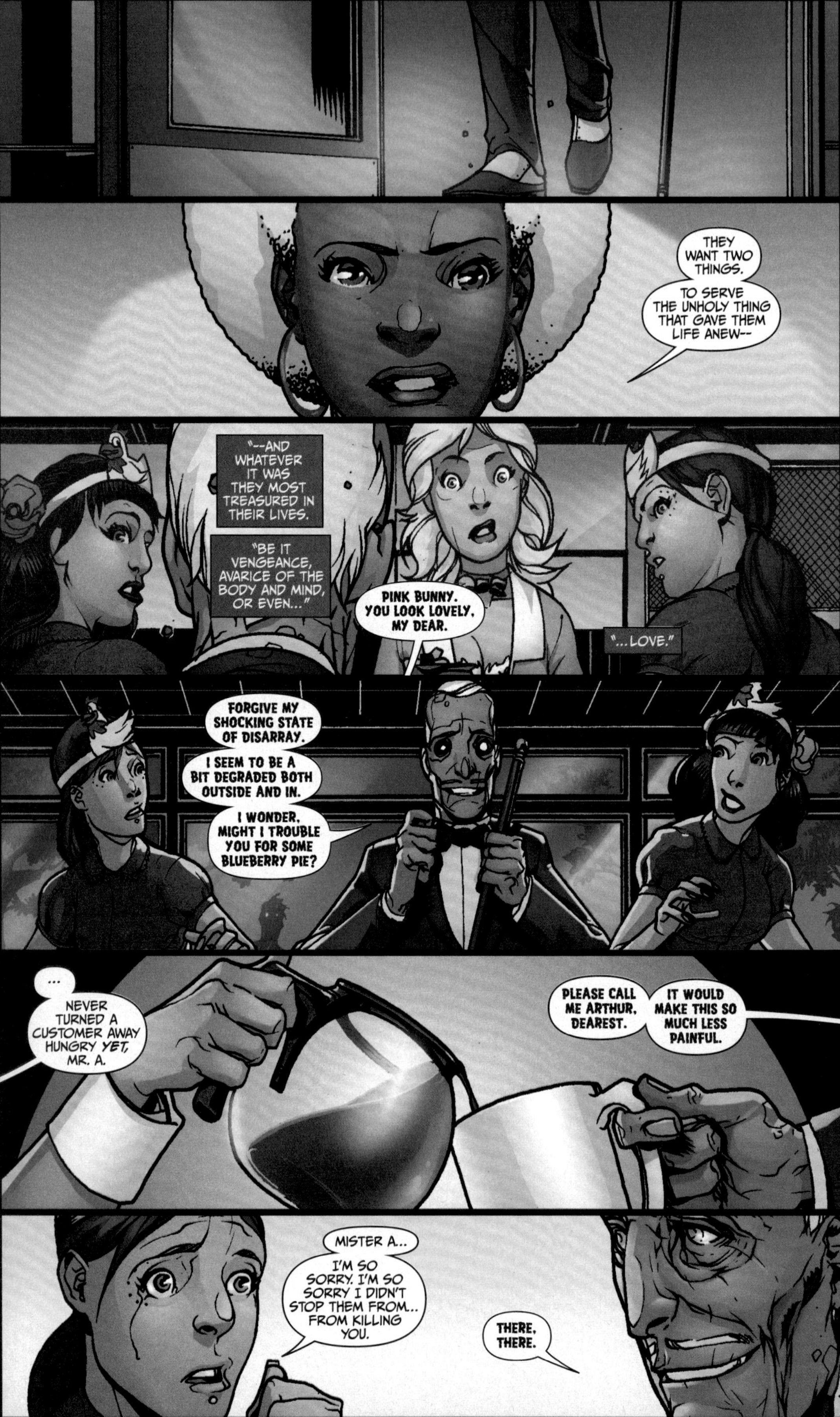
THEY WANT TWO THINGS.
TO SERVE THE UNHOLY THING THAT GAVE THEM LIFE ANEW--
"--AND WHATEVER IT WAS THEY MOST TREASURED IN THEIR LIVES.
"BE IT VENGEANCE, AVARICE OF THE BODY AND MIND, OR EVEN..."
PINK BUNNY. YOU LOOK LOVELY, MY DEAR.
"...LOVE."
FORGIVE MY SHOCKING STATE OF DISARRAY.
I SEEM TO BE A BIT DEGRADED BOTH OUTSIDE AND IN.
I WONDER, MIGHT I TROUBLE YOU FOR SOME BLUEBERRY PIE?
...
NEVER TURNED A CUSTOMER AWAY HUNGRY YET, MR. A.
PLEASE CALL ME ARTHUR, DEAREST.
IT WOULD MAKE THIS SO MUCH LESS PAINFUL.
MISTER A...
I'M SO SORRY. I'M SO SORRY I DIDN'T STOP THEM FROM... FROM KILLING YOU.
THERE, THERE.

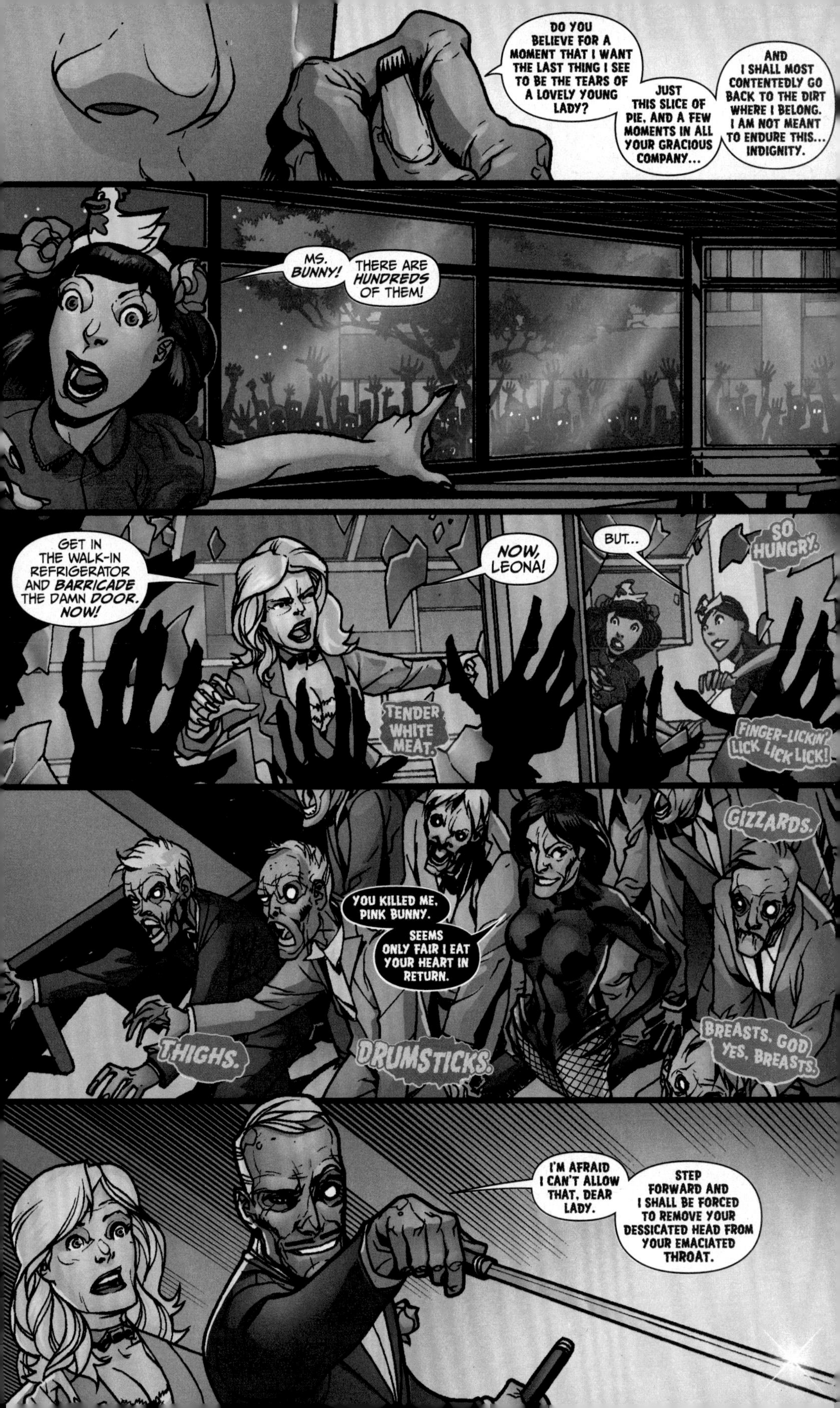
DO YOU BELIEVE FOR A MOMENT THAT I WANT THE LAST THING I SEE TO BE THE TEARS OF A LOVELY YOUNG LADY?
JUST THIS SLICE OF PIE, AND A FEW MOMENTS IN ALL YOUR GRACIOUS COMPANY...
AND I SHALL MOST CONTENTEDLY GO BACK TO THE DIRT WHERE I BELONG. I AM NOT MEANT TO ENDURE THIS... INDIGNITY.
MS. *BUNNY!*
THERE ARE *HUNDREDS* OF THEM!
GET IN THE WALK-IN REFRIGERATOR AND *BARRICADE* THE DAMN *DOOR. NOW!*
NOW, LEONA!
BUT...
SO HUNGRY.
TENDER WHITE MEAT.
FINGER-LICKIN' LICK LICK LICK!
GIZZARDS.
YOU KILLED ME, PINK BUNNY.
SEEMS ONLY FAIR I EAT YOUR HEART IN RETURN.
THIGHS.
DRUMSTICKS.
BREASTS, GOD YES, BREASTS.
I'M AFRAID I CAN'T ALLOW THAT, DEAR LADY.
STEP FORWARD AND I SHALL BE FORCED TO REMOVE YOUR DESSICATED HEAD FROM YOUR EMACIATED THROAT.

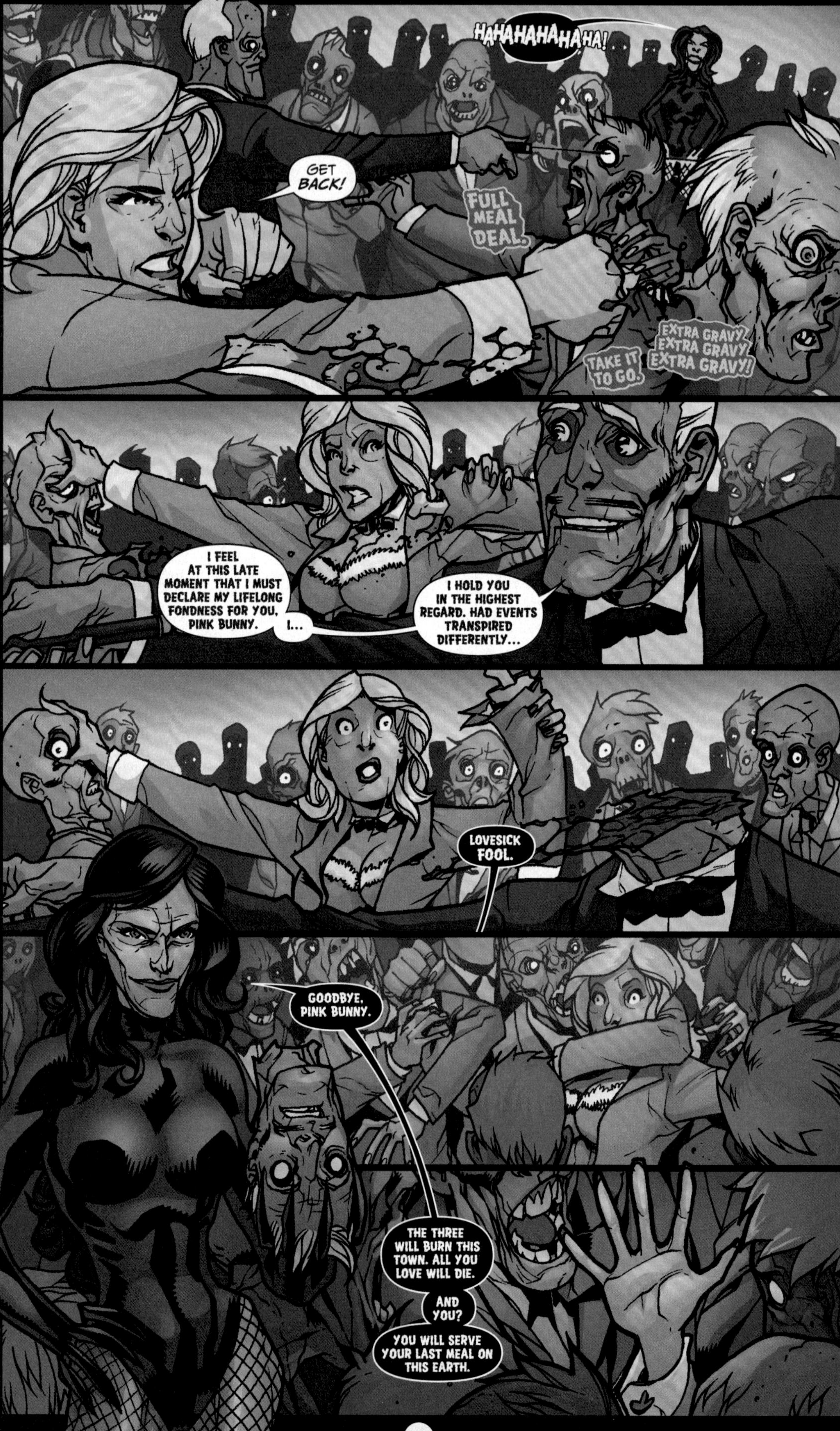
HAHAHAHAHAHA!
GET BACK!
FULL MEAL DEAL.
TAKE IT TO GO.
EXTRA GRAVY, EXTRA GRAVY, EXTRA GRAVY!
I FEEL AT THIS LATE MOMENT THAT I MUST DECLARE MY LIFELONG FONDNESS FOR YOU, PINK BUNNY.
I...
I HOLD YOU IN THE HIGHEST REGARD. HAD EVENTS TRANSPIRED DIFFERENTLY...
LOVESICK FOOL.
GOODBYE, PINK BUNNY.
THE THREE WILL BURN THIS TOWN. ALL YOU LOVE WILL DIE.
AND YOU?
YOU WILL SERVE YOUR LAST MEAL ON THIS EARTH.

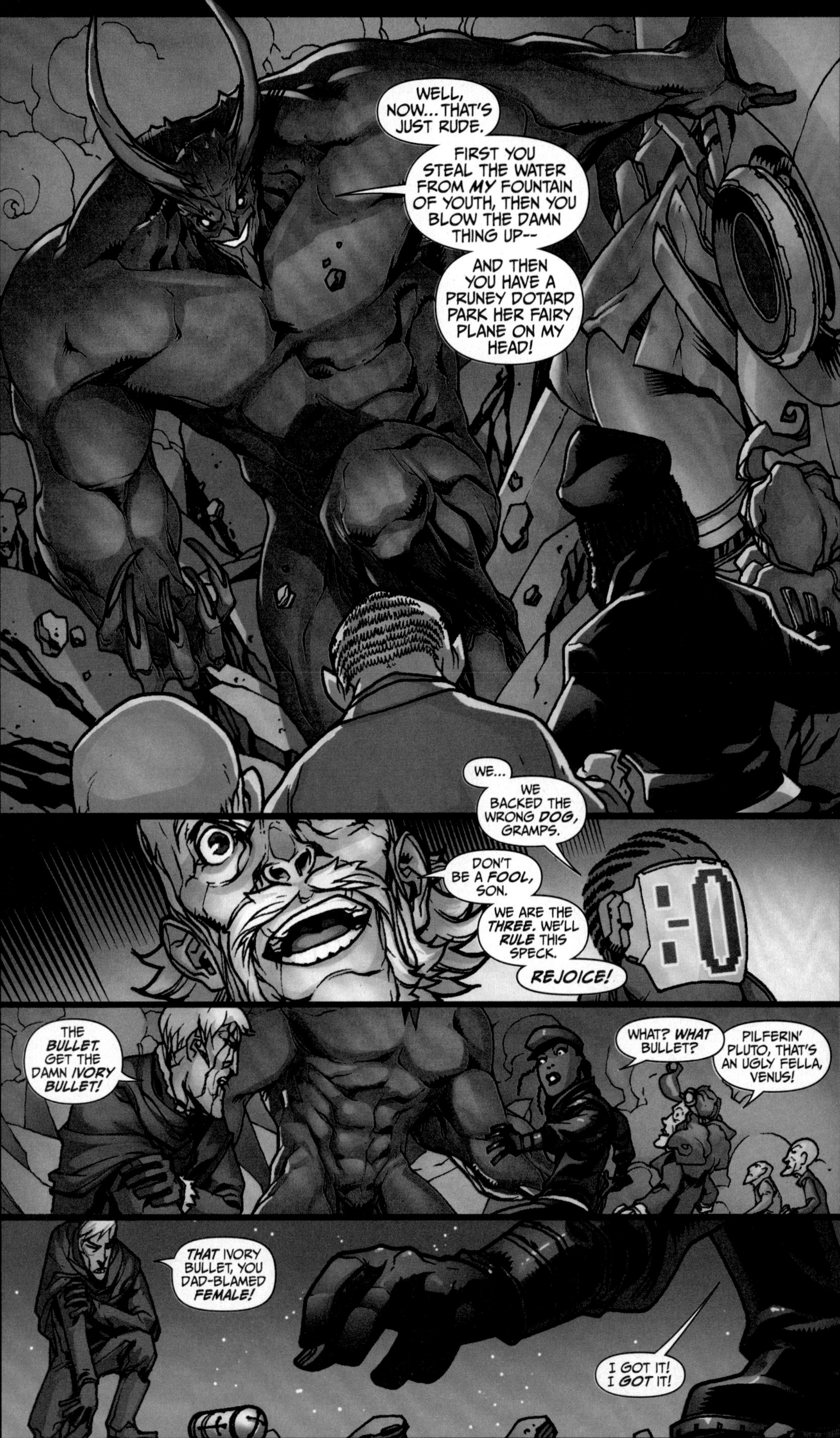
WELL, NOW... THAT'S JUST RUDE.
FIRST YOU STEAL THE WATER FROM *MY* FOUNTAIN OF YOUTH, THEN YOU BLOW THE DAMN THING UP--
AND THEN YOU HAVE A PRUNEY DOTARD PARK HER FAIRY PLANE ON MY HEAD!
WE... WE BACKED THE WRONG *DOG*, GRAMPS.
DON'T BE A *FOOL*, SON.
WE ARE THE *THREE*. WE'LL *RULE* THIS SPECK.
REJOICE!
:-0
THE *BULLET*. GET THE DAMN *IVORY BULLET!*
WHAT? *WHAT* BULLET?
PILFERIN' PLUTO, THAT'S AN UGLY FELLA, VENUS!
THAT IVORY BULLET, YOU DAD-BLAMED *FEMALE!*
I GOT IT! I *GOT* IT!

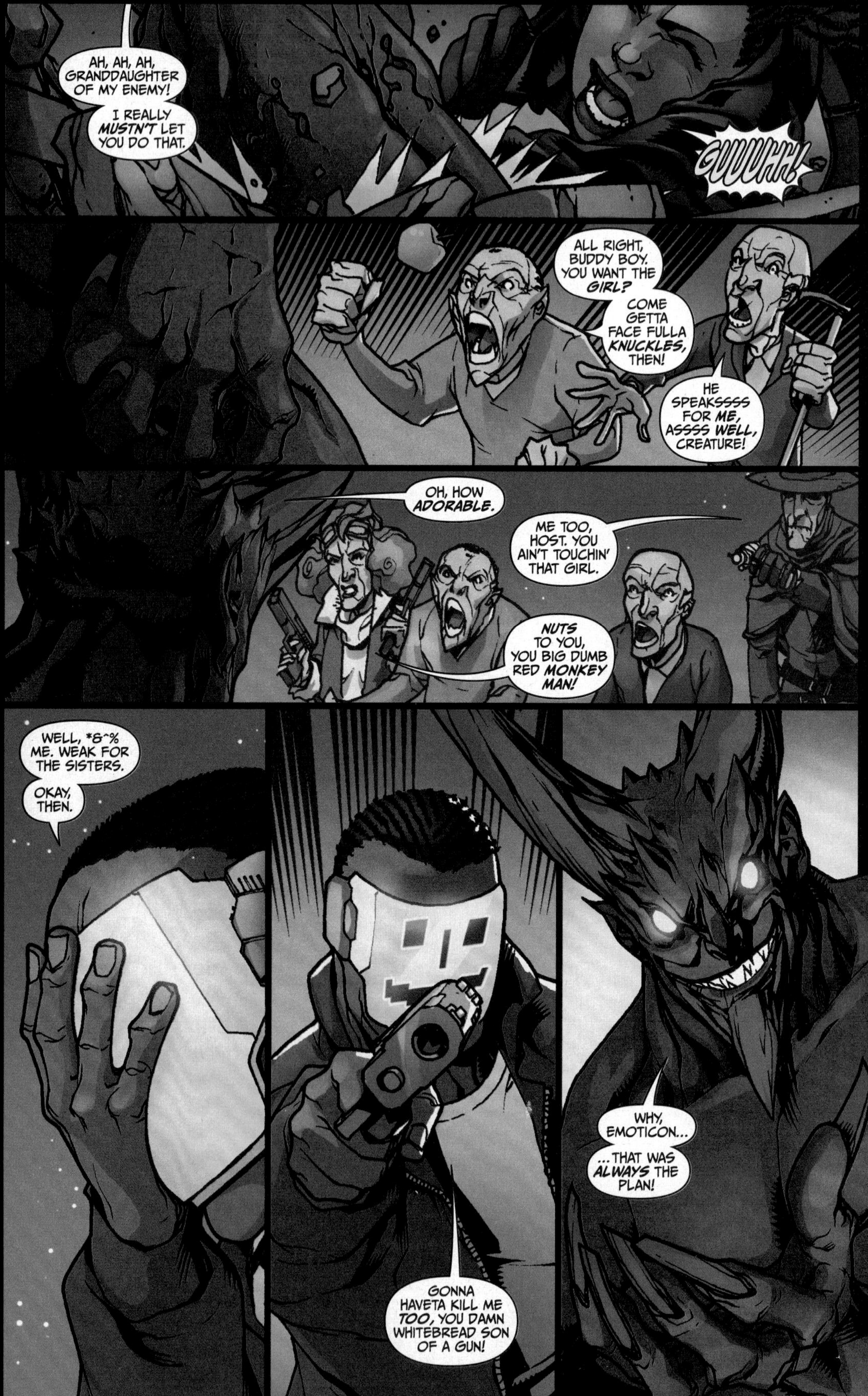
AH, AH, AH, GRANDDAUGHTER OF MY ENEMY!
I REALLY MUSTN'T LET YOU DO THAT.
GUUUHH!
ALL RIGHT, BUDDY BOY. YOU WANT THE GIRL?
COME GETTA FACE FULLA KNUCKLES, THEN!
HE SPEAKSSSS FOR ME, ASSSS WELL, CREATURE!
OH, HOW ADORABLE.
ME TOO, HOST. YOU AIN'T TOUCHIN' THAT GIRL.
NUTS TO YOU, YOU BIG DUMB RED MONKEY MAN!
WELL, *&^% ME. WEAK FOR THE SISTERS.
OKAY, THEN.
GONNA HAVETA KILL ME TOO, YOU DAMN WHITEBREAD SON OF A GUN!
WHY, EMOTICON...
...THAT WAS ALWAYS THE PLAN!

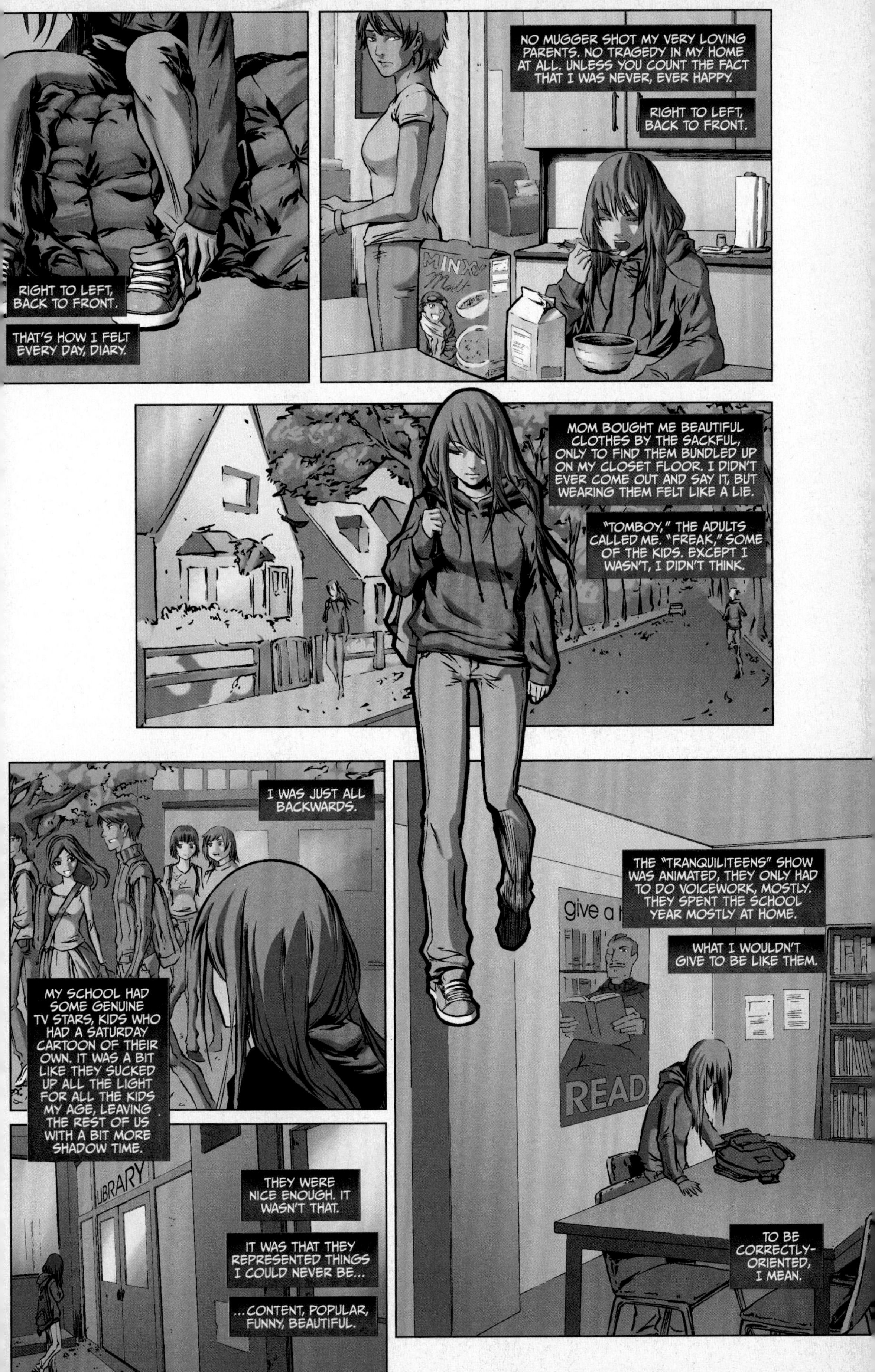
RIGHT TO LEFT, BACK TO FRONT.
THAT'S HOW I FELT EVERY DAY, DIARY.
NO MUGGER SHOT MY VERY LOVING PARENTS. NO TRAGEDY IN MY HOME AT ALL. UNLESS YOU COUNT THE FACT THAT I WAS NEVER, EVER HAPPY.
RIGHT TO LEFT, BACK TO FRONT.
MINXY Malt
MOM BOUGHT ME BEAUTIFUL CLOTHES BY THE SACKFUL, ONLY TO FIND THEM BUNDLED UP ON MY CLOSET FLOOR. I DIDN'T EVER COME OUT AND SAY IT, BUT WEARING THEM FELT LIKE A LIE.
"TOMBOY," THE ADULTS CALLED ME. "FREAK," SOME OF THE KIDS. EXCEPT I WASN'T, I DIDN'T THINK.
I WAS JUST ALL BACKWARDS.
MY SCHOOL HAD SOME GENUINE TV STARS, KIDS WHO HAD A SATURDAY CARTOON OF THEIR OWN. IT WAS A BIT LIKE THEY SUCKED UP ALL THE LIGHT FOR ALL THE KIDS MY AGE, LEAVING THE REST OF US WITH A BIT MORE SHADOW TIME.
LIBRARY
THEY WERE NICE ENOUGH. IT WASN'T THAT.
IT WAS THAT THEY REPRESENTED THINGS I COULD NEVER BE...
...CONTENT, POPULAR, FUNNY, BEAUTIFUL.
THE "TRANQUILITEENS" SHOW WAS ANIMATED, THEY ONLY HAD TO DO VOICEWORK, MOSTLY. THEY SPENT THE SCHOOL YEAR MOSTLY AT HOME.
WHAT I WOULDN'T GIVE TO BE LIKE THEM.
give a
READ
TO BE CORRECTLY-ORIENTED, I MEAN.

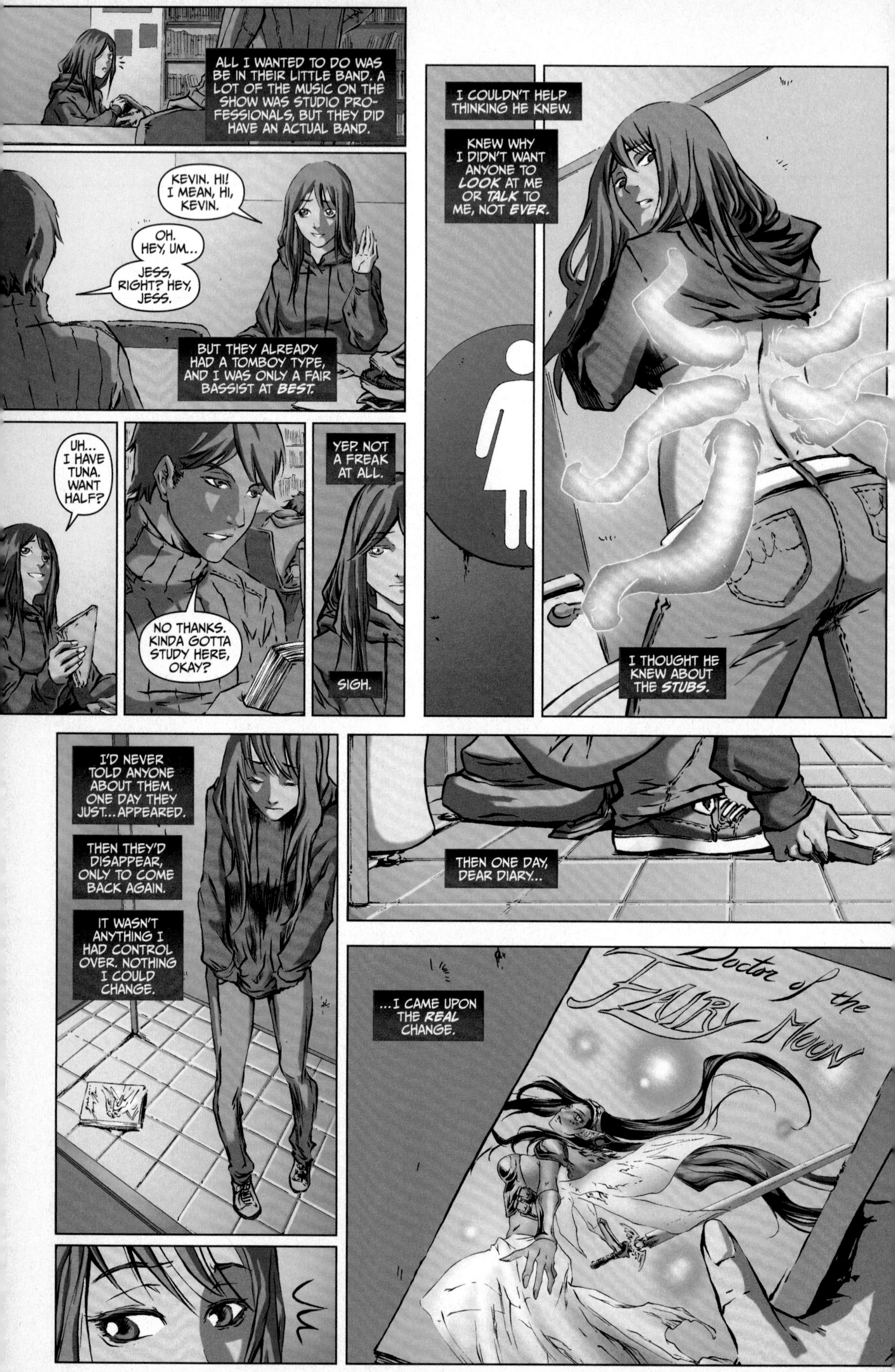
ALL I WANTED TO DO WAS BE IN THEIR LITTLE BAND. A LOT OF THE MUSIC ON THE SHOW WAS STUDIO PROFESSIONALS, BUT THEY DID HAVE AN ACTUAL BAND.
KEVIN. HI! I MEAN, HI, KEVIN.
OH. HEY, UM...
JESS, RIGHT? HEY, JESS.
BUT THEY ALREADY HAD A TOMBOY TYPE, AND I WAS ONLY A FAIR BASSIST AT BEST.
UH... I HAVE TUNA. WANT HALF?
NO THANKS. KINDA GOTTA STUDY HERE, OKAY?
YEP. NOT A FREAK AT ALL.
SIGH.
I COULDN'T HELP THINKING HE KNEW.
KNEW WHY I DIDN'T WANT ANYONE TO LOOK AT ME OR TALK TO ME, NOT EVER.
I THOUGHT HE KNEW ABOUT THE STUBS.
I'D NEVER TOLD ANYONE ABOUT THEM. ONE DAY THEY JUST...APPEARED.
THEN THEY'D DISAPPEAR, ONLY TO COME BACK AGAIN.
IT WASN'T ANYTHING I HAD CONTROL OVER. NOTHING I COULD CHANGE.
THEN ONE DAY, DEAR DIARY...
...I CAME UPON THE REAL CHANGE.
Doctor of the FAIRY MOON

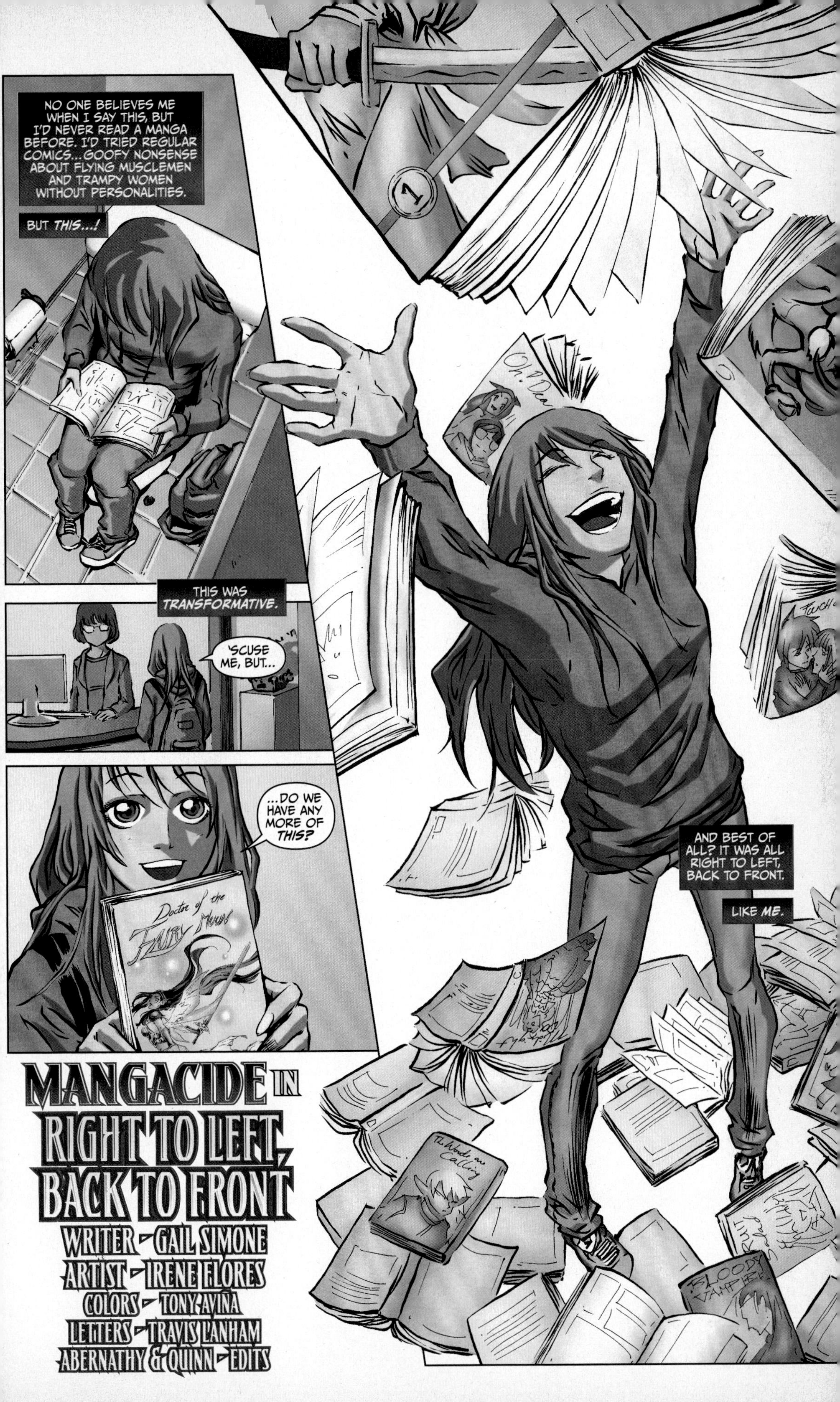
NO ONE BELIEVES ME WHEN I SAY THIS, BUT I'D NEVER READ A MANGA BEFORE. I'D TRIED REGULAR COMICS...GOOFY NONSENSE ABOUT FLYING MUSCLEMEN AND TRAMPY WOMEN WITHOUT PERSONALITIES.
BUT *THIS*...!
THIS WAS *TRANSFORMATIVE.*
'SCUSE ME, BUT...
...DO WE HAVE ANY MORE OF *THIS?*
Doctor of the Fairy Moon
AND BEST OF ALL? IT WAS ALL RIGHT TO LEFT, BACK TO FRONT.
LIKE *ME.*
The Words are Calling
BLOODY VAMPIRE
MANGACIDE IN
RIGHT TO LEFT, BACK TO FRONT
WRITER - GAIL SIMONE
ARTIST - IRENE FLORES
COLORS - TONY AVIÑA
LETTERS - TRAVIS LANHAM
ABERNATHY & QUINN - EDITS

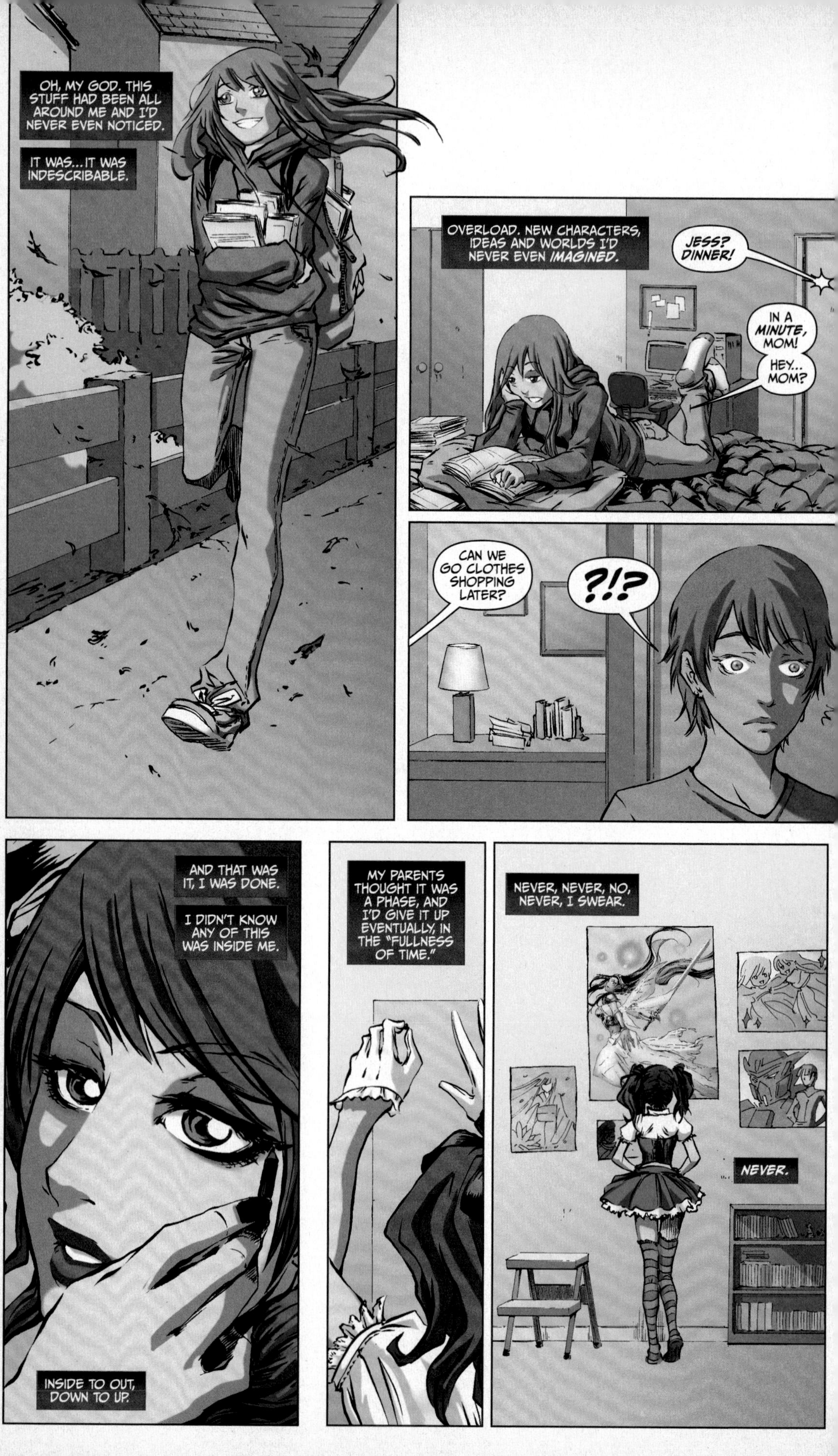
OH, MY GOD. THIS STUFF HAD BEEN ALL AROUND ME AND I'D NEVER EVEN NOTICED.
IT WAS... IT WAS INDESCRIBABLE.
OVERLOAD. NEW CHARACTERS, IDEAS AND WORLDS I'D NEVER EVEN *IMAGINED*.
JESS? DINNER!
IN A *MINUTE*, MOM!
HEY... MOM?
CAN WE GO CLOTHES SHOPPING LATER?
?!?
AND THAT WAS IT, I WAS DONE.
I DIDN'T KNOW ANY OF THIS WAS INSIDE ME.
INSIDE TO OUT, DOWN TO UP.
MY PARENTS THOUGHT IT WAS A PHASE, AND I'D GIVE IT UP EVENTUALLY, IN THE "FULLNESS OF TIME."
NEVER, NEVER, NO, NEVER, I SWEAR.
NEVER.

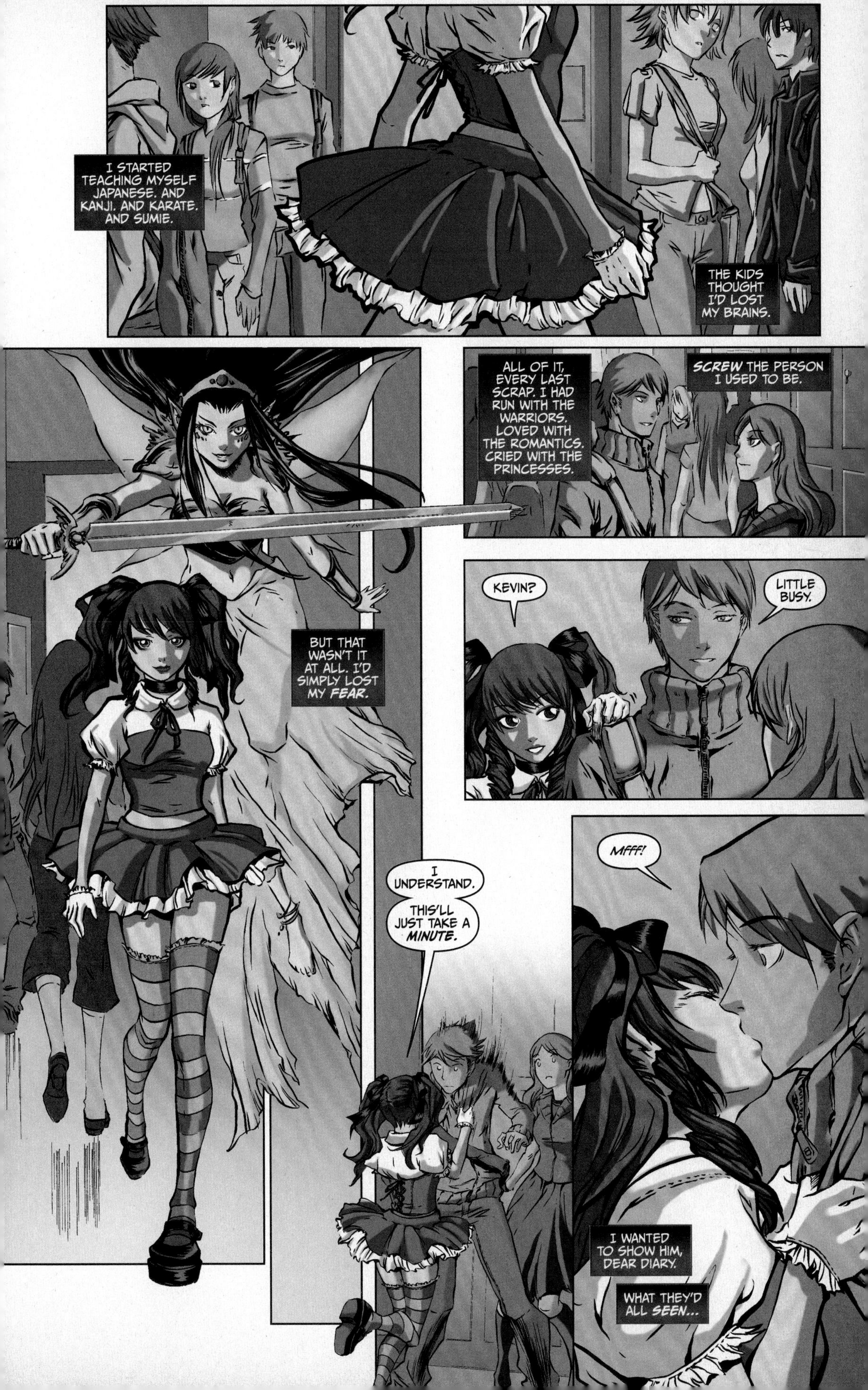
I STARTED TEACHING MYSELF JAPANESE. AND KANJI. AND KARATE. AND SUMIE.
THE KIDS THOUGHT I'D LOST MY BRAINS.
BUT THAT WASN'T IT AT ALL. I'D SIMPLY LOST MY FEAR.
ALL OF IT, EVERY LAST SCRAP. I HAD RUN WITH THE WARRIORS. LOVED WITH THE ROMANTICS. CRIED WITH THE PRINCESSES.
SCREW THE PERSON I USED TO BE.
KEVIN?
LITTLE BUSY.
I UNDERSTAND.
THIS'LL JUST TAKE A MINUTE.
MFFF!
I WANTED TO SHOW HIM, DEAR DIARY.
WHAT THEY'D ALL SEEN...

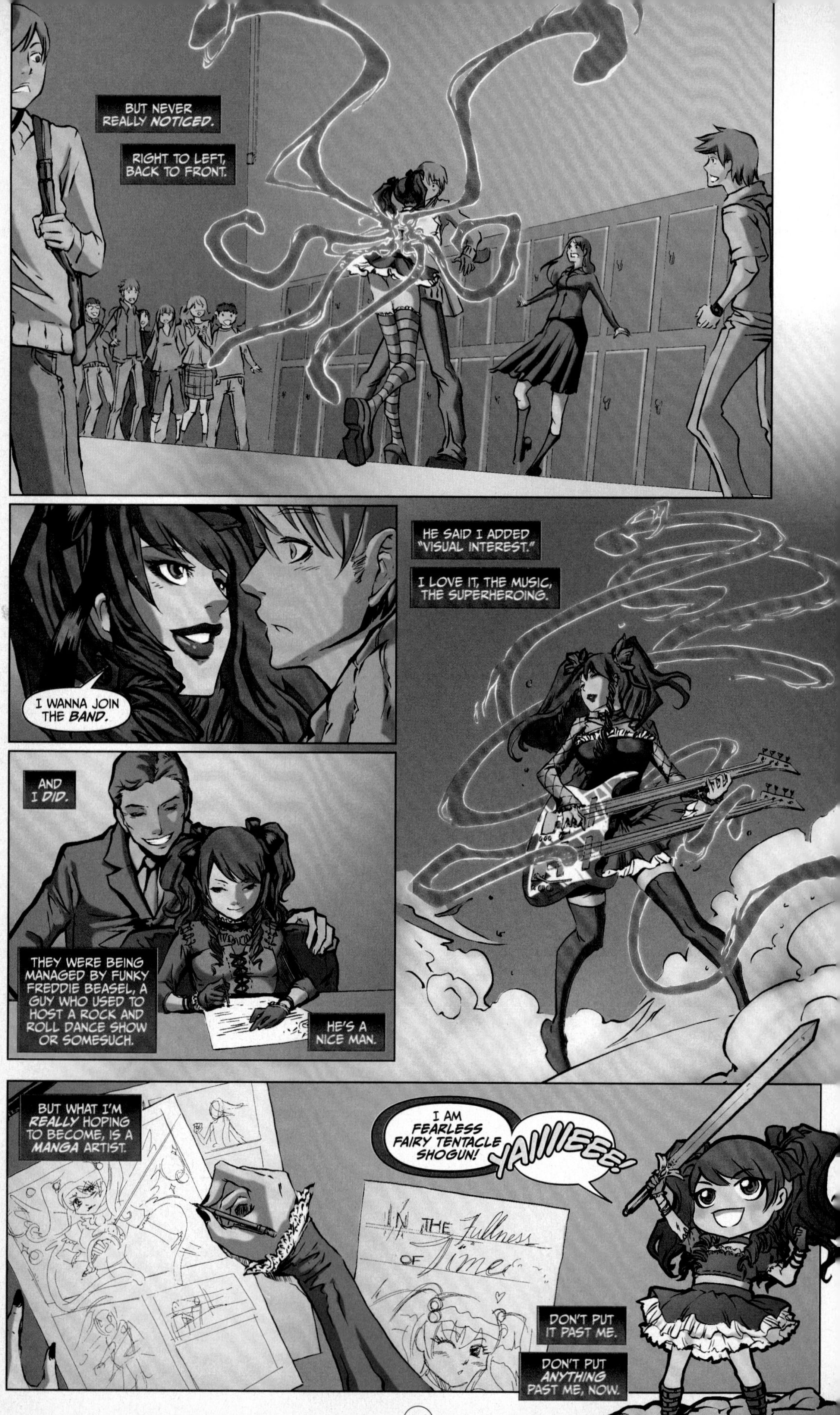
BUT NEVER REALLY *NOTICED*.
RIGHT TO LEFT, BACK TO FRONT.
I WANNA JOIN THE *BAND*.
AND I *DID*.
THEY WERE BEING MANAGED BY FUNKY FREDDIE BEASEL, A GUY WHO USED TO HOST A ROCK AND ROLL DANCE SHOW OR SOMESUCH.
HE'S A NICE MAN.
HE SAID I ADDED "VISUAL INTEREST."
I LOVE IT, THE MUSIC, THE SUPERHEROING.
BUT WHAT I'M *REALLY* HOPING TO BECOME, IS A *MANGA* ARTIST.
I AM *FEARLESS* FAIRY TENTACLE SHOGUN!
YAIIIIEEE!
IN THE Fullness OF Time
DON'T PUT IT PAST ME.
DON'T PUT *ANYTHING* PAST ME, NOW.

CHAPTER SIX

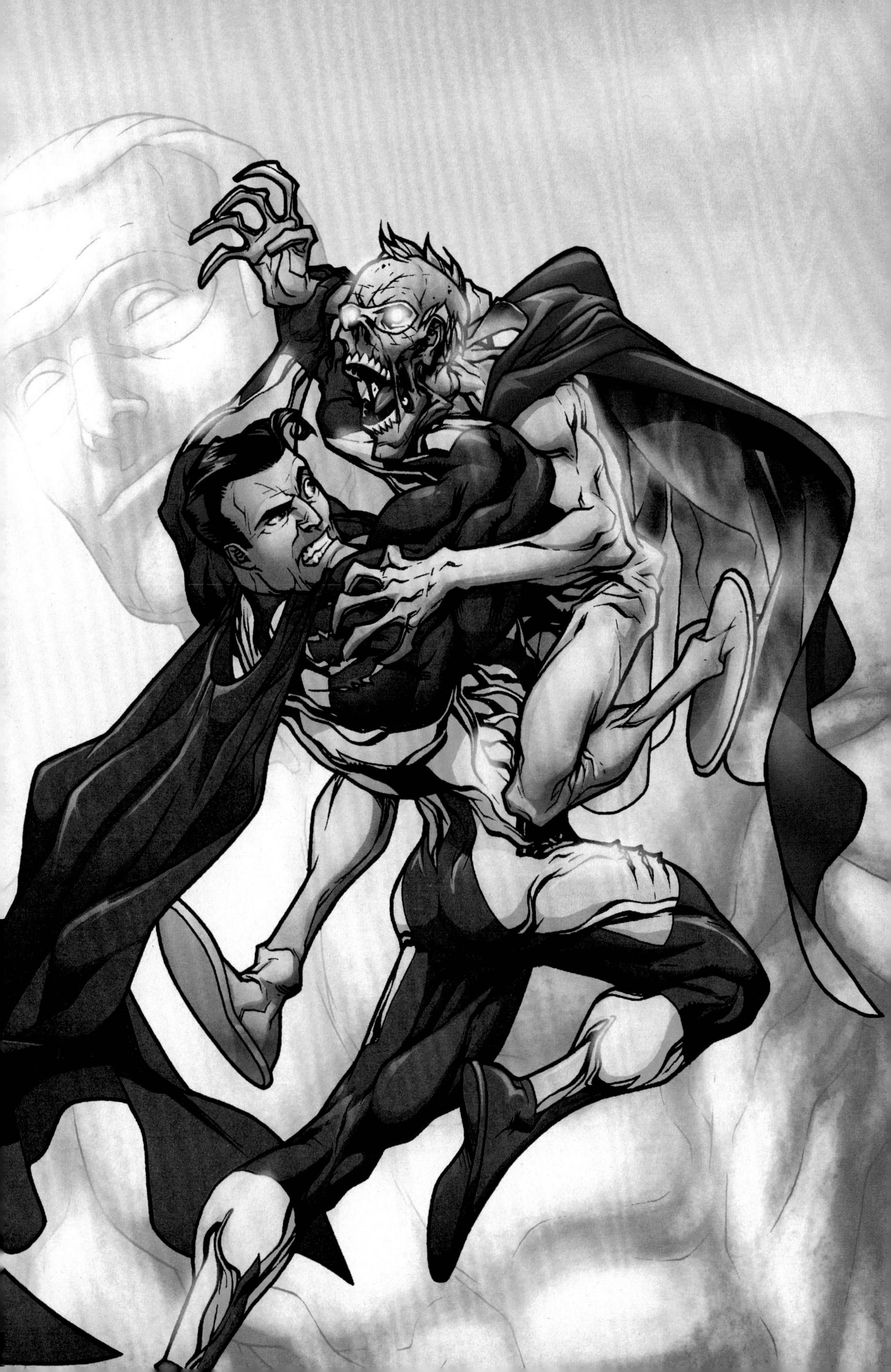

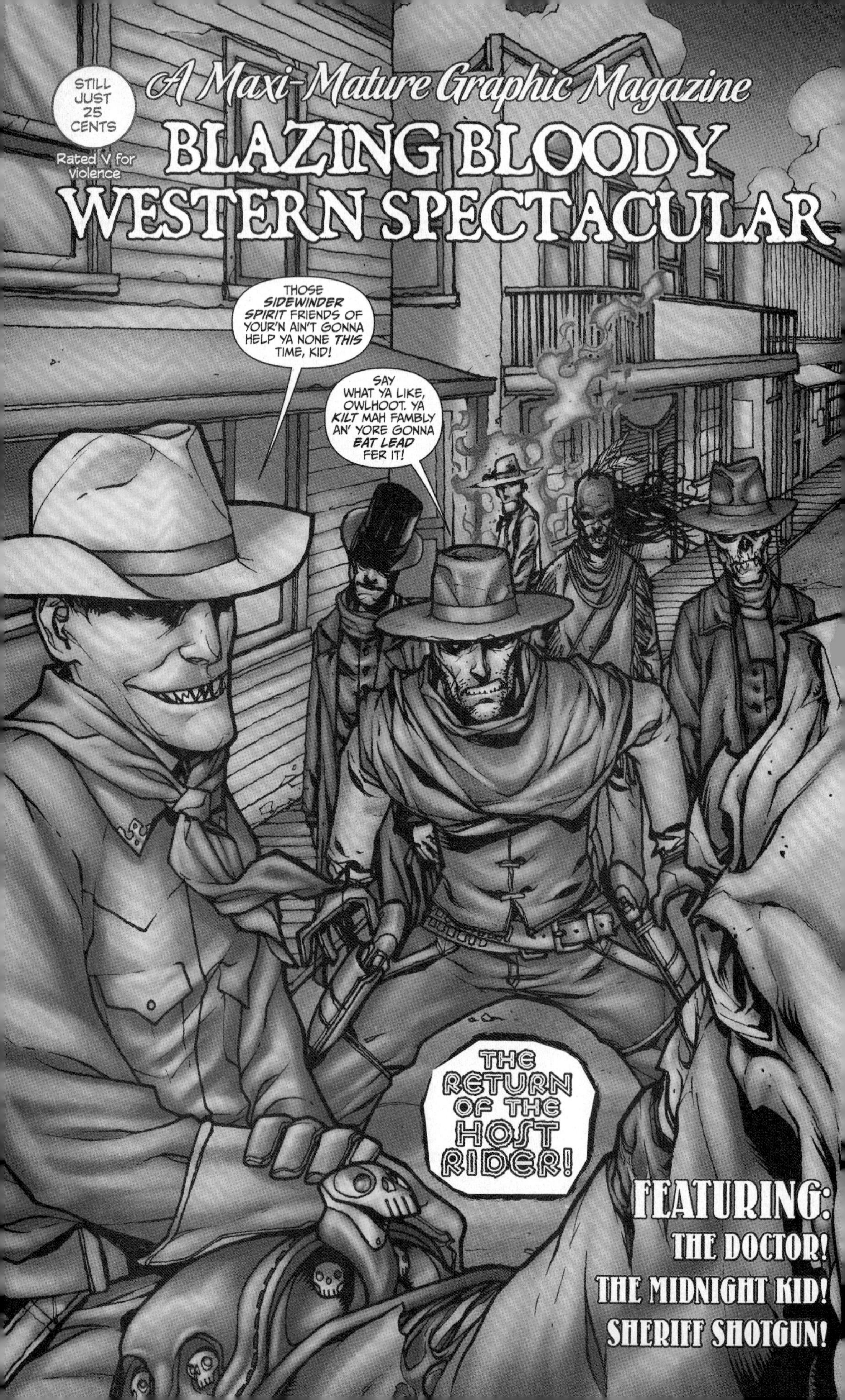
STILL JUST 25 CENTS
A Maxi-Mature Graphic Magazine
Rated V for violence
BLAZING BLOODY WESTERN SPECTACULAR
THOSE SIDEWINDER SPIRIT FRIENDS OF YOUR'N AIN'T GONNA HELP YA NONE THIS TIME, KID!
SAY WHAT YA LIKE, OWLHOOT. YA KILT MAH FAMBLY AN' YORE GONNA EAT LEAD FER IT!
THE RETURN OF THE HOST RIDER!
FEATURING:
THE DOCTOR!
THE MIDNIGHT KID!
SHERIFF SHOTGUN!

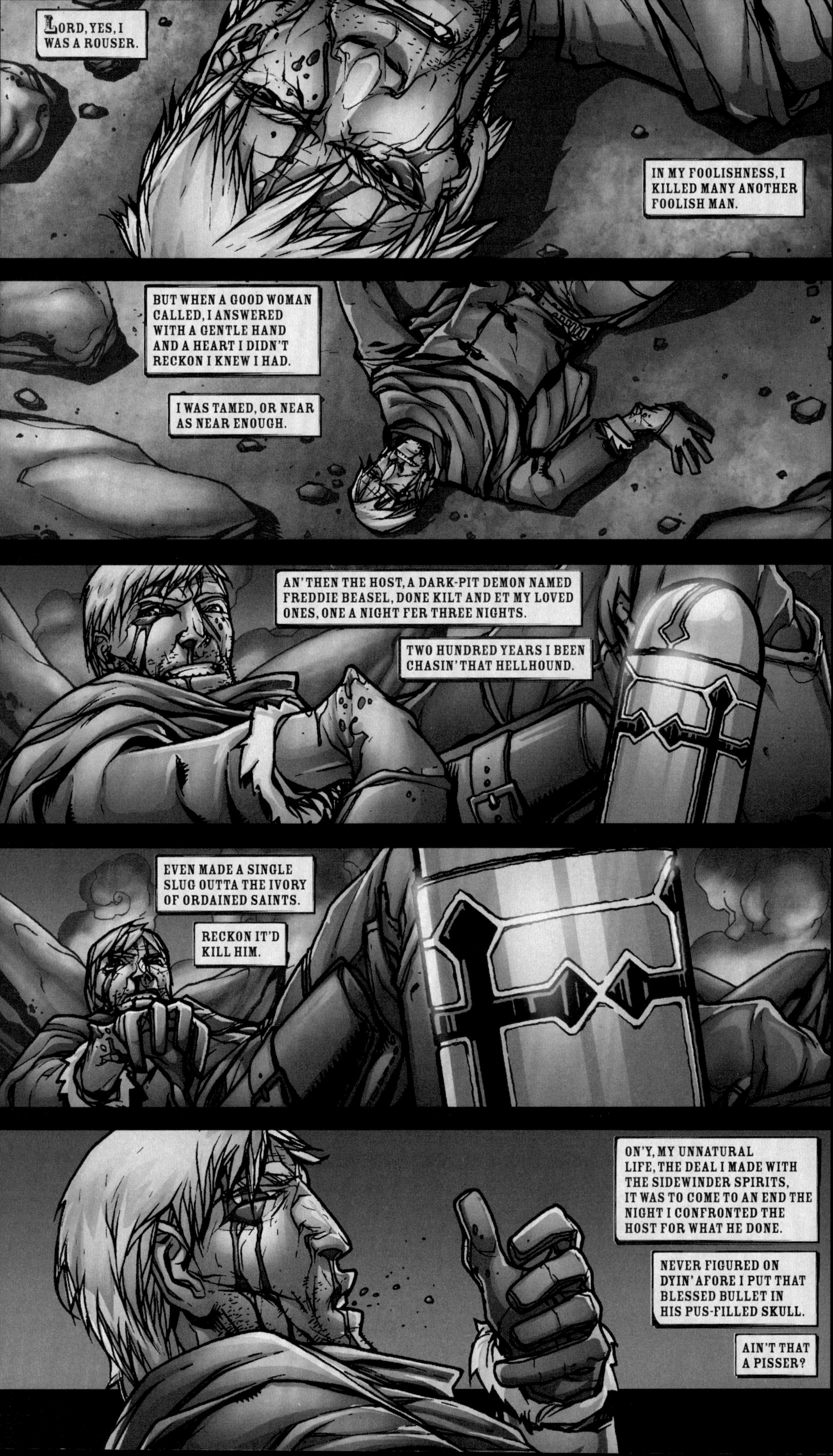
LORD, YES, I WAS A ROUSER.
IN MY FOOLISHNESS, I KILLED MANY ANOTHER FOOLISH MAN.
BUT WHEN A GOOD WOMAN CALLED, I ANSWERED WITH A GENTLE HAND AND A HEART I DIDN'T RECKON I KNEW I HAD.
I WAS TAMED, OR NEAR AS NEAR ENOUGH.
AN' THEN THE HOST, A DARK-PIT DEMON NAMED FREDDIE BEASEL, DONE KILT AND ET MY LOVED ONES, ONE A NIGHT FER THREE NIGHTS.
TWO HUNDRED YEARS I BEEN CHASIN' THAT HELLHOUND.
EVEN MADE A SINGLE SLUG OUTTA THE IVORY OF ORDAINED SAINTS.
RECKON IT'D KILL HIM.
ON'Y, MY UNNATURAL LIFE, THE DEAL I MADE WITH THE SIDEWINDER SPIRITS, IT WAS TO COME TO AN END THE NIGHT I CONFRONTED THE HOST FOR WHAT HE DONE.
NEVER FIGURED ON DYIN' AFORE I PUT THAT BLESSED BULLET IN HIS PUS-FILLED SKULL.
AIN'T THAT A PISSER?

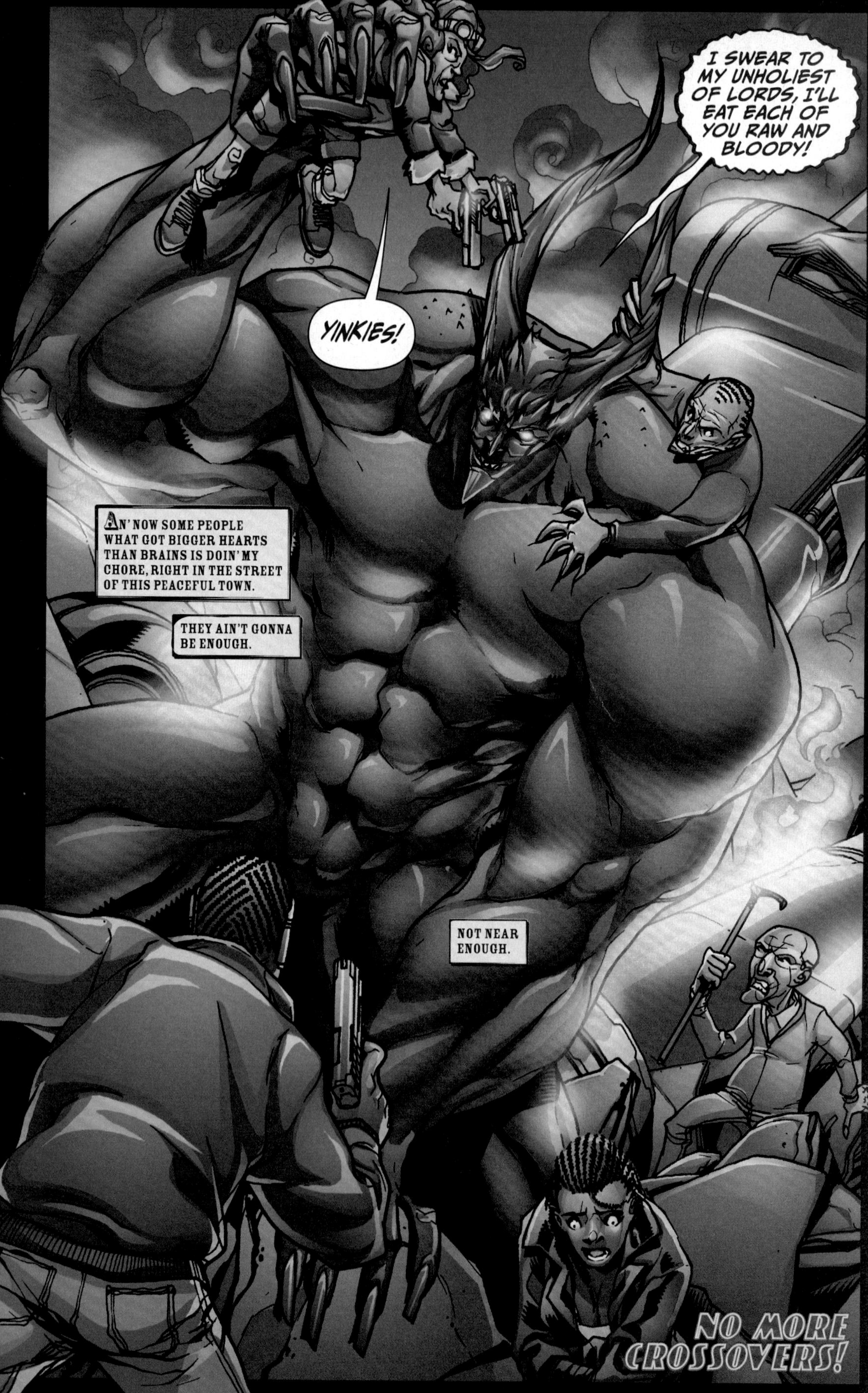
I SWEAR TO MY UNHOLIEST OF LORDS, I'LL EAT EACH OF YOU RAW AND BLOODY!
YINKIES!
AN' NOW SOME PEOPLE WHAT GOT BIGGER HEARTS THAN BRAINS IS DOIN' MY CHORE, RIGHT IN THE STREET OF THIS PEACEFUL TOWN.
THEY AIN'T GONNA BE ENOUGH.
NOT NEAR ENOUGH.
NO MORE CROSSOVERS!

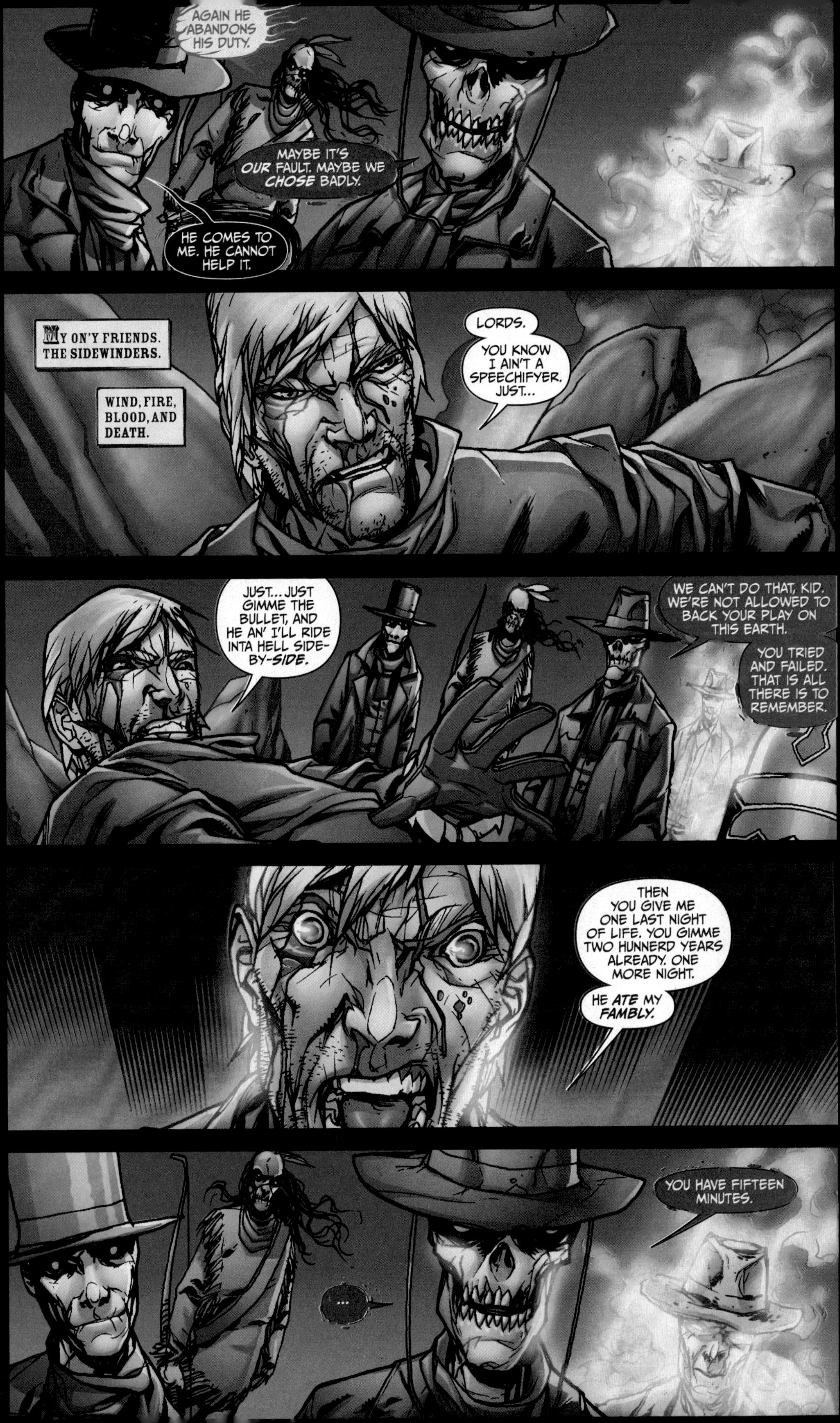
AGAIN HE ABANDONS HIS DUTY.
MAYBE IT'S OUR FAULT. MAYBE WE CHOSE BADLY.
HE COMES TO ME. HE CANNOT HELP IT.
MY ON'Y FRIENDS. THE SIDEWINDERS.
WIND, FIRE, BLOOD, AND DEATH.
LORDS.
YOU KNOW I AIN'T A SPEECHIFYER. JUST...
JUST... JUST GIMME THE BULLET, AND HE AN' I'LL RIDE INTA HELL SIDE-BY-SIDE.
WE CAN'T DO THAT, KID. WE'RE NOT ALLOWED TO BACK YOUR PLAY ON THIS EARTH.
YOU TRIED AND FAILED. THAT IS ALL THERE IS TO REMEMBER.
THEN YOU GIVE ME ONE LAST NIGHT OF LIFE. YOU GIMME TWO HUNNERD YEARS ALREADY. ONE MORE NIGHT.
HE ATE MY FAMBLY.
...
YOU HAVE FIFTEEN MINUTES.

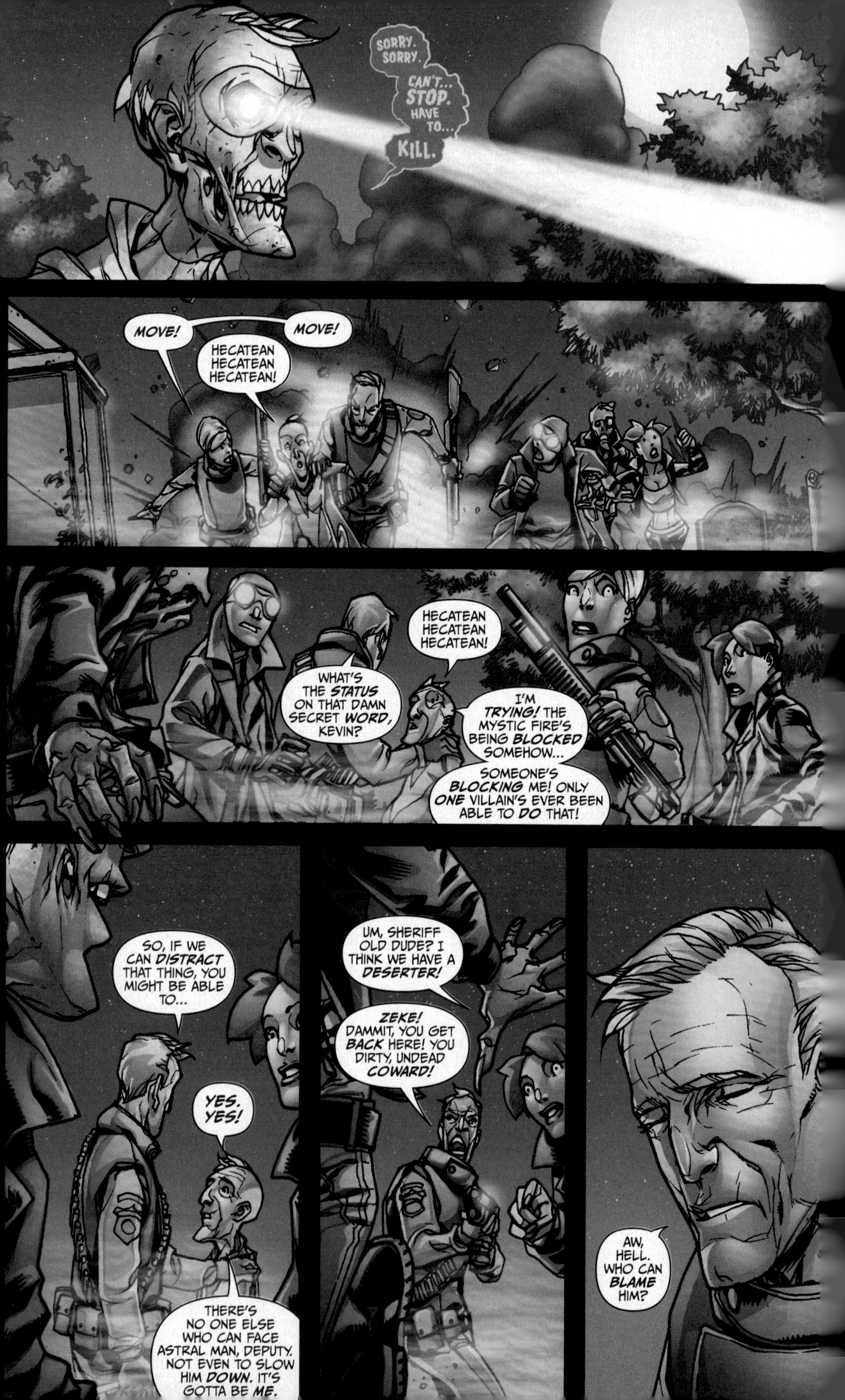
SORRY. SORRY. CAN'T... STOP. HAVE TO... KILL.
MOVE!
HECATEAN HECATEAN HECATEAN!
MOVE!
WHAT'S THE STATUS ON THAT DAMN SECRET WORD, KEVIN?
HECATEAN HECATEAN HECATEAN!
I'M TRYING! THE MYSTIC FIRE'S BEING BLOCKED SOMEHOW...
SOMEONE'S BLOCKING ME! ONLY ONE VILLAIN'S EVER BEEN ABLE TO DO THAT!
SO, IF WE CAN DISTRACT THAT THING, YOU MIGHT BE ABLE TO...
YES. YES!
THERE'S NO ONE ELSE WHO CAN FACE ASTRAL MAN, DEPUTY. NOT EVEN TO SLOW HIM DOWN. IT'S GOTTA BE ME.
UM, SHERIFF OLD DUDE? I THINK WE HAVE A DESERTER!
ZEKE! DAMMIT, YOU GET BACK HERE! YOU DIRTY, UNDEAD COWARD!
AW, HELL. WHO CAN BLAME HIM?

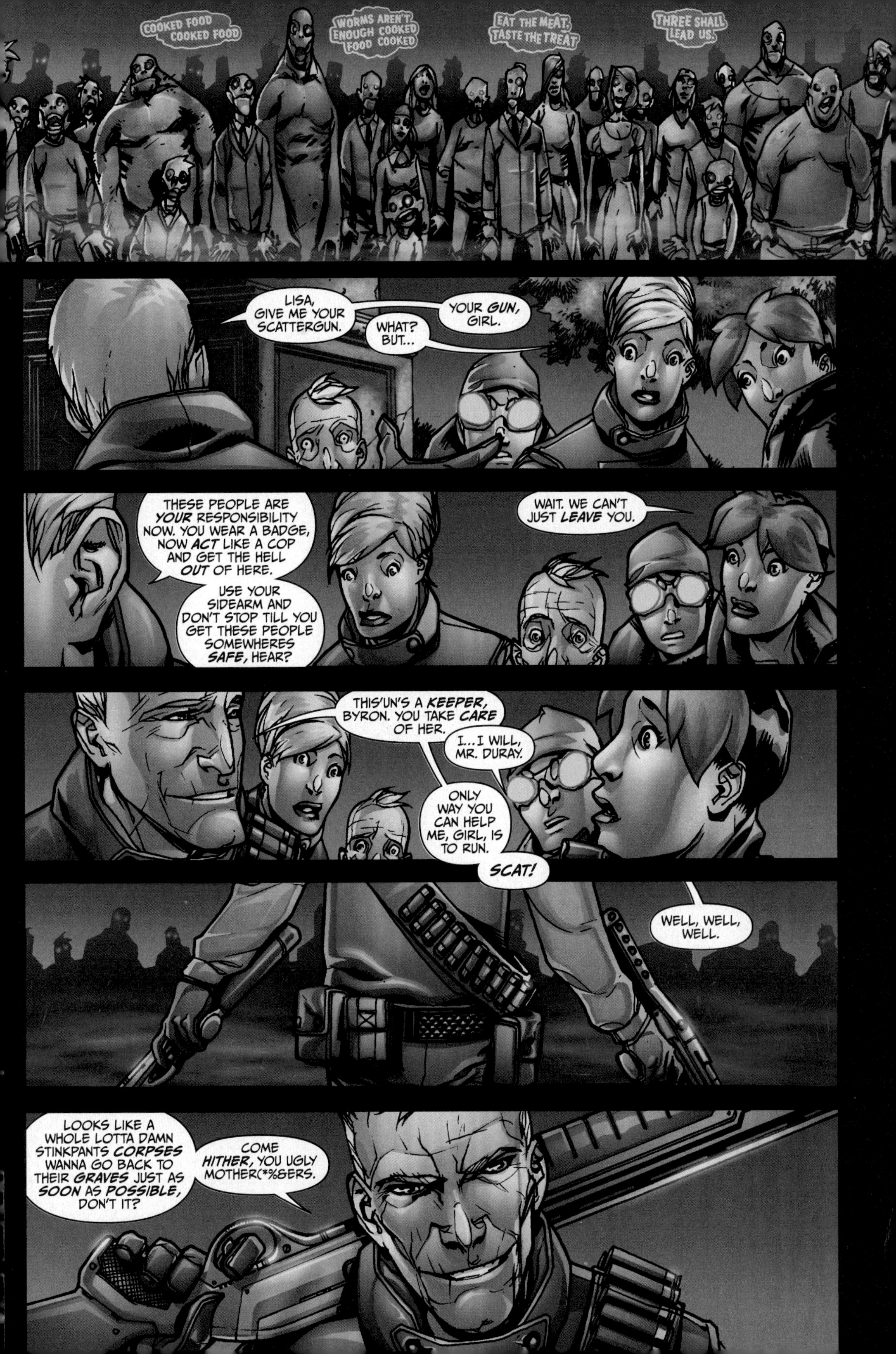
COOKED FOOD COOKED FOOD
WORMS AREN'T ENOUGH COOKED FOOD COOKED
EAT THE MEAT. TASTE THE TREAT
THREE SHALL LEAD US.
LISA, GIVE ME YOUR SCATTERGUN.
WHAT? BUT...
YOUR GUN, GIRL.
THESE PEOPLE ARE YOUR RESPONSIBILITY NOW. YOU WEAR A BADGE, NOW ACT LIKE A COP AND GET THE HELL OUT OF HERE.
USE YOUR SIDEARM AND DON'T STOP TILL YOU GET THESE PEOPLE SOMEWHERES SAFE, HEAR?
WAIT. WE CAN'T JUST LEAVE YOU.
THIS'UN'S A KEEPER, BYRON. YOU TAKE CARE OF HER.
I...I WILL, MR. DURAY.
ONLY WAY YOU CAN HELP ME, GIRL, IS TO RUN.
SCAT!
WELL, WELL, WELL.
LOOKS LIKE A WHOLE LOTTA DAMN STINKPANTS CORPSES WANNA GO BACK TO THEIR GRAVES JUST AS SOON AS POSSIBLE, DON'T IT?
COME HITHER, YOU UGLY MOTHER(*%&ERS.

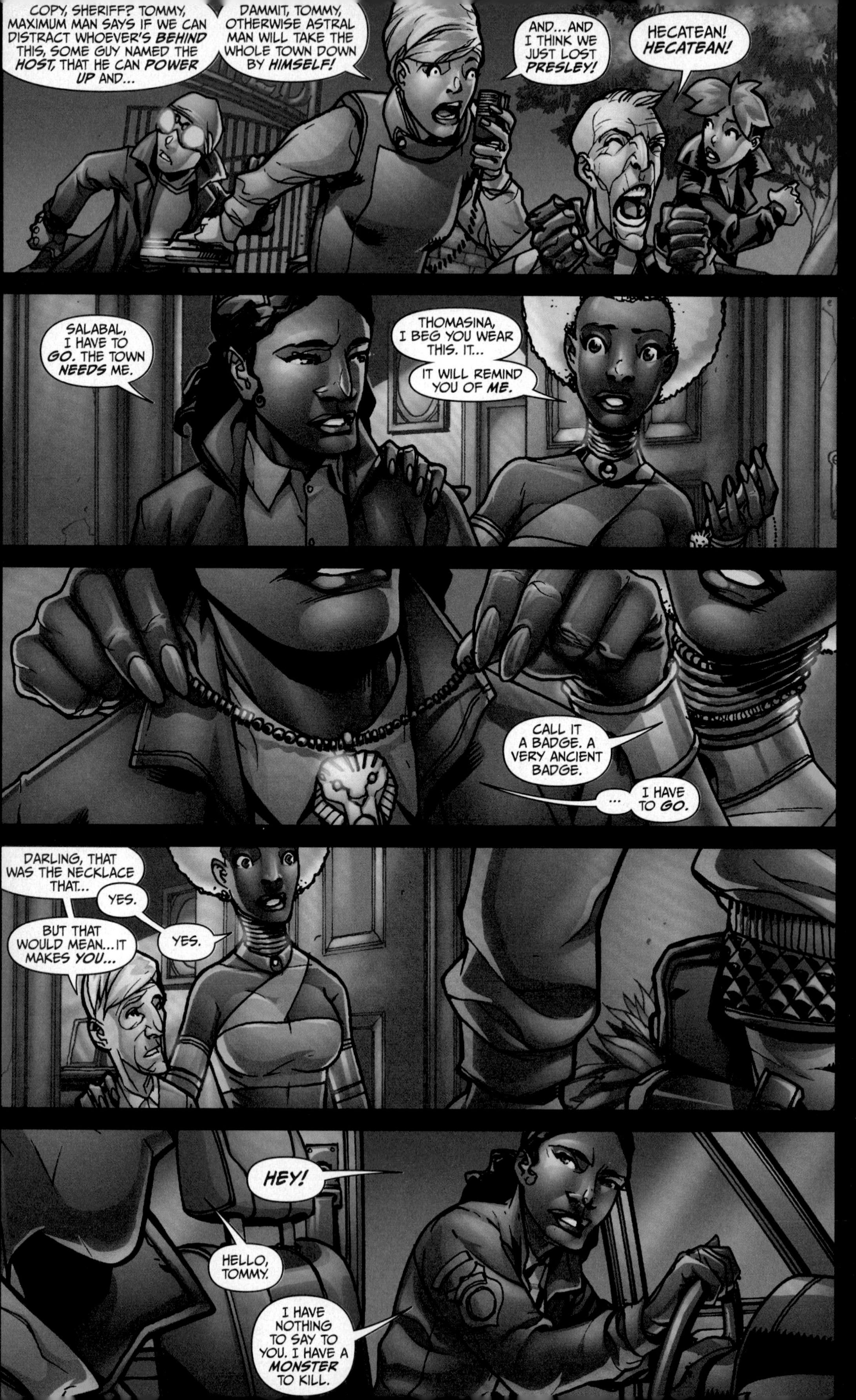
COPY, SHERIFF? TOMMY, MAXIMUM MAN SAYS IF WE CAN DISTRACT WHOEVER'S BEHIND THIS, SOME GUY NAMED THE HOST, THAT HE CAN POWER UP AND...
DAMMIT, TOMMY, OTHERWISE ASTRAL MAN WILL TAKE THE WHOLE TOWN DOWN BY HIMSELF!
AND... AND I THINK WE JUST LOST PRESLEY!
HECATEAN! HECATEAN!
SALABAL, I HAVE TO GO. THE TOWN NEEDS ME.
THOMASINA, I BEG YOU WEAR THIS. IT...
IT WILL REMIND YOU OF ME.
CALL IT A BADGE. A VERY ANCIENT BADGE.
... I HAVE TO GO.
DARLING, THAT WAS THE NECKLACE THAT...
YES.
BUT THAT WOULD MEAN... IT MAKES YOU...
YES.
HEY!
HELLO, TOMMY.
I HAVE NOTHING TO SAY TO YOU. I HAVE A MONSTER TO KILL.

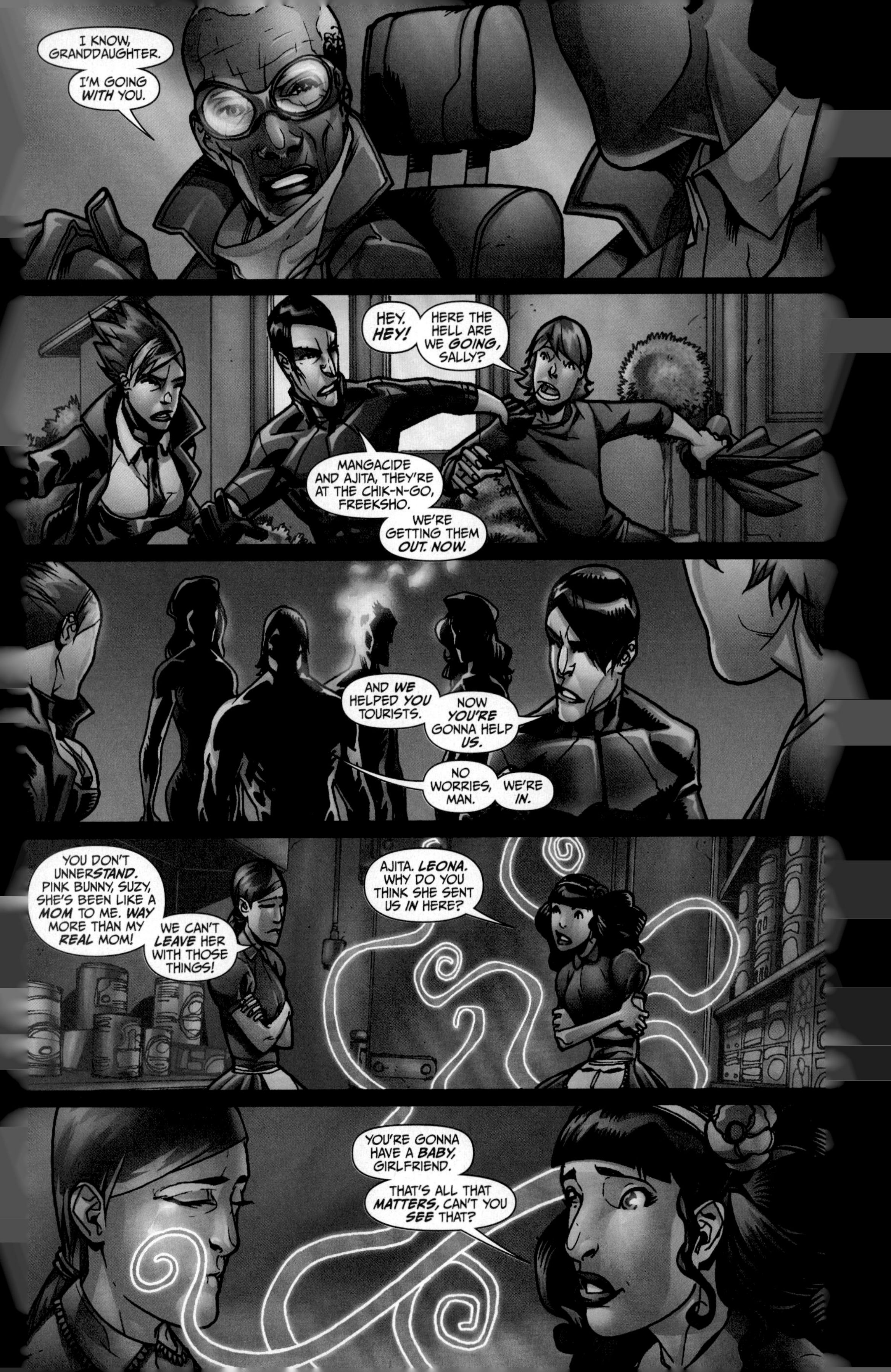

I KNOW, GRANDDAUGHTER.
I'M GOING WITH YOU.
HEY. HEY!
HERE THE HELL ARE WE GOING, SALLY?
MANGACIDE AND AJITA, THEY'RE AT THE CHIK-N-GO, FREEKSHO.
WE'RE GETTING THEM OUT. NOW.
AND WE HELPED YOU TOURISTS.
NOW YOU'RE GONNA HELP US.
NO WORRIES, MAN.
WE'RE IN.
YOU DON'T UNNERSTAND. PINK BUNNY, SUZY, SHE'S BEEN LIKE A MOM TO ME. WAY MORE THAN MY REAL MOM!
WE CAN'T LEAVE HER WITH THOSE THINGS!
AJITA. LEONA. WHY DO YOU THINK SHE SENT US IN HERE?
YOU'RE GONNA HAVE A BABY, GIRLFRIEND.
THAT'S ALL THAT MATTERS, CAN'T YOU SEE THAT?

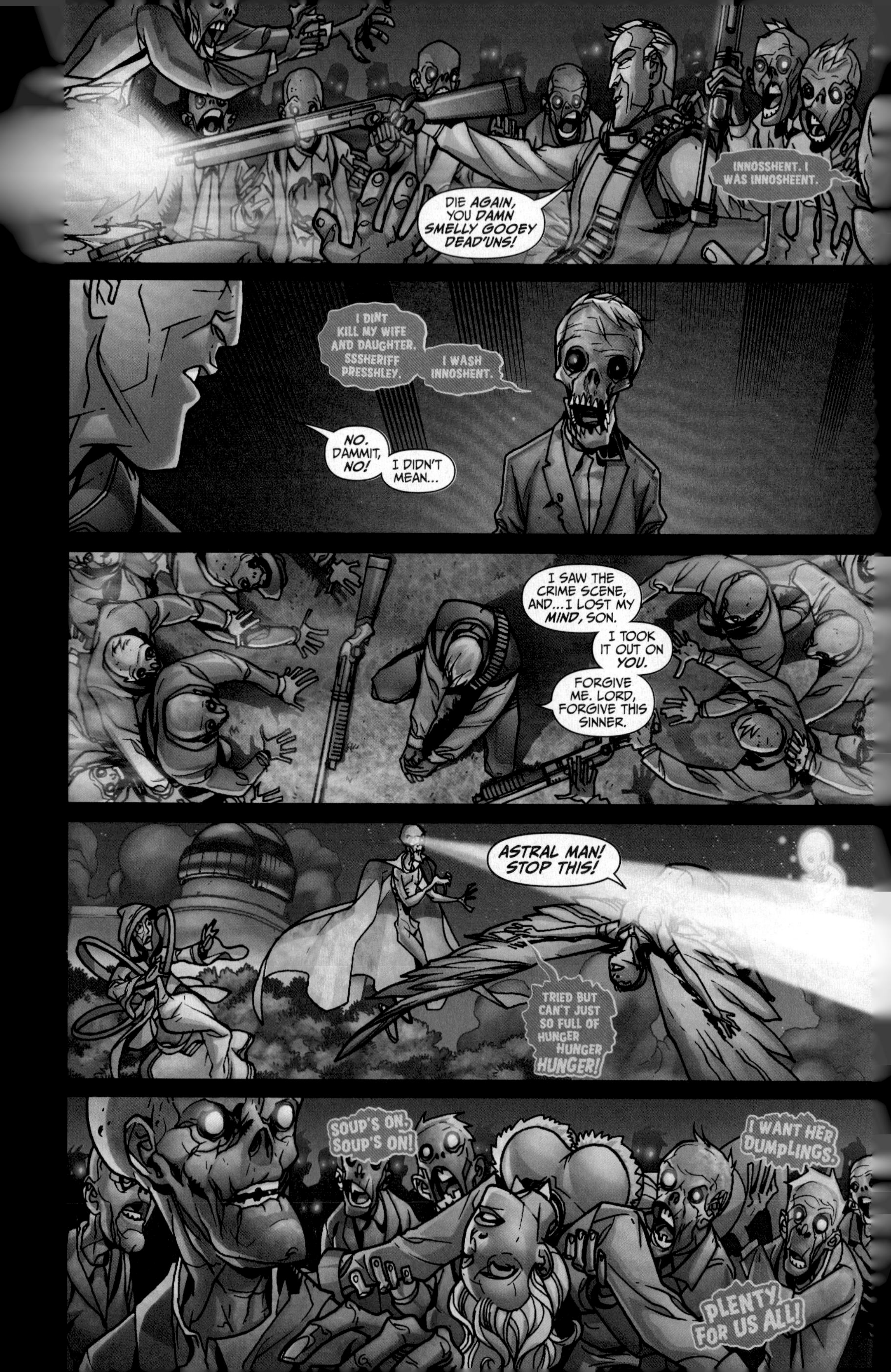
DIE AGAIN, YOU DAMN SMELLY GOOEY DEAD'UNS!
INNOSSHENT. I WAS INNOSHEENT.
I DINT KILL MY WIFE AND DAUGHTER. SSSHERIFF PRESSHLEY.
I WASH INNOSHENT.
NO. DAMMIT, NO!
I DIDN'T MEAN...
I SAW THE CRIME SCENE, AND...I LOST MY MIND, SON.
I TOOK IT OUT ON YOU.
FORGIVE ME. LORD, FORGIVE THIS SINNER.
ASTRAL MAN! STOP THIS!
TRIED BUT CAN'T JUST SO FULL OF HUNGER HUNGER HUNGER!
SOUP'S ON, SOUP'S ON!
I WANT HER DUMPLINGS.
PLENTY FOR US ALL!

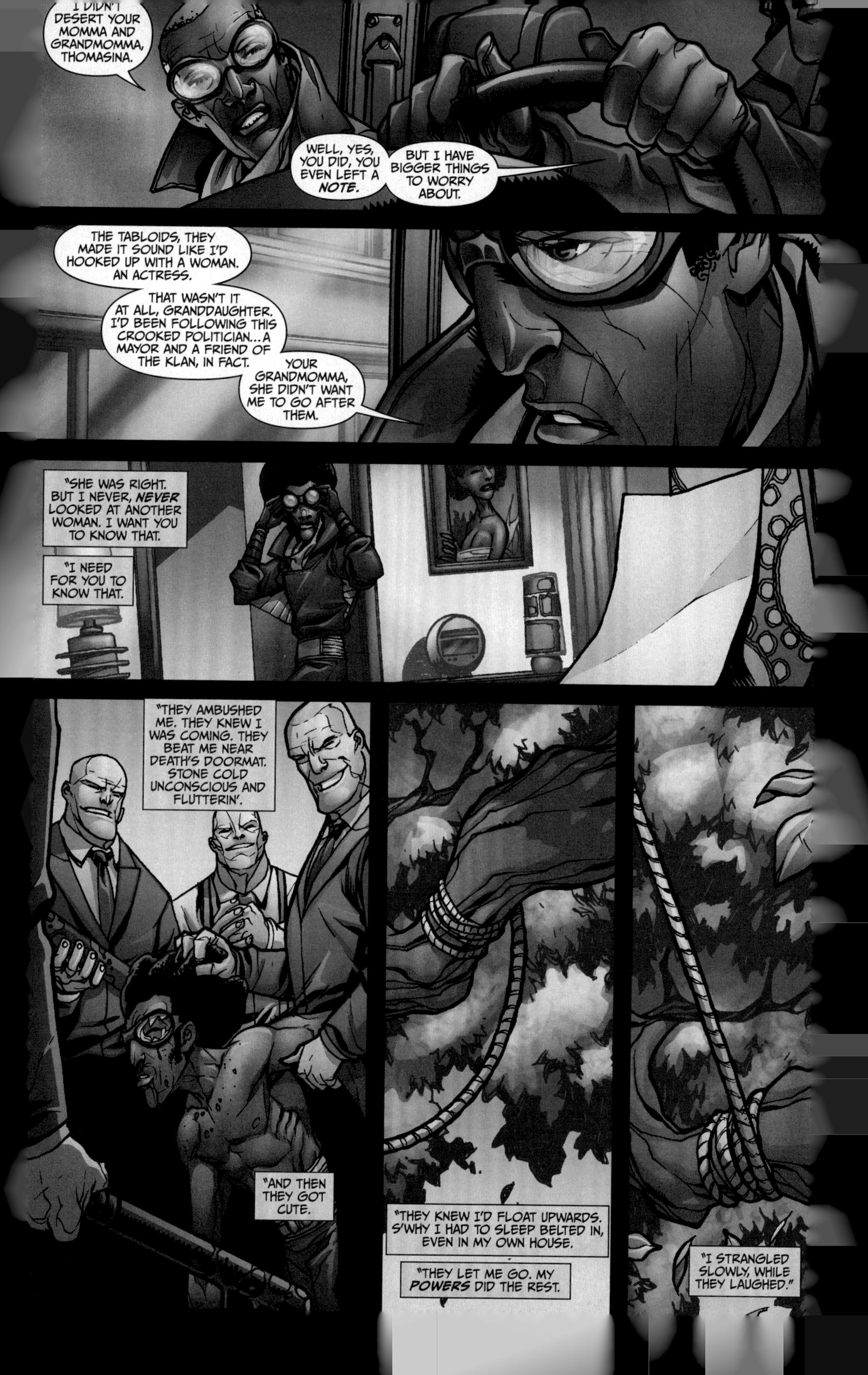
I DIDN'T DESERT YOUR MOMMA AND GRANDMOMMA, THOMASINA.
WELL, YES, YOU DID, YOU EVEN LEFT A NOTE.
BUT I HAVE BIGGER THINGS TO WORRY ABOUT.
THE TABLOIDS, THEY MADE IT SOUND LIKE I'D HOOKED UP WITH A WOMAN. AN ACTRESS.
THAT WASN'T IT AT ALL, GRANDDAUGHTER. I'D BEEN FOLLOWING THIS CROOKED POLITICIAN...A MAYOR AND A FRIEND OF THE KLAN, IN FACT.
YOUR GRANDMOMMA, SHE DIDN'T WANT ME TO GO AFTER THEM.
"SHE WAS RIGHT. BUT I NEVER, NEVER LOOKED AT ANOTHER WOMAN. I WANT YOU TO KNOW THAT.
"I NEED FOR YOU TO KNOW THAT.
"THEY AMBUSHED ME. THEY KNEW I WAS COMING. THEY BEAT ME NEAR DEATH'S DOORMAT. STONE COLD UNCONSCIOUS AND FLUTTERIN'.
"AND THEN THEY GOT CUTE.
"THEY KNEW I'D FLOAT UPWARDS. S'WHY I HAD TO SLEEP BELTED IN, EVEN IN MY OWN HOUSE.
"THEY LET ME GO. MY POWERS DID THE REST.
"I STRANGLED SLOWLY, WHILE THEY LAUGHED."

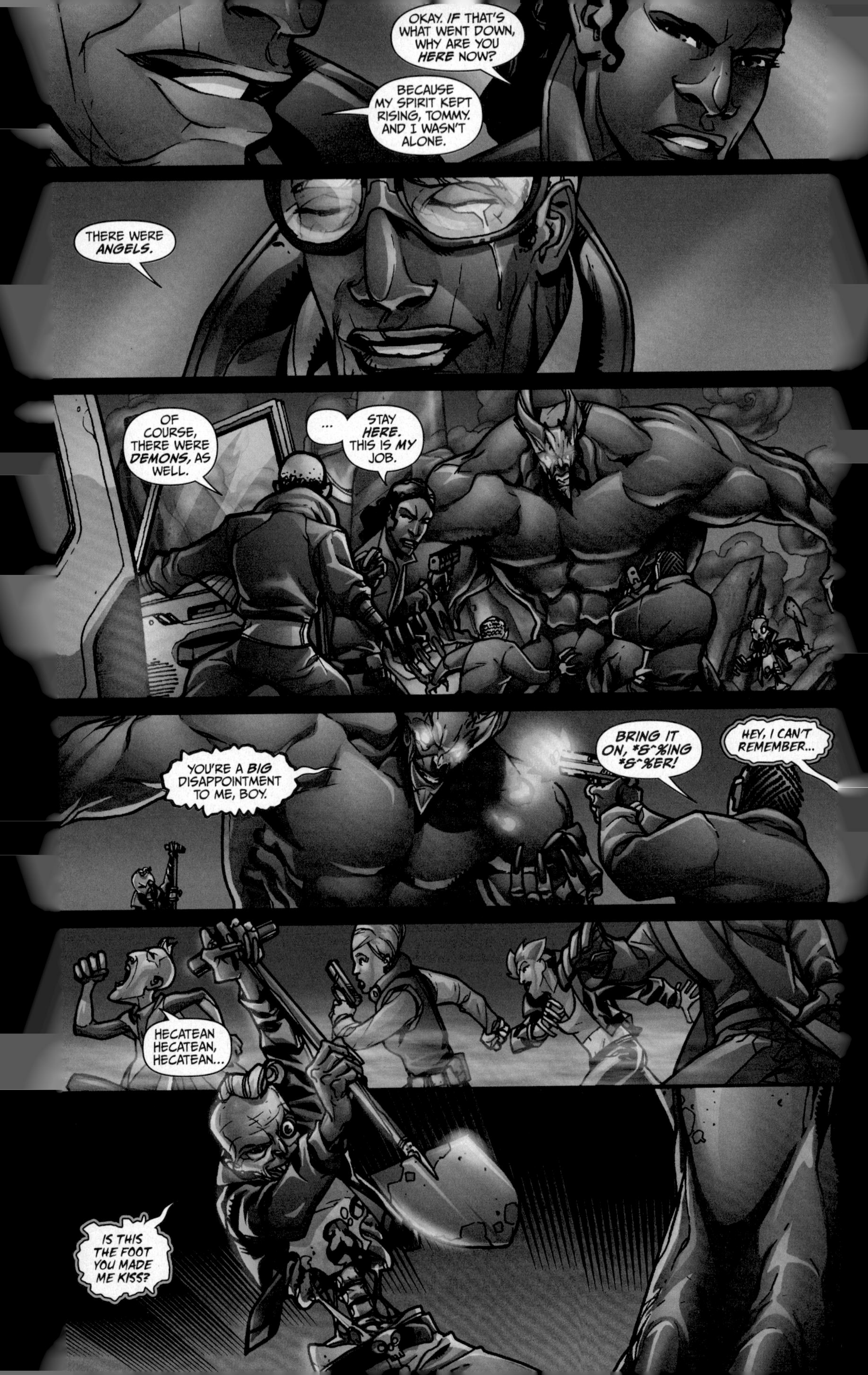
OKAY. IF THAT'S WHAT WENT DOWN, WHY ARE YOU HERE NOW?
BECAUSE MY SPIRIT KEPT RISING, TOMMY. AND I WASN'T ALONE.
THERE WERE ANGELS.
OF COURSE, THERE WERE DEMONS, AS WELL.
...
STAY HERE. THIS IS MY JOB.
YOU'RE A BIG DISAPPOINTMENT TO ME, BOY.
BRING IT ON, *&^%ING *&^%ER!
HEY, I CAN'T REMEMBER...
HECATEAN HECATEAN, HECATEAN...
IS THIS THE FOOT YOU MADE ME KISS?

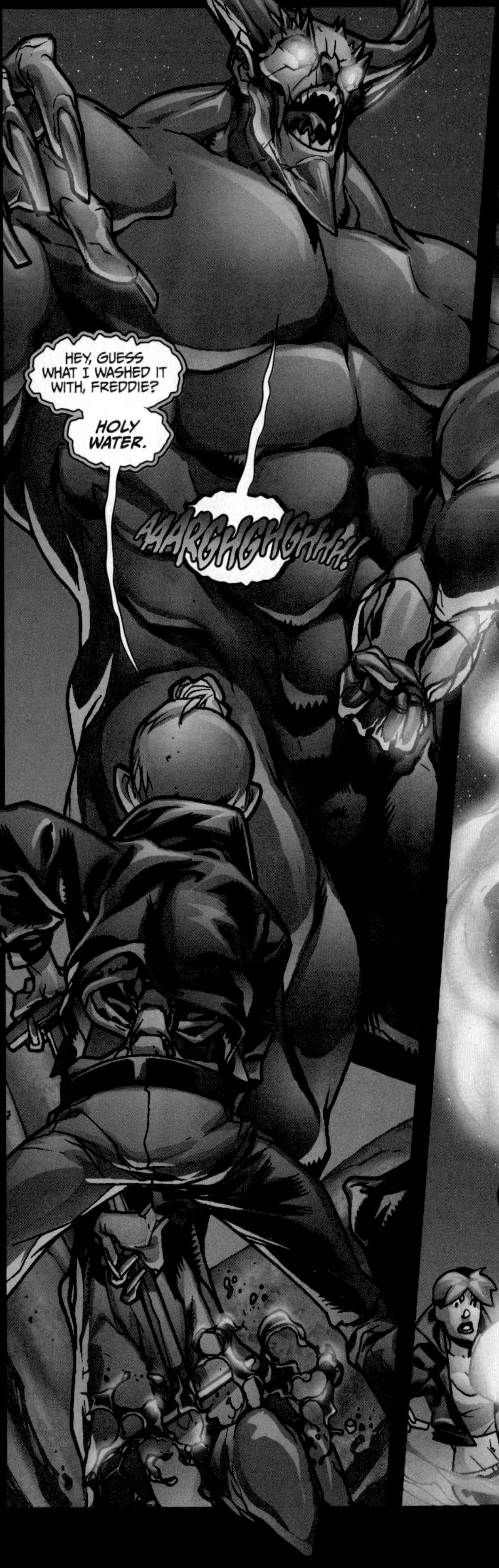
HEY, GUESS WHAT I WASHED IT WITH, FREDDIE?
HOLY WATER.
AAARGHGHGHHH!

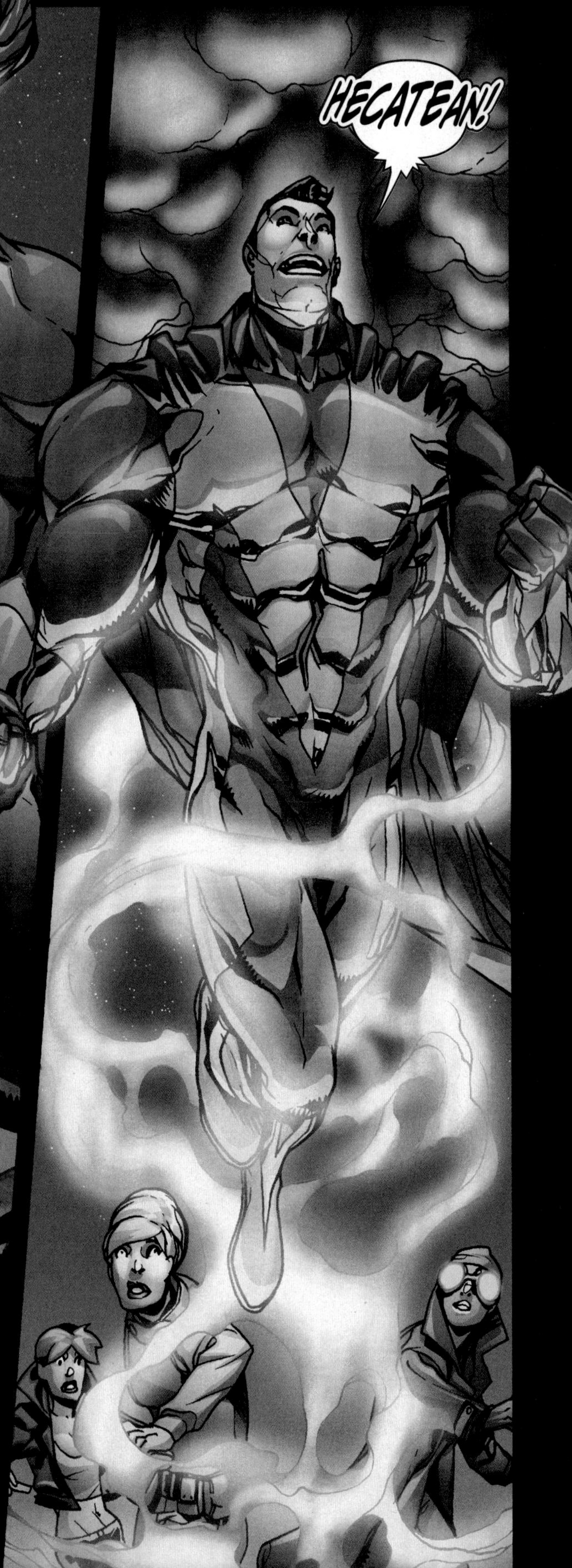
HECATEAN!

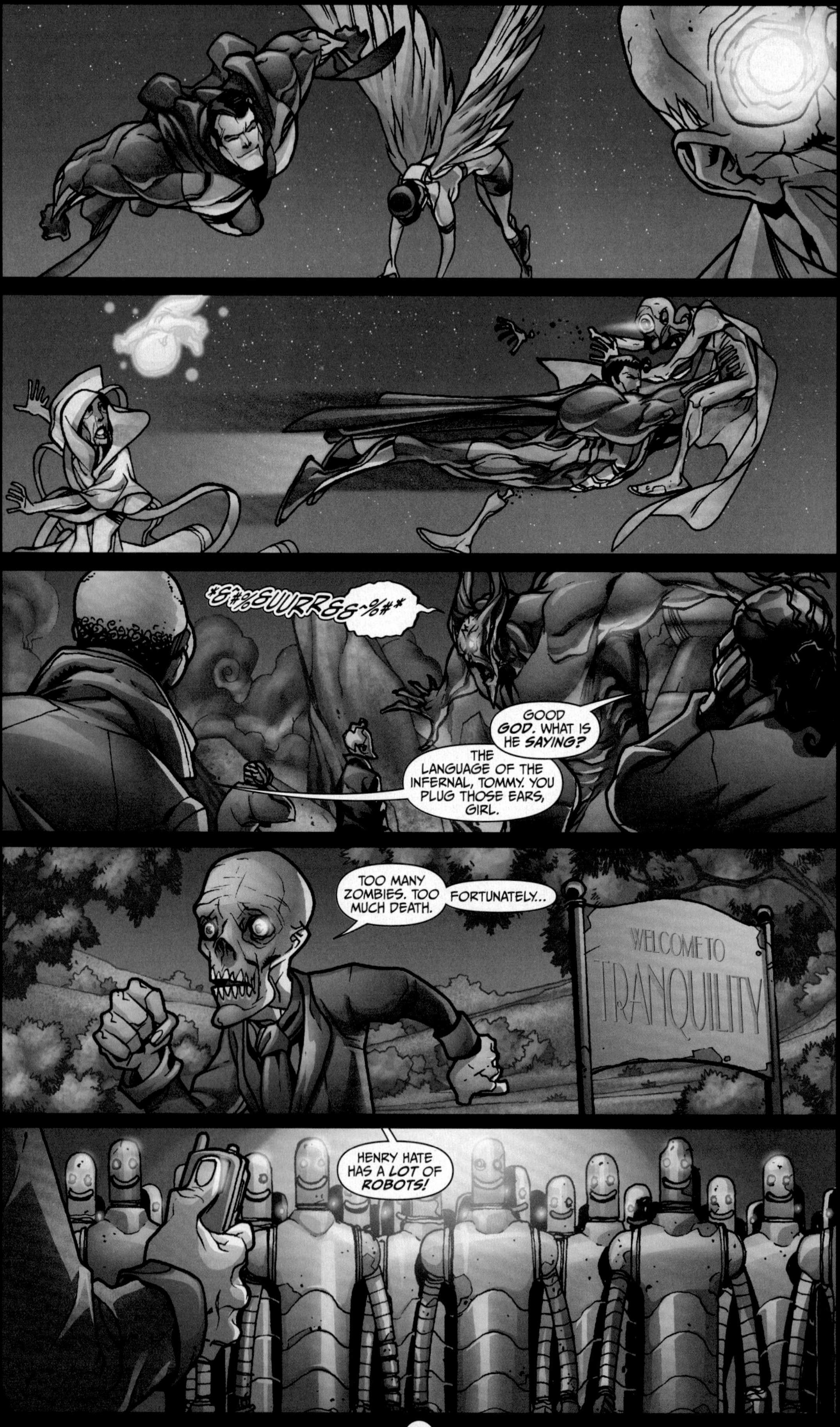

$#%GUURRGG~%#
GOOD GOD. WHAT IS HE SAYING?
THE LANGUAGE OF THE INFERNAL, TOMMY. YOU PLUG THOSE EARS, GIRL.
TOO MANY ZOMBIES. TOO MUCH DEATH.
FORTUNATELY...
WELCOME TO TRANQUILITY
HENRY HATE HAS A LOT OF ROBOTS!

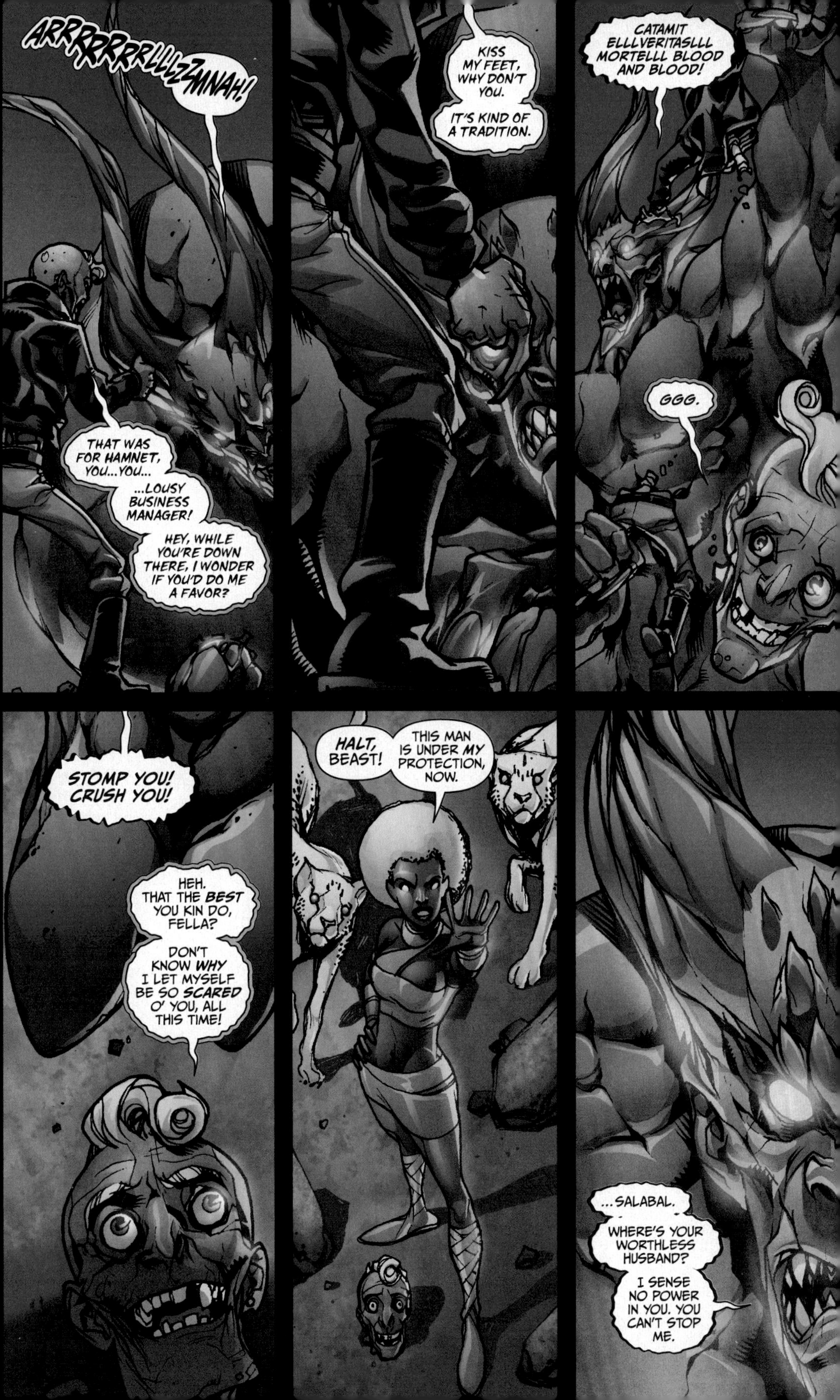
ARRRRRRRLLLZZMNAH!
THAT WAS FOR HAMNET, YOU...YOU...
...LOUSY BUSINESS MANAGER!
HEY, WHILE YOU'RE DOWN THERE, I WONDER IF YOU'D DO ME A FAVOR?
KISS MY FEET, WHY DON'T YOU.
IT'S KIND OF A TRADITION.
CATAMIT ELLLVERITASLLL MORTELLL BLOOD AND BLOOD!
GGG.
STOMP YOU! CRUSH YOU!
HEH. THAT THE BEST YOU KIN DO, FELLA?
DON'T KNOW WHY I LET MYSELF BE SO SCARED O' YOU, ALL THIS TIME!
HALT, BEAST!
THIS MAN IS UNDER MY PROTECTION, NOW.
...SALABAL.
WHERE'S YOUR WORTHLESS HUSBAND?
I SENSE NO POWER IN YOU. YOU CAN'T STOP ME.

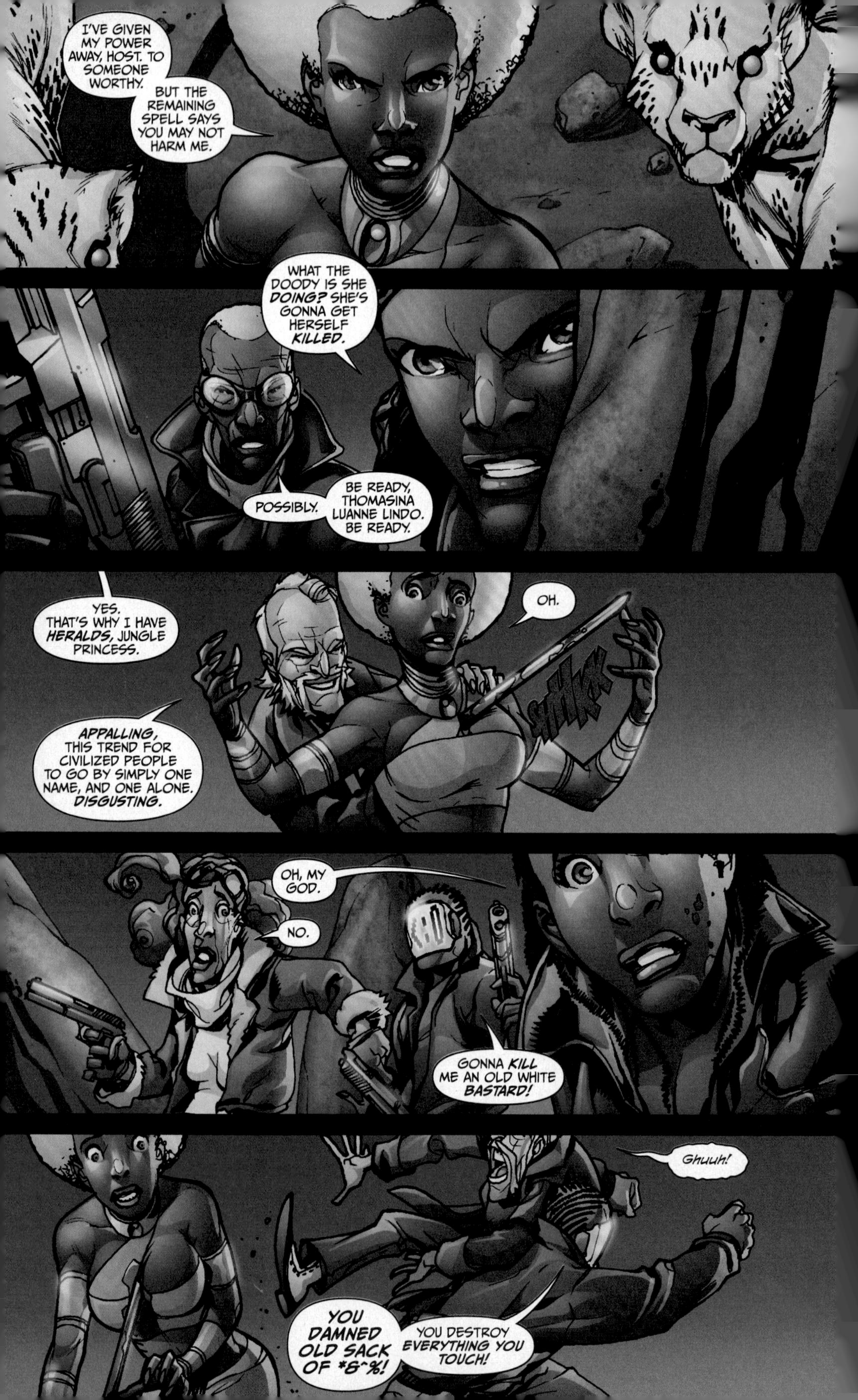
I'VE GIVEN MY POWER AWAY, HOST. TO SOMEONE WORTHY.
BUT THE REMAINING SPELL SAYS YOU MAY NOT HARM ME.
WHAT THE DOODY IS SHE DOING? SHE'S GONNA GET HERSELF KILLED.
POSSIBLY.
BE READY, THOMASINA LUANNE LINDO. BE READY.
YES. THAT'S WHY I HAVE HERALDS, JUNGLE PRINCESS.
APPALLING, THIS TREND FOR CIVILIZED PEOPLE TO GO BY SIMPLY ONE NAME, AND ONE ALONE. DISGUSTING.
OH.
SHHKK
OH, MY GOD.
NO.
GONNA KILL ME AN OLD WHITE BASTARD!
Ghuuh!
YOU DAMNED OLD SACK OF *&^%!
YOU DESTROY EVERYTHING YOU TOUCH!

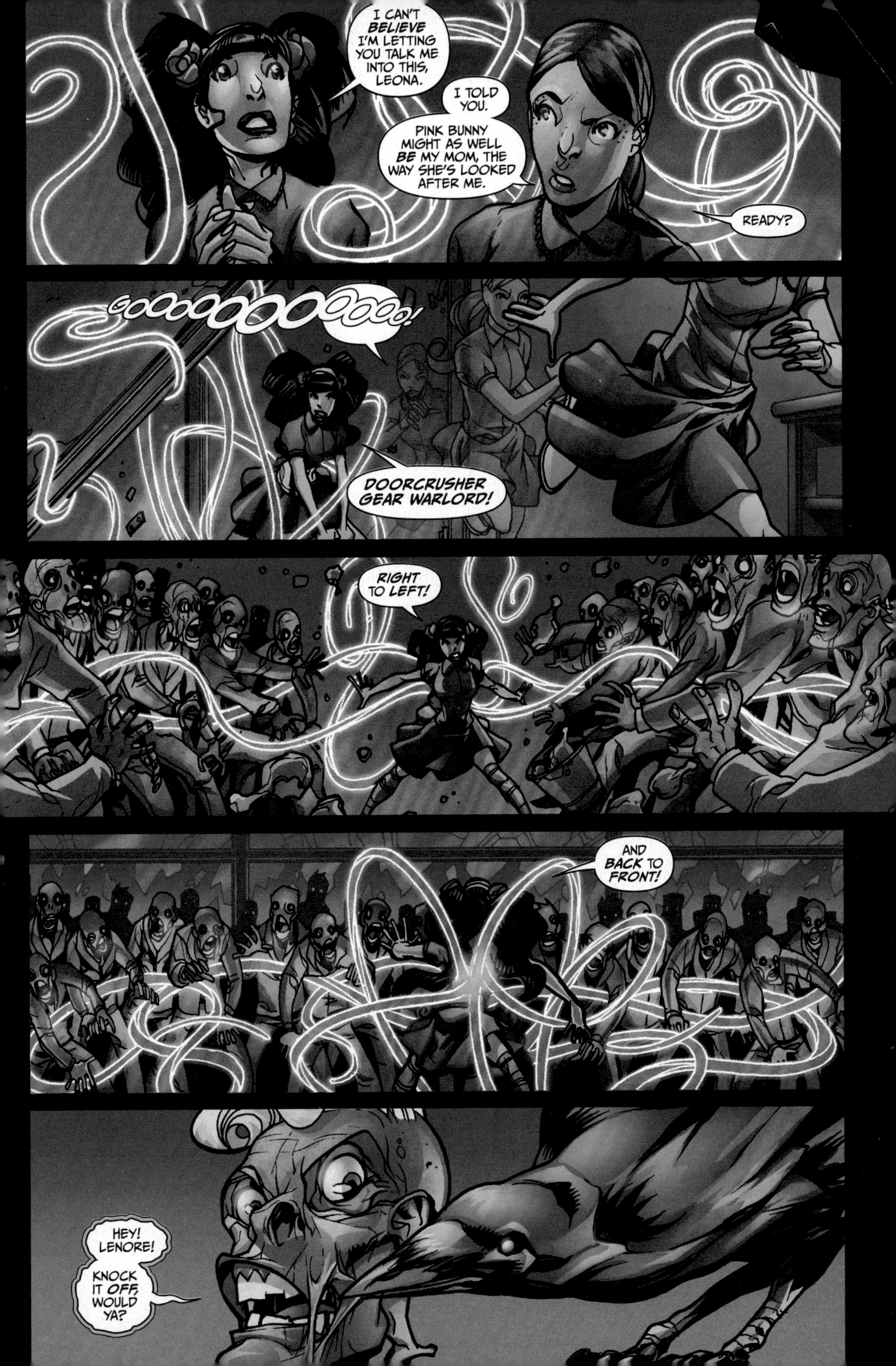
I CAN'T *BELIEVE* I'M LETTING YOU TALK ME INTO THIS, LEONA.
I TOLD YOU.
PINK BUNNY MIGHT AS WELL *BE* MY MOM, THE WAY SHE'S LOOKED AFTER ME.
READY?
GOOOOOOOOOOOOOOO!
DOORCRUSHER GEAR WARLORD!
RIGHT TO LEFT!
AND BACK TO FRONT!
HEY! LENORE!
KNOCK IT *OFF*, WOULD YA?

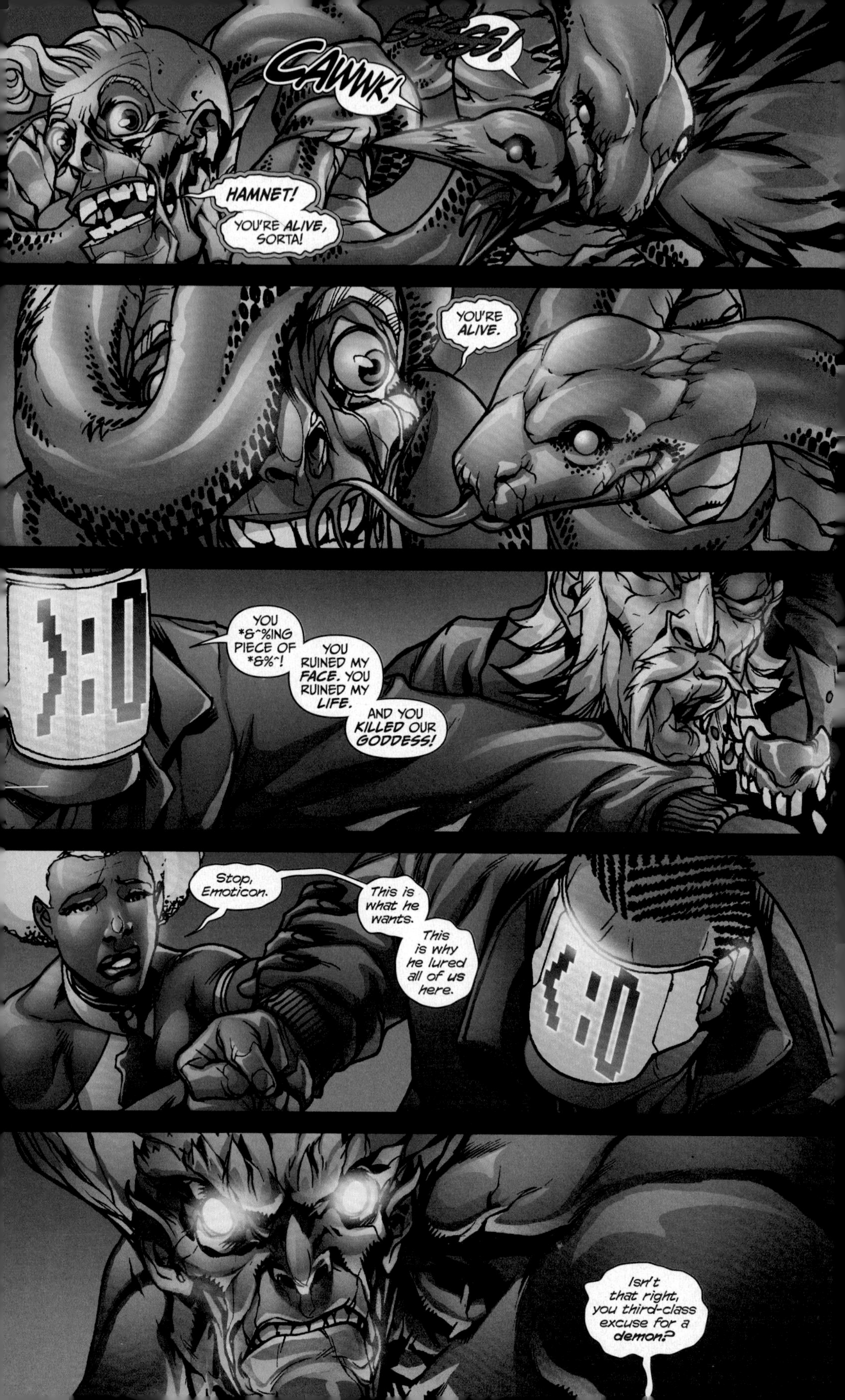
CAWWK!
SSSSS!
HAMNET!
YOU'RE ALIVE, SORTA!
YOU'RE ALIVE.
YOU *&^%ING PIECE OF *&%^!
YOU RUINED MY FACE. YOU RUINED MY LIFE.
AND YOU KILLED OUR GODDESS!
Stop, Emoticon.
This is what he wants.
This is why he lured all of us here.
Isn't that right, you third-class excuse for a demon?

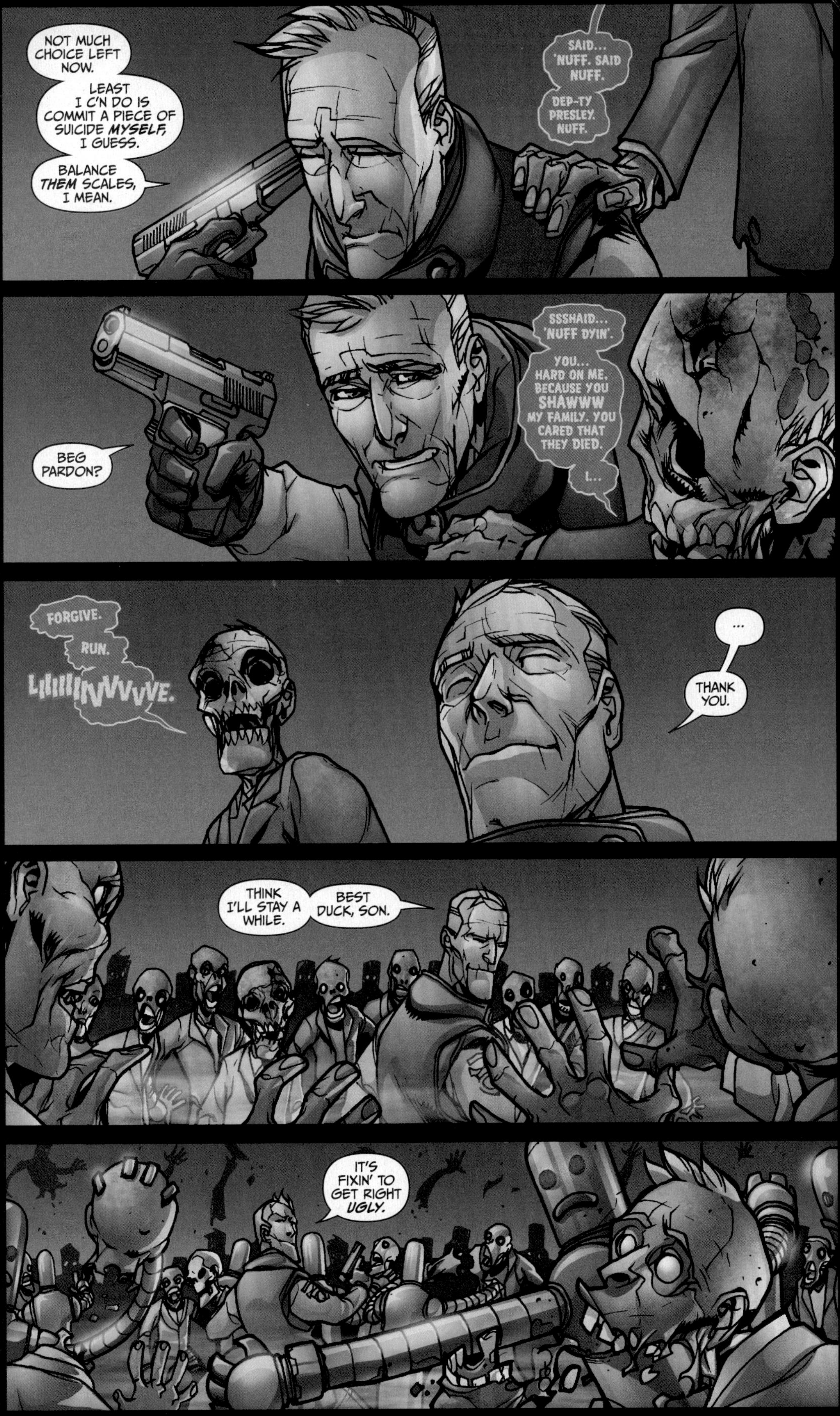
NOT MUCH CHOICE LEFT NOW.
LEAST I C'N DO IS COMMIT A PIECE OF SUICIDE *MYSELF*, I GUESS.
BALANCE *THEM* SCALES, I MEAN.
SAID... 'NUFF. SAID NUFF.
DEP-TY PRESLEY. NUFF.
BEG PARDON?
SSSHAID... 'NUFF DYIN'.
YOU... HARD ON ME. BECAUSE YOU SHAWWW MY FAMILY. YOU CARED THAT THEY DIED.
I...
FORGIVE.
RUN.
LIIIIIIVVVVVE.
...
THANK YOU.
THINK I'LL STAY A WHILE.
BEST DUCK, SON.
IT'S FIXIN' TO GET RIGHT *UGLY*.

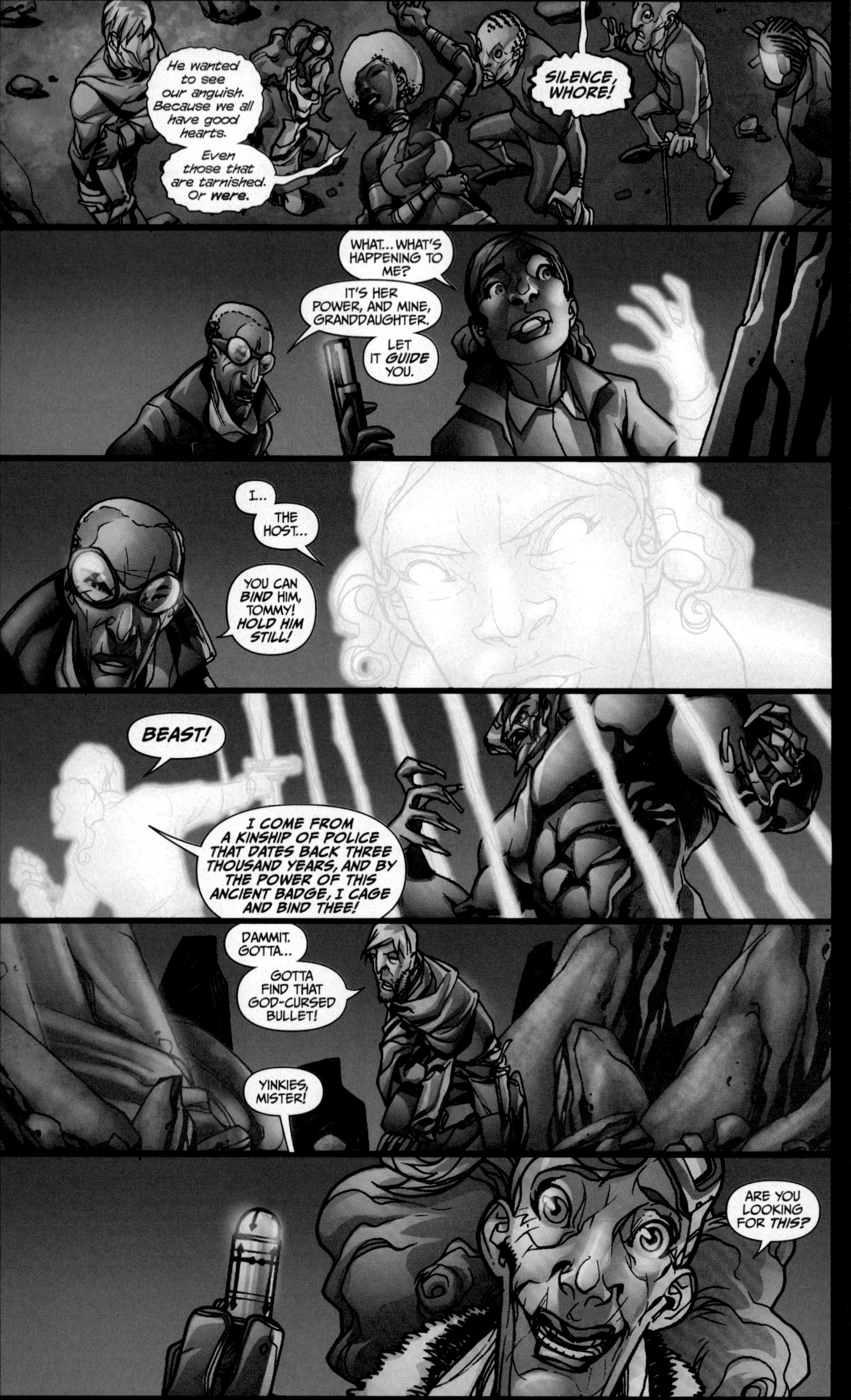
He wanted to see our anguish. Because we all have good hearts.
Even those that are tarnished. Or were.
SILENCE, WHORE!
WHAT... WHAT'S HAPPENING TO ME?
IT'S HER POWER, AND MINE, GRANDDAUGHTER.
LET IT GUIDE YOU.
I... THE HOST...
YOU CAN BIND HIM, TOMMY! HOLD HIM STILL!
BEAST!
I COME FROM A KINSHIP OF POLICE THAT DATES BACK THREE THOUSAND YEARS, AND BY THE POWER OF THIS ANCIENT BADGE, I CAGE AND BIND THEE!
DAMMIT. GOTTA...
GOTTA FIND THAT GOD-CURSED BULLET!
YINKIES, MISTER!
ARE YOU LOOKING FOR THIS?

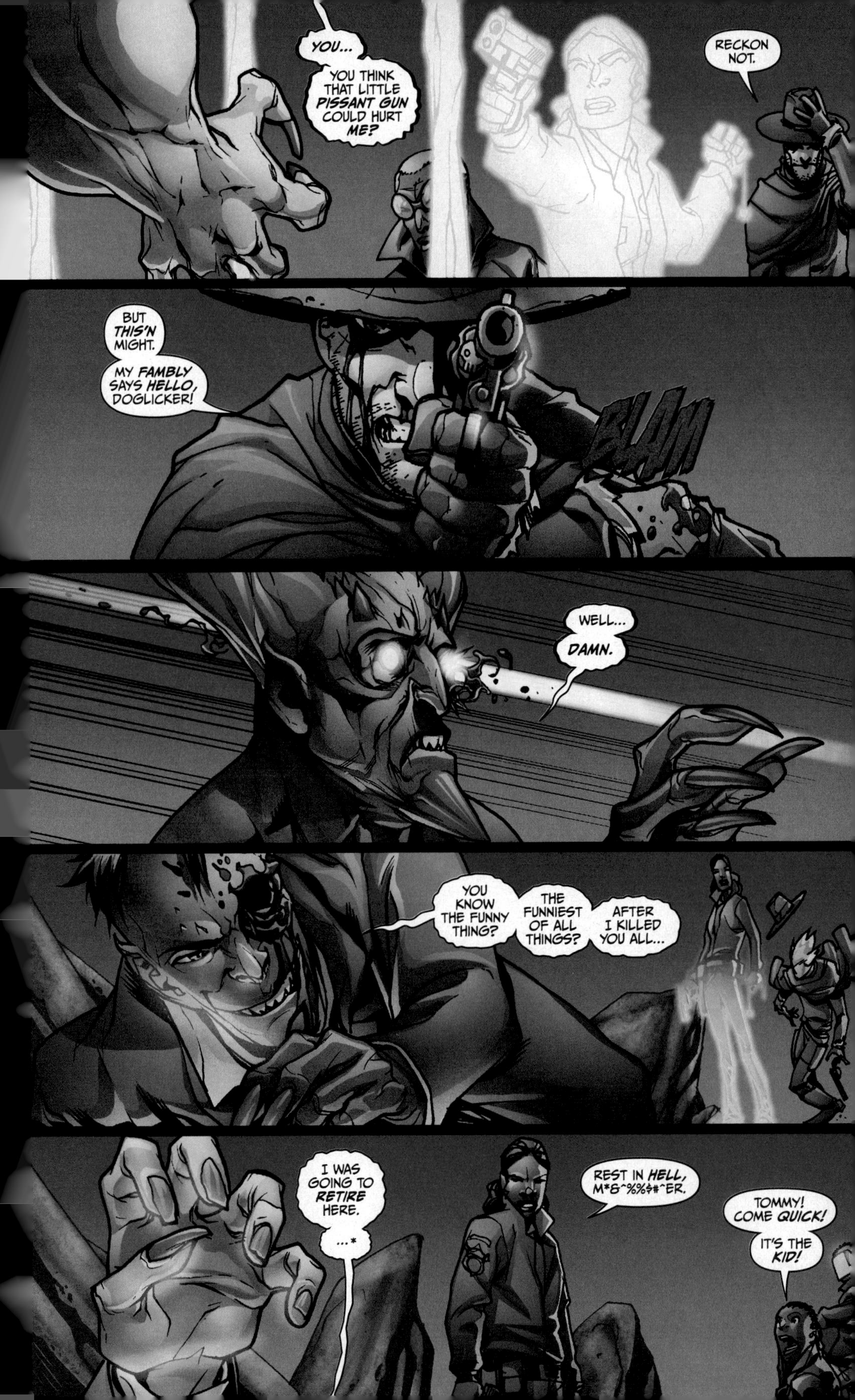
YOU...
YOU THINK THAT LITTLE PISSANT GUN COULD HURT ME?
RECKON NOT.
BUT THIS'N MIGHT.
MY FAMBLY SAYS HELLO, DOGLICKER!
BLAM
WELL... DAMN.
YOU KNOW THE FUNNY THING?
THE FUNNIEST OF ALL THINGS?
AFTER I KILLED YOU ALL...
I WAS GOING TO RETIRE HERE.
...*
REST IN HELL, M*&^%%$#^ER.
TOMMY! COME QUICK!
IT'S THE KID!

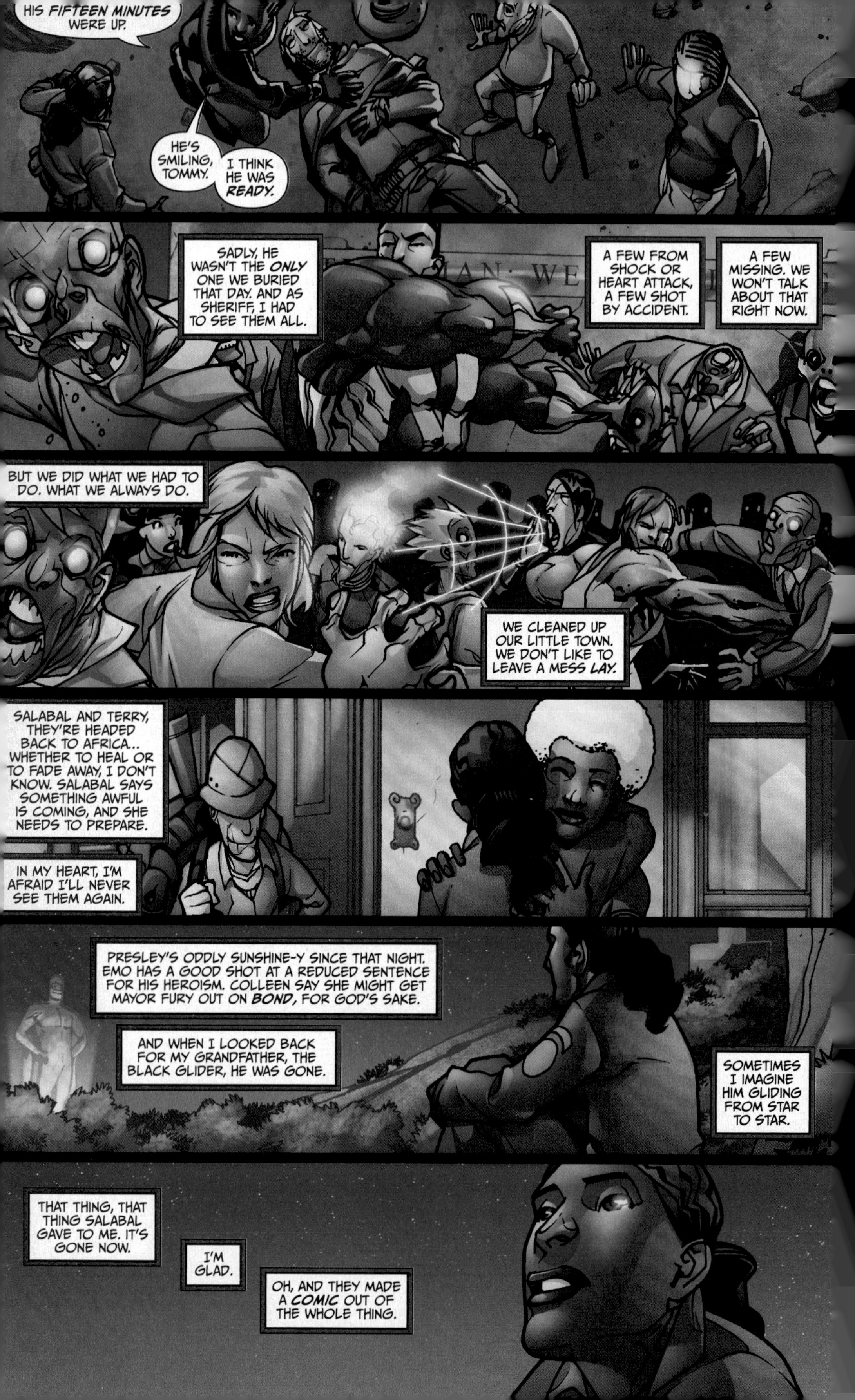
HIS FIFTEEN MINUTES WERE UP.
HE'S SMILING, TOMMY.
I THINK HE WAS READY.
SADLY, HE WASN'T THE ONLY ONE WE BURIED THAT DAY. AND AS SHERIFF, I HAD TO SEE THEM ALL.
A FEW FROM SHOCK OR HEART ATTACK, A FEW SHOT BY ACCIDENT.
A FEW MISSING. WE WON'T TALK ABOUT THAT RIGHT NOW.
BUT WE DID WHAT WE HAD TO DO. WHAT WE ALWAYS DO.
WE CLEANED UP OUR LITTLE TOWN. WE DON'T LIKE TO LEAVE A MESS LAY.
SALABAL AND TERRY, THEY'RE HEADED BACK TO AFRICA... WHETHER TO HEAL OR TO FADE AWAY, I DON'T KNOW. SALABAL SAYS SOMETHING AWFUL IS COMING, AND SHE NEEDS TO PREPARE.
IN MY HEART, I'M AFRAID I'LL NEVER SEE THEM AGAIN.
PRESLEY'S ODDLY SUNSHINE-Y SINCE THAT NIGHT. EMO HAS A GOOD SHOT AT A REDUCED SENTENCE FOR HIS HEROISM. COLLEEN SAY SHE MIGHT GET MAYOR FURY OUT ON BOND, FOR GOD'S SAKE.
AND WHEN I LOOKED BACK FOR MY GRANDFATHER, THE BLACK GLIDER, HE WAS GONE.
SOMETIMES I IMAGINE HIM GLIDING FROM STAR TO STAR.
THAT THING, THAT THING SALABAL GAVE TO ME. IT'S GONE NOW.
I'M GLAD.
OH, AND THEY MADE A COMIC OUT OF THE WHOLE THING.

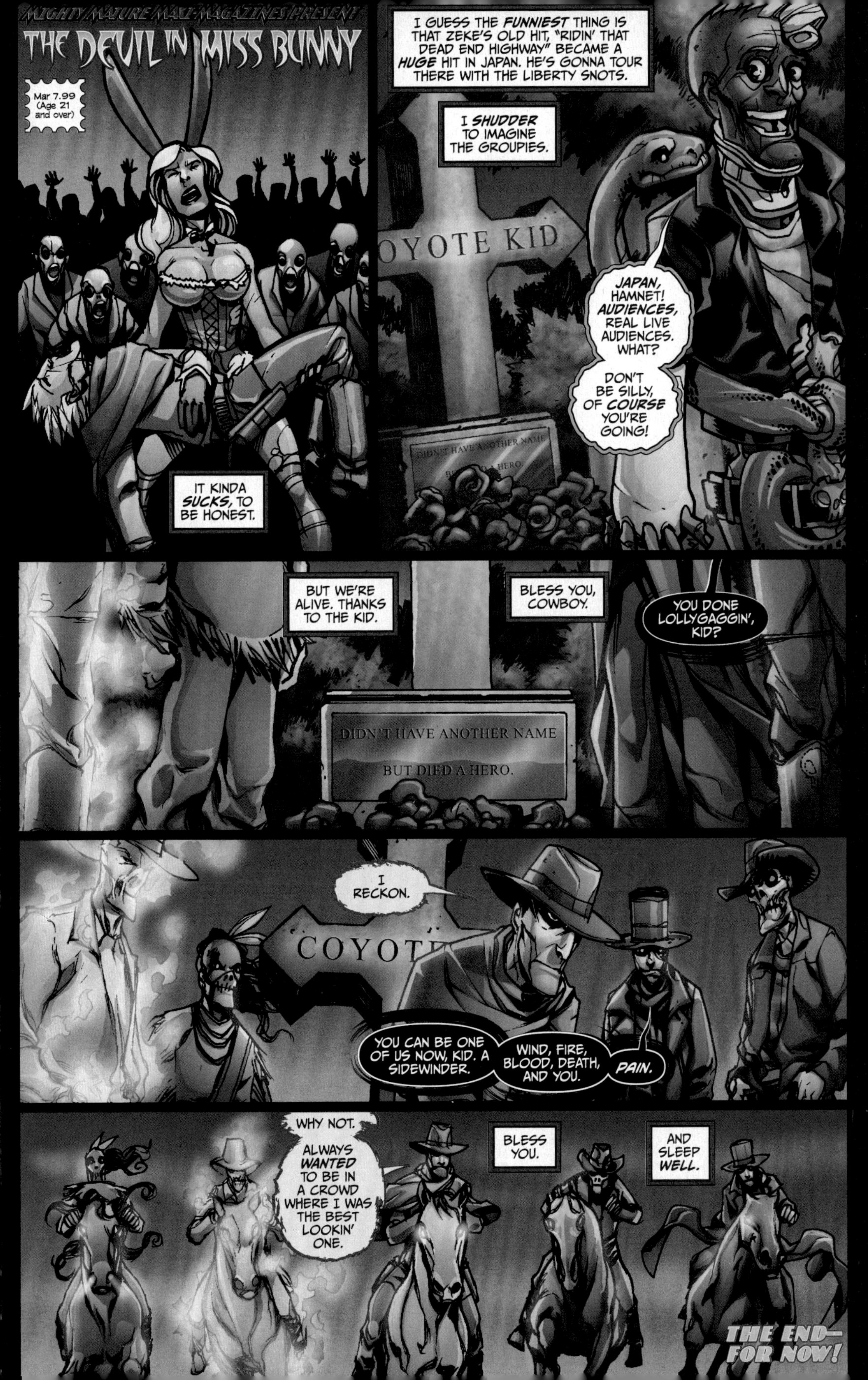
MIGHTY MATURE MAXI-MAGAZINES PRESENT
THE DEVIL IN MISS BUNNY
Mar 7.99 (Age 21 and over)
IT KINDA SUCKS, TO BE HONEST.
I GUESS THE FUNNIEST THING IS THAT ZEKE'S OLD HIT, "RIDIN' THAT DEAD END HIGHWAY" BECAME A HUGE HIT IN JAPAN. HE'S GONNA TOUR THERE WITH THE LIBERTY SNOTS.
I SHUDDER TO IMAGINE THE GROUPIES.
OYOTE KID
JAPAN, HAMNET! AUDIENCES, REAL LIVE AUDIENCES. WHAT?
DON'T BE SILLY, OF COURSE YOU'RE GOING!
BUT WE'RE ALIVE. THANKS TO THE KID.
BLESS YOU, COWBOY.
YOU DONE LOLLYGAGGIN', KID?
DIDN'T HAVE ANOTHER NAME
BUT DIED A HERO.
I RECKON.
COYOT
YOU CAN BE ONE OF US NOW, KID. A SIDEWINDER.
WIND, FIRE, BLOOD, DEATH, AND YOU.
PAIN.
WHY NOT.
ALWAYS WANTED TO BE IN A CROWD WHERE I WAS THE BEST LOOKIN' ONE.
BLESS YOU.
AND SLEEP WELL.
THE END— FOR NOW!

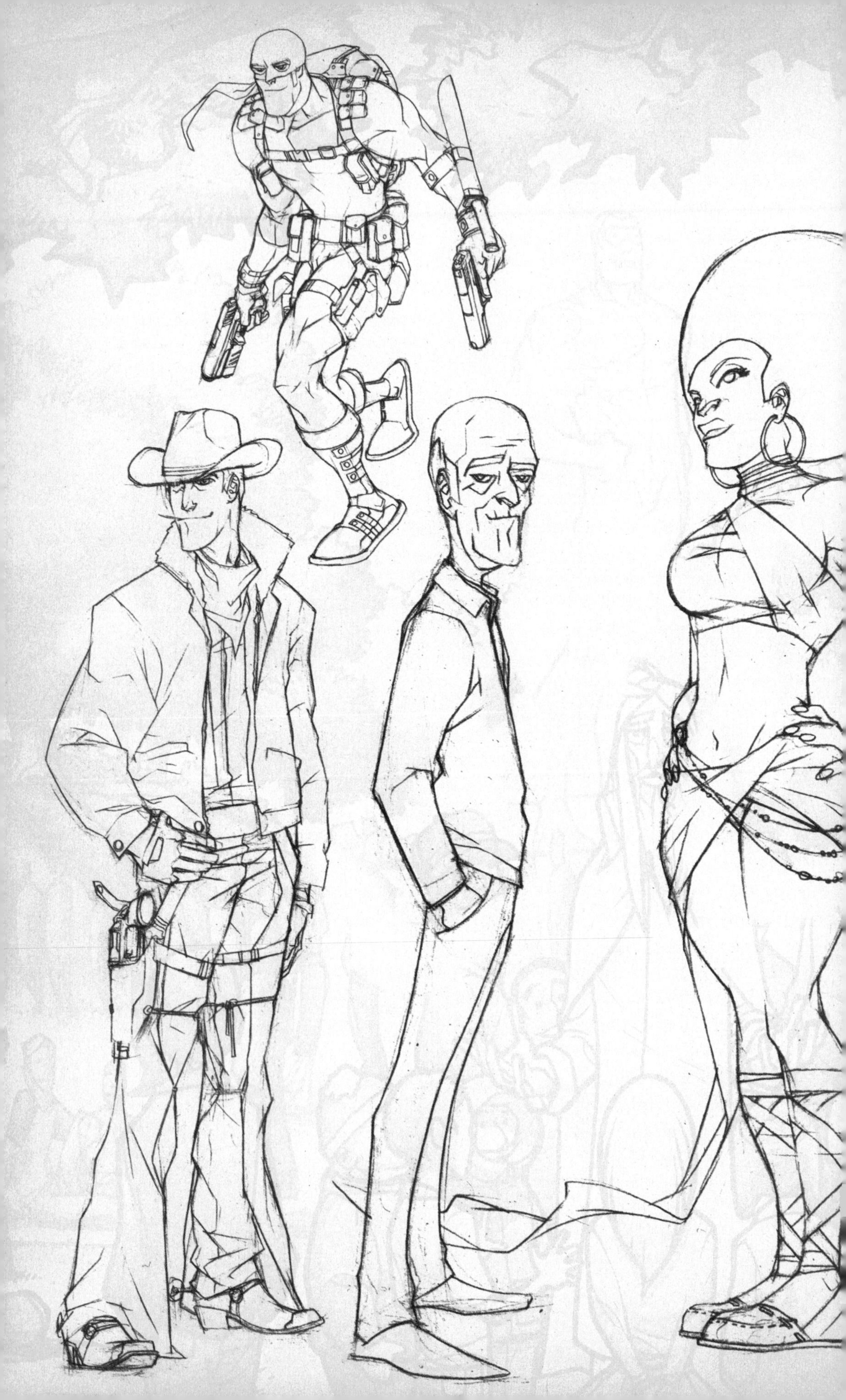

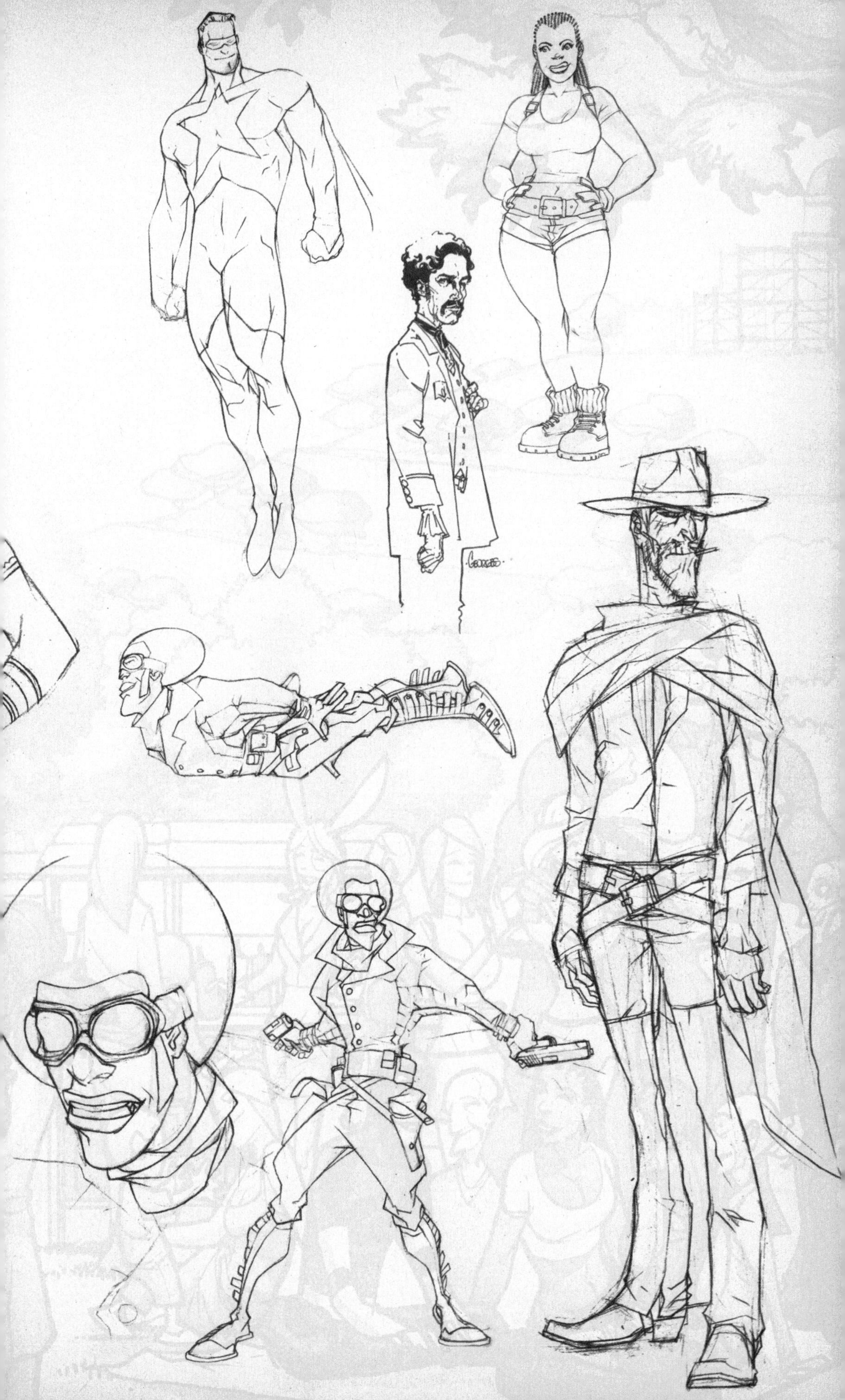

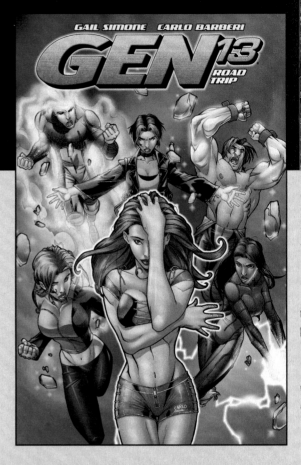

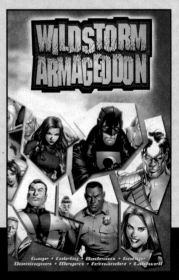